KU-781-310

NUCLEAR WEAPONS IN A TRANSFORMED WORLD

THE CHALLENGE OF VIRTUAL NUCLEAR ARSENALS

EDITED BY MICHAEL J. MAZARR

MACMILLAN

© Michael J. Mazarr 1997

All rights reserved. No reproduction, copy or transmission of
this publication may be made without written permission.

No paragraph of this publication may be reproduced, copied or
transmitted save with written permission or in accordance with
the provisions of the Copyright, Designs and Patents Act 1988,
or under the terms of any licence permitting limited copying
issued by the Copyright Licensing Agency, 90 Tottenham Court
Road, London W1P 9HE.

Any person who does any unauthorised act in relation to this
publication may be liable to criminal prosecution and civil
claims for damages.

First published 1997 by
MACMILLAN PRESS LTD
Houndmills, Basingstoke, Hampshire RG21 6XS
and London
Companies and representatives
throughout the world

ISBN 0-333-72369-4

A catalogue record for this book is available
from the British Library.

10 9 8 7 6 5 4 3 2 1
05 04 03 02 01 00 99 98 97 96

Printed in the United States of America by
Haddon Craftsmen
Scranton, PA

CONTENTS

PART FIVE: CONCLUSION

ACKNOWLEDGMENTS

The editor would like to extend his warmest thanks and appreciation to the people who made this volume a reality:

First, to the authors, who agreed to tackle an unusual and challenging subject, did so with energy and expertise, and completed their work in a remarkably timely fashion.

Second, to our editor at St. Martin's Press, Michael Flamini, who saw value in the subject when the project was only a glimmer in the editor's eye.

And third and most importantly, to the W. Alton Jones Foundation and its program officer in this field, Mr. George Perkovich, for their consistent and kind support over a number of years. This book, the project from which it has emerged, and the rapid growth in thinking about virtual nuclear arsenals would not have been possible without their leadership.

FOREWORD

FRED CHARLES IKLÉ

Some two hundred years ago—so it says in our history books—the Industrial Revolution ushered in the modern age, with its ceaseless advances in science and technology. One hundred and fifty years later these advances reached the stage in which the leading industrial nations, by dint of a concerted effort, could build nuclear weapons. Today, another half-century later, the problem of reconciling the existence of these weapons with a world of many sovereign nation-states is as unresolved as it was in 1945. And not for lack of trying. For fifty years senior statesmen, military leaders, diplomats, arms-control experts, plus a wholly new international profession—the nuclear strategist—have struggled to find solutions.

Three undisputable facts tower above everything that has been said and done about the problem of nuclear weapons:

- First, the fact of the arsenals. Tens of thousands of these weapons have been built, many of them a thousand times more destructive than the two used in 1945, and most of them continue to be kept ready for use.
- Second, the fact of the spread of nuclear weapons. At least three dozen nations are now technically capable of building nuclear weapons, an option inextricably embedded in their scientific-technological know-how. That is to say, if political developments in any one of these nations led to the decision to acquire atomic bombs, and if this decision were sustained with discipline and perseverance, such a nation would have the technical wherewithal to build an arsenal of, say, ten to a hundred

weapons within three to five years. These *potential* nuclear arsenals will be part and parcel of the global strategic order, whether or not the major powers agree to transform their ready-to-use nuclear arsenals into "virtual"ones, as proposed in this book.

- Third, the fact of nonuse. Since 1945 not a single nuclear weapon has been used destructively. This fact goes a long way to explain the insouciance with which most people accept (and many indeed support) the continued existence of thousands of nuclear weapons that are being maintained in a state of high readiness. Alas, the dispensation of nonuse that has now lasted for half a century can come to an end any day.

In fairness it must be recognized that many political and military arrangements have been put in place during the last fifty years to avert situations that might lead to the use of nuclear weapons. And much of what has been done came about because of U.S. leadership. Many of these arrangements, however, are mutually contradictory, and most have been overtaken by events. They have been designed for the bipolar world of the Cold War, not for the "transformed world" addressed in this book.

For example, the largest nuclear powers still cling to the Cold War idea that maintaining large and highly ready strategic forces is a necessary condition of stable deterrence. To deter our potential enemies from launching a surprise attack, so this argument goes, part of our own forces must always be ready to execute a massive retaliatory strike instantly. But it is precisely the readiness of our forces that induces other nuclear powers that are not our close allies to keep their "retaliatory" forces at a high state of readiness. And their readiness, of course, compels us to be more alert. The result is increased danger all around. The greater the emphasis on readiness, the greater the risk of a cataclysmic accident. Time is the best healer of mistakes, while a hair-trigger posture leaves no room for error.

Perhaps during the height of the Cold War there was no escape from this vicious circle of the fear of surprise attack leading to a high state of readiness, which in turn confirmed the danger of surprise attack. Yet even then there were some of us who dissented. I wrote back in 1973 that we and the Russians should "jointly decide to replace the doomsday catapults invented in the 1950s with arms that are incapable of being launched swiftly." Today, it should at last be possible to escape from the Cold War mind-set, which regards readiness for "prompt" retaliation as a virtue and any arrangement for a delayed response as sinful. Yet even now, after the Cold War has ended, several technical problems need to be solved to render such a transformation feasible. In the pages that follow Micheal Mazarr is right in emphasizing technical and operational hurdles that must be overcome on the road to "virtual nuclear arsenals."

Equally conflicted Cold War thinking still governs the approach to reductions in the number of offensive forces. The START Treaty and other such agreements presumably are meant to reduce the immense potential for nuclear destruction, yet these agreements are coupled with the ABM Treaty, which is meant, precisely, to preserve an immense potential for nuclear destruction. Similar contradictions afflict the policies against nuclear proliferation. Agreements to ban the worldwide export of nuclear materials and know-how are intertwined in a Faustian bargain with commitments by the nuclear powers to provide the very materials and much of the nuclear know-how in exchange for other nations' pledges not to to use these gifts for making bombs.

The justification given for this Faustian bargain has been that the International Atomic Energy Agency (IAEA) would prevent nuclear technology that was bestowed for peaceful purposes from being diverted to bombs. While most people involved in these matters knew better all along, those who did not should have been disabused of their illusion by the revelations from Iraq. As Iraq kept nudging closer, year after year, to completing the construction of nuclear bombs (exploiting various technology imports to that end), the IAEA kept certifying that Iraq was using nuclear technology for peaceful purposes only. For an international organization to verify that virtual nuclear arsenals are not being transformed into ready-to-use arsenals would be a mission even more difficult than that given to the IAEA. The skeptical views expressed on this issue in some of the essays that follow are warranted.

To create and preserve a world order that will keep nuclear weapons from being used destructively is a project that requires strong leadership, organizational cohesion and discipline, and a sustained exertion of political will. None of these qualities can be found in any of the international organizations that have come into existence. Arms-control experts would do well to keep this in mind and to eschew proposing some new international organization as the centerpiece of their solution.

At the same time, nuclear strategists, who tend to be the more skeptical experts involved in these matters, must wake up to the fact that most of their concepts are out of date.

For four decades nuclear strategists have been working on what cosmologists call a "singularity"—that early phase in the creation of a new universe when the laws of nature are still curiously warped and incompatible with the long-term order of things. The strategists' singularity, of course, has been the bipolar nuclear confrontation between "East" and "West" that warped their initial "laws." Those who keep reiterating these allegedly universal laws—and some of our good friends in France and England (among many others) come to mind here—might be given this homework assignment:

> Please write a brief essay explaining why ready nuclear weapons prevent war, how only mutual deterrence can keep the peace, and why preparations for instant retaliation and "first use" help maintain stability. But, instead of justifying these concepts by assuming a replay of the first half-century of the nuclear age, explain their validity—if any!—for a world in which the Soviet Union has broken up peacefully, in which NATO ambles eastward in a vain search for the lost Warsaw Pact, and in which our best intelligence services cannot keep track anymore of the numbers and whereabouts of nuclear bombs in the world. Then reconsider your assessment of virtual nuclear arsenals.

PART ONE

INTRODUCTION

ONE

THE NOTION OF
VIRTUAL ARSENALS

MICHAEL J. MAZARR

THE END OF THE COLD WAR has created an unfortunate dilemma for
advocates of nuclear arms control: now that it has finally become
possible, it no longer seems necessary.[1] John Lepingwell has put the
problem nicely: in the immediate aftermath of the Cold War, "it seemed
that the old approaches to arms control had simultaneously reached
their summit and become irrelevant." As the U.S.-Soviet nuclear
confrontation receded, so did "the urgency attached to the destruction
of nuclear weapons."[2]

This volume stems from the simple belief that the abandonment
of strategic nuclear arms control—by scholars, the media, founda-
tions, and governments—is both premature and dangerous. The
dangers posed by nuclear weapons remain very real. If anything, in the
more unpredictable and disorderly world that has emerged in the wake
of the Cold War, addressing the risks inherent in operational nuclear
forces is as important as ever.

Many, but not all, of the contributors to this book belong to the
growing number of experts who believe that some form of limited or
radical nuclear arms control stands to benefit U.S. national interests
more directly and powerfully than at any time in the last half-century.
Indeed, as the following section will document, this argument has

transformed the arms-control community from a generally liberal group of collective security advocates into a diverse array of analysts from all parts of the political spectrum, carrying any number of positive and negative assumptions about the future of international relations. The case for nuclear arms control no longer rests, if it ever did, on flimsy appeals to the unity of humankind and the need for international cooperation. It can now call upon a hardheaded catalog of U.S. and allied interests to support its arguments.

As the subtitle suggests, this book examines one specific arms-control proposal—the notion of virtual nuclear arsenals (VNAs). This concept, which will be explained in more detail later in this essay, focuses on the operational status of nuclear weapons rather than their number. It seeks to remove all nuclear weapons from operational status by partially dismantling them—removing the warheads from the missiles, for example. Virtual nuclear arsenals aim to achieve some of the advantages of complete nuclear disarmament, removing all nuclear weapons from day-to-day operational status and thereby seeking to push them to the margins of world politics while allowing current nuclear powers to retain some of the core missions for nuclear forces by threatening to rebuild a few dozen weapons within a period of a few days or weeks. Whether VNAs could conceivably achieve these twin aims is the overarching question that inspires this book.

But our purpose here is at once more modest and more ambitious than a comprehensive verdict on VNAs. It is more modest because a single book cannot answer all the questions surrounding a scheme as complicated, and as different from current ways of doing business, as virtual arsenals. Rather than rendering a final judgment on VNAs, the purpose of the essays that follow is twofold: to *identify the key issues* surrounding the idea and to *ask the right questions* about its feasibility. Their aim is to get debate started, rather than to end it. To this purpose we have intentionally recruited authors whose views of VNAs range from cautiously supportive to intellectually intrigued to resoundingly skeptical. We hope that the resulting dialog, at times bordering on debate, builds a fertile base of analysis for subsequent thinking.

Because our purpose is to introduce rather than end a debate, we have been less concerned here about a common failing of many edited volumes—that their individual essays are imperfectly divided, overlapping and duplicating treatment of many issues. We have made every effort to insure that the pieces of this book work well together: all the authors of the core technical essays met to discuss their outlines; several met once again to discuss completed drafts; and the editor provided detailed suggestions on each draft for cross-referencing and avoiding unhelpful duplication. But some duplication can be a positive strength, providing readers with various perspectives on a given issue. Thus, Peter Wilson's essay includes a brief discussion of strategic defense, which is the focus of Keith Payne's essay, but Wilson's outlook is somewhat different, and the two together offer a more complete analysis than one would alone. Several issues, such as reconstitution and verification, bear heavily on the subjects of various authors and have been discussed in a number of pieces.

These justifications are relevant to a book whose goal is not to provide a definitive verdict on its subject. In another way, however, our purpose here is much bolder than a mere consideration of VNAs. For the concept opens a window onto an entirely different model of world politics: one in which nuclear weapons have been abolished. Virtual arsenals offer a way of testing the strategic implications and practical feasibility of a world in which nuclear weapons have been shunted firmly to the margins of international relations.

One recognition critical to understanding the debate in this book is that virtual arsenals are not, or at least aspire not to be, tantamount to complete and total nuclear disarmament as traditionally understood. Under VNAs, nation-states would retain components of strategic nuclear arsenals—missiles, guidance sets, fissile material, warheads—that could be reassembled within a given amount of time. The exact number of such reconstitutable arsenals and their precise status are among the most important issues to be resolved in any VNA agreement, but the decisive fact about VNAs is that such arsenals do exist and that nation-states could therefore theoretically continue to rely on nuclear weapons for such missions as ultimate homeland defense and nuclear retaliation once their virtual arsenals have been reassembled. This is very different from complete nuclear disarmament, which envisions the utter destruction of all nuclear materials and components and is based on the clear and verifiable *in*ability of any nations to reconstitute a nuclear arsenal.

Nonetheless, in a virtual nuclear world the role of nuclear weapons in world politics would be transformed. The credibility of some of the more elaborate deterrent policies, such as the U.S. policy of extended nuclear deterrence, might decline substantially. Power relations between nuclear and nonnuclear states might change. Simply put, the currency of nuclear weapons would be significantly devalued, and states that have relied upon them for security would have to learn to live without any nuclear warheads ready for use on a regular basis. Thus, some analysts, such as Kenneth Waltz in his reaction essay, argue that, for all intents and purposes, VNAs do suffer the same basic faults as disarmament.

It is hardly surprising, then, that much of the analysis that follows focuses on the strategic implications of a nonnuclear world for the five declared nuclear powers and other nations. One can see this in the case studies, which assess the reactions of various states to a denuclearized world. One can sense it in the perspectives of nations such as the United Kingdom and France, whose likely reactions to VNAs emphasize the threat they pose to the war-avoiding qualities of nuclear weapons. One can appreciate the transformative strategic implications of VNAs as well in the essay by Keith Payne, which contends that, while many see strategic defenses as potentially destabilizing today, in a world of VNAs they might be one of the most stabilizing defense policies imaginable.

In short, our aim in this book is to raise the ultimate questions at the root of debates about nuclear policy and nuclear arms control: What are the purposes of nuclear weapons in international relations? Do they continue to serve those purposes in the wake of the Cold War? If not, what are the strategic implications of a denuclearized world?

Fred Iklé, former undersecretary of defense in the Reagan administration and currently a distinguished scholar with the Center for Strategic and International Studies in Washington, has put these questions in a different way, with customary wit and insight. "Let us imagine the inherited [U.S. and Russian nuclear] arsenals did not exist," he posits. "Would Russian defense planners now argue that Russia must build and deploy a missile force to hurl thousands of nuclear weapons at the United States? Would the U.S. secretary of defense testify before Congress that the United States must purchase 3,500 strategic warheads to threaten the destruction of Russia?"[3] Presumably not; but *if* not, then what nuclear arrangement is suitable for the present strategic environment? The concept of VNAs serves as a useful analytical tool to raise these questions.

In the sections that follow, I examine three distinct questions. First, I lay out the basis for the new consensus on the value of strategic arms control. Second, I provide more explanation and details of the concept of VNAs. And, finally, I examine a number of critical issues and questions surrounding VNAs.

VISIONS OF NUCLEAR ARMS CONTROL

In the wake of the Cold War, analysts of every political stripe and academic persuasion have called for a reorientation of the place of nuclear weapons in world politics and U.S. policy. Many writers now contend that, if the Cold War energized the East-West nuclear competition, then its end should allow some reduction in the degree to which the United States, and indeed all states, rely on nuclear weapons to keep the peace.

The recent international relations literature is therefore filled with proposals for nuclear arms control. In the early post–Cold War years, from perhaps 1988 through about 1992, a series of studies argued for reductions in U.S. and Russian strategic nuclear arsenals from their Cold War peaks of 20,000 or more to roughly 2,000 weapons. Few of these works challenged the basic assumption that nuclear weapons should remain, in some form and for some time, an adjunct to deterrence. They merely contended that the deterrent requirements of the major world powers could be fulfilled with a fraction of the weapons that had been deployed during the previous forty years. Some went as far as to propose a more radical reduction of nuclear arms, perhaps to levels commonly associated with "minimum deterrence"—some 50 to 300 nuclear weapons or even lower.[4] Each analyst writing on the subject focused on a different theme, a different rationale, for a postnuclear world.

One report that represented the intersection between these two approaches was *Toward a Nuclear Peace,* issued as a panel report in 1993 by the Center for Strategic and International Studies and published in book form the following year. In this report a study group including former secretary of defense Harold Brown, former national security advisor Zbigniew Brzezinski, and the noted scholar Thomas Schelling argued that the United States should aim to reduce U.S. and Russian strategic nuclear arsenals to no more than 1,000 warheads each by the year 2010, slash the operational tempo of nuclear forces, and declare a policy of no-first-use toward nonnuclear weapons states. In this it had much in common with the preceding analyses. But it also suggested more far-reaching steps, proposing that the United States initiate discussions to establish an international treaty prohibiting nuclear first use and begin consideration of various nuclear end-states, including, in the very long-term, complete disarmament.[5]

Other observers have taken up this same theme and extended the analysis even further. Paul Nitze, the author of NSC-68 and one of the originators of containment, argued that high-tech conventional weapons were far more credible and effective as deterrent threats than nuclear weapons.[6] "As a coldly rational approach to a new security strategy and as a morally correct foreign policy choice," Nitze wrote in a later elaboration on the theme, the U.S. government should convert "the principal focus of our strategic deterrent from nuclear to conventional weapons. The idea that the future peace and well-being of the world should rest upon the threat of the nuclear annihilation of large numbers of noncombatants is unacceptable."[7]

As Nitze suggests, a nonnuclear world would maximize U.S. conventional military dominance. Through its advanced technologies and pursuit of what is now commonly known as the "Revolution in Military Affairs," the United States now has, and will retain for some years, a substantial degree of dominance in the field of conventional warfare.[8] Nuclear weapons in the hands of potential U.S. adversaries, especially in the developing world, only degrade this advantage. This represents the inverse of the situation during the Cold War, when U.S. officials believed only their threats of nuclear retaliation offset Soviet conventional strength in Europe. Now Washington is the one being deterred by nuclear weapons, and a program to reduce their influence in world politics would maximize U.S. power.

Other analysts joined Nitze in proposing dramatic new avenues of nuclear arms control. Fred Iklé pointed out the dangerous role nuclear weapons could play in reinvigorating a U.S.-Russian hostility. Writing with other top U.S. and Russian defense experts, Iklé recommended a strict no-first-use policy and a path to de-alerted nuclear forces, with the vast majority of warheads removed from operational status.[9]

Robert Manning of the Progressive Policy Institute brought a third rationale to bear on the case for a dramatic approach to nuclear arms control: the dangers of nuclear proliferation. While its importance and the degree to which it must dominate U.S. national security policy are sometimes exaggerated,[10] proliferation certainly constitutes a growing concern for the United States; since the late 1980s nonproliferation has achieved top billing on almost all lists of foreign policy and defense priorities. If a global arms-control regime could help address the threat of proliferation—by establishing rigid new verification and inspection requirements, for example, and by focusing even more intense world approbrium and pressure on new proliferators—it would therefore promote a chief U.S. national interest. In recognition of this fact, Manning proposed movement toward a "postnuclear ethic" for the declared nuclear powers and new proliferants alike. Manning recommended movement toward a level of 100 to 200 or less "actual" nuclear weapons, with a substantially larger "virtual" arsenal of disassembled or deactivated weapons held in reserve.[11]

A similar focus on the connection between arms control and nonproliferation underlay the argument of Barry Blechman and Cathleen Fisher, who wrote at the end of 1994 that "America's continued reliance on nuclear weapons cripples its efforts to persuade others not to seek nuclear capabilities" and suggested that "the gradual elimination of *all* such weapons from *all* countries—including America—should be the U.S. objective."[12] And this same issue prompted some startling comments in the summer of 1994 by Air Force Gen. Charles Horner. A chief planner of Gulf War air operations and at the time head of the U.S. Space Command, Horner said flatly:

> The nuclear weapon is obsolete. I want to get rid of them all. I want to go to zero. I'll tell you why. If we and the Russians can get to zero nuclear weapons, think what that does for us in our efforts to counter the new war. The new war is this [proliferation of] weapons of mass destruction in an unstable world. Think how intolerant we will be of nations that are developing nuclear weapons if we have none. Think of the moral high ground we secure by having none.[13]

Like Nitze, Horner contended that nuclear weapons are essentially unusable by the United States against a developing world nation, and General Horner elaborates on these thoughts in his piece in this volume.

In short, by the end of 1994 discussions of dramatic arms control were no longer confined to a narrow fringe of left-wing defense analysts.[14] The idea had graduated into the big leagues of policy proposals, being proposed as an actual option or a topic for detailed investigation by a group of analysts spanning the ideological spectrum. And, rather than raising ill-defined concerns about the terrible potential of nuclear weapons and the need for peace among nations, these studies now make their case with hardheaded arguments that dramatic reductions in nuclear arms benefit U.S. national security interests. Roger Molander and Peter Wilson of the RAND Corporation have summarized the growing consensus:

> In the U.S. military . . . there appears to be a rising belief that a United States properly armed with conventional weapons may not need to rely on thousands of at-the-ready nuclear weapons to satisfy its future defense and deterrence needs. At the same time . . . there is a rapidly growing appreciation that a small nuclear arsenal in the hands of a regional predator (such as Iraq in 1991) would present any U.S. or U.S.-led military force with a daunting set of basic military problems. From this conjunction of factors there emerges an interest in exploring what it would take to de-emphasize in a profound fashion the role of at-the-ready nuclear arsenals in international security.[15]

This consensus, it is important to recognize, has not yet advanced throughout the entire U.S. military, and remains especially alien to the civilian leaders of the U.S. defense establishment, even under the Clinton administration. For that reason the proposals for substantial nuclear reductions made by proponents of this view remain in the category of policy options in need of study—and one such proposal is for virtual nuclear arsenals.

NUCLEAR WEAPONS IN WORLD POLITICS

What, then, is the role of nuclear weapons in the new, post–Cold War world? For the last forty years skeptics countered proposals for substantial nuclear reductions with two arguments. They first pointed out that Washington could hardly trust Moscow to implement such an agreement faithfully. But, with the change of government in Russia and recent Russian cooperation on verifying and implementing the START accords, that argument—while not disappearing altogether, especially given recent political trends in Moscow—has declined radically in force.

Second, and more fundamentally, those who opposed deep cuts in nuclear arms argued that such weapons in fact represented the world's best hope for peace. In an anarchic system of states, the argument goes, nuclear weapons provide an indispensable deterrent to war. With them the United States and the Soviet Union avoided war from 1945 to 1990. Without them, and cut loose from their Cold War moorings, the great powers might easily come into conflict yet again.

On this latter point there are two basic schools of thought. A minority view holds that nuclear weapons are basically irrelevant to peace, that the "long peace" of the Cold War was due to many factors that will continue irrespective of nuclear weapons.[16] The dominant school argues to the contrary that nuclear weapons, by making major war unthinkably destructive, have been central in eliminating war as a policy option for the great powers and, more fundamentally, that nuclear weapons have had a critical calming effect on the naturally anarchic nature of the international system.[17] To eliminate nuclear weapons, according to this school, would be to invite major war back into world politics—a line of thinking reflected in Kenneth Waltz's unflattering assessment of the VNA concept included in this volume.

New proposals for reductions in nuclear arms have thus run head-on into an ancient theoretical debate. Each school—the nuclear-weapons-are-irrelevant school and the nuclear-weapons-are-indispensable school—makes its argument with persuasive force and with reference to historical evidence. And the simple fact is that we will never truly know which is correct; or, to be more specific, it is impossible to *disprove* the thesis that nuclear weapons are indispensable to preventing the major powers from considering recourse to war. The only way to tell for sure would be to pursue complete and total disarmament and see what happens, a risky and politically untenable strategy. Subsequent essays discuss this debate and its implications, both for VNAs and, more broadly, for the goal of a denuclearized world.

Short of deterring conventional war, nuclear weapons can take on an additional role besides deterring nuclear use by other countries: deterring or preventing the use of chemical and biological weapons. Often, though perhaps wrongly, grouped with nuclear arsenals as "weapons of mass destruction," chemical and biological weapons pose a major threat to the United States, its allies, and especially its military forces. In the period before the Persian Gulf War, U.S. officials feared that Saddam Hussein's Iraq possessed both in substantial quantities and would use them against U.S. troops, and the U.S. reaction to this threat carried important implications for the future of nuclear weapons. The Bush administration, in a letter delivered to the Iraqi foreign minister, made a vague threat of nuclear retaliation for chemical or biological use. Because the United States has forsworn the use of both chemical and biological weapons, some believed that Washington's only recourse to deter their employment was to threaten to hit back with the one weapon of mass destruction it retained the right to use, nuclear weapons.

Some observers now contend that this threat was instrumental in heading off Iraqi use of chemical and biological weapons. And yet, if it became accepted practice, the use of nuclear deterrence for this purpose might constitute a barrier to arms control. What U.S. president, for example, could agree to a proposal for virtual arsenals knowing that it might undermine the credibility of U.S. deterrent threats and make U.S. military forces vulnerable to chemical and biological attack?

This issue goes to the heart of the VNA proposal, testing the advocates' claim that virtual arsenals could continue to deter because they could be reconstituted and used. If, for example, an aggressor hit U.S. forces in the field with a massive biological attack, the U.S. president could then order the remating and use of one, or five, or a dozen nuclear weapons. To augment deterrence of such an attack in the first place—if, for example, U.S. forces were preparing to engage in hostilities against an adversary that had threatened the use of biological weapons—the president might order the remating of a half-dozen weapons as a signal of resolve regarding the U.S. commitment to retaliate with nuclear weapons. Skeptics would reply that a leader like Saddam Hussein might bank on the fact that U.S. public opinion would prevent a president from reassembling and using a nuclear weapon in retaliation and thus would be undeterred from using other weapons of mass destruction.

Yet the question is immensely complicated, because at least two former Bush administration officials have publicly stated that they would *not* have actually retaliated with nuclear weapons in the Gulf War. They were using the threat of such retaliation as a deterrent but had absolutely no intention of carrying out that threat, because to do so would have provoked a strong international protest—and perhaps accelerated nuclear proliferation around the world.[18] This policy highlights a possible distinction between *operational* and *declaratory* nuclear policy: the civilian leaders of the U.S. government may not expect to launch a nuclear retaliation against a chemical or biological attack (although the U.S. military almost certainly has contingency plans to allow such a strike), but they will refuse to make that decision public in the hope that potential future leaders like Saddam Hussein might think that the U.S. would do so. Whether such ambiguity is a good thing and whether it could be preserved under arms-control schemes like VNAs are subjects that require attention.

VIRTUAL NUCLEAR ARSENALS

To a significant degree, then, the established consensus in favor of further nuclear arms control is a viewpoint in search of an ultimate implication—the long-term nuclear future that it might support. Many of the analysts proposing deeper reductions in nuclear weapons favor cuts to at least 1,000 weapons in the United States and Russia; others favor a global transition to truly minimum deterrents of perhaps 300 weapons in the United States and Russia and 100 to 200 in the other three declared nuclear powers. Most support near-term steps such as the Comprehensive Test Ban Treaty (CTBT) and a global end to the production of new fissile material.

Each of these proposals, however, begs the ultimate question of where the overall process is heading. To marginalize nuclear weapons in world politics is not necessarily to eliminate them, and at least in the governments and defense-policy communities of the declared nuclear powers, arguments for complete nuclear disarmament continue to fall on deaf ears. Vulnerable to cheating through covert nuclear weapons programs, offering no effective response to nuclear programs in the developing world, running squarely into the complaint that it would make the world safe for conventional (and perhaps chemical and biological) warfare, disarmament as traditionally understood enjoys little support among the declared nuclear powers or their allies. And yet this indisputable fact resides uneasily alongside the growing recognition that a process of nuclear arms control, while undoubtedly carrying important risks, might also stand to benefit U.S. and worldwide interests in important ways.

This discussion raises a powerful question—perhaps the single most important question in the field of nuclear arms control for the next two decades and a question that constitutes the underlying motivation for this book: Is there some arrangement of nuclear weapons that would achieve some of the advantages of complete disarmament while avoiding its most important pitfalls?

A hint can be found in the fact that many nations will always possess the ability to constitute a nuclear arsenal in relatively short order: the technology and fissile material to assemble a sizable number of nuclear devices within several days, weeks, or months. For most developed and a few developing states the question is not whether they could have nuclear weapons but, rather, how long it would take to deploy them. The key criterion becomes the cushion of time between a given stage of nuclear technology and a deployed nuclear force.

For nuclear weapons states, creating such a cushion means banning the existence of assembled, ready-to-use nuclear weapons. The United States and Russia have already begun to move in this direction by reducing the alert levels of portions of their nuclear arsenals. The goal for a VNA would be a situation in which no nuclear weapons were assembled and ready for use. Gradually, nuclear weapons states would dismantle all assembled nuclear devices and place the resulting parts—perhaps including warheads, delivery vehicles, and fissile material—under bilateral, multilateral, and/or international inspection. The weapons would be separated from the delivery systems in such a way that any attempt to marry the two could be verified. Several writers have labeled the resulting nuclear forces virtual nuclear arsenals.[19]

Many of the essays in this book describe how a virtual nuclear arsenal might work. Not all of them offer the same model of a VNA, and it is important to note the fine distinctions that crop up in the pages that follow. My own description here attempts to offer the bare bones of a possible VNA arrangement and to highlight the main areas of contention about how it might be arranged.

To begin with, in the early phases of a transition to virtual arsenals all the declared nuclear powers might keep a reserve of operational nuclear weapons—a handful of submarines at sea or mobile missiles on land or some combination of the two. Gradually, however, the operational readiness of the reserve could be reduced—for example, by removing guidance sets from missiles at sea. In the *final* stage of a program of establishing virtual arsenals, no nuclear weapon would exist in assembled form. Advocates argue that moving toward virtual arsenals would establish a two-phase process of deterrence: former nuclear powers would deter one another from reconstructing their nuclear arsenals with the threat to match such a move; and if two or more arsenals were ever reconstructed, the nations holding them would deter one another from actual use by the same sort of deterrence that prevails today. A regime of virtual arsenals, like the NPT itself, would need to have a clause through which member states could withdraw from the agreement—that is, indicate their intention to reassemble part or all of their nuclear arsenal. Provisions for such a withdrawal process would have to be very clearly spelled out to insure that, should one or more states make such a decision, the transition to a reassembled world would be a stable one. Whether such a system could work reliably and in a stable fashion is one of the major questions facing VNAs.

The critical measurable criteria at the core of a VNA regime would be the *time* required for weapons to be reassembled. Already, as described in Bruce Blair's essay, many nuclear weapons have been rendered unready for prompt use or for use in a matter of minutes; VNAs would extend that existing process to a more fundamental level. The basic distinction might be that, whereas existing reductions seek to create a cushion of hours, or at most a day, before nuclear weapons could be used, VNAs would attempt to create a cushion measured in days or weeks. Once the VNAs were in place, governments could decide to lengthen that time line to weeks or months.

No black-and-white dividing lines exist between these various levels of operational readiness. At what point VNAs would turn into "disarmament," for example, is probably more of a theological than an objective issue. For our purposes, however, the critical distinction lies on the other side of the spectrum: the one that separates a relatively traditional, fully operational, but low-alert nuclear force from a VNA. This, too, is a subjective question, but for the time being it is probably enough to think of the two as involving a matter of "hours" versus "several days or weeks" to prepare nuclear weapons for use.

To give this new deterrent regime teeth, the nuclear powers would need to establish a program for storing the dismantled weapons in a survivable fashion. No state should be capable, through the reassembly of 100 or 200 weapons, of achieving a first-strike ability against one or more of the other nuclear weapons states. By storing warheads and delivery vehicles in secret (though monitored) or survivable locations, and by keeping a certain number of submarines and mobile missiles operational (although not ready for launch on a day-to-day basis), a number of hedges could be built against the risk of breakout. Again, though, as many of the following essays suggest, the reliability of such hedges is open to question. Virtual arsenals in fact raise a powerful dilemma between verification and survivability: the two trade off fairly directly, and it is not clear that the trade-off can be resolved.

As noted, virtual arsenals are not equivalent to disarmament by abolition, at least as that latter concept is traditionally understood. Individual nations would retain the components of nuclear weapons and the reassuring knowledge that they could reassemble them within a fixed amount of time. No international body would take possession of the weapons. Advocates of VNAs hope that this distinction will answer many of the most obvious criticisms of disarmament. They suggest that no renegade state could obtain leverage by constructing a handful of nuclear weapons, because the nuclear powers would simply reassemble a few dozen of their own, and deterrent by threat of retaliation would have been reestablished. Knowing this in advance would presumably persuade the renegade state not to waste its effort. Moreover, proponents suggest that the supposed existential value of nuclear weapons—deterring the prospect of major war by rendering it unimaginably horrific—would remain, as any all-out war would lead to reassembly and thence to nuclear use. For this same reason, advocates contend, those nations that now rely on security pledges from nuclear powers as a rationale for eschewing their own arsenals could continue to do so.

All of this matches very closely the proposal made by Jonathan Schell in 1984 (and updated by an exhaustive, three-year study by the RAND Corporation in the 1990s[20]). Schell envisioned a world in which nuclear weapons had been dismantled, but which also "would permit some particular, defined level of armament to be achieved in a fixed lead time to nuclear rearmament—say, 6 weeks:"[21]

> The task for strategy in a nuclear-weapon-free world would be to design a capacity for nuclear rearmament which could not be

destroyed in a first strike by a nation that took the lead in rearmament by abrogating the abolition agreement, secretly or openly. . . . If that requirement was satisfied, possession in a nuclear-weapon-free world of the capacity for rebuilding nuclear weapons would deter nations from rebuilding them and then using them, just as in our present, nuclear-armed world possession of the weapons themselves deters nations from using them.

Today, Schell continued, "missile deters missile, bomber deters bomber, submarine deters submarine. Under what we might call weaponless deterrence, factory would deter factory, blueprint would deter blueprint, equation would deter equation."[22]

Schell pointed out in defense of his scheme that, while "it has often been said that the impossibility of uninventing nuclear weapons makes their abolition impossible," in fact "under the agreement described here the opposite would be the case. The knowledge of how to rebuild the weapons is just the thing that would make abolition *possible,* because it would keep deterrence in force." If one nation raced into nuclear rearmament, Schell contended, this act would "set in motion all over the world the countermeasures that would prevent any repetition: not only the victimized nation but every other nuclear-capable nation in the world would rearm with nuclear weapons to confront the violator."[23]

VIRTUAL ARSENALS: ISSUES AND PROBLEMS

The proposal to move toward virtual nuclear arsenals—or, in Schell's terminology, weaponless deterrence—raises a host of related issues and problems. It is the purpose of subsequent essays to assess these subjects in detail; here I will skim over them briefly. Together they raise the key questions that must be answered before virtual nuclear arsenals attain the status of a worthwhile idea, let alone a meaningful policy proposal.

To begin with, advocates of any arms control scheme must address the question of whether international events will be hospitable to the further reduction of nuclear arms. The essays in this book generally assume that the time required before virtual arsenals could be implemented ranges somewhere between ten and twenty or thirty years. The essays propose no firm time frame within that range, but the key fact is that reaching the end-state of virtual arsenals will take at least a decade. Virtual arsenals, therefore, will be the result of a fairly extensive process of arms control stretching over many years, not a rapid, one-move transition. Analyses of the likely political and other reactions to the idea must take this fact into account: objections to (or arguments for) the proposal today may no longer be relevant after the substantial learning curve involved in a two- or three-decade arms-control process. On the other hand, it is impossible to predict the future, and neither this study as a whole nor its individual essays make any grand assumptions about the specific world system that will be in place twenty, thirty, or fifty years from now. All the authors recognize that the nature of world politics—whether it is cooperative, conflictual, or somewhere in between—will carry important implications for the feasibility and desirability of virtual arsenals.

Taken together, these various issues raise the first question that must energize research into VNAs and related arms control proposals:

> Question 1: What is the context for arms control over the next decade? What role will there be for the use of force in the international system, and what implications does the answer hold for virtual nuclear arsenals and other arms control proposals?

Many of the essays note the important distinction between the character of world politics during the transition to virtual arsenals and their character once such a deterrent arrangement has been fully established. A period of relatively benign trends in world politics—that is, a world short of intense new great-power rivalries—may well be necessary to bring about such a dramatic reorientation of nuclear weapons in world politics, though authors may differ about the range of world systems that would allow virtual arsenals to be established. Yet it is also clear that, for VNAs to be defensible, they must not assume that a cooperative world order becomes a permanent fixture of the international system; they must, instead, be capable of surviving a substantial growth in interstate hostility once they have been established.

When we then turn to the specific characteristics of a VNA regime, perhaps most fundamental is the issue of what, exactly, virtual nuclear arsenals would look like. Would the warheads simply be removed from the missiles? Would the fissile material also be separated from the warheads? Would the physical warheads and delivery vehicles be destroyed or merely stored? Each of these various options comes complete with a somewhat distinct definition: de-mating, dismantlement, disassembly, and so on.

Part of the answer emerges in the simple fact that the process would inevitably begin with the simplest procedure and move from there. Indeed, as Bruce Blair explains in his essay, the first steps toward virtual arsenals have already begun, with the de-targeting and partial de-alerting agreements reached by the United States and Russia. From the current position, the most fundamental next step would be the de-mating of nearly all nuclear warheads from their missiles, with one or two hundred left as an operational reserve. Eventually these weapons, too, would be dismantled. Thus, after a period of, say, ten to fifteen years, all the declared nuclear powers (and perhaps several threshold states as well) would possess a certain number of nuclear warheads and a number of delivery vehicles, each stored separately from the other and all under close international monitoring.[24]

From that point a host of further steps could be imagined. States could destroy all the dismantled warheads save one or two hundred, the fissile material of the rest placed under close guard or burned in nuclear reactors. Or, rather than destroying them, nuclear weapons states could bring the weapons to a further stage of disassembly, perhaps by removing the fissile material and guidance sets and storing them separately. Or the delivery vehicles themselves (the missiles and bombers) could be destroyed.[25]

The problem of finding an acceptable transitional arrangement is especially acute for nuclear missile submarines. As the most survivable leg of several nuclear arsenals—and, in the case of the United Kingdom, France and perhaps soon China, the dominant leg—submarines offer an important residual guarantee against a first strike. It would be important for a regime of virtual arsenals to preserve that guarantee. Removing the undetectable submarine from the deterrent equation would inevitably render nuclear arsenals more vulnerable, even to conventional attack. In the first stage of the transition to virtual arsenals this would not be a significant problem; each declared nuclear power could keep all or most of its allowed residual force of 200 or so operational nuclear warheads at sea. Eventually, however, even those weapons would be disassembled, and the architects of a virtual deterrence regime would then have to find some way of keeping a nuclear deterrent at sea without allowing it to be operational on a day-to-day basis.

A number of specific procedures might achieve this goal. Initially, all nations operating nuclear missile submarines could remove the guidance sets from the missiles and store them either on land or in conventional attack submarines or surface ships, where they could be claimed in case of attack. Submarines would be tagged for identification, and "once or more per month each side would be allowed to request a random surfacing" and examination of the missiles on a given submarine. "A sufficient number of random call-ups could establish a statistical improbability that a significant number of submarines were violating the agreement."[26] Alternately, whole warheads could be removed and stored separately, although this might require drastic modifications of the missiles and submarines to allow at-sea remating.

The basic character and organization of VNAs is the foundation for all other analysis of the proposal. The specific aspects of one or another model of VNAs—and slightly different versions are offered here by Bruce Blair, Peter Wilson, Michael Wheeler, and others—will carry important ramifications for issues like verification and stability. These issues therefore raise the second policy question surrounding VNAs:

> Question 2: What, specifically, would a virtual nuclear world look like? What would be the elements of a VNA agreement, in such areas as: force structure; doctrine; reconstitution requirements; allowable strategic defenses and stages through which the countries would pass?

The specific organization of VNAs is highly contingent, and not all the authors in this book agree on precisely the same transition strategies and end points in the process. Whether the nuclear warheads themselves would eventually be disassembled and whether delivery vehicles would be destroyed—these and many other specific aspects of VNAs are flexible and a matter of individual preference.

A particularly notable point of disagreement centers around the role of missile defenses that might be deployed to complement virtual arsenals. As Keith Payne discusses in his essay, whereas strategic defenses are destabilizing in a world of operational nuclear forces by threatening to support a first strike, they might help stabilize a disarmed world by undermining the early value of rearmament. If an aggressor nation were considering a rapid breakout in which it would quickly assemble 200 or 300 warheads and if its intended victim had a strategic defense capable of reliably intercepting twice that number, the aggressor might be deterred from its plans.

On the other hand, at least four potential drawbacks of strategic defense might remain even in a virtual nuclear world: their vulnerability, their ineffectiveness against certain forms of attack, their cost, and their role in fomenting instability. If the defenses relied heavily on space-based sensors and weapons, an aggressor might believe it could attack the defense directly to clear the way for its nuclear blackmail. Given the similarity of anti-satellite (ASAT) weapons to traditional military and civilian space technologies, a clandestine ASAT program might be even easier to maintain than a secret rearmament program. Nor could even a space-based defense respond adequately to all forms of attack, such as depressed-trajectory submarine-launched missiles fired from waters close to shore or ground-hugging, sea-launched cruise missiles. An aggressor might focus its rearmament in these areas and attempt to skirt the deterrent power of the defense. Any strategic defense, and especially one employing space-based components, will be enormously expensive, an expense that the cash-strapped nations of the West might be unwilling to bear in the coming decades. Finally, the assumption that defenses would produce stability in a VNA regime may be wrong: a combination of rapid breakout from the agreement and strategic defense may prove highly *de*stabilizing in the early phases of reconstitution.

Verification in a world of virtual arsenals would require a significant upgrading of the staff and powers of the International Atomic Energy Agency (IAEA) or the creation of some parallel organization. Any monitoring agreement underlying a regime of virtual nuclear arsenals must give the agency the ability to verify, with high confidence, both the provisions of the dismantlement agreement itself (such as the separation of warheads and delivery vehicles) and the nondiversion of civilian nuclear material for a clandestine weapons program. As David Kay explains in his essay, this would require extraordinarily broad-based powers of short-notice inspection and continuous monitoring of key nuclear weapons–related facilities. Important, too, the monitoring organization must have this ability, not only among the declared weapons states but in borderline proliferants as well. Whether nations like North Korea, Iran, Iraq, India, Pakistan—and even Russia and China—would be willing to subject themselves to much tougher verification measures in exchange for disarmament among the declared nuclear powers may prove a critical variable in the feasibility of VNAs.

As discussed in a number of essays, these requirements raise the powerful question of whether any of the declared nuclear powers would allow the sort of verification required to monitor adequately a VNA regime—a third broad policy issue facing the concept.

> Question 3: What would be the verification criteria for a VNA regime, and would the agreement be verifiable according to those criteria?

Developing clearly-understood criteria for verifying VNAs will be especially important and difficult. How perfectly must monitoring work? Would the secret reassembly of five weapons be catastrophic to the system? Or twenty? The issue cannot be considered in isolation, but must be examined in the context of the answers to question 2: precisely *what kind* of VNA regime is established. A VNA system with substantial strategic defenses, for example, might guard against low levels of cheating better than one without them. Similarly, a regime that managed to preserve an invulnerable deterrent—such as nuclear missile submarines constantly at sea yet not ready to fire their weapons—could help deal with cheating by insuring that the cheater could not obtain a first-strike advantage.

A virtual arsenal treaty will also need to resolve the thorny question of the circumstances under which parties would be allowed to reassemble nuclear weapons. One obvious example is the withdrawal clause mentioned earlier: states will want to preserve a right to withdraw from the treaty in a stable manner, with enough warning time and verification of the steps to rearmament that others will not fear for their security. But there are bound to be hundreds of intermediate questions. What if a country wants to reassemble one weapon? Or five? Or twenty?

The fundamental requirement for any reassembly might be a formal notification, presumably at the United Nations, of a nation's intention to reassemble a given number of weapons. A limit on partial rearmament might be established—say, ten or twenty warheads; if a nation felt the need to reassemble more than that, it might need to declare a full withdrawal from the treaty.[27] Once a nation had declared its intention to conduct a partial rearmament, its reasons for doing so, and the expected duration of the rearmament, other states could make their own decisions about whether to match that number. If the United States, for example, stated a need to reassemble five bombs to deter Iraqi biological weapons attack, one might expect other nuclear powers not to reassemble any of their own weapons, at least initially. Indeed, the effect of such statements might be to make them unnecessary: the world community, seeking to avoid nuclear reassembly and use, might demand an Iraqi pledge of nonuse of biological weapons, with threats of nonnuclear sanctions if Iraq did not comply.[28]

But all of this is highly suggestive. The precise way in which reconstitution would work, in legal as well as practical terms, remains to be decided. And these questions—the legal procedures for reconstitution—are especially important because they also provide the basis for discussing the fourth critical policy issue of the VNA proposal: stability. Whether an arrangement like this could survive crises, and even wars, without giving rise to destabilizing reassembly races, races that might be far *more* destabilizing than continued deterrence at current levels, leads to the fourth major question:

> Question 4: How stable would the VNA regime be? Could reconstitution procedures be established that would help insure a stable reassembly process if one became necessary?

The Cold War criteria would be that each state should retain a survivable nuclear retaliatory force—that the transition process and the virtual arsenals end-state should not make any state's nuclear components vulnerable to preemptive attack by any other state (the traditional offensive deterrence-through-threat-of-retaliation model of the last half-century). But this mode of thought may no longer be appropriate for a nuclear arrangement designed specifically to transcend such thinking. Individual authors in this book will differ on their exact thinking about the nature of and requirements for deterrence; nonetheless, because the Cold War deterrent mind-set remains in place, it is safe to assume that a virtual arsenals scheme will be asked to meet the traditional definition of stability, at least initially.

Perhaps the most serious challenge to be overcome is the risk of asymmetries in reaction times that could emerge in a virtual arsenal context. If one nation could reconstitute its forces more rapidly than others it might have a strategic advantage; in particular, dictatorships might have an edge over democracies, in which legislatures and pressure groups might serve to obstruct a rapid reconstitution in time of crisis. This risk is magnified by another challenge to stability: the risk of virtual proliferation. If the impression arose that possession of a virtual arsenal was acceptable, many nations might build up to a robust virtual capability to match the level to which the declared nuclear powers had come down. The result would be to put many more nations as the starting line of a potential reconstitution race, with possibly negative implications for security.

A related but distinct set of stability problems relate to great powers' attempts to deter regional adversaries. Virtual arsenals must answer stability questions attendant to the stability of deterrent relationships aimed at such nations as Iraq and North Korea. Would a U.S. transition to such arsenals undermine the stability of regional deterrence? The issue is complicated by the fact that different actors are likely to have very different ideas of stability. Stability for the United States, for example, might involve, through the dominance of U.S. conventional forces, instability for countries like Russia and China. Some countries might also see the U.S. lead in missile defense technologies as conferring an unstable advantage to the United States in a reconstitution process.

A further element of complexity will be the fact, as argued by Peter Wilson in his essay, that the relationship between nuclear and nonnuclear weapons will become much murkier in a world of virtual nuclear arsenals, with important implications for stability. Dismantled nuclear forces might become vulnerable to long-range conventional precision weapons; in thirty or forty years states seeking retaliation against a rogue aggressor's nuclear strike may not need to reconstitute virtual weapons; and the threat posed by chemical and biological weapons is likely to grow.

The idea of virtual nuclear arsenals also raises broader, systemic questions of stability. One is the issue of extended deterrence. This mission of U.S. and, to a lesser extent, Russian and (increasingly) French nuclear forces is held to be critical in forestalling proliferation among the allies of these nuclear powers. But whether and how extended deterrence would function in a virtual world are questions that demand close analysis, and the potential implications for stability are clear enough: if U.S. allies worried about the future U.S. commitment to their security, they might seek more independent means of defense, including nuclear weapons. This, in turn, could begin a process of unraveling alliances and undermining Western solidarity. These risks point us to an important broader issue—the effect of a transition to VNAs on U.S. power and prestige in a wider sense. Thus the question:

> Question 5: Would VNAs enhance or undermine U.S. power and leadership in the international community?

The answer to this question is, of course, complicated by the fact that it might be contingent on who is asking it—the United States, its allies, or its potential rivals.

One particular development in a world of VNAs that would bear on relative U.S. power would be the presumed elevation of the opaque nuclear states—India, Israel and Pakistan—to the level of the five declared nuclear powers. This would change power relationships and perceived influence in significant ways and thus carry important implications for stability in the Middle East and South Asia. Such considerations encourage us to ask a further question.

> Question 6: What are the strategic implications, and ramifications for U.S. national interests, of moving from a P-5 of recognized nuclear powers to an N-8 of officially recognized virtual powers?

In other words, would VNAs represent a more equitable distribution of nuclear weapons capabilities worldwide, or would they merely trade a P-5 for a P-8? And what are the implications for stability?

Finally, the ultimate question regarding systemic stability focuses on the theme with which this essay began—the role of nuclear weapons in deterring major war. If such a role exists, VNAs might threaten to undermine it; thus a critical issue to be resolved by VNA proponents is:

> Question 7: Would VNAs represent something different from true disarmament in that they would preserve an existential deterrent to other forms of warfare, or not? Are the conditions in

world affairs that would allow VNAs fundamentally different from those that would make disarmament possible, or not?

Many of the essays that follow examine this question either explicitly or by implication. It is perhaps the most important single issue confronting the virtual nuclear idea, and it is also one of the most difficult to address. We do not know, for certain, exactly how critical nuclear weapons have been to avoiding war since 1945, and so we cannot know for sure how dangerous their dismantlement might be. Like all the other questions outlined here, however, this is one that must be confronted if the nations of the world are to contemplate a future in which nuclear weapons have been pushed to the margins of world politics. And like the other questions, confronting it requires an informed, articulate debate—a debate we hope to begin in the pages that follow.

NOTES

1. For an argument that *all* arms control suffers from this dilemma, see the quotation from Colin Gray in Keith Payne's essay, "Strategic Defenses and Virtual Nuclear Arsenals," in this volume, n. 17.
2. John W. R. Lepingwell, "START II and the Politics of Arms Control in Russia," *International Security* 20, no. 2 (Fall 1995): 63, 90.
3. Fred C. Iklé, "The Second Coming of the Nuclear Age," *Foreign Affairs* 75, no. 1 (January-February 1996): 125.
4. See, for example, Harold A. Feiveson and Frank N. von Hippel, "Beyond START: How to Make Much Deeper Cuts," *International Security* 15, no. 1 (Summer 1990); Carl Kaysen, Robert S. McNamara, and George W. Rathjens, "Nuclear Weapons after the Cold War," *Foreign Affairs* 70, no. 4 (Fall 1991); Michael May, George Bing, and John Steinbruner, *Strategic Arms Reductions* (Washington, D.C.: Brookings Institution, 1988); Michael J. Mazarr, "Military Targets for a Minimum Deterrent," *Journal of Strategic Studies* 15, no. 2 (June 1992); and The National Academy of Sciences, *The Future of the U.S.-Soviet Nuclear Relationship* (Washington, D.C.: National Academy of Sciences, 1991).
5. See Michael J. Mazarr, project director, *Toward a Nuclear Peace: The Future of Nuclear Weapons in U.S. Foreign and Defense Policy* (Washington, D.C.: Center for Strategic and International Studies, June 1993); and Mazarr and Alexander T. Lennon, eds., *Toward a Nuclear Peace* (New York: St. Martin's Press, 1994).
6. Paul H. Nitze, "Is It Time to Junk Our Nukes?" *Washington Post,* January 16,

1994, C1-C2.

7. Paul H. Nitze, "A Conventional Approach," U.S. Naval Institute, *Proceedings*, (May 1994), 46 ff. Nitze was not recommending immediate disarmament. His primary goal was a stronger and more credible U.S. defense policy; in fact he went on to argue that "the United States would be wise to continue to maintain a secure and widely dispersed array of nuclear weapons and their delivery systems" until such time as "the nuclear weapons of other nations constitute no threat to the *overwhelming strategic nuclear superiority* of U.S. forces" (emphasis added.) Instead, his argument, as he summed it up, was that "even though the current world situation requires us to maintain an overwhelming nuclear strategic capability, it would appear unwise and unnecessary for us to use that capability, even in retaliation." For a similar argument, see Seth Cropsey, "The Only Credible Deterrent," *Foreign Affairs* 73, no. 2 (March-April 1994): 14-20.

8. The *revolution in military affairs* refers to capabilities for information dominance and precision strike, partly displayed in the Persian Gulf War, that are changing the nature of major war. For a superb introduction to the issue, see Eliot Cohen, "A Revolution in Warfare," *Foreign Affairs* 75, no. 2 (March-April 1996): 37-54. For a more detailed examination, see MTR Study Group, *The Military-Technical Revolution* (Washington, D.C.: Center for Strategic and International Studies, 1993).

9. Fred C. Iklé and Sergei A. Karaganov, cochairmen of the Joint Project on U.S. and Russian Defense Policy, *Harmonizing the Evolution of U.S. and Russian Defense Policies* (Washington, D.C. and Moscow: Center for Strategic and International Studies and the Council on Foreign and Defense Policy, 1993): 23-31. More recently, Iklé has added another twist to his argument: control of nuclear arms, he now contends, is also essential to the preservation of democracy: "Whether by accident, because of a terrorist act, or as part of a military campaign, a nuclear bomb might explode someday, unleashing forces that would transform the international system far more profoundly than did the collapse of the Soviet empire." Given the "emotional shock destructive nuclear detonations would generate," Iklé worries, and the intrusive government powers that would be required to address the risk in advance, "democracy cannot survive in a highly uncertain world in which a smuggled nuclear bomb might be detonated in Paris or Manhattan and in which such calamities might recur." A bold initiative in nuclear arms control is therefore required, among other reasons, "so that open societies could continue to flourish" ("Second Coming of the Nuclear Age," 119, 128, 127).

10. See Michael J. Mazarr, *North Korea and the Bomb: A Case Study in Nonproliferation* (New York: St. Martin's Press, 1995), esp. chaps. 9, 10.

11. Robert A. Manning, *Back to the Future: Toward a Post-Nuclear Ethic—The New Logic of Nonproliferation* (Washington, D.C.: Progressive Foundation, 1994): 29. Thanks partly to Manning's efforts, the Democratic Leadership Council—significantly, the organization of *moderate and conservative* Democrats—adopted in 1994 as part of its 10-point "Progressive Alternative"

for President Clinton the notion that the United States should push for a nuclear-free world by the year 2045 (see Robert A. Manning, "Ending the Nuclear Century," *New Democrat* [January-February 1995]: 54-56). Also making the connection between arms control and nonproliferation, and offering a "thought experiment" remarkably similar to Manning's proposal, is Michael Wheeler, in "Nuclear Disarmament: Preconditions and Prospects" (paper prepared for the NGO Committee on Disarmament, the United Nations, New York, April 21, 1993).

12. Barry M. Blechman and Cathleen S. Fisher, "Phase Out the Bomb," *Foreign Policy*, no. 97 (Winter 1994-95): 79, 82-83.

13. Horner cited in "Horner Advocates Negotiating Elimination of Nuclear Weapons," *Inside the Air Force*, July 22, 1994, 12-13; and John Diamond, "Air Force General Calls for End to Atomic Arms," *Boston Globe*, July 16, 1994, 3.

14. See also Dr. Thomas W. Graham, "Abolishing Weapons of Mass Destruction: Realistic Goal or Fantasy?" (Paper prepared for Seminar on Global Cooperation for the 21st Century, Zao, Japan, July 8-16, 1994.)

15. Roger C. Molander and Peter A. Wilson, "On Dealing with the Prospect of Nuclear Chaos," *Washington Quarterly* 17, no. 3 (Summer 1994): 24-25.

16. This argument is made most forcefully in John Mueller, *Retreat from Doomsday: The Obsolescence of Major War* (New York: Basic Books, 1989).

17. Kenneth Waltz is the foremost modern theorist to emphasize the role of nuclear weapons in moderating the anarchic competition of states; see *Theory of International Politics* (Reading, Mass: Addison-Wesley, 1979).

18. It is important to note that this reticence to use nuclear weapons was not the position of all Bush administration officials. Secretary of Defense Richard Cheney, for one, apparently fought for consideration of nuclear options if Iraq used chemical or biological weapons. Thus it was not necessarily the official position of the administration to play the nuclear card only as a bluff, yet, given the strong opposition to nuclear use in some quarters of the government, in effect that might have been what happened.

19. The term *virtual arsenals* is used in Roger Molander and Peter Wilson, *The Nuclear Asymptote: On Containing Nuclear Proliferation*, MR-214-CC (Santa Monica, Calif.: RAND Corporation, 1993). Other authors who have discussed similar proposals include Jonathan Dean, "The Final Stage of Nuclear Arms Control," *Washington Quarterly* 17, no. 4 (Autumn 1994): 1-52; Peter Gray, *Briefing Book on Non-Proliferation of Nuclear Weapons* (Washington, D.C.: Council for a Livable World Education Fund, 1993): 19; Arjun Makhijani and Katherine Yih, "What to Do at Doomsday's End," *Washington Post*, March 29, 1992; Manning, *Back to the Future*, 29-30; Mazarr, *Toward a Nuclear Peace*, 73-75; Wheeler, "Nuclear Disarmament: Preconditions and Prospects"; and Jonathan Schell, *The Abolition* (New York: CITE, 1984).

20. Molander and Wilson, *Nuclear Asymptote*; and Marc Dean Millot, Roger Molander, and Peter Wilson, *The Day After . . . Study: Nuclear Proliferation*

in the Post-Cold War World, vol. 1: Summary Report (MR-266-AF); vol. 2: Main Report (MR-253-AF); vol. 3: Exercise Materials (MR-254-AF) (Santa Monica, Calif: RAND Corporation, 1993).

21. Schell, *Abolition,* 118.

22. Ibid., 119.

23. Ibid., 120, 144.

24. While Schell refers to a very thorough dismantling as the final goal, he notes that "any increase [in the lead time required to use nuclear weapons] would be beneficial. For example, if the nuclear powers today did nothing more than remove the nuclear warheads from their missiles and store them nearby, so that it would take, say, 6 hours to put them in again, the gain would be great. It would increase the lead time by several thousand percent" (*Abolition,* 135).

25. As Schell recognizes, control of delivery vehicles might in the long run be "even more important than the abolition of warheads," because without a bomber or missile to deliver them, nuclear warheads become largely irrelevant (Ibid., 153).

26. Mazarr, *Toward a Nuclear Peace,* 24. The report offered this methodology in support of a different idea—an agreement to keep submarines a certain distance away from coasts—but the principle is the same.

27. Choosing that number will involve a delicate balancing act: on the one hand, ensuring that no nation could rearm sufficiently to pose a first-strike threat to the disassembled nuclear storage facilities of another; but on the other hand, allowing a sufficiently large exception so that parties to the treaty were not constantly tempted to withdraw completely.

28. This process would offer many of the advantages of a proposal, made by George Quester and Victor Utgoff, that nuclear powers consult at the United Nations before using nuclear weapons (see Quester and Utgoff, "Toward an International Security Policy," *Washington Quarterly* 17, no. 4 [Autumn 1994]: 5-18).

PART TWO

ELEMENTS
OF VIRTUAL
DETERRENCE

Nuclear Doctrine and Virtual Nuclear Arsenals

Michael Brown

SINCE THE END OF THE COLD WAR in the late 1980s, fundamental changes have taken place in relations between some of the world's biggest military powers. It is therefore a propitious moment to reassess the role that nuclear weapons should play in international and national security affairs.

One of the most innovative ideas that has been put forward is for all declared and undeclared nuclear powers to transform whatever operational nuclear capabilities they have into "virtual nuclear arsenals."[1] The idea, as Michael Mazarr has written, is "to ban the existence of all assembled, ready-for-use nuclear weapons, and thus to push them to the background of world politics."[2] Over time, bombs and warheads would be decoupled from delivery vehicles and dismantled, and their component parts would be placed under international inspection. The reconstitution of nuclear weapons would be declared contrary to international law. It is argued that states would be deterred from re-arming or trying to acquire nuclear weapons by the threat of rearmament. This, it is said, would make the world a less dangerous place.

The natural starting point for investigating the merits of this conception of the future is by taking a close look at nuclear doctrine. In this essay, I will endeavor to do three main things. First, I will define *nuclear doctrine* in more elaborate terms and delineate the main elements of nuclear doctrine. Second, I will provide an overview of nuclear thinking in the United States, Russia, China, France, and Britain, seeking to identify areas of continuity and change since the end of the Cold War. Third, I will discuss how nuclear doctrines would have to change in a world of virtual nuclear arsenals.

I advance three main arguments. First, to understand nuclear doctrine properly, one must look at both the general ideas that leaders have about the roles nuclear weapons play in international and national security affairs and the specific plans that states make to use nuclear weapons in time of war. The latter include assumptions and decisions about timing, targeting, and the size of one's attack. Second, although nuclear weapons have become less important in some respects with the passing of the Cold War, there is still considerable attachment to large, fully operational nuclear arsenals and provocative nuclear doctrines. This is true even in the United States, which has seen its most formidable strategic challenges evaporate with the collapse of Soviet power in Eastern Europe and the breakup of the Soviet Union itself. Russia and China are in some ways more attached than ever to their nuclear arsenals. China's nuclear doctrine and forces are evolving in particularly worrying ways. Third, transforming the nuclear forces of the five declared nuclear powers into virtual nuclear arsenals will require profound changes in attitudes in all five countries. It will require adopting a nuclear doctrine that is fundamentally different from long-established and deeply entrenched modes of thinking and planning. In short, the intellectual and organizational barriers to the adoption of virtual nuclear arsenals are formidable.

ELEMENTS OF NUCLEAR DOCTRINE

I define *nuclear doctrine* broadly to include both the ideas that leaders have about the roles nuclear weapons play in international and national security affairs and the specific plans that states make to use nuclear weapons for deterrence and defense. The former include beliefs about whether or not nuclear weapons contribute to strategic stability, whether or not they are essential for national security, and whether or not they are important to have for political or status reasons.

Plans to use nuclear weapons have three main elements.[3] First, nuclear war plans reflect assumptions and decisions about timing. Do plans exist to use nuclear weapons first, either in a campaign of aggression, as a preventive attack, or to preempt an adversary who is about to strike? Or do plans reflect an operational commitment—as opposed to a rhetorical declaration—to "no first use?" Even if one is committed to no-first-use as an operational guideline, plans can be geared to either a quick response (launch on warning) or riding out an attack and responding hours or days later.

Second, nuclear war plans reflect assumptions and decisions about the kinds of targets that should be attacked. In theory, five main sets of targets can be attacked: (1) the nuclear forces and nuclear infrastructure of one's adversary; (2) other military targets, such as conventional forces, naval bases, and depots; (3) economic and industrial targets, including transportation and communications networks; (4) leadership targets, including bunkers for civilian and military decision makers; and (5) cities and population centers. In practice, some target sets and specific targets within these sets are given higher priority than others. For example, U.S. nuclear war plans have historically emphasized the first four of these five target sets, and priorities within and between these sets have ebbed and flowed over time.[4]

Third, nuclear war plans reflect assumptions and decisions about the size of one's attack. Do plans contain options for limited nuclear attacks, or do they feature only massive attacks involving most of one's arsenal? Military organizations tend to favor the latter, believing that limited nuclear options take important forces away from main attack plans and that limited attacks would leave remaining forces in a vulnerable position. It is also believed that it will be difficult if not impossible to carry out limited nuclear exchanges because of command and control vulnerabilities and because adversaries might not be willing or able to distinguish between selective and massive nuclear attacks. Military leaders also fear that civilian decisionmakers will not be able to grasp the intricacies of nuclear operations in the very short amount of time the latter typically devote to their study. In any event, military leaders do not want civilians micromanaging military operations in time of war. This, it is fervently believed, is the domain of military command-ers. It is not surprising, therefore, that a recurring theme in the history of U.S. nuclear doctrine is the civilian struggle to introduce limited nuclear options into U.S. nuclear war plans.[5]

Students of public policy, bureaucratic politics, and organizational behavior will find it easy to understand why nuclear war plans are slow to change.[6] If plans have been in place a long time, it will be easier to see them or characterize them as successful. If plans are elaborate, changes can involve enormous amounts of work. Ideas about how nuclear operations should be conducted can evolve into belief systems and become part of an organizational culture; belief systems and organiza-tional cultures are not predisposed to change. Changing nuclear doc-trines and operational plans is especially difficult if particular doctrines and plans become closely identified with the "essence" of specific military organizations.[7] In short, bureaucratic, organizational, and intellectual inertia can be considerable.

NUCLEAR THINKING IN THE POST–COLD WAR ERA

Given the magnitude of the transformation that has taken place in the strategic landscape since the late 1980s, it is not surprising that there have been changes in the nuclear policies of the five declared nuclear powers. That said, the post–Cold War era has seen more continuity than change in nuclear doctrine in the United States, Russia, China, France, and Britain. Post–Cold War nuclear thinking and nuclear war plans have much in common with their Cold War antecedents. In addition, although some of the changes that have taken place in nuclear doctrine have created an environment more conducive to the adoption of virtual nuclear postures, others have had precisely the opposite effect. Russia and China, in particular, are more attached than ever to large, operation-al nuclear arsenals and provocative nuclear doctrines. For advocates of virtual nuclear postures, attitudinal and policy changes in these coun-tries are part of the problem—not part of the solution.

At the most general level, many still argue that nuclear weapons contribute to international stability in important ways. In the United States, former secretary of defense Les Aspin maintained that "some states seek evidence and reassurance that America will protect their interests and help them safeguard their security. . . . The United States cannot ignore the fact that its military posture and, particularly, its nuclear posture may influence the decisions by others to either acquire or forgo their own nuclear weapons and other weapons of mass destruction."[8] The argument, in other words, is that the United States can dampen incentives to acquire nuclear weapons and enhance international stability by continuing to maintain a nuclear posture that extends deterrent benefits to allied states. Policymakers in Britain still see nuclear weapons as stabilizing influences in an unsettled and dangerous world.[9] Strategic thinkers in France, looking back on the many failures of conventional deterrence in the twentieth century, continue to place great emphasis on the stabilizing virtues of nuclear weapons.[10]

The consensus about the utility of nuclear weapons is even stronger with respect to national security calculations. The established nuclear powers continue to believe that nuclear weapons contribute to national security in important ways.

It is undeniably true that, with the end of the Cold War, the United States faces a less challenging set of strategic and military problems and that it is less preoccupied with nuclear weapons. Policymakers and military planners no longer worry about the Soviet Union launching a massive, counterforce nuclear attack against the United States or a conventional blitzkrieg into Western Europe. Strategic deterrence and extended deterrence have consequently become much more manageable problems, and policy makers in Washington have become less obsessed with the nuclear balance. This, in turn, has led to a series of sweeping agreements with Moscow with respect to strategic, theater, and tactical nuclear weapons. Force structures have been reduced, many programs have been canceled, and commitments have been made to make even deeper cuts in nuclear forces in the future.[11] The United States and Russia have pledged to destroy all of their ground-launched tactical nuclear weapons. The United States, Russia, and Britain have promised to stop deploying tactical nuclear weapons on naval vessels in peacetime. The U.S. military—the army and navy, in particular—has de-emphasized nuclear weapons to a considerable degree. Indeed, it sees nuclear programs as budgetary competitors to conventional undertakings, to which it attaches a higher priority.

That said, there is no doubt that policymakers in Washington continue to believe that nuclear weapons constitute one of the main pillars of U.S. national security. The Clinton administration's Nuclear Posture Review, launched with great fanfare in October 1993 as a comprehensive effort aimed at "rewriting the rules for the Post–Cold War world,"[12] concluded in September 1994 and embraced the status quo. Nuclear weapons, it was said, would be needed for the foreseeable future, first, as a "hedge" against a turn for the worse in Russia and, second, to deal with the threats posed by rogue states eager to acquire nuclear weapons or other weapons of mass destruction.[13] The strategic triad—long-range bombers, intercontinental ballistic missiles (ICBMs), and submarine-launched ballistic missiles (SLBMs)—would be preserved. Large numbers of strategic nuclear weapons would be retained, and a new strategic arms reduction treaty (START III) would not be pursued in the near term. Those who had hoped for a radical reassessment of the role nuclear weapons would play in U.S. defense policy were disappointed by the outcome of the Nuclear Posture Review. Although some "adjustments," as the Pentagon put it,[14] would be made to the U.S. nuclear force structure, the main result of the review was to identify force levels below which the United States would not go and to promulgate rationales for maintaining those robust force levels. Traditionalists within the U.S. defense establishment clearly carried the day.

In Moscow, the last time the strategic landscape looked bleaker was 1941. With the collapse of Soviet power in Eastern Europe, Moscow lost what were, from a defensive standpoint, important buffer states. Making matters worse, the United States and its Western European allies have promised to bring some of Moscow's former allies into the North Atlantic Treaty Organization (NATO) in the not-too-distant future. Many people in Russia see these developments as threatening. Things are seen as equally bad on the eastern and southern fronts. China, which has a long history of troubled relations with Russia, has a booming economy, a modernizing military, and a burning desire to reassume its place as a dominant world power. The southern front poses more fractured but nonetheless worrying problems: here, too, strategic buffers have been lost, and Russian leaders worry about an Islamic revival sweeping from Iran and Afghanistan into Azerbaijan, Tajikistan, Uzbekistan, and points farther north.[15]

From Moscow's standpoint, strategic buffers have disappeared and threats have grown just as Russia's economy has collapsed and its conventional military capabilities, once formidable, have evaporated.

The pathetic performance of the Russian military in Chechnya was not just embarrassing to Moscow—it was terrifying. Many Russian leaders see their country under siege on all fronts and virtually defenseless. If nuclear weapons are *one* of the pillars of U.S. defense policy, they are *the* pillar of Russian defense policy, given the perceived lack of near-term conventional alternatives. This is one of the main reasons why many Russian leaders would like to scrap or rewrite the START II agreement and why some in the Russian nuclear establishment are unenthusiastic about cooperating with the United States on denuclearization initiatives.[16]

Although China's strategic position has improved with the collapse of Soviet military power in East Asia and the reduced U.S. military presence in the region, it has long-term strategic concerns and strategic aspirations that have led it to place considerable emphasis on the development of its nuclear arsenal. China's main strategic concern is Japan's economic and technological prowess, which gives Tokyo the ability to field the kinds of sophisticated conventional forces that were devastatingly effective during the Gulf War. Japan also has latent (arguably, virtual) nuclear capabilities. Although China's conventional military forces are large and becoming more advanced as time goes by, Japan still has decisive technological advantages that it will continue to enjoy for the foreseeable future. From Beijing's perspective nuclear weapons equalize the equation and make it possible for China to pursue its goal of regaining its dominant position in East Asian affairs, which it is determined to do. China's leaders also believe that they need to improve their nuclear capabilities vis-à-vis the United States. They believe that Washington has already adopted a containment strategy designed to keep China from challenging the United States as the world's leading political, economic, and military power. They are also keen to deter the United States from interfering in whatever unfolds between mainland China and Taiwan. As far as Beijing is concerned, Japan and the United States will inevitably resist China's efforts to improve its relative position, they are formidable powers that have to be dealt with from a position of strength, and improving China's nuclear capabilities is therefore essential.

France and Britain operate in radically different strategic circles, but leaders in both countries nonetheless believe that retaining nuclear arsenals is vitally important for national security reasons. Although the problem is not articulated in these terms, British and French policymakers believe that their countries need to retain nuclear capabilities as hedges against the emergence of an aggressive Russia and an isolationist United States: there are good historical reasons for worrying about both of these possibilities. In addition, leaders in both countries worry about threats posed by rogue states, regional troublemakers, and the proliferation of weapons of mass destruction. Nuclear weapons continue to constitute the foundation of national security planning for these two countries, which no longer have the resources of vast overseas empires to draw on.

Powerful nuclear arsenals are also believed to be important for political or status reasons. For better or worse, policymakers in all five countries continue to see a state's international standing being closely tied to the possession of nuclear weapons.

Although the United States has the world's largest economy and most powerful conventional military forces, many Americans see the country's massive nuclear arsenal as an important, tangible manifestation of its superpower status. Policymakers in Washington were willing to enter into agreements with Moscow that eliminated excess capabilities, reduced force structures, and stabilized the nuclear balance, but they have shown no interest in slashing the U.S. nuclear arsenal to a point at which it would be comparable in size to the Chinese, French, and British arsenals. Policymakers in Washington refuse to think of the United States as a "medium-sized" power—it would be political suicide to propose moving in this direction—and they therefore instinctively oppose the idea of abdicating the country's status as a nuclear superpower.

These feelings are even more intense in Moscow, which struggled for decades to achieve nuclear parity with the United States, believing that the establishment of nuclear parity was a precondition to being taken seriously as a superpower. Since the late 1980s, Moscow's empire in Eastern Europe, the Caucasus, and Central Asia has collapsed, its conventional military capabilities have withered, and its economy has imploded. Russia remains a superpower in one and only one area: nuclear affairs. Moscow is desperate to remain respected as an international power, and its attachment to its nuclear arsenal is therefore stronger than ever.

China's leaders also have a long tradition of equating nuclear capabilities with international standing and prestige. Mao Zedong, for example, stated in 1958: "As for the atomic bomb, this big thing, without it people say you don't count for much. Fine, then we should build some." A Chinese strategist insisted in 1992 that if China did not have strategic nuclear capabilities, "people would look down upon us and our country's major power status would be hard to establish and preserve." In a 1993 study on China's military it was said that China's nuclear forces were an "important pillar of our country's great power status."[17] There is no doubt that China's great power aspirations have grown since the mid-1980s: Soviet military power in East Asia has collapsed; the U.S. military presence in the region has declined; and China's economy has grown by leaps and bounds, with no end in sight. Extrapolations from recent trends suggest that China's economy will be the world's largest in the first two or three decades of the twenty-first century. All of this has made China's leaders more, not less, committed to enhancing China's nuclear position.[18]

Reinforcing this trend is the mounting weakness of the Communist Party's monopoly on power in China's domestic affairs. Given that China has in essence embraced capitalism (albeit capitalism with "Chinese characteristics"), the rationale for Communist rule weakens with each passing day. Indeed, it is hard to think of a group less qualified to run a booming capitalist economy than the Chinese Communist Party. It is not surprising, therefore, that party leaders in Beijing have embraced nationalism and made a concerted effort to justify their continued rule on nationalistic grounds, such as bringing Taiwan back into the fold. Nuclear weapons are potent symbols of a government's accomplishments, and they can be used to promote national unity.

In France and Britain, retaining nuclear capabilities is seen as essential if their increasingly tenuous claims to great power status are to have any credibility. France's attachment to its nuclear arsenal is intimately linked to French beliefs in the country's "grandeur" and its central place on the world's stage. Britain's motivations are reinforced by its desire to preserve the "special" British-American relationship, which is one of London's unique claims to international fame and which is rooted in Anglo-American nuclear cooperation.[19]

In sum, there is still deep attachment to nuclear arsenals for both strategic and political reasons in the United States, Russia, China, France, and Britain. Nuclear policies and force structures have changed in some respects with the passing of the Cold War, but fundamental strategic and political assessments of the utility of possessing nuclear weapons have not. The biggest changes that have taken place, moreover, have taken place in Russia and China, where attachments to nuclear arsenals are greater than ever.

Not surprisingly, much less information is available in the public domain about specific nuclear war plans. The United States and Russia have undoubtedly de-emphasized tactical nuclear weapons in operational planning, having promised to destroy all ground-launched tactical nuclear weapons and many air-delivered weapons and having pledged not to deploy tactical nuclear weapons on naval vessels in peacetime. At the strategic level, Washington and Moscow have agreed to take all long-range bombers off alert as well as missiles scheduled to be deactivated under the terms of the START I agreement. In January 1994 the two agreed not to target strategic nuclear missiles against each other on a day-to-day basis. It is generally understood, however, that this de-targeting initiative is mainly a symbolic gesture because missiles could be re-targeted in a matter of minutes or, at most, hours.[20]

The most dramatic change in U.S. operational policy is that the number of installations targeted in U.S. nuclear war plans has dropped sharply—from 10,000 in October 1989 to approximately 3,000 in October 1995. Some of these changes came about because of an internal review of the Single Integrated Operational Plan (SIOP) that was launched in November 1989 and continued through 1990 and into 1991. The SIOP Targeting Review, as it came to be known, scrubbed the target set, eliminating installations of marginal value such as reserve airfields and alternate command posts. Through improved network analysis of transportation, communication, and industrial systems, critical nodes were identified. This also allowed U.S. nuclear war planners to eliminate installations from the target set. Weapon allocation procedures were revised, which led to a reduction in cross-targeting. As a result, the SIOP was streamlined.

The fact that the SIOP Targeting Review was under way made it easier for U.S. nuclear war planners to take into account the implications of the collapse of Soviet power in Eastern Europe and the breakup of the Soviet Union. Around 1,000 targets in Eastern Europe were taken out of the SIOP that went into effect in October 1990: Soviet forces in Eastern Europe were in the process of being withdrawn; bases were being closed; and Eastern European military forces and defense industries were no longer seen as threats. The breakup of the Soviet Union in December 1991 led to even more dramatic changes to U.S. nuclear war plans in 1992 and 1993. The number of nuclear installations in the target set dropped because thousands of tactical nuclear weapons were shipped from a wide variety of places in the former Soviet Union to military bases in Russia. Non-Russian republics were taken out of main attack plans. With the collapse of Communist Party rule the number of leadership targets in U.S. war plans declined significantly. By October 1993 the number of installations targeted in the SIOP had plummeted to around 3,500.

Although dramatic changes have taken place in the SIOP since 1989, U.S. nuclear war plans remain rooted in the past in many important respects. A wide-ranging Nuclear Posture Review was conducted in 1993-94, but the basic philosophy and deterrent strategy that guide the formation of the SIOP have not changed. The kinds of targets in the SIOP and targeting priorities have not changed. More specifically, the SIOP still places tremendous emphasis on counternuclear targeting, and the levels of damage expected of attack options are still high. This translates into plans for prompt, massive attacks on a wide range of nuclear and other military facilities in Russia. In short, the plans that have been developed with respect to Russia in the 1990s are streamlined versions of the plans that were designed during the Cold War to deter and, if necessary, devastate the Soviet Union.

Furthermore, although U.S. strategic bombers have been taken off alert, U.S. ICBMs and SLBMs are still kept on very high alert rates. Some experts believe that the United States has a *de facto* launch-on-warning policy; otherwise, it would not be able to carry out the massive attacks its nuclear war plans call for.[21] This is extremely dangerous, for obvious reasons. It is also highly unnecessary, given that a Russian nuclear attack on the United States is unlikely in the extreme.

Overall, U.S. policymakers receive mixed marks for adapting U.S. nuclear war plans to the new strategic circumstances of the 1990s. Great progress has been made in taking a large number of countries and a large number of targets out of the SIOP. Little has been done, however, to reformulate the basic principles, strategic assumptions, and operational objectives that guide the formation of U.S. nuclear war plans. As a result, the basic features of U.S. nuclear war plans—prompt, massive attacks on a wide range of nuclear targets—have not changed with the passing of the Cold War. Intellectual and organizational inertia is considerable.

In his first major speech on nuclear policy, Boris Yeltsin, the president of the newly independent Russian Federation, declared in January 1992 that many Russian nuclear programs would be scrapped or scaled back, Russia and the United States should reduce their strategic arsenals dramatically, and Russia and the United States should not target their nuclear forces at each other.[22] Yeltsin's January 1993 signing of the START II treaty—which called for the complete elimination of multiple-warhead ICBMs, the backbone of the Russian nuclear force structure—suggested that Russia was moving away from its traditional reliance on nuclear weapons and that profound changes were taking place in Russian thinking about nuclear doctrine.

The "new" Russian military doctrine approved in November 1993, however, showed that Russian nuclear doctrine still exhibited more continuity than change.[23] Nuclear deterrence was reaffirmed as one of the cornerstones of Russian military policy. The new Russian guidance also specified that "the whole complex of strategic weapons" would have as one of its tasks deterring conventional attacks against Russia and its allies. This reinforced Moscow's willingness to consider using nuclear weapons first in a crisis. Perhaps the biggest change in Russian policy was the revocation of Moscow's 1982 no-first-use pledge. Although Moscow declared in November 1993 that it would not use nuclear weapons against any nonnuclear state that was a party to the Nuclear Nonproliferation Treaty (NPT), it left open the door to using nuclear weapons against nonnuclear states that were allied to a nuclear power. This shift in policy seems to have been directed at states in Central and Eastern Europe that have been lobbying to join NATO. In short, Russia's latest statements about its nuclear doctrine reflect what one analyst has called Russia's "renewed infatuation with nuclear weapons."[24]

The most authoritative study of Chinese nuclear doctrine in the 1990s suggests that the problem in this case is not continuity but change—change in provocative directions. According to Iain Johnston, starting in the late 1980s, Chinese nuclear strategists began to refine what they called a doctrine of "limited nuclear deterrence."[25] Johnston explains:

> Limited deterrence rests on a limited war-fighting capability
> aimed at communicating China's ability to inflict costly damage
> on the adversary at every rung on the escalation ladder and thus

denying the adversary victory in a nuclear war. . . . Limited
deterrence therefore requires the development of a greater number of tactical, theater, and strategic weapons that are accurate
enough to hit counterforce targets, are mobile, can be used in the
earliest stages of a nuclear crisis, and . . . are capable of penetrating
ballistic missile defense systems. . . . Given that China does not
now have such capabilities, the straight-line prediction would be
that over the next decade or so, we should expect to see a
discernible effort to shift the forces away from a minimum strike-
back assured destruction posture, which China now has, toward
limited war-fighting.[26]

This new Chinese nuclear doctrine, which is based on the idea that
nuclear weapons play critical roles in deterring both conventional and
nuclear wars and that nuclear weapons might have to be used early in a
crisis, flies directly in the face of proposals to adopt virtual nuclear
postures. As Johnston puts it: "The deterrent and war-fighting value of
nuclear weapons, in the eyes of these strategists, has not declined over
the past decades, but has, in fact, increased. . . . Regrettably, in an era
where much international effort is being put into de-legitimizing the
utility of nuclear weapons, Chinese military strategists have apparently
been moving in the opposite direction."[27]

Nuclear doctrine in Britain and France, on the other hand,
continues to be influenced by the constraints that shaped British and
French nuclear policy during the Cold War.[28] Because of economic and
financial limitations, Britain and France were never able to deploy more
than a few hundred nuclear weapons during the Cold War. It therefore
made little sense for these countries to adopt counterforce nuclear
doctrines that placed a high priority on attacking Soviet nuclear forces:
it was inconceivable that British or French nuclear attacks could do more
than dent the Soviet nuclear arsenal. Both Britain and France consequently favored counter-cities targeting options that evolved, as the two
countries deployed larger numbers of more accurate warheads in the
1980s, into plans to attack a wider range of economic and administrative
"vital centers." The idea, as British officials put it, was to emphasize
attacks on "key aspects of Soviet state power." This, it was hoped, would
deter aggression in the first place. British and French nuclear modernization plans have been scaled back since the end of the Cold War, and

this has only reinforced Britain's and France's attachment to these established doctrinal principles. It appears that British and French nuclear war plans continue to emphasize retaliatory countervalue strikes and eschew prompt counterforce options.

NUCLEAR DOCTRINE IN
A VIRTUAL NUCLEAR WORLD

The nuclear doctrines of the five declared nuclear powers will have to change in fundamental ways if proposals for creating virtual nuclear arsenals are to be implemented effectively. Currently, policymakers in the five declared nuclear states believe that having operational nuclear arsenals is closely linked to the promotion of international stability, national security, and political status. They also believe—certainly in the United States and Russia and increasingly in China—that being able to launch prompt, powerful attacks against an adversary's nuclear forces is extremely important. All of this will have to change if a world of virtual nuclear arsenals is to be created and if it is to be sustained over time.

In essence, nuclear weapons would have to be "decoupled" from both broad strategic calculations and specific war plans. Starting at the broadest level, strategic thinkers would have to abandon their reliance on nuclear weapons as stabilizing influences in international affairs and devise other ways of promoting interstate stability and, where necessary, extended deterrence. Policymakers and military planners would have to abandon their deep reliance on nuclear weapons as the ultimate guarantors of national security and devise other ways of providing for the common defense. This will not be easy, given that different states face different kinds of threats, have different economic and technological resources on which to draw, and are able to field conventional forces with dramatically different capabilities. The United States is better suited to a virtual nuclear world than any of its great power counterparts because it faces no continental threat, because it has a strong economy and technological base, and because it has a head start in applying advanced technologies to conventional forces. Other states will be less inclined to adopt virtual nuclear postures because these strategic asymmetries work against them and because these asymmetries are not likely to go away.

National leaders will also have to decouple the possession of nuclear arsenals and international status. This will not be easy because, as noted earlier, all five declared powers closely associate their nuclear capabilities with their international standing. India, which is desperate and determined to be taken seriously as a great power, is deeply attached to its nuclear program for this reason as well. Although changing these attitudes will be difficult, this might be a more manageable proposition than taking nuclear weapons out of national security calculations: attitudes change slowly, but they do change; objective strategic circumstances, such as continental vulnerabilities and economic and technological bases, change at a glacial pace, if at all. Since none of the five declared nuclear powers is likely to voluntarily and unilaterally denuclearize, the best way to proceed might be to elevate the standing of nonnuclear powers. Making Germany and Japan permanent members of the United Nations (UN) Security Council would, for example, elevate their standing and decouple possession of nuclear weapons with being part of the "inner club" of international affairs. Making India a permanent member of the Security Council, provided that it agreed to join the NPT as a nonnuclear state and enter into the creation of a nuclear weapon–free zone in South Asia, would serve the same purpose. In short, elevating the international status of leading nonnuclear powers is probably the best way of enticing established nuclear powers to give up their nuclear arsenals: denuclearizing would then involve a smaller drop in status and would therefore be more bearable.

At an operational level, nuclear war plans would have to be reconceived. Currently, nuclear war plans in the United States and Russia, for example, feature prompt, massive attacks on a wide range of nuclear targets. In a virtual nuclear world, nuclear doctrine would have to change across the board. First, the main purpose of shifting to virtual nuclear postures is to make first use of nuclear weapons extremely difficult and to reduce response times from minutes and hours to days and weeks. At a doctrinal level this means changing strategic and organizational cultures: from first use, prevention, preemption, and launch on warning to no first use, delayed response, and riding out attacks. The idea of using nuclear weapons in support of conventional operations would have to be de-emphasized: nuclear and conventional operations would have to be decoupled. Attitudinal shifts of this kind are not inconceivable, but they will not come about on their own, nor will they come about overnight: attitudinal shifts of this magnitude would involve overturning decades of entrenched thinking and deeply held beliefs about how nuclear operations can best serve national security.

Second, ideas about targeting would also have to change. Currently, the United States and Russia consider the nuclear forces and facilities of one's adversary to be high-priority targets. As previously discussed, China appears to be moving in this direction as well. One of the keys to making a virtual nuclear world attractive and viable is convincing policymakers that virtual nuclear capabilities would be available in a crisis, particularly if an adversary began to rearm. This means that nuclear facilities would have to be capable of surviving a sudden attack. Moving away from the current emphasis on first-strike, counternuclear targeting would be a step in the right direction, but declarations about operational intentions would not by themselves reassure policymakers about the survivability of their own virtual capabilities. Point defenses of fissile material storage sites and nuclear facilities might be needed. To be effective, these defenses would have to include both ballistic missile and air defenses as well as defenses against commando units and saboteurs.

Shifting away from counternuclear targeting would not force a responder to attack cities indiscriminately, as some contend.[29] Instead, the responder's target list could feature—and, indeed, should feature—conventional and naval forces, transportation and communication centers, key industrial facilities, and leadership targets. For a responder to have assured penetration and assured retaliation capabilities, a ban on area defenses might be needed.

Third, and last, although virtual nuclear arsenals would not necessarily have to be small, in all probability they would be small: virtual nuclear capabilities would probably be counted in dozens rather than hundreds or thousands of reconstitutable weapons.[30] Nuclear planners will therefore have to shift away from their current attachment to massive attacks and responses and think creatively about using small numbers of weapons to maximum effect. Nuclear doctrine will have to shift away from its current emphasis on war fighting—which places a premium on prompt, massive, counternuclear attacks—and stress selective strikes on conventional and naval forces, vital economic centers, and leadership targets. Since the numbers of available weapons will probably be low, this would also argue for a ban on area defenses.

In sum, nuclear doctrines and targeting policies for virtual nuclear arsenals would have to be based on the following principles:

- Timing: Shifting away from first use, prevention, preemption, and launch on warning to no first use, delayed response, riding out attacks, and using nuclear weapons as weapons of last resort.
- Targeting: Shifting away from counternuclear targeting and relying instead on plans to attack conventional and naval forces, transportation and communication networks, vital economic centers, and key leadership targets.
- Sizing: Shifting away from attachments to massive, crushing attacks and responses and relying, instead, on options involving handfuls or dozens of weapons.

Devising nuclear doctrines and targeting policies for virtual nuclear arsenals would be easier for some countries than others. Countries such as Israel, India, and Pakistan, which are in essence virtual nuclear powers now, would presumably be able to make the adjustment to a virtual nuclear world without too much difficulty. Of the five declared nuclear powers, Britain and France would clearly find the transition easier to manage than the other three: Britain and France have small arsenals; they do not place particular emphasis on being able to make prompt nuclear responses; they have already eschewed massive counterforce operations; and they consider nuclear weapons to be weapons of last resort. Although China is beginning to place more emphasis on counterforce options, this has not yet become an entrenched way of thinking: it has not yet become part of China's nuclear strategic culture. Therefore, there are good reasons for believing that China might re-embrace the idea that nuclear weapons are weapons of last resort and that they can play a marginal role in national security affairs.

Russia and the United States are more problematic from a doctrinal standpoint. National security planning in both countries has long placed tremendous emphasis on having the ability to launch prompt, massive counternuclear attacks. Intellectual and organizational inertia is considerable in both countries. That said, there are signs of fluidity in Russian and American policy-making circles: Moscow and Washington have agreed to make unprecedented cuts in their nuclear arsenals, and they are clearly less obsessed with the nuclear balance than they used to be.

Their new thinking on nuclear issues has not yet had a correspondingly dramatic impact on nuclear doctrine and targeting policy, but one cannot exclude this as a possibility for the future.

CONCLUSIONS

The obstacles to eliminating operational nuclear arsenals and creating virtual nuclear arsenals are formidable. They include entrenched ideas about the contributions nuclear weapons make to international and national security and the political standing of one's country. They also include rigid beliefs about how nuclear weapons should be used and organizational commitments to certain modes of action. These strategic, political, intellectual, and organizational obstacles are formidable, but it would be foolish to assume that they are insurmountable. The strategic landscape changed in fundamental ways between 1985 and 1995 and is currently quite fluid. As noted at the outset, this is a propitious moment to take a hard look at the role nuclear weapons can—and should—play in international security affairs.

NOTES

1. See, in particular, Michael J. Mazarr, "Virtual Nuclear Arsenals," *Survival* 37, no. 3 (Autumn 1995): 7-26; Bruce G. Blair, *Global Zero Alert for Nuclear Forces* (Washington, D.C.: Brookings Institution, 1995).

2. Mazarr, "Virtual Nuclear Arsenals," 8.

3. For more discussion of planning and targeting issues, see Henry S. Rowen, "Formulating Strategic Doctrine," in *Commission on the Organization of the Government for the Conduct of Foreign Policy* (Washington, D.C.: U.S. Government Printing Office [GPO], 1975) 4, app. K, 217-34; Lynn Etheridge Davis, *Limited Nuclear Options: Deterrence and the New American Doctrine,* Adelphi Paper no. 121 (London: International Institute for Strategic Studies [IISS], 1975-76); Lawrence Freedman, *The Evolution of Nuclear Strategy* (London: Macmillan, 1981); Desmond Ball, *Targeting for Nuclear Deterrence,* Adelphi Paper no. 185 (London: [IISS], 1983); Fred Kaplan, *The Wizards of Armageddon* (New York: Simon and Schuster, 1983); Scott Sagan, *Moving Targets: Nuclear Strategy and National Security* (Princeton, N. J.: Princeton University Press, 1989); Janne E. Nolan, *Guardians of the Arsenal: The Politics of Nuclear Strategy* (New York: Basic Books, 1989); U.S. General

Accounting Office (GAO), *Strategic Weapons: Nuclear Weapons Targeting Process,* GAO/NSIAD-91-319FS (Washington, D.C.: U.S. GAO, 1991); Bruce G. Blair, *The Logic of Accidental Nuclear War* (Washington, D.C.: Brookings Institution, 1993).

4.   For an excellent overview of U.S. nuclear doctrine, see Sagan, *Moving Targets,* chap. 1; Kaplan, *Wizards of Armageddon.*

5.   For more details on the struggle to introduce limited options into U.S. nuclear war plans, see Rowen, "Formulating Strategic Doctrine"; Davis, *Limited Nuclear Options;* Freedman, *Evolution of Nuclear Strategy,* chaps. 7-8, 15, 25; Ball, *Targeting for Nuclear Deterrence;* Kaplan, *Wizards of Armageddon,* chaps. 12-18, 22, 25; Sagan, *Moving Targets,* chap. 1; Nolan, *Guardians of the Arsenal,* chap. 6.

6.   For a discussion of organizational inertia and change, see James G. March and Herbert A. Simon, *Organizations* (New York: Wiley, 1958); Anthony Downs, *Inside Bureaucracy* (Boston: Little, Brown, 1967); Herbert Kaufman, *The Limits of Organizational Change* (University, Ala.: University of Alabama Press, 1971); Morton H. Halperin, *Bureaucratic Politics and Foreign Policy* (Washington, D.C.: Brookings Institution, 1974); John D. Steinbruner, *The Cybernetic Theory of Decision: New Dimensions of Political Analysis* (Princeton, N. J.: Princeton University Press, 1974); Daniel A. Mazmanian and Jeanne Neinaber, *Can Organizations Change?* (Washington, D.C.: Brookings Institution, 1979).

7.   See Halperin, *Bureaucratic Politics and Foreign Policy,* chap. 3.

8.   See Les Aspin, *Report of the Secretary of Defense to the President and the Congress* (Washington, D.C.: U.S. GPO, January 1994): 57.

9.   For more on British thinking, see Stuart Croft's chapter in this volume.

10. For more on French thinking, see Michael Mazarr's chapter on the established nuclear powers, in this volume.

11. For an overview of these initiatives and agreements, see Michael E. Brown, "Recent and Prospective Developments in Nuclear Arsenals," in *Nuclear Deterrence: Problems and Perspectives in the 1990s,* ed. Serge Sur (New York: United Nations, 1993): 17-44.

12. Aspin, *Report of the Secretary of Defense,* 63.

13. For an overview of the findings of the Nuclear Posture Review, see "Remarks Prepared for Delivery by Secretary of Defense William J. Perry to the Henry L. Stimson Center" (news release, Office of the Assistant Secretary of Defense [Public Affairs], September 20, 1994); "DOD Review Recommends Reduction in Nuclear Force" (news release, Office of the Assistant Secretary of Defense [Public Affairs], September 20, 1994). For critical assessments of the Nuclear Posture Review, see R. Jeffrey Smith, "Clinton Decides to Retain Bush Nuclear Arms Policy," *Washington Post,* September 22, 1994, A1; William J. Arkin, "Bad Posture," *Bulletin of the Atomic Scientists* 50, no. 4 (July-August 1994): 64.

14. See "DOD Review," 1.

15. For more on the view from Moscow, see the essays by Alexei Arbatov and

Konstantin Sorokin, both in this volume.

16. For more on Russian attitudes toward START II, see John W. R. Lepingwell, "START II and the Politics of Arms Control in Russia," *International Security* 20, no. 2 (Fall 1995): 63-92. For a thorough analysis of U.S.-Russian denuclearization efforts, see Graham Allison, Owen Coté, Richard Falkenrath, and Steven Miller, *Avoiding Nuclear Anarchy: Controlling the Threat of Loose Russian Nuclear Weapons and Fissile Material* (Cambridge, Mass.: MIT Press, 1996).

17. Mao Zedong, the Chinese strategist, and the study of China's military are all quoted in Alastair Iain Johnston, "China's New 'Old Thinking,'" *International Security* 20, no. 3 (Winter 1995-96): 8.

18. This suggests a paradox: when a country's economy declines, as Russia's has, leaders place more emphasis on nuclear weapons as a way of trying to maintain great power status; when a country's economy booms, as China's has, leaders place more emphasis on nuclear weapons as a way of trying to establish great power status.

19. On France, see Philip Gordon's contribution to this volume. See also David S. Yost, "France's Nuclear Dilemmas," *Foreign Affairs* 75, no. 1 (January-February 1996): 108-18. On Britain, see Stuart Croft's chapter in this volume.

20. On tactical nuclear weapons and lower alert levels, see Brown, "Recent and Prospective Developments," 18-27. On de-targeting of strategic nuclear missiles, see "U.S.-Russian Strategic Missile Detargeting Complete," *Arms Control Today* 24, no. 6 (July-August 1994), 26; "U.S. Reaches Understanding with Ukraine, Russia on Denuclearization," *Arms Control Today* 24, no. 1 (January-February 1994): 19-20; Michael R. Gordon and Eric Schmitt, "U.S. Considers Aiming Missiles at Oceans, Not the Russians," *International Herald Tribune,* December 6, 1993, 1; Blair, *Global Zero Alert.*

21. See Blair, *Logic of Accidental Nuclear War,* 272-76.

22. See "Russian Arms Control Initiatives," *Survival* 34, no. 2 (Summer 1992): 122-24.

23. My discussion of developments in Russian nuclear doctrine draws on Alexei Arbatov's contribution to this volume.

24. See Konstantin Sorokin, in this volume.

25. See Johnston, "China's New 'Old Thinking.'"

26. Ibid., 41.

27. Ibid., 12, 42.

28. For an overview of British nuclear doctrine, see Lawrence Freedman, "British Nuclear Targeting," in *Strategic Nuclear Targeting* , eds. Desmond Ball and Jeffrey Richelson (Ithaca, N.Y.: Cornell University Press, 1986): 109-26. On France, see David S. Yost, "French Nuclear Targeting," in Ball and Richelson, *Strategic Nuclear Targeting,* 127-56.

29. For a devastating critique of the idea that small nuclear arsenals can only engage in city-busting attacks, see Michael J. Mazarr, "Military Targets for a Minimum Deterrent: After the Cold War, How Much Is Enough?" *Journal of Strategic Studies* 15, no. 2 (June 1992): 147-171.

30. Virtual nuclear arsenals will probably be small, first, because states will find it easier to make quantitative reductions in their nuclear arsenals than qualitative changes in the basic configurations of their nuclear assets: quantitative reductions, perhaps a series of step-by-step reductions, will probably precede decisions to eliminate all operational nuclear weapons. Second, virtual nuclear arsenals will probably be small because of the concerns states will have about verification: small arsenals will be easier to verify than large arsenals, and states will not enter into virtual nuclear arrangements unless the verification problem can be addressed to everyone's satisfaction.

THREE

COMMAND, CONTROL, AND WARNING FOR VIRTUAL ARSENALS

BRUCE BLAIR

THE PROPONENTS' BRIEF FOR VIRTUAL ARSENALS touts a multitude of benefits.[1] Deactivating the world's nuclear arsenals would downgrade the salience of nuclear weapons in international affairs, promote non-proliferation, improve weapons security and safety, and eliminate the technical ability of states to mount a sudden intentional attack. The residual arsenals would also constitute a latent threat of retaliation sufficient to deter a prospective nuclear aggressor.

The activities of the command organization that would embody the new principles of inactive deployment would revolve around the aims of operational safety and deterrence.[2] The command system would need to provide reliable stewardship of dismantled weapons in peace-time and stand ready to direct the redeployment and possible employ-ment of forces during a crisis. A key task is maintaining effective safeguards—the prevention of theft, accidents, inadvertent or illicit use—not only during peacetime but also when preparing to conduct wartime missions in crisis circumstances. The other key task is preserv-ing an ability to reconstitute nuclear forces to the strength necessary to project a convincing performance of the wartime mission. Deterrence would hinge on this capacity.

Nuclear doctrine, strategy, targeting, force structure, and other facets of virtual arsenals will shape the supporting command, control, communications, and early warning arrangements. For instance, sea- and land-based missiles require different command system design. Different assumptions about nuclear release authority, timing, and targeting also produce large variations in system design. A host of other factors will affect the ultimate form and function of a command system designed for virtual arsenals. These determinants, though explored throughout this volume, remain too speculative to hazard predictions on the exact contours of the arrangements that will evolve.

The general characteristics of such a system are discernible, however. Some are familiar attributes. As suggested earlier, any command system will concentrate on two basic aims: safety and deterrence. A transition to virtual arsenals will not relieve the system of its continuous, laborious effort to balance these objectives.

The basic mechanism for adjusting this balance also will not change. Using various means of intelligence gathering, the command system will continuously monitor its environment and raise or lower the alert level of nuclear weapons accordingly. By regulating the overall response time of nuclear weapons, it seeks equilibrium between main- taining a high standard of operational safety and upholding deterrence. The operation of this mechanism was especially visible during Cold War crises, when the alert level of U.S. and Soviet nuclear forces ratcheted up; this act compromised safety for the sake of magnifying the deterrent effect.[3] During that era the command systems worked within a narrow band of nuclear response time. The launch readiness of the vast majority of strategic forces varied from a couple of minutes to a couple of days under normal daily conditions. In crisis circumstances the command systems planned to shorten the response time to a few minutes for all the strategic forces.

Today, the alert curves are being redrawn as the basic priorities are being reformulated. Most observers acknowledge that the appropriate balance between safety and deterrence has undergone a fundamental shift. Safety claims higher priority because the easing of deterrent requirements in the post–Cold War era allows it and because safety has become more tenuous as a result of Russian disintegration and global proliferation. The new circumstances warrant a sharp shift in priorities and mandate sharp reductions in the alert levels of nuclear weapons.

Virtual arsenals represent the biggest shift; the fuse on nuclear forces would be lengthened considerably, extending the response time of nuclear forces to weeks, months, and years, while setting a much higher international standard of safety and control.

An initial adjustment in priorities in fact was made several years ago. In the wake of the August 1991 Moscow coup, Presidents Bush and Gorbachev relaxed the combat disposition of thousands of nuclear weapons. The U.S. Strategic Command took all strategic bombers off alert and downloaded and stored their weapons in nearby depots. It also took 450 Minuteman II missiles off alert, removed the launch keys from the underground control posts, and installed safety pins in each missile to block the possibility physically of rocket motor ignition.[4] Russia followed suit, deactivating a substantial portion of its strategic land-based missile force and pledging to keep its bomber force at a low level of readiness. The two governments implemented these measures in a matter of days. In addition, both the United States and Russia removed all tactical nuclear weapons from surface naval ships over the course of the next twelve months.

This wholesale deactivation partially reflected the decreasing tension in U.S.-Soviet relations, but its driving motivation within the U.S. government was to prevent any further erosion of Soviet nuclear control. The worsening social, political, and economic conditions in the former Soviet Union had earlier raised the specter of a breakdown of nuclear control; the coup reinforced the anxiety. In the judgment of many U.S. officials, shoring up the operational safety of Soviet weapons took precedence over deterrence. The latter had not eroded; the large arsenals left over from the Cold War indeed exceeded reasonable requirements of deterrence. Both sides could thus deactivate large portions of their nuclear forces, for the sake of safety, without endangering deterrence in the slightest.

Deactivation of nuclear forces will continue under START II, assuming Russia ratifies and implements it, and many forecast further movement down this path in the next decade. Although the pace and ultimate extensiveness of the process remain to be seen, this book assumes that in two decades or so conditions might be ripe enough for complete deactivation.[5] The Bush-Gorbachev deactivation demonstrated, however, that lengthening the fuse on nuclear weapons—that is, slowing their response time—can be accomplished expeditiously if desired. Furthermore, certain unexpected events could greatly accelerate the schedule of deactivation. The accidental explosion of even a single nuclear weapon, for instance, could create irresistible public demand for rapidly de-alerting all the nuclear forces of all countries.

COMMAND SYSTEM OPERATIONS: 1996

The transition from the current nuclear posture to virtual arsenals will dictate major changes in command system operations. Safety and deterrence will still be the guiding principles, but a major redesign of the U.S. and Russian command systems will be required to support the radical new pattern of low-tempo nuclear operations.

DETERRENT PRACTICES

The current practices of the U.S. and Russian command systems set the stage and need to be grasped. These practices support nuclear postures (and related activities such as submarine trailing) carried over from the Cold War, stances designed to insure the rapid destruction of many thousands of enemy targets in wartime. These postures and their attendant command practices may embody the tired old concepts of a previous era in U.S.-Russian relations, but the fact remains that neither government has replaced them.

The command systems continue their past targeting practices, though both have been scaling back the number of targets. Soviet-Russian targets, for example, in the U.S. strategic war plan fell by 84 percent during the past decade, dropping from about 16,000 targets in 1985 to 2,500 in 1995, as a result of a very extensive realignment and reduction of Russian forces.[6] Nevertheless, the command systems remain saddled with responsibility for insuring coverage of an extensive and diverse set of military and industrial targets and for inflicting severe and comprehensive damage to the entire target set in wartime. Neither side has altered this long-standing requirement.

Another feature carried over from the Cold War is a strong predisposition to rapid reaction. Thousands of weapons in both arsenals stand ready for launch on short notice. Both the U.S. and Russian command systems in fact remain geared to launch on warning—that is, launching strategic missiles after an enemy missile attack is detected but before the incoming enemy missiles arrive. Their early warning and nuclear release procedures are pegged to an option that allows only three or four minutes for detecting an attack and another three or four minutes for top-level decision making.[7]

A doctrinal shift toward minimum deterrence based on retaliation after riding out an attack appears to be under serious consideration by Russian planners, but its adoption hinges on strengthening command and control and settling the issue of ballistic missile defense (BMD).[8]

The primary option of launch on warning may seem academic since the end of the Cold War. Nevertheless, it remains an operational reality. The Russian and the U.S. command systems regularly exercise their nuclear quick draw, and Russia evidently entered the early phases of the firing procedures in January 1995, when the launch of a Norwegian scientific rocket triggered a false warning that activated Yeltsin's nuclear suitcase and initiated an emergency telecommunications conference with his nuclear advisors.[9]

Although the U.S. BMD program poses a larger political than strategic problem to Russia at this juncture, it works to reinforce Russian reliance on rapid reaction. Russian war-gamers cannot ignore the prospect that a U.S. ABM system designed only to shield U.S. territory from very limited strikes could severely weaken Russian retaliatory capability. Such a system might be able to blunt the ragged response of their decimated forces if they were forced to ride out an attack.[10]

The perpetuation of fast response times by both sides suggests that the 1994 agreement between Russia and the United States to stop aiming missiles at each other is practically meaningless. Its symbolism may comfort the public, but the agreement produced no significant change in launch readiness. Today, launching a first or second strike of massive proportions takes no longer for the U.S. command system than it took before the agreement went into effect, and the Russian system also remains practically unencumbered.[11]

Let me turn next to some command system operations that lie outside the arena of U.S.-Russian central deterrence, beginning with nuclear contingencies involving China. The United States took China out of the active strategic war plan in the early 1980s,[12] but that decision might be challenged if relations deteriorate further and if China's modernization of its strategic missiles creates a major operational nuclear threat to the United States. Meanwhile, about 700 Chinese facilities remain targets for the U.S. strategic reserve force.[13]

Russia's command system also regulates the operations of nuclear weapons aimed at China, and Russian conventional weakness insures a continuation of that war plan (called "Barrier"). Conventional weakness also dictates nuclear targeting of NATO forces. Russia's command system may be reassigning forces to cover these targets in light of the elimination and obsolescence of forces assigned to the NATO theater, such as variable-range SS-19 forces in Ukraine, and older SSBNs. Additional reassignments of strategic, theater, and tactical nuclear forces presumably will occur if NATO expands eastward.

As for regional targeting by U.S. nuclear forces, the hit list includes North Korea, Iran, Libya, and other hostile countries acquiring weapons of mass destruction.[14] Targeting such countries by the U.S. strategic reserve force began many years ago, but the recent emphasis on counterproliferation has raised the priority of this mission. Although the Pentagon envisions the use of conventional weapons to deal with the threatening weapons in the Third World, it does not exclude the use of nuclear forces, including nonstrategic as well as strategic weapons. For example, Tomahawk sea-launched nuclear cruise missiles apparently have been earmarked for possible use against Iran, and target packages have been developed for the contingency.[15]

SAFETY PRACTICES

As indicated earlier, safety problems especially plague the Russian command-control and warning system.[16] Several already significant weaknesses appear to be worsening. First, as the Russian military decays, the likelihood of unauthorized actions by Russian nuclear commanders grows, while the ability to quickly counter such actions declines. Although Russian safeguards on nuclear forces of all types are generally technically impressive, they are really, in the final analysis, just gimmicks designed to buy time, and their effectiveness depends crucially on the overall cohesion of the Russian military. Alas, that cohesion is weakening.

Second, the inherent danger of the quick-draw postures mentioned earlier is compounded by the deterioration of Russia's early warning network, which is falling on hard times, like the rest of the military infrastructure. The risk of false alarms and nuclear inadvertence would increase if Russia shortens the response time of its command system to counter Trident D-5 missile deployments, whose high accuracy and short flight times might otherwise negate Russia's option of quick launch.[17]

A third adverse trend is that Russia, at U.S. insistence, plans to shift the bulk of its strategic warheads out of silo-based ICBMs and into mobile ICBMs and submarines. Ironically, safeguards on silo-based rockets are vastly superior to those on mobile forces on land and sea. Although to fire any of these forces their commanders normally need an unblocking code held by the general staff, submarines have much weaker safeguards, mainly because of the crew's autonomy during their long patrols at sea.[18] Safeguards at the intermediate levels of submarine command are also weaker because of vulnerable communications links with the general staff. This vulnerability encourages, in a crisis, the implementation of established procedures for distributing launch authority and the unblocking codes to the level of the fleet or navy front commander.[19] As for mobile ICBMs, their safeguards are stronger than submarines but weaker than silo-based rockets.

The fourth weakness concerns the difficulty of maintaining cohesion at the top of the nuclear chain of command in Moscow, given an unstable political system that lacks effective institutional checks and balances and which depends almost completely on personal loyalties at the apex. The potential exists for a sudden shift of allegiance that causes a breakdown at the very heart of the system. Depending on the circumstances, this potential instability could be heightened or ameliorated by the fact that the Russian general staff has access to the unlock and authorization codes needed to initiate a missile attack and can exercise direct launch control over a portion of the strategic forces. This access, however, depends on a dual-key arrangement that involves the KGB.[20]

The perpetuation of the traditional deterrent practices makes it difficult indeed to distinguish Cold War from post–Cold War nuclear postures and command system operations. The public harbors an impression of change that is mostly illusory.

COMMAND SYSTEM OPERATIONS DURING THE TRANSITION TO VIRTUAL ARSENALS

After reviewing the U.S. nuclear posture, the Clinton administration endorsed a hedging strategy with a plan for the year 2003 that calls for an arsenal of 5,000 operational warheads (strategic and tactical), several thousand reserve warheads earmarked for crisis redeployment, and another cache of many thousands of plutonium pits to support even more extensive reconstitution if Russia revives nuclear hostility toward the West. Under this plan the United States deploys 3,500 strategic warheads allowed by START II and seeks no further reductions for the indefinite future.

Russia on the other hand seeks to lower the START ceiling to about 2,000 warheads, the maximum level that the Russian defense economy could sustain. Russia shows little more inclination than the U.S. to go lower than that. Indeed, Russia depends more than ever on nuclear weapons. The demise of the Red Army that protected Russia from NATO and Chinese conventional forces shifted the burden of security onto nuclear forces. Russia's new military doctrine abandons its former pledge of no-first-use of nuclear weapons and widens the conditions under which it might resort to their use. As suggested earlier, some prospective developments viewed by the Russians as adverse to their security, such as NATO expansion, could enlarge the role of nuclear weapons and militate against de-alerting measures. In the face of NATO expansion Russia would likely increase the numbers and readiness of tactical and theater nuclear forces in particular.

Achieving further large reductions in alert levels probably depends, first and foremost, on reducing the insecurity of Russia and the regional proliferator states and, secondarily, on driving home to a broad audience the safety and nonproliferation benefits. The basic argument will posit that deterrence no longer represents an endangered objective and therefore no longer warrants large arsenals on launch-ready alert. A much smaller force on lower launch readiness can easily satisfy reasonable requirements of deterrence. It will also advance the view that impeding proliferation and preventing the loss of control over nuclear weapons are much harder and more urgent than deterring deliberate aggression. It will solicit a much stronger international commitment to remove nuclear weapons from alert, going eventually to "zero alert" en route to the next stage: virtual arsenals—disassembled weapons under multilateral inspection and monitoring.

In trying to forge a consensus on the desirability of de-alerting, the proponents must establish the safety virtues and nonproliferation benefits. A quantum improvement in peacetime safety can be clearly presented by contrasting a deactivated arsenal with the one kept on "hair-trigger" alert. The salutary effect on nonproliferation is also clear: the exact accounting and internationalized monitoring required to establish zero alert is almost certainly a necessary condition for the virtual elimination of nuclear arsenals, and projecting their eventual virtual elimination is very likely to be a necessary condition for effectively managing the general process of weapons proliferation.[21]

The intermediate and transitional stage of zero alert would involve separating nuclear warheads, shrouds, or other vital components from their delivery vehicles and arranging for continuous verification of the separation. An end-state of zero alert would clearly require systematic cooperation, and transparency, among all the countries that maintain active nuclear forces. This might be easier to secure, since China, India, Pakistan, and Israel have a de-alerted posture anyway.

Monitoring would need to be especially stringent to insure that no party could gain a decisive preemptive advantage by breaking out of a zero-alert commitment.[22] As a further precaution, it would be prudent to deploy the arsenals in such a way that a portion of them would remain invulnerable and reconstitutable even if an egregious failure of verification occurred and warning of a breakout was not provided.

Global Zero Alert for Nuclear Forces outlines a crude scheme designed along these lines.[23] For current purposes, suffice it to illustrate briefly the basic idea. To de-alert the bomber forces, bomber payloads would be moved to storage facilities far away from the bombers' home bases. The retrieval and uploading of the payloads would require elaborate, time-consuming, and observable procedures. Similarly, warheads would be removed from land-based missiles and put in storage—a standard Soviet practice for all land-based strategic forces until the late 1960s. Mobile land-based missiles and their warheads would be separated, but they could both be protected from sudden attack by means of mobile basing schemes. Although warheads could also be removed from ballistic missile submarines, reinstalling them in a crisis would pose numerous difficulties. A preferable alternative might be to take guidance sets off the sea-based missiles and place them in survivable storage, perhaps on board attack submarines deployed at sea. Under routine practices the components would remain separated at all times and yet invulnerable to attack. If necessary during a nuclear crisis, the missile and attack submarines could rendezvous and quickly transfer the guidance sets, which could be installed on all 24 Trident missiles in about three days.

The implications of zero alert for command system operations are extensive and profound. The requisite command system would scarcely resemble the current system in several key respects.

DETERRENCE TO CRISIS MANAGEMENT

The command system that manages deactivated arsenals acquires much greater responsibility for managing crises. Preventing a crisis from reaching an intensity that tempts or pressures the parties to invoke nuclear threat will be among its chief aims. The salient threshold of a crisis will be the redeployment of nuclear weapons, which would likely induce a nuclear reaction and further escalation of alert readiness. A basic mission of the command system will be to diffuse nuclear tensions before feuding states cross the threshold and, failing that, to regulate the redeployment to the extent possible in the interest of stability.

To these ends the system will have an outward and inward view of crisis management. Its outward view involves diplomacy aimed at prevention but also includes negotiation on "rules of the road" for crises. The need would exist to anticipate and systematically examine various plausible situations that might lead to the crisis redeployment of weapons and to negotiate in advance a set of mechanisms for regulating the re-alerting process.[24]

The general rule to be followed would be that the party breaking out of its inactive posture would notify the other parties of its intentions, identify the pertinent weapons to be redeployed for possible use, and clarify the alerting steps and combat actions to be taken. This norm could be strengthened by designating a special storage area from which a small number of weapons could be returned to alert if that ever proved to be necessary. The limited number would provide reassurance that a larger regeneration was not being screened by the smaller contingency. This arrangement, coupled with joint monitoring already in place and national technical means of verification, should provide ample reassurance to the other parties in cases of very small operations such as those intended to deal with Third World contingencies. A small option prepared for that purpose should not trigger uncontrolled escalatory interaction among the major nuclear powers.

A more difficult but manageable situation would develop if deteriorating relations between the major nuclear powers impelled them to adopt a more aggressive alert posture. Starting from a baseline of zero alert, the steps taken to raise alert levels could be regulated by prior agreement, measured and instituted cautiously to avoid triggering an uncontrolled spiral in combat readiness. There should be protocols to notify others and to define and limit this process in advance should it ever be deemed necessary.

The least tractable but also least probable scenario engaging the major nuclear powers in escalatory alert features a classic confrontation with one party anticipating a conflict that might involve military hostilities and deciding to break out of a zero-alert regime. One or more powers could annul their cooperative partnership and dissolve the regime, and an uncontrolled escalatory spiral could ensue. Ideally, all parties would then receive unambiguous warning from joint monitoring teams and other sources that large-scale preparations were under way to bring nuclear forces quickly to a state of wartime readiness.

The chances are remote that this scenario would unfold without first passing through a phase in which a deterioration of relations leads to a gradual heightening of combat readiness for some forces. This precursor phase could have the effect of moderating the instability of the subsequent phase, as alert forces already in place, combined with invulnerable inactive weapons, would provide ballast. If a sudden breakout occurs without passing through the first phase, and if crisis alerting responses were unduly delayed on one side for political or military reasons, then stability would depend on having a zero-alert posture that provides for invulnerable and reconstitutable forces in any case.

CENTRALIZATION OF OFFENSIVE FORCE RECONSTITUTION

The inward view of the command system would reflect the critical importance of tightly regulating the regeneration of nuclear forces in an emergency. Zero alert requires the command systems to take a major discontinuous step to regenerate strategic capability. This vastly increases the likelihood that nuclear alerting would be a deliberate act of a national policy. Crisis alerting thus becomes less the diffuse process it presently is, with less chance that incremental steps could be taken by a decentralized command system driven by military exigencies.[25] Under zero alert the threshold would be raised to such heights that only a deliberate decision by a top civilian authority could cross it. This strengthens top-level control over the process and inhibits spontaneous escalation. Prior agreements and protocols devised by central political authorities before the outbreak of crisis tensions would govern alerting operations devoted to offensive force regeneration. Furthermore, the ad hoc management of offensive preparation would also be centralized to insure its correct alignment with crisis diplomacy.

The sharpened dichotomy between civilian and military control implied by these revisions of the alerting process and authority raises the possibility of creating a special custodial organization to manage the nuclear warheads or other critical components. This organization would be separate from military organizations and have its own chain of command and communications network. The Russians in fact already maintain such organizational separation: the Twelfth Main Directorate of the Defense Ministry manages nuclear warheads and other military organizations operate the delivery systems and all the other support infrastructure. This model also exists in NATO to insure the proper custody of U.S. nuclear warheads. The model could be extended to the case of virtual arsenals. A separate national custodial organization would support all the nuclear combat units.

Centralization can become excessive, however, especially if it removes all de facto checks and balances at the apex of command. Despite the legal launch authority vested in the presidents of Russia and the United States, the command systems should not be designed to enable those individuals to bypass the entire chain of command and remotely fire nuclear weapons. The Russian system went quite far down this road during the Cold War. No future system on any side should concentrate physical control to such an extent.

REFORMULATION OF DEFENSE READINESS CONDITION LEVELS

The existing levels of combat readiness for U.S. and Russian nuclear forces and the established procedures for raising and lowering those levels presently have no relation whatsoever to the idea of cooperative regulation. Virtual arsenals require a cooperative effort to subject alerting and redeployment to protocols and other covenants. The reconstitution of forces thus must conform to new rules of the road. The basic military steps taken at each higher rung of the alert ladder should correspond to these rules. Extensive revision of existing alerting procedures is necessary to align the elaborate procedures for bringing nuclear forces to launch readiness with rules formulated to impose limitations on the process, insure transparency, and otherwise provide reassurance.

STRENGTHENING REDEPLOYMENT SAFEGUARDS

Moving up the ladder of alert readiness inevitably erodes operational safety. Combat readiness takes precedence over safety for the sake of projecting threat to deter a potential aggressor. At some stage warheads would be mated to delivery vehicles, and the command systems would revert to their Cold War predilection for rapid reaction to signs of impending or actual attack. In consequence, the risks of accidental, unauthorized, or inadvertent use of nuclear weapons would rise. These risks might exceed the customary risks insofar as rusty command systems, forced to move from zero to high alert without the benefit of recent experience in mating warheads to missiles and in generally managing high-tempo operations, would be more prone to errors and accidents.

Extra precautions against these hazards need to be adopted by the command organizations. Unlock codes needed to fire nuclear forces should not be distributed as widely as they presently are, and no single code should unlock the entire arsenal. (Russian unlock codes are far more restrictive in this regard.) Predelegations of contingent launch authority (to predesignated national command authorities) should be revoked. A comprehensive review of nuclear safeguards should be undertaken to identify other correctives.

The loss of experience presently gained by daily alert operations could be substantially compensated by extensive exercising of the procedures and protocols of reconstitution. Realistic exercises would be regularly undertaken to practice redeployment and iron out the wrinkles in the cooperative monitoring arrangements. Furthermore, regular operational test firings of missiles and other weapons systems tests would be permitted, though under a strict regime of joint monitoring.

This exercise and test activity would certainly fall short of the experience necessary to manage alert operations safely during a crisis. But, then again, so do daily alert operations. The standards of safety that have evolved through repetitive learning over the past forty years have not been extended to the circumstances of advanced crisis or to the actual initiation of combat operations. There is scant reason to believe that past experience would enable the organization necessary to cope well with the stress and unpredictability of an intense nuclear crisis. Such an event would be inherently dangerous. The creation of agreed redeployment rules, however, should alleviate these dangers, and extensive practice of the procedures could well raise the standards of operational safety in a crisis above the present standards.

As suggested earlier, the command systems should also be safeguarded against the possibility of overconcentration of physical launch authority at the top of the chain of command. This cautionary note suggests that the systems should impose checks and balances on any leader empowered by law to exercise launch authority. The Russian and American presidents should not be exempt from "personnel reliability program" standards and should not in any case have the physical ability to push the launch button.

INCREASED RELIANCE ON STRATEGIC WARNING

The traditional nuclear posture of the United States assumes the possibility of a surprise attack. In the words of a former defense secretary, U.S. planners were "obliged to make the contingency of a Soviet surprise attack on our strategic forces the fundamental test of the adequacy of those forces and the main basis for our strategic nuclear planning."[26] This guidance evidently remains in effect today.

Under a regime of zero alert or virtual arsenals, similar guidance might continue to apply to at least a portion of the arsenals. Strategic warning that provides early indications of an adversary's preparation to attack—in this case, detecting the redeployment of de-alerted forces—actually would be easier than usual. The preparations an adversary needs to complete would be more extensive and time-consuming than in the past, and, moreover, the parties to an agreement would submit to continuous on-site monitoring. Nevertheless, strategic warning historically has been ambiguous or worse, and, if the parties lack confidence in the absolute reliability and timeliness of intelligence on the operational status of other states' arsenals, then it would be prudent for them to hedge against an intelligence failure by configuring the inactive arsenals to survive a surprise attack. (During the Cold War the Soviets raised the alert level of their strategic nuclear forces on numerous occasions during crises; U.S. intelligence missed every one of them.)[27]

The extensive monitoring arrangements would nonetheless enable the parties to increase their confidence in and reliance on strategic early warning. Redundant means—national and cooperative—of surveillance would provide greater daily reassurance of adherence to an accord, greater confidence that a legal redeployment follows protocol, and greater assurance that a gross violation of the accord would be detected in time to take counterbalancing responses.

ELIMINATION OF LAUNCH-ON TACTICAL WARNING

As a safety precaution, the command systems should not reconstitute an option of launch-on warning as part of their crisis redeployment operations. Strategic organizations should drop this option from their repertoire because it depends on a nearly flawless performance by sensor networks and decisionmakers operating in a highly compressed period of time (no greater than about 20 minutes). Placing the forces on a hair trigger during a crisis would reinstate the risk that miscalculation or a false alarm would trigger an inadvertent nuclear war.

DEVELOP THE OPTION OF RETALIATION AFTER RIDE-OUT

The corollary to eliminating launch-on warning is providing a viable option for retaliating after a nuclear attack has been ridden out.

This aspiration carries major implications for both the command systems and the force structures. The transition from peacetime to wartime operations would require a complex transformation of command system operations. Peacetime command operations devoted to the peacetime stewardship of inactive arsenals and to the continuous surveillance and monitoring of opposing arsenals would yield to operations devoted to the redeployment of forces to invulnerable combat positions.

As the command system itself would require protection during and after this transformation, survivable command posts and communications networks would be activated along with the dispersed forces. The elements of a resilient wartime command system would thus need to be maintained in peacetime. This system would also be extensively exercised under normal daily circumstances.

The force structures would consist of mobile weapons systems that achieve invulnerability through stealth. Submarines undoubtedly would become the backbone of the U.S. (and British, French, and possibly Chinese) strategic arsenals, while land-based mobile strategic rockets would presumably monopolize the Russian portfolio. These forces would regularly participate in redeployment exercises designed to optimize their survivability and ability to carry out orders from higher authority after an attack has been ridden out. They would go through the motions using (verifiably) dummy warheads or other artifacts that prevent actual rearmament.

DECENTRALIZATION OF SURVIVABILITY MEASURES

Under current alerting arrangements and planned responses to strategic and tactical warning, protective dispersal and other survival actions are related organically to preparations for rapid offensive action.[28] Under zero alert or virtual arsenals, the response to impending or actual enemy nuclear attack would initially be strictly restricted to insuring the reconstitution and survival of the forces and command systems. Survival actions would be separate from and would take strong precedence over offensive preemption or counterstrike coordination.

Although the authority to conduct offensive operations would remain highly centralized across the spectrum of hostilities, activities dedicated to force and command survival could be highly decentralized.

If a zero-alert agreement had been breached by a large-scale breakout of opposing forces, and the rules of the road thus scrapped, the latitude for decentralization could be very large. For purely defensive ends, nuclear units at all echelons could be programmed for rapid dispersion and granted leeway to improvise if necessary to minimize their exposure to attack. Early warning systems including tactical sensors could be modified to support this defensive action. Direct links between sensors and individual weapons units, for instance, could be established.

CONCLUSION

Taking all nuclear weapons off alert as a transitional stage toward more comprehensive dismantling of forces would create a strict international standard of operational safety and ease nuclear tensions by removing the threat of sudden deliberate attack. Zero alert would drastically reduce the risk of a catastrophic failure of nuclear control. It would also relax the nuclear postures, bringing them into harmony with improved political relations.

But it would also require nuclear planners to scale back the requirements of deterrence and redirect nuclear policy toward an emphasis on safety. That basic adjustment, along with the extensive changes in command system operations discussed earlier, will not happen without broad public support and presidential leadership. The bureaucracies that created the standard practices of deterrence cannot be expected to move toward virtual arsenals on their own. Proponents of this option must assume a heavy burden of original study and intensive outreach to pave the way.

NOTES

A note on sources: the factual material largely derives from interviews with Russian and U.S. officials who wish to remain anonymous.

1. A lucid discussion is Michael J. Mazarr, "Virtual Nuclear Arsenals," *Survival* (Autumn 1995): 7-26. The basic concept corresponds closely in many respect to Bruce G. Blair, *Global Zero Alert for Nuclear Forces* (Washington, D.C.: Brookings Institution, 1995).

2. These requirements correspond to oft-used, if more abstract, concepts of

negative and positive control. See Bruce G. Blair, *Strategic Command and Control: Redefining the Nuclear Threat* (Washington, D.C.: Brookings Institution, 1985), esp. 68-69. Important literature on the topic of safety includes Scott D. Sagan, *The Limits of Safety: Organizations, Accidents, and Nuclear Weapons* (Princeton: Princeton University Press, 1993); and Peter Douglas Feaver, *Guarding the Guardians: Civilian Control of Nuclear Weapons in the United States* (Ithaca: Cornell University Press, 1992).

3. Sagan, *Limits of Safety;* Bruce G. Blair, "Alerting in Crisis and Conventional War," in *Managing Nuclear Operations,* eds. Ashton B. Carter, John D. Steinbruner, and Charles A. Zraket (Washington, D.C.: Brookings Institution): 75-120; Bruce G. Blair, *The Logic of Accidental Nuclear War* (Washington, D.C.: Brookings Institution, 1993); testimony of Col. (Ret.) Gennadi A. Pavlov, *Command and Control of Soviet Nuclear Weapons: Dangers and Opportunities Arising from the August Revolution,* Hearing before the Subcommittee on European Affairs of the Senate Committee on Foreign Relations, 102d Cong., 1st Sess. (Washington, D.C.: USGPO, 1992).

4. Blair, *Global Zero Alert,* esp. 79-90.

5. In his opening chapter, in this volume, Mazarr outlines many of the aspects of cooperation that the transition to virtual arsenals presupposes.

6. Blair, *Global Zero Alert,* 73.

7. The role of launch-on warning in U.S. and Russian nuclear postures is extensively analyzed in Blair, *Logic of Accidental Nuclear War,* and *Global Zero Alert.* The old nuclear rivals retained their postures of rapid reaction for similar reasons. First, their latest war plans did not downgrade the traditional mission of nuclear counterforce. The dominant target set still consists of a long list of time-urgent military targets, particularly nuclear forces (and associated control posts). Russia's standing strategic attack plan (called "Sphere"), for example, draws heavily on SS-18 land-based rockets on high-combat alert and aimed at U.S. nuclear forces. In the U.S. Single Integrated Operational Plan every major attack option still requires, at a minimum, a full-scale attack on Russian nuclear forces.

Second, missiles in silos play a big role in this counterforce mission, and, being vulnerable themselves, they need to be fired before incoming warheads pulverize them. (U.S. ballistic missile submarines on combat patrol, normally two each in the Atlantic and Pacific, are also dedicated completely to this nuclear counterforce mission and would promptly launch all their missiles despite the boat's invulnerability.)

Third, the vulnerability of command, control, and communications networks puts a premium on prompt launch. To hedge against the massive disruption or decapitation of command control, the U.S. command system not only came to rely on LOW but also routinely delegated launch authority to certain senior military commanders, to insure the dissemination of launch orders before U.S. forces were forced to absorb the brunt of an attack.

Russia's command system depends no less on rapid reaction. During the 1980s Soviet planners estimated that, if their strategic forces were not launched promptly on tactical warning of a decapitating U.S. first strike, then only 2 to 10 percent of those forces, and possibly none at all, would be able to retaliate after absorbing the attack. START I and II forces fare no better in the models, reinforcing prompt launch in Russian command system operations. This option is the centerpiece of current nuclear release procedures that the Russian general staff can exercise in either of two ways. One is to send unblocking and launch authorization codes directly to individual weapons commanders, who then perform the launch procedures. (That is also how the United States would do it.) The other method, unique to Russia, is for the general staff personally to push the launch button from war rooms in the Moscow vicinity. (The primary wartime command post for the general staff is at Chekov, 60 km south of Moscow.) This is a remote, robotic-like launch of land-based strategic missiles that would totally bypass the subordinate commanders and missile launch crews down the chain of command.

8.   To improve the resilience of nuclear command, Russia continues to build deep underground command posts to protect top nuclear commanders during wartime (e.g., the massive excavation ongoing at Beloretsk in the Urals) and to upgrade a last-ditch method of retaliatory missile launch known as the "dead hand." If top Russian leaders do not get a clear picture of an apparent missile attack, or if for any reason they fail to give timely authorization to retaliate, the general staff can activate the dead hand, a special complex outside Moscow created to insure quasi-automatic retaliation in the event of their decapitation (Bruce G. Blair, "Russia's Doomsday Machine," *New York Times,* October 8, 1993; Blair, *Global Zero Alert,* 51-55).

This complex consisting of special underground radio stations, control posts, and communications rockets became operational around 1985. Although its operational performance and safety are hard to evaluate, the Soviets at least designed the system to fire missiles only after it registers certain objective conditions of enemy attack; notably, the detection of nuclear explosions and a complete outage of communications with the general staff. By contrast, the two methods of launching on warning mentioned earlier depend on data from warning sensors alone.

9.   Blair, *Global Zero Alert,* 47.

10.   Today, owing to economic austerity and maintenance shortfalls, only about 100 Russian strategic missiles could ride out a surprise U.S. attack (20 percent of the mobile SS-25 force, plus one or two SSBNs at sea—typically, a Typhoon or Delta IV in Northern Fleet and/or a Delta III in the Pacific). Russian planners could lack confidence that their residual forces could penetrate a future U.S. national defense system, even one limited to the 100 interceptors allowed by the ABM Treaty, in sufficient numbers to underwrite even minimum deterrence.

11.   For a technical explanation of the de-targeting measures and their reversibility, see Blair, *Global Zero Alert,* esp. 78-84.

12.   Ibid., 7.

13.   For instance, the onboard computers of U.S. Trident submarines in the Pacific

carry target coordinates for China. The U.S. command system assigns the strategic reserve target package including China to off-alert SSBNs at sea as well as to off-alert strategic bombers and ICBMs.

14. Blair, *Global Zero Alert,* 5-7.

15. Strategic Command in Omaha has assumed major responsibility for planning nuclear strikes against these Third World targets in part because of the large-scale withdrawal of tactical nuclear weapons from ships and from regional theaters around the world. Strategic Command increasingly performs nuclear planning for those theaters.

16. These problems as well as the danger of nuclear smuggling are assessed in detail in *Loose Nukes, Nuclear Smuggling, and the Fissile-Material Problem in Russian and the NIS,* Hearings before the Subcommittee on European Affairs, Senate Committee on Foreign Relations, 104th Cong., 1st Sess. (Washington, D.C.: USGPO, 1995).

17. I have in mind the sort of extraordinary shortcuts the Soviets considered during the early 1980s to cope with the perceived threat of decapitation posed by Pershing II missiles. For example, they designed and tested a command link meant to give the top political leadership direct push-button launch control over a portion of the ICBM force, bypassing even the general staff and thereby shaving a few minutes off the time needed to launch.

18. U.S. ballistic missile submarines also represent the least-well-safeguarded strategic weapons in the U.S. arsenal, partly because, unlike Russian boats, they have not been equipped with blocking devices. (U.S. bombers and ICBMs were configured with coded locking devices to prevent unauthorized employment physically during the early and late 1970s, respectively.) The Pentagon will install such safeguards on Trident subs during 1996 and 1997; for the first time in history the SSBN crews will need to receive a code from higher authority to unlock a safe containing a key needed to effect launch.

19. Interview material.

20. Interview material.

21. I am indebted to John Steinbruner for this point.

22. The challenges of verification are addressed by Kay in his essay in this volume.

23. This notional scheme of de-alerting generally fits the overall framework of virtual arsenals developed by Mazarr in the opening essay of this volume. My blueprint perhaps differs slightly in its emphasis on keeping warheads intact, though it does not preclude further steps toward the disassembly of warheads.

24. The essay on reconstitution by Wheeler concentrates on the problems of stability that might accompany an *un*regulated redeployment. Provisions would need to be made, however, to permit some legal regulated rearming of some portion of the virtual arsenals.

25. The decentralized authority traditionally vested in the military command structure to adopt precautionary alert measures during a crisis is discussed in Blair, "Alerting in Crisis and Conventional War."

26. Brown, *Department of Defense Annual Report, Fiscal Year 1979,* 53.

27. These episodes are discussed in Blair, *Logic of Accidental Nuclear War,* and

Global Zero Alert.

28. This section draws heavily on Bruce G. Blair, *Strategic Command and Control* (Washington, D.C.: Brookings Institution, 1985), esp. 289-85.

FOUR

ISSUES OF FORCE STRUCTURE, NUCLEAR INFRASTRUCTURE, AND SURVIVABILITY

PETER WILSON

OVERVIEW

THE ADVOCATES of moving toward a virtual nuclear arsenal (VNA) end-state for the global military environment will have to address a wide range of new "stability" issues. "The devil will be in the details" in dealing with both the challenges of any transition from the current nuclear weapon environment and the maintenance of a stable virtual nuclear arsenal end-state. As in many idealized end-states, the most daunting problems may reside in designing a nondestabilizing transition process. For that reason it will be necessary to explore the implications of moving to a steady state of virtual nuclear arsenals through another plausible end-state of "virtual abolition or minimum deterrence." The former case can be clearly defined as an end-state in which there are no operational nuclear arsenals, while the military environment of "virtual abolition" is one in which the declared nuclear weapon states (NWSs) maintain only small arsenals of operational nuclear weapons.[1]

These new types of stability problems can be categorized in the following fashion. The first problem is that of instabilities during the transition to the desired end-state of virtual nuclear arsenals. Second is the problem of crisis stability between nation-states.

FROM "VIRTUAL ABOLITION" TO "VIRTUAL NUCLEAR ARSENALS"

From the perspective of the current international environment, a conscious decision by the declared nuclear weapon states, the Perm-Five, to move to a nuclear de-emphasis strategy that leads to virtual abolition should be viewed as a revolutionary change in attitude by the political military elites of those "great powers."[2]

The rationale for virtual nuclear abolition is rather straightforward. Even with the successful effort by the Perm-Five to renew indefinitely the Nuclear Nonproliferation Treaty (NPT) during April 1995, the prospects for the longevity of the NPT regime can be described as problematic. There is the argument by the nonnuclear weapon states (NNWSs) that the current arrangement of five nuclear haves and nuclear have-nots is only tolerable over the medium term (next decade) if the Perm-Five move vigorously to downsize their nuclear forces with the clear intent of ultimately creating a virtual nuclear arsenal end-state.[3]

There is the argument that, by moving to a state of virtual abolition, the Perm-Five and other great powers will have enhanced legitimacy to take more vigorous measures to insure the continued maintenance of the NPT regime. These more vigorous measures flowing from an overt strategy that de-emphasizes the role of nuclear weapons could include much more intrusive global inspection procedures and monitoring capabilities beyond the current IAEA regime. Further, a consensus that the collective use of force by the great powers to enforce the NPT may gain international legitimacy.[4] Finally, the argument for limited operation nuclear arsenals is based upon the proposition that all sources of major international conflict will not have been resolved and require that the Perm-Five maintain a nuclear "lid on the jar."

Putting aside the question of the medium-term (the next decade) feasibility of moving to a state of virtual abolition, there are a host of new challenges to insure that the lid on the jar is in fact tight and not itself a source of political and strategic instability. Most important will be the requirement for the international security community to reconceptualize the meaning of a "nuclear military balance." Brought up in the Cold War environment of very large, at-the-ready nuclear forces, most members of the U.S., European, and former Soviet national security communities tended to ignore the other elements of a national nuclear weapon infrastructure, apart from the operational arsenal of a particular NWS that was on either day-to-day or rapidly mobilizable ("generated") alert. Nuclear strategy and planning was truly based upon a "come as you are" bias to war planning and evaluation.

Since the end of the Cold War, that bias has tended to erode as the U.S. and Russian national security communities have had to wrestle with the consequences of conducting a major demobilization of their at-the-ready nuclear arsenals. Since 1989, with the ratification of the Intermediate Nuclear Forces (INF) Treaty, both the United States and the former Soviet Union (now the Russian Federation) have embarked upon a massive downsizing and consolidation of their nuclear arsenals. Noteworthy are the Bush-Gorbachev September 1991 agreement to eliminate and/or consolidate whole classes of tactical/theater nuclear weapons and the START I Treaty ratified in December 1994. Simultaneously, the United States had to confront a new strategic challenge in 1991 with the breakup of the Soviet Union, which led to the protracted but successful process by which the nuclear arsenal of the Soviet Union was consolidated under the control of a single state, the Russian Federation. Out of this "Russification" of the former Soviet nuclear arsenal, the United States and the Russian Federation have developed a new, albeit tentative, strategic relationship via the Cooperative Threat Reduction (CTR) program.

Flowing from this experience, the concept of a virtual nuclear arsenal has become apparent. Put simply, as the size of the operation nuclear arsenals of the United States and the Russian Federation shrink substantially, the strategic significance of the other components of their nuclear weapon infrastructure rises. With very deep reductions to a few hundred operational nuclear weapons, the United States and the Russian Federation will have to pay very close attention to the operational capabilities of the other declared and undeclared nuclear weapons states and the nuclear weapons mobilization base of other significant nonnuclear weapons states.[5]

THE NUCLEAR WEAPONS MOBILIZATION BASE

The nuclear weapons mobilization base of a declared or an undeclared nuclear weapons state (NWS) will have the following components:

- *Day-to-day operational weapons* and their associated delivery vehicles.
- *"Generated" weapons and their associated delivery vehicles* that can be made ready within a matter of hours or days.
- *Nonoperational weapons* that can be made ready within a matter of days or weeks: these may be nuclear weapons in "cold storage" or in a "nuclear reserve stockpile" status. These weapons provide an immediate mobilization base either to upload operational delivery vehicles or to expand the overall arsenal by providing weapons to an expanded inventory of delivery vehicles.
- *Nuclear weapons physics packages* that can be made ready within a matter of days, weeks, or months depending upon the availability of the other components of the bomb or warhead.
- *Stockpiles of weapons-grade fissile material* that can be fabricated into weapons within a matter of months.
- *Nuclear weapons assembly facilities* that are used to assemble and/or manufacture new weapons.
- *Fissile material production facilities* that could include either uranium enrichment or plutonium production infrastructure and associated uranium mining capability.
- *Civilian nuclear research and power reactors* that can be a source of weapons-grade plutonium.
- *Nuclear waste-disposal facilities* that might be a source of fissile material that can be mined.

All of these elements of a nuclear weapons mobilization base are controlled by a national command authority that relies upon a command, control, communications, and intelligence (C3I) system. In the case of the five declared nuclear weapons states, this C3I infrastructure is designed (as are the operational delivery vehicles) to be deployed in a mode to make them resilient to various forms of attack. In theory, the difference between a nuclear weapons state and a nonnuclear weapons state is very clear-cut as defined by the NPT regime. The former is permitted to have *all components* of the nuclear weapon mobilization infrastructure. The latter is allowed to have *only the last three elements,* which are designed to support a civilian nuclear power production cycle.

After fifty years of the "Atomic Age," the nuclear weapons mobilization potential of any particular state can cover a wide spectrum or have a "gray scale." Currently, there are examples of undeclared nuclear weapons states such as Israel, India, and Pakistan. Public evidence suggests that Israel is likely to have the full range of the nuclear weapons mobilization base, including several hundred nuclear weapons that are or can rapidly be placed on alert. The status of the Indian and Pakistani programs remain more ambiguous. Public evidence suggests that both do not have an operational nuclear arsenal on either a day-to-day or generated alert posture. In essence, both have a virtual nuclear arsenal with a high-speed mobilization capability.[6]

It is noteworthy that other major industrial powers have an inherent virtual arsenal with their extensive nuclear power infrastructure that may include facilities for the chemical reprocessing of plutonium as a future source of reactor fuel. (This configuration of a NNWS nuclear infrastructure is not prohibited by the NPT.) Most remarkable in this category is Japan, with its extensive nuclear power infrastructure, including a plutonium reprocessing and storage capacity.[7]

"STABILITY" AND VIRTUAL ABOLITION (MINIMUM DETERRENCE)

The argument in favor of virtual abolition rests on several assumptions. The first is that a global security environment in which the declared nuclear weapons states "de-emphasize" the role and significance of nuclear weapons will have a powerful salutary effect on the prospects of sustaining the NPT regime. Second, a nuclear de-emphasis strategy will not create new types of instabilities that confirm the "law of unintended consequences." Third is that a passage to an environment of virtual arsenals can only be made through a period of virtual abolition during which the international community becomes convinced that operational nuclear arsenals have now become "impotent and obsolete" insofar as military security is concerned.[8]

A key variable that will affect the stability of either the end-state of virtual abolition or virtual arsenals is the geopolitical environment. If anything has been learned from the Cold War arms control and disarmament experience, it is that the success or failure of any particular arms control and/or disarmament initiative is profoundly dependent upon the political environment between the negotiating parties. The nuclear arms competition of the Cold War era was clearly as much a symptom of the profound geostrategic, political, and ideological struggle between the industrial democracies and the Soviet Empire as a cause of acute interstate tension.

The concept of virtual abolition presumes that a broad consensus can be gained between the declared nuclear weapon states to de-emphasize the role of nuclear weapons while hedging against future serious international conflict. How might this hedge break down?

GEOSTRATEGIC STRESS

Three sources of geopolitical stress on a virtual abolition regime are identifiable. The first is serious deterioration in relations between the great powers. Even if a virtual abolition regime came into place during the first two decades of the twenty-first century, there is the distinct prospect the members of the Perm-Five might have a major falling-out. Most plausible is renewed strain over a wide range of issues between the United States and either the Russian Federation or China. Second is the possibility that one, or more, of the important regional powers becomes very dissatisfied with the global status quo. What some have labeled "rogue states" may in fact prove to be more formidable opponents to the international status quo. One plausible source for major "disturbers of the peace" are countries such as Iran and Iraq, which could be part of a larger Islamic "rejectionist front." Third is the prospect that nonstate actors may play a much larger role in the international environment for both good and evil. One or more major powers may be subject to severe internal political and economic upheaval; currently, the greatest source of international concern flows from events from the states that have been created by the collapse of the Soviet Union. Out of severe internal chaos one or more criminal organizations or factions within a regime may acquire nuclear weapons or, more plausibly, the components for a small nuclear weapons capability. These "loose nukes" might either become part of a civil war drama or be the object of international criminal commerce.[9]

Aside from working the larger international system to reduce the causes of future conflict, there are likely to be a range of practical measures to be taken to insure that a virtual abolition regime is resilient to future shocks. These range from enhanced global monitoring/inspection regimes to deploying the virtual abolition arsenals in "hard to kill" configurations. Some old and new concepts are worthy of examination.

BEYOND THE CURRENT IAEA REGIME

The inadequacies of the current IAEA inspection process to insure that a declared nonnuclear weapons state remains at that status is apparent in the context of a virtual abolition, much less a virtual arsenal environment. To put it simply, the current inadequacies of the IAEA inspection regime are accepted by the declared NWSs because all five have substantial operational arsenals and the consequences of a NNWS breakout scenario would not put the vital interest of any NWS at immediate risk.

In the context of a virtual abolition regime the NWSs would demand that the international community accept a new and far more intrusive monitoring regime to insure that one or more NNWS does not use its inherent nuclear mobilization infrastructure to overturn the international status quo. Several authors have suggested that the global monitoring system would have to be at least as intrusive and responsive to perceived violators as that of the Chemical Weapons Convention (CWC).[10]

An enhanced monitoring and inspection system would be only a necessary but not sufficient condition to make a virtual abolition regime resilient to shocks. In parallel, there would have to be a credible and effective means of the enforcement of this more complete nuclear de-emphasis regime. It is hard to believe that a virtual abolition regime with enhanced monitoring and inspection components could be agreed upon unless there were broad consensus among at least the great powers that any attempt to "break out" of this regime would be viewed as a grave threat to international peace—not unlike the joint Perm-Five statement in January 1992. The key question is whether the use of force can be legitimated in this circumstance.

ON ENFORCEMENT

The viability of a virtual arsenal will flow from the central question of whether and how the regime will be enforced. Several possible options are conceivable. First, the enforcement of the regime could be solely in the hands of the UN Security Council. As in any other case of an act of international aggression, the Security Council could organize and/or legitimate a great power response, which could include the full range of political, economic, and military sanctions. Against an internationally isolated rogue such as Saddam's Iraq, the Security Council process can work quite effectively to legitimate a U.S. decision to use decisive military force. As seen in a protracted crisis such as the Yugoslavia civil war, there may be future paralyzing circumstances in which a violator of the virtual abolition regime is either an aspiring regional hegemon, has great power allies, or is one of the great powers that was a party to the regime.

This aggressor may even be prepared to take military advantage of the virtual abolition regime and conduct a strategic preemption operation against one or more of the NWSs, most specifically the United States.

ON PROTECTING THE U.S. NUCLEAR MOBILIZATION BASE

It became a strategic analytical conventional wisdom during the Cold War that crisis stability was maintained through a large and diverse nuclear offensive force structure. By definition an operational arsenal in the context of a virtual abolition regime will be small but possibly diverse. There are several models for small operational nuclear arsenals. The first is the planned early-twenty-first-century posture of the United Kingdom.[11] This is a strategic "monad" of four high-performance SSBNs each equipped with sixteen Trident II (ICBM-class) SLBMs.

Another option is one that is more diverse, such as the U.S. plan to maintain land-based ICBMs, a fleet of SSBNs, and a small number of long-range bombers as an operational "triad."[12]

For the sake of argument, one could posit a 2020 U.S. nuclear arsenal with the following attributes:

- At-the-ready nuclear weapons:
  - 100 silo-based single RV ICBMs (MaRV?)
  - 8 *Trident* class SSBNs x 16 single RVSLBMs (MaRV?)

  or

  - 100 silo-based single RV ICBMs (MaRV?)
  - 6 *Trident* class SSBNs x 96 *Tomahawk* follow-on SLCM

- Rapidly operational nuclear weapons:
  - 600 nuclear bombs in three underground storage sites
  - 100 long range bombers and fighter-bombers that can be modified to deliver nuclear weapons within 10 days

- A nuclear "reserve":
  - 600 "pits" in three underground storage sites
  - Several hundred long-range fighter-bombers that can be modified to carry nuclear weapons within 360 days

- Nuclear production infrastructure:
  - One production facility with a capacity to remanufacture 600 bombs from extant pits within 360 days
  - No stockpile of weapon-grade fissile material
  - No nuclear weapon–grade fissile material production facility
  - Extant nuclear power infrastructure
  - Several temporary and one deeply buried nuclear waste storage site.

The two different at-the-ready force structures reflect different assumptions about the scope of permitted ballistic missile defenses and the requirement for assured retaliation in the face of these enhanced defenses. It might be worth considering a shift away from a pure dyad of ballistic missiles to one that has a mix of ballistic and cruise missiles. This mix may not be necessary if all parties have deployed Maneuvering Re-Entry Vehicles (MaRV) designed to defeat most plausible early-twenty-first-century ballistic missile defense systems.[13]

As for the undeclared NWSs, it is assumed that all have virtual vice operational arsenals. In the event of a political military crisis how might this force structure be vulnerable to preemption? As previously noted, the overall stability and a virtual abolition regime would rely much more heavily on the prospect that threats to geostrategic stability will be detected and acted on in a collective fashion. In the event that the United States and its allies do not react to the strategic warning indicators, this smaller force structure might become acutely vulnerable to various types of preemptive attack.

POSSIBLE EARLY-TWENTY-FIRST-CENTURY COUNTERFORCE THREATS

One of the most striking features of a small operational force consistent with a virtual nuclear arsenal (VNA) regime is the likely small number of aim points. The small operational force structure may become acutely vulnerable to nonnuclear precision strike attacks. Furthermore, the small number of mobile systems such as land-based ICBMs and/or SSBNs are likely to be vulnerable to special operation forces (SOF) type attacks. If the current "Revolution in Military Affairs" has any meaning, it is in the domain of a radical improvement in the military orchestration of advanced multispectral sensors, high-performance munitions, Internetted wide-band communications, and decision aids. This revolution in nonnuclear military performance is likely to be encouraged by the prospect of a nuclear de-emphasis strategy, which is a central feature of the virtual abolition regime.[14]

One can posit a scenario in which a major revisionist power has decided to paralyze the will of the United States to sustain its extended deterrent commitments to a key ally. The so-called nuclear lid on the jar could become the object of "strategic" attack along with a broader campaign to cause maximum disruption to the strategic infrastructure of the United States.

The danger of not implausible preemption scenarios increases if only because of the likely phenomenon of "out of sight, out of mind." In essence, the very success of a virtual abolition regime, much less a virtual nuclear arsenal regime, will induce a powerful sense of political ennui if not indifference about all matters dealing with nuclear weapons. A strong case can be made that such a process is well under way among the current senior U.S. military leadership. Without any immediate threat to the viability of a smaller operational nuclear force, the tendency of bureaucratic indifference would likely come into play in which near-term financial and other concerns take clear priority over the "remote worries about survivability." Aside from the vulnerability of direct attack on operational nuclear stockpiles and their means of delivery, the residual command, control, communications, and intelligence system may become a prime target. On the other hand, the precise vulnerability of a 2020 command and control system to strategic attack may be very difficult to ascertain. By this time the first phase of the creation of the global informational infrastructure, or cyberspace, will be complete. This Internetted communications system will likely insure that the "message will get through." Therefore "strategic information warfare" campaigns using software and electronic attack techniques may not cripple a nuclear command and communications system.[15]

On the other hand, it remains unclear at this time whether this command system, which exploits commercially derived technology, will be very vulnerable to the use of high-altitude nuclear detonations to generate wide-area temporary and permanent electronic damage. Certainly, the selected use of high-altitude nuclear detonations as an information warfare weapon might seem as an outrageous affront to many great powers that are committed to a nuclear-de-emphasis regime. Yet the military leverage of such nuclear-weapons use might be viewed as very attractive to an ambitious regional power that was attempting to paralyze the advanced military capacity of the United States, especially one built upon the components made of silicon.[16]

All of this points to the likely need to maintain some diversity in the deployment scheme of a small operational nuclear force. A small fleet of SSBNs is attractive, since several can be maintained at sea at any one time. Unfortunately, this small fleet is likely to be based at only one or two ports. Given the operational tempo and size of the force, an opponent may be able to conduct a precision nonnuclear attack on those

SSBNs in port. Most worrisome is the prospect that the one or two operational SSBNs will become vulnerable to attack if they have been tagged. Dispersing a portion of the small force among actively defended land-based silos or in deeply buried tunnel fortifications may prove a high-confidence way to thwart either nonnuclear precision or special forces attack.

Aside from possible counterforce attacks there is the question about how small nuclear arsenals deal with high performance active defenses.

VIRTUAL ABOLITION (MINIMUM DETERRENCE) AND ACTIVE DEFENSES

A major variable in the virtual abolition environment is the size and characteristics of active missile defenses. Even in this geostrategic environment, a number of major powers including the United States may want to deploy high-performance theater missile defenses. The motivation will be quite straightforward if there is a broad international consensus that some enhanced active defense capabilities are an important complement to an effort to suppress, much less "neutralize," a widely proliferating threat of theater-range (300-1000 km) ballistic and cruise missiles. The traditional Cold War syllogism labels strategic defenses as "destabilizing." In an environment of virtual abolition, the negative effect of the deployment of "strategic defenses" may be obviated by the fact that the destablilizing effect is insignificant or irrelevant. Even in the face of a high-performance theater or national missile defense, the small residual operation nuclear forces of the Perm-Five are likely to have "assured penetration." By 2020 it should not be too demanding to develop and deploy on single-RV long-range ballistic missiles a Maneuvering Re-Entry Vehicle that will defeat most plausible missile defense systems. Finally, there is the technological alternative of the low observable cruise missile, which could become a central feature of a small residual nuclear force designed to be relatively insensitive to the presence of robust missile defenses.

Even with a robust missile defense, the assured retaliation requirement for the virtual abolition forces of the Perm-Five members should be very modest—the theoretical capacity to hold a small number of high-value targets at risk. After all, the main purpose of the residual operational force is to insure that no opponent of the virtual abolition status quo has an early nuclear breakout option with a small number of nuclear weapons.[17]

Although it is not the focus of this essay, there are some major challenges about how the Perm-Five might navigate from the turn-of-the-century offensive force structure down to virtual abolition levels in the presence of robust missile defenses. In essence, the Perm-Five will have to decide what is more important: the continued maintenance of assured nuclear retaliation at some high level against each other or the deployment of high-performance counterproliferation capabilities including robust active missile defenses.

Certainly, the dilemmas of maintaining assured retaliation options in a world of high-performance missile defenses disappear during an end-state of virtual nuclear arsenals.

THE WORLD OF VIRTUAL NUCLEAR ARSENALS

Traditional worries associated with nuclear crisis stability disappear if all states no longer find the need to maintain an operational assured nuclear retaliation capability. In this environment all major powers would have a nuclear mobilization infrastructure without any operational nuclear forces and would likely be less concerned about the size and scope of global active defenses.

It is likely that this end-state will appear after a somewhat protracted period of virtual abolition (minimum deterrence). Put simply, the current NWSs will have gotten used to the idea that nuclear deterrence no longer needs a real but only a virtual capability. A virtual arsenal will have the following nuclear force mobilization infrastructure:

UNDER NATIONAL CONTROL WITH TIGHT IAEA MONITORING

- *Nonoperational weapons* that can be made ready within a matter of days or weeks: these may be nuclear weapons in "cold storage" or in a "nuclear reserve stockpile" status. These weapons provide an immediate mobilization base either to upload operational delivery vehicles or to expand the overall arsenal by providing weapons to an expanded inventory of delivery vehicles.

- *Nuclear weapon physics packages* that can be made ready within a matter of days, weeks, or months depending upon the availability of the other components of the bomb or warhead.
- *Stockpiles of weapon-grade fissile material* that can be fabricated into weapons within a matter of months.
- *Nuclear weapon assembly facilities* that are used to assemble and/or manufacture new weapons.
- *Fissile material production facilities* that could include either uranium enrichment or plutonium production systems and associated uranium mining capability.
- *Civilian nuclear research and power reactors* that can be a source of weapon-grade plutonium.
- *Nuclear waste–disposal facilities* that might be a source of fissile material that can be mined.

In this end-state of virtual arsenals there will be more than five states with a capacity to convert their nuclear mobilization base rapidly into an operational arsenal. It is easy to imagine that more than the current Perm-Five would have the infrastructure close to the one described here. It is plausible that every permanent member on an expanded UN Security Council would be allowed to maintain a virtual arsenal. Having this infrastructure would become the new definition of a nuclear weapons state.[18]

Expanding the Permanent Membership of the Security Council may be one plausible route by which the inherent geostrategic instability of virtual arsenals can be dealt with. A variable in the virtual arsenal end-state design is whether sovereign states would still have national control over a stockpile of either nuclear physics packages or weapon-grade fissile material or whether this weapon material would be under international control—a super IAEA. The storage and maintenance of weapon-grade fissile material appears to be a major design question for two types of virtual arsenal concepts. The first will be labeled VNA (national control) and the other VNA (international control). Each has its own advantages and disadvantages.

VIRTUAL NUCLEAR ARSENALS
(NATIONAL CONTROL)

In the same way that virtual abolition represents a potential transition stage to a virtual nuclear arsenal end-state, the concept of nationally controlled virtual arsenals may be a transition to virtual arsenals under international control. Suffice it to say that the core assumption is that the major powers who remain declared nuclear weapon states (NWSs) will want to maintain the unilateral option of reconstituting their virtual arsenal into an operational one. In essence, the issue is a matter of trust about whether the major powers are prepared to hand over a profound element of sovereignty to the United Nations.

Even in a virtual abolition regime the NWSs will continue to worry about the possibility of preemption, although the most important issue of stability will revolve around the broad issues that cause geostrategic instability. Much of the problems that might occur with a virtual arsenal regime will have less to do with the technical characteristic of that regime than with the underlying political stability of the international environment.[19]

MAINTAINING "STABLE" VIRTUAL
NUCLEAR ARSENALS

Even with the issue of the macrostability of the international environment in mind, there are a variety of practical challenges about how virtual nuclear arsenals might be maintained in configurations that are less vulnerable to preemptive scenarios. There will remain the more than hypothetical worry that a VNA regime proves vulnerable to a significant international predator that chooses to break out.[20] It is during the transition from a virtual to an operational arsenal that one or more major states within the regime may be very vulnerable to preemptive military operations designed to paralyze the reconstitution of their nuclear arsenals and means of long-range delivery.

For the sake of argument, one could posit a 2040 U.S. virtual nuclear arsenal with the following features:

- Rapidly operational nuclear weapons:
  - 180 nuclear bombs at three deep underground storage sites
  - 180 intercontinental range cruise missiles on mobile launchers in three deep underground storage sites (separate for the nuclear weapon storage sites); in essence, this part of the arsenal would play the role of SSBNs at sea.

- A nuclear "reserve":
  - 300 fissile material "pits" in three deep underground storage sites.
  - Several hundred long-range bombers and/or fighter-bombers that can be modified to carry nuclear weapons within 360 days.

- A nuclear production infrastructure:
  - One production facility in a deeply buried site capable of remanufacturing 300 bombs within 360 days.
  - No other stockpile of weapon-grade fissile material.
  - No nuclear weapon–grade fissile material production facility.
  - Extant nuclear power infrastructure.
  - Several temporary and one deeply buried nuclear waste storage sites.

As part of the virtual nuclear arsenal regime, all ballistic missiles with a range greater than 500 kilometers would be destroyed and banned.[21] This is based on the philosophy that the maintenance of high-speed transoceanic-range delivery systems are inconsistent with the idea that any reconstituted virtual arsenal need be used in a hurry. Further, a ban on solid-propellant ICBMs and SLBMs and their related production facilities provides the international community with another strategic signal that a major power was choosing to overturn the VNA regime. By the mid-twenty-first century many countries are likely to be using ICBM-class small space launchers. These would have to be banned or their production and use placed under close international supervision as part of the overall VNA regime.[22]

As for constructing deep underground facilities, the technology of tunneling has made major advances as seen by the successful completion of the Channel Tunnel in 1994. Deep tunneling technology has flourished and is part of massive worldwide civil infrastructure industry. Such deep tunneled storage sites for the separate storage of the residual nuclear arsenal and secure means of delivery are attractive for several reasons. First, these clearly identifiable sites can be placed under international monitoring.[23] Second, these facilities are likely hard to kill, even with improved nonnuclear earth penetrating warhead (EPW) munitions. It may prove useful to try to constrain the development of EPW munitions, although it is likely that the United States will have made a major investment in this munitions technology in the name of counterproliferation.[24] To insure that a particular tunnel complex cannot be blocked by single or small special operations–type attack using either nonnuclear or nuclear munitions, each facility would have the capacity to dig out through a number of blind portals.

Some might object to this configuration, arguing that the reconstitution option should include some type of submarine-based option.[25] In the final analysis the concept of a virtual nuclear arsenal requires such massive change in the political attitudes of the major powers that there is the opportunity to reconfigure totally the residual virtual nuclear arsenals on operational and cost grounds.

Building these large tunnel complexes will be expensive and time consuming, but one can presume that construction of these facilities could begin during the period that virtual abolition operational forces are maintained. This transition will likely take more than a decade. One of the major challenges of any future U.S. administration is convincing the public and Congress that investing in a robust and secure virtual nuclear arsenal is worth the cost so that "peace is at hand."

For the three continental-sized powers—the United States, Russian Federation, and China—the technical and operational shift from small operational nuclear forces will be far easier than for geographically smaller powers such as the United Kingdom and France.[26] All three could easily accept a land-based only configuration. The UK and France would face the very large relative cost of scrapping their SSBN forces in favor of a deep tunnel option in the next twenty years.

Both countries might chose to construct deep tunneled facilities on their territory or accept greater vulnerability to a low-probability threat of military preemption. One may assume that the Atlantic Alliance is still viable, and both countries might accept a higher degree of vulnerability based upon the assumption that the United States and possibly the Russian Federation will provide a "strategic nuclear reserve" for the industrial democracies. Similar but smaller-scale virtual nuclear arsenal configurations are plausible for the three undeclared nuclear weapon states, Israel, India, and Pakistan.

ON ACTIVE DEFENSES AND A VNA REGIME

The role of active defenses in a virtual nuclear arsenal regime is likely to be transformed from the current views of the relationship between offense and defense in a world of large operational nuclear arsenals.[27] As noted previously, all nuclear weapon states may have a much more relaxed attitude about the deployment of high-performance active defense during a virtual abolition (minimum deterrence) regime. After all, the move to virtual abolition posits a major breakthrough in great power security relations.

A strong case can be made that robust active theater defenses will still be viewed as desirable with the likely global proliferation of very high-performance nonnuclear armed 300 to 1000 kilometer-range cruise and ballistic missiles. As for national missile defense options, a case can be made that a thin but high-performance active defense of the United States would act as complement to the virtual arsenal configuration described earlier. First, the active defenses would be part of global capacity to monitor possible aggressive action by a potential state or nonstate perpetrator. Second, an effective air and missile defense would increase the complexity and difficulty of any hypothetical attack on the virtual arsenal infrastructure. Third, a thin but high-performance ballistic missile defense would raise the threshold to any plausible breakout option that involved the use of small space launch vehicles and/or the early production of a new generation of ICBMs.[28]

VIRTUAL ARSENAL (NATIONAL CONTROL) COLLAPSE SCENARIOS

The optimist will point to the prospect that, once the major nations get into the habit of a virtual arsenal regime, they will be prepared to invest blood and treasure to maintain that end-state. The pessimist will note that the presence of a virtual arsenal regime does not preclude a major deterioration of that regime. In fact, the regime might collapse quite quickly in the event of a serious downturn in major state relations.

The longevity of a virtual nuclear arsenal regime during the mid- and late-twenty-first century has to be examined. As noted, the optimist will argue that a fundamental shift in interstate relations will have occurred. In essence, major war will become "obsolete," and that "history will have ended" with the global dominance of the commercial/market-oriented democracies. On the other hand, there may remain major fault lines within the international community. There will remain the uncertain future of the Eurasian "elephants," China, India, and the Russian Federation. Major quarrels between them, with their neighbors, and with the United States are still possible.

Another possible source of major international tension is the successful rise of an Islamic or other religious fundamentalist coalition that might attempt to overthrow the mid-twenty-first century political and economic status quo. Finally, there is the second Dark Age scenario during which the very cohesion of the nation-state is challenged by benign and malevolent forces. These could include the rise of powerful transnational criminal organizations that could exploit the internal chaos that could beset major portions of Eurasia, Africa, and Latin America. Even North America may face major centrifugal challenges over language, culture, and race, as seen by the outcome of the recent referendum in Quebec.

One of the worrisome aspects of a virtual arsenal regime is its virtue—all major powers are now more nearly equal in their status as potential nuclear weapons states. In response to a major international provocation or deterioration of the international environment, a future U.S. administration would face an acute dilemma about whether to exercise the right to convert a virtual arsenal into an operational one. A unilateral decision to create an operational arsenal might prove as difficult as the decision actually to use nuclear weapons during a future conflict. One major worry and impediment to a decision to exercise the option to deploy is the prospect that the decision might trigger instant proliferation, with many nuclear weapons–capable states rapidly deploying a nuclear operation capability.[29] While viewed as a virtue by some advocates of the virtual arsenal concept, it does undermine one of the underlying presumptions of the virtual nuclear arsenal concept that the deterrent effect of the threat of rapid nuclear rearmament is meaningful to a powerful international predator.

The specific design features of a virtual arsenal regime may be unable meaningfully to address the stresses caused by renewed geostrategic instability. The most powerful determinant is the likelihood about whether the major states are still prepared to use the full range of their power—political, perception management, economic, and military—to thwart the reappearance of major threats to the international peace. Unless powerfully institutionalized through a modified Security Council, many economically powerful states may choose to "free ride" and avoid future hard commitments of blood and treasure in the name of international law and order.

This suggests that a virtual arsenal regime may be made more resilient if eventually the latent nuclear weapons states give up their unilateral option to create operational nuclear arsenals rapidly.

VIRTUAL ARSENALS
(INTERNATIONAL CONTROL)

Put simply, the concept of a virtual arsenal regime under international control has many elements of the originally radical nuclear disarmament proposal, the Acheson/Lilienthal Plan. In this case the nuclear mobilization infrastructure would have the following elements:

UNDER DIRECT SECURITY COUNCIL CONTROL

- *Nuclear weapon physics packages* that can be made ready within a matter of days, weeks, or months depending upon the availability of the other components of the bomb or warhead
- *Stockpiles of weapon-grade fissile material* that can be fabricated into weapons within a matter of months
- *Nuclear weapons assembly facilities* that are used to assemble and/or manufacture new weapons

UNDER NATIONAL CONTROL WITH VERY TIGHT IAEA MONITORING

- *Fissile material production facilities* that could include either uranium enrichment or plutonium production systems and associated uranium mining capability
- *Civilian nuclear research and power reactors* that can be a source of weapon-grade plutonium
- *Nuclear waste disposal facilities* that might be a source of fissile material that can be mined

The central challenge of this arrangement is the reconfiguration of the UN Security Council. Permanent membership will have to be expanded to other major powers, which will represent the geostrategic, religious, racial, and economic interests of all seven continents. By 2020 the list of permanent members might include the original Perm-Five, and Brazil, Egypt, Germany, India, Indonesia, Japan, and South Africa.

In this circumstance the current veto system would be unworkable, since a future predator might be able to paralyze the Security Council decision process, especially if the council were dealing with the controversial decision to initiate the limited production and deployment of a nuclear arsenal in response to a major threat and/or act of international aggression. The precise design of the supramajority veto scheme for a profoundly altered and expanded Security Council is beyond the scope of this essay. Suffice it to say, this issue will be central to the design of any plausible process that leads to the global end-state of virtual nuclear arsenals under international control.

NOTES

1. See Michael J. Mazarr, "Virtual Nuclear Arsenal," *Survival* (Autumn 1995), for a rationale of moving to a global security environment in which no country or international institution controlled an operational nuclear arsenal—the end-state of "virtual nuclear arsenals." For a description of the end-state of "virtual abolition," in which only the declared nuclear weapon states would

maintain very small (fewer than several hundred) nuclear arsenals, see Roger C. Molander and Peter A. Wilson, "On Dealing with the Prospect of Nuclear Chaos," in *Weapons Proliferation in the 1990s,* ed. Brad Roberts (Cambridge, Mass: MIT Press, 1995), 8-9.

2. The near-term prospects for the Perm-Five to engage in a nuclear de-emphasis strategy that leads to a virtual abolition type multistate agreement appears increasingly remote at this time (winter 1996). Until the spring of 1995 there was a widespread assumption by much of the U.S. national security community that START II would be ratified rather rapidly. With the success of the former communists and nationalists during the elections for the Russian Duma in December 1995, followed by Russian and U.S. presidential election campaigns in 1996, it is possible that ratification, if at all feasible, will not occur until late 1997 or early 1998. Current public evidence indicates that a majority of the new Duma opposes the ratification of START II. Without a U.S. and Russian commitment to cut its "strategic nuclear" forces to START II limits, it is unlikely that the other three Perm-Five members will be interested in joining negotiations about limits much less about cuts of their much smaller nuclear arsenals.

3. For a discussion of the implications of Article 6 of the NPT, see Jack Mendelson and Dunbar Lockwood, "The Nuclear-Weapon States and Article 6 of the NPT," *Arms Control Today* (March 1995): 11-16. For an excellent summary of the politics of the unchanged renewal of the NPT on May 11, 1995, see Lewis A. Dunn, "High Noon for the NPT," *Arms Control Today* (July-August 1995): 3-9.

4. The discovery of the scope and size of the Iraqi WMD programs after Desert Storm in 1991 had damaged the reputation of the IAEA's inspection regime. Further predators may successfully cheat against the IAEA, even though the Iraqi experience has led to a toughening of the IAEA's inspection approach toward the DPRK. Any move toward deep reduction in the nuclear arsenals of declared nuclear weapon states will require a new level of IAEA-type surveillance and the prospect of challenge inspections not unlike the CWC. See David A. Kay, "Denial and Deception Practices of WMD Proliferators: Iraq and Beyond," in Roberts, *Weapons Proliferation,* 305-25. Also see David Kay's essay in this volume.

5. See Molander and Wilson in Roberts, *Weapons Proliferation,* 11, for a description of the relationship between at-the-ready and mobilizable nuclear forces (virtual arsenals).

6. Although it is not the focus of this essay, another major barrier to the rapid movement toward a virtual abolition, much less a virtual nuclear arsenal regime, is the presence of the three undeclared nuclear weapon states, India, Israel, and Pakistan. Whether all three would be allowed to maintain their current nuclear arsenals, which may or may not have an at-the-ready component as virtual arsenals, is a major geostrategic question that would involve the security interests of all three states' regional neighbors.

7. See Molander and Wilson in Roberts, *Weapons Proliferation,* 11, for a

description of Japan's nuclear mobilization potential.

8. Both Alexei Arbatov and Konstantin E. Sorokin clearly indicate in their essays, in this volume, that the historical timing for a virtual nuclear arsenal is poor, with Russian national security elites now convinced that nuclear weapons are more important than ever after the collapse of Russia's geostrategic and military position following the rapid demise of the Soviet Union. The trend in China toward a nuclear de-emphasis strategy is not good. See Alastair Iain Johnston, "Chinese Perspective on Nuclear Doctrine: The Concept of Limited Deterrence," *International Security* 20, no. 3 (Winter 1995-96), for evidence that the Chinese military might adopt a military concept of operations that calls for the limited use of nuclear weapons in future regional conflicts. The recent crisis over the presidential elections in Taiwan, during which the U.S. displayed its naval power, is likely to stimulate Chinese interest in deploying a larger and more diverse nuclear arsenal.

9. For a pessimistic scenario of a chaotic near future, see Peter Schwartz, "The New World Disorder," *Scenarios: WIRED,* (1995). For a more benign view with the prospect of only moderate disturbances to the international system, see Hamish McRae, *The World in 2020* (Boston: Harvard Business School Press, 1994), and Peter Schwartz and Peter Leyden, "The Long Boom," *WIRED,* July 1997.

10. For a discussion of the need to maintain a deterrent response as a complement of the inspection regime planned for both the CWC and BWC, see Graham S. Pearson, "Prospects for Chemical and Biological Arms Control: The Web of Deterrence," in Roberts, *Weapons Proliferation,* 287-304. See David Kay's article in this volume for a more complete discussion of this issue.

11. For a description of the UK decision to rely upon single RV Trident SLBMs to provide a "substrategic" nuclear strike option, see *The Military Balance,* 1995-1996 (Oxford: Oxford University Press, 1995), 35

12. The Nuclear Posture Review (NPR) had laid out a U.S. nuclear "triad" for the early twenty-first century based upon the assumption that START II will be ratified in the near future. The results of the NPR signaled a major shift in U.S. thinking about the size and shape of its nuclear strategic forces with the emphasis being given to the maintenance of a large ICBM force (500 in silos) with single RVs and a somewhat smaller fleet (14 vice 18) *Trident* SSBNs. A very small bomber force of some 66 B-52Hs and 20 B-2s would be kept as nuclear capable long-range aircraft without being placed on high levels of day-to-day alert. See *Military Balance, 1995-96,* 15-17. Public reports indicate that the U.S. will maintain several thousand nuclear weapons in a reserve storage even after START II comes into force.

13. For summaries of the current theater missile defense programs, see Mark Hewish and Barbara Starr, "Catching the Bullet," *International Defense Review* 6 (1994): 30-41; and Mark Hewish, "Providing the Umbrella," *International Defense Review* 8 (1995): 28-34.

14. For a discussion of the 1991 Persian Gulf War as precursor of the "revolution in military affairs," see C. Kenneth Allard, "The Future of Command and

Control: Toward a Paradigm of Information Warfare," in *Turning Point: The Gulf War and U.S. Military Strategy,* ed. L. Benjamin Ederington and Michael J. Mazarr (Boulder: Westview Press, 1995). Both Arbatov and Sorokin, in this volume, note that a clear U.S. superiority in the new nonnuclear warfare technology will tend to strengthen the case for nuclear weapons within Russia. Bragging about the U.S. early-twenty-first century advantage in a silicon-based revolution in military affairs is not likely to help the cause for a global nuclear de-emphasis regime. See Joseph Nye and William Owens, "The Information Edge," *Foreign Affairs* (March-April 1996).

15. For a description of the concept of "cyber war" or "strategic information warfare," see Roger C. Molander, Andrew S. Riddile, and Peter A. Wilson, *Strategic Information Warfare: A New Face of War,* RAND MR-661-OSD: RAND (1966, 1995); and Oliver Morton, "The Information Advantage," *The Economist,* June 10, 1995.

16. See Bruce Blair, in this volume, for a more complete discussion of the command and control issues raised by a shift to a VNA regime. For a discussion of the vulnerability of U.S. communication systems to HEMP attacks, see Timothy J. Hannigan, "Analysis of the Feasibility of Degrading U.S. National Technical Means and Affecting Associated Communications by the Effects of a High Altitude Nuclear Detonation," JAYCOR (draft technical report to the Defense Nuclear Agency, December 1994).

17. See Keith B. Payne, in this volume, for the argument that national missile defenses would be stabilizing in an environment of virtual abolition (minimum deterrence) regime. Others take a more skeptical view of the role that enhanced defense might play in a virtual abolition environment (see Bruce Blair, in this volume). This author believes that national air and missile defenses will play on balance a stabilizing role in the context of a minimum deterrent regime, since they could preclude effective nonnuclear strategic counterforce campaigns against the smaller operational arsenal, as suggested by Arbatov in this volume.

18. See David Kay, in this volume, for a more complete discussion of the monitoring and verification challenge associated with a VNA regime.

19. This point is repeatedly stressed in the companion essays by Arbatov, Croft, Heisbourg, and Sorokin.

20. For a more complete discussion see Blair, Roberts, and Wheeler, in this volume.

21. It is this author's belief that, by the time of any politically plausible VNA, say 2020, most major military forces will have large inventories of 300 to 1000-kilometer range ballistic and cruise missiles on ground and sea platforms. Given the likely superiority of U.S. and European air forces equipped with "piloted" combat aircraft, many major powers such as China, India, and the Russian Federation are likely to be loath to give up their theater ballistic and cruise missiles equipped to deliver advanced conventional munitions with very high accuracy. The Chinese use of their M-9 SRBMs as long-range artillery during the political-military crisis surrounding the election of the president of

Taiwan, on March 23, 1996, is likely a sign of "things to come."

22. Small solid propellant space launch vehicles such as the air-launched *Pegasus* and ground-launched *Taurus* are likely to be used by a wide range of nations during the early twenty-first century.

23. See Michael Wheeler, in this volume, for a more complete discussion of the international monitoring concepts for a VNA regime. In essence, many of the concepts and issues explored by the essays in this volume are the requirements for maintaining the "family atomics" as described by Frank Herbert in *Dune*.

24. If ICBMs and SLBMs are banned, then advanced EPW could only be delivered by aircraft or cruise missiles. The VNA facilities could be protected by robust air defenses.

25. Bruce Blair, in this volume, has made the imaginative suggestion that a fleet of SSBNs could be maintained with their SLBMs and warheads without guidance packages. The latter would be maintained on SSNs to insure that the entire package is not vulnerable to nonnuclear preemptive attacks. This concept appears to be too clever by half. There would still remain the hypothetical possibility that guidance packages could be clandestinely mated at sea.

26. The Russian Federation will have a hard time maintaining a substantial fleet of SSBNs during the early twenty-first century and that the modern fleet of SSBNs recently being built by the United States, the United Kingdom, and France will reach their end of service lives by 2020-30, roughly the time that a VNA regime might come into force. The Russians and Chinese have made major investments in deeply buried facilities. A VNA configuration as described above would not seem revolutionary from their military institutional or historical perspective. For the United States, United Kingdom, and France, giving up the SSBN option might be viewed as a traumatic change.

27. High-performance national active defenses could provide additional protection to the deeply buried VNA infrastructure during the potential destabilizing phase of a future nuclear weapon breakout scenario or the formal decision by one or more parties to the VNA to make some of their nuclear arsenals operational.

28. Breakout scenarios involving SLBMs are uninteresting, given the long lead time associated with the production of new SSBNs. The problem of SLCMs is another matter. Long- range nonnuclear armed SLCMs will be an important deep strike armament for many navies by the early twenty-first century. A survivable early breakout and response option to the collapse of a VNA regime could be the rapid discussion of nuclear armed SLCMs to a wide range of warships and submarines. Unfortunately, SSNs equipped with nuclear armed SLCMs may provide new preemption options during the critical and potentially unstable breakout period.

29. It would be naive to believe that a number of major powers other than the declared and undeclared nuclear weapons states would not maintain a nuclear weapon mobilization potential after a VNA regime has come into place. Further, the U.S. extended deterrent commitment to a number of major states

along the Eurasian periphery, such as Japan and Germany, will likely erode. On seeing one or more members of the "nuclear club" exercising their option to make ready a portion of their VNA during a twenty-first century crisis might prompt either to respond with a nuclear weapon mobilization as a strategic "defense and deterrence maneuver." The precise response of the international community to a decision by one or more parties to VNA regime to "go operational" is unknowable, given the wide range of mid- to late-twenty-first-century political strategic crises scenarios.

FIVE

THE CHALLENGE OF INSPECTING AND VERIFYING VIRTUAL NUCLEAR ARSENALS

DAVID KAY

THIS ESSAY WILL NOT ATTEMPT TO PROVE THE UNPROVABLE—that a virtual nuclear arsenal arrangement could or could not be satisfactorily verified. As with all complex arrangements between states, and especially those yet to be negotiated, the devil is in the details. The attempt here will be to identify the major "devils" and to suggest some of the areas in which research should be focused as additional work is done to give greater substance to the virtual arsenal alternative future. The lack of substance and understanding of the complex arrangements necessary to comprehend the implications of virtual arsenals should in no sense be taken as a measure of the long-term worth of the concept itself. In this regard it is worth remembering that the concept of strategic nuclear deterrence—the concept that guided U.S. national security through the Cold War—evolved considerably over the forty-five years of the Cold War and remained, in several of its most fundamental aspects, in dispute even at the end of the Cold War.

A good place to begin is to identify a few of the most important issues that arise in any arms-control verification arrangement and to explore their implications for a world of virtual nuclear arsenals.

The specific verification environment—that is, the political context within which inspections take place—has varied over time and between arms-control agreements, and influences significantly the way in which the verification system in each of these agreements has operated. Three principal arms-control verification environments, cooperative, adversarial and coercive, can be identified. Two wars, the Cold War and the Gulf War, have had dramatic impacts on the process of verification and most particularly upon the conduct of on-site inspections. Arms-control treaties such as INF, START, CFE, and CWC, negotiated in the last years of the Cold War, when the parties still were suspicious of each other's intentions, called for stringent, intrusive, complex verification. The oft-repeated motto, "Trust, but Verify," or its Soviet version, "Verify, then Agree," underlined an insistence on proof of compliance.

Within a short period, however, implementation of the INF and START I Treaties demonstrated a high level of compliance on the part of the Former Soviet Union (FSU) and the former Warsaw Pact countries. Treaty-related activities, in particular on-site inspections, were characterized by good cooperation, verification proceeded in a satisfactory manner, and the atmosphere was one of transparency and confidence. This type of verification environment became characterized as generally cooperative.

There is always a basic conflict in designing a verification regime between the wish to know more about another country's activities and facilities and the desire to protect one's own national security and proprietary activities and facilities. Cooperative verification starts with overcoming the reluctance to let other parties have a close look at one's own military structures. Political will dictates a voluntary openness; when it is a shared openness, the primary verification tasks become demonstrating compliance with an agreement and/or constructively resolving ambiguous activities or events—termed here a cooperative verification environment.

For example, the IAEA/NPT safeguards system, as it existed before the Gulf War, can be considered the model of cooperative verification because safeguards were primarily intended to provide assurance to neighbors of a country's peaceful intentions. Those countries that were not prepared to give such assurances or that simply wanted to maintain their options and some degree of ambiguity about their nuclear intentions stayed outside of the NPT safeguards system. This system is cooperative, in that member states have agreed to submit to inspections of their declared nuclear facilities, which are designed to confirm their safeguards' undertakings. Member states know that if a diversion of nuclear material from declared, safeguarded facilities is found, the country concerned could be declared in violation of its safeguards obligation. The dominant expectation before the Gulf War was that any state that wanted to seek nuclear weapons would not join the NPT or, if it had joined the NPT, would either withdraw or pursue its weapons efforts through a clandestine program that would not be detected through inspections of declared facilities.

As a result of this dominant belief about the purpose of nuclear safeguards, they came to be viewed before the Gulf War largely as confidence-building measures carried out in a cooperative verification environment. Confidence-building measures, which are supported by verification methods such as data exchanges, notifications, and on-site inspections, are often based on the same assumptions of reassurance, no intentional violations, and cooperative security.

A second type of verification environment can be termed adversarial. In an adversarial verification environment the arms limitations and nonproliferation commitments are entered into freely, but the level of suspicion between the parties is sufficiently great that the parties view noncompliance as a realistic possibility and seek verification measures that will detect such noncompliance. If no violations are found over a long period or if basic political relations change in major ways—as they did with the end of the Cold War—then the adversarial verification environment may move toward the cooperative end of the spectrum. Before the end of the Cold War relations between the United States and the Soviet Union could be generally characterized as adversarial, and arms-control measures of that period reflected this fact. The adversarial verification environment will have three primary characteristics: verification methods will be extensive and intrusive because some parties may not comply with the agreement; there will be anomalous events and ambiguous activities requiring investigation; and, since there can be no absolute guarantee to prevent, or even detect, all noncompliance, the level of intrusive verification agreed to should at the very least raise the political and economic costs of large-scale, clandestine noncompliance by making it probable that major violations will be detected.

The end of the Gulf War has signaled an entirely different context in which verification activities can take place.[1] The verification environment in which the Iraqi inspections have taken place can be termed a coercive verification environment. A coercive verification environment is dominated by two factors. First, the arms limitation itself is imposed and not a voluntary undertaking. Second, the working assumption is that noncompliance and active deception measures to avoid detection will be present, so intrusive, extensive verification methods must be employed. While the exact context in which the Iraqi inspections have taken place is unique, many of the verification lessons may have application to other agreements in which the basic agreement is established through coercion or imposition (e.g., by victorious states or the UN Security Council) and there is strong reason to suspect noncompliance.

The linkages between verification environments and verification methods sketched out here are summarized in the following matrix (in table 5.1).

While arms-control agreements reflect the verification environment at the time they were concluded, this environment may change with considerable impact upon the expectations of how on-site inspection will operate. The clearest example of such change is the pre- versus post–Gulf War IAEA/NPT safeguards. In the pre–Gulf War the dominant verification environment was cooperative. After the discoveries of the extent of Iraq's clandestine nuclear program emerged from the aftermath of the war and the possibility of noncompliant behavior became recognized as a realistic possibility, numerous changes in the IAEA/NPT safeguards regime were instituted, and the environment moved somewhat in the direction of an adversarial system. The bulk of the U.S.-Soviet agreements that were signed in the Cold War era provide additional examples of changes in the verification environment that are moving in a more hopeful direction, from adversarial to cooperative.

The arm-in-arm linkage of verification and arms control is not quite as seamless as this quick chronology would indicate. One major arms-control agreement concluded during the adversarial phase of the post–World War II period did not embody any inspection measures.[2] At the time the Biological Weapons Convention (BWC) was signed in 1972, it was apparent that the level of inspection that would have been required to provide reasonable confidence that the treaty's obligations

TABLE 5.1

Verification Environment	Dominant Orientation	Verification Methods	Verification Goal
Cooperative	Provide reassurance; no intentional violations; cooperative security or externally provided security system. Ambiguous events will be viewed as errors in inspection methodology and effort will be made to reduce sensitivity of inspection process.	Data exchanges; notifications of relevant developments; limited on-site inspections or visits to agreed-upon sites; general concern that methods not become too onerous or expensive.	Provide reassurance that parties are meeting their commitments.
Adversarial	Noncompliance viewed as realistic possibility, and considerable suspicions exist about motivations and future intentions of parties. Ambiguous events will be viewed as probable violations.	Extensive and intrusive verification activities, including: extensive data exchanges; use of nationally derived intelligence to guide inspections; inspections with short notice and to sites not previously designated; resident inspectors at sensitive facilities; cost of verification process will not be viewed as important criteria. Reciprocity will, however, limit each side to methods and controls that it is prepared to have applied to itself.	Detect violations before they become militarily significant for other parties.
Coercive	Obligations are imposed and viewed as one-sided. Assumption is that state being controlled will engage in noncompliant behavior and will attempt to hide its cheating. Ambiguous events will be viewed as violations and indication of undetected noncompliance.	Extensive and highly intrusive inspections; whole economy and society will be subject of attention, not just military sector; export controls and limitations on permissible R&D as well as military forces. Threat of military/economic sanctions will be in play. Methods will be unconstrained by concerns with reciprocity, and cost will be minor consideration.	Prevent all noncompliance until new political developments allow verification regime to be relaxed.

were being met was neither politically sustainable nor technically reachable. Both the political climate of the Cold War and the ease with which biological weapons research could be shielded in civil programs argued against attempting to construct a verification regime for this treaty. The United States concluded that even if the Soviets were to cheat on their obligation to abandon any offensive biological weapons program—as they indeed did—they would gain no substantial military advantage. It is interesting that even though the chill of the Cold War climate has evaporated and the revelations of the Iraqi biological program have made the prospect of biological warfare more real and the United States much less confident that a biologically armed opponent will not pose a significant military problem, the treaty remains without any verification regime. The principal reason that this is the case is that the underlying spread of biological technology and capabilities have grown to such an extent that no feasible inspection regime is thought to offer reasonable confidence. In all probability the BWC as it now stands would not be ratified today by the U.S. Senate.

ENVISAGING THE WORLD OF VIRTUAL ARSENALS

Any arms-control inspection regime—and certainly none more than that required for a world of virtual nuclear arsenals—is shaped by the political and technical environment of the regime. What would be the environment of the world of virtual nuclear arsenals? As there is no "correct" answer at this point for the uncertain and distant point at which this world would arise, the best that can be done is to consider this world in one of two bands. The first band would be the minimum conditions that would have to prevail for virtual arsenals to become a reality, and the second band would be the most desirable state that can be realistically envisaged.

Three broad groupings of states would be affected differently by a world of virtual nuclear arsenals: first would be the world of the currently five declared nuclear powers (Britain, China, France, Russia, and the United States); second would be the world of the "unconfirmed but known" nuclear states (India, Israel, and Pakistan); and, finally, the rest of the world.[3] What a world of virtual nuclear arsenals would mean for these three groupings of states is laid out in table 5.2. The purpose

TABLE 5.2

States	Minimum Condition	Optimistic Conditions
Five Nuclear Powers	Assembled weapons in low hundreds; delivery systems off alert and de-targeted; no testing; Special Nuclear Material not being produced, and no new weapons being produced, but production capability maintained; disassembled weapons under some type of observation; dominant attitude is adversarial.	Assembled weapons below 100 and all demated from delivery systems and partially disassembled; Special Nuclear Material production capacity not immediately available; no new warhead production permitted; disassembled weapons under strict control, with procedures applied to make them unusable in short time frame; dominant attitude is cooperative.
"Unconfirmed but Known" Nuclear States	No weapons mated to delivery systems; weapons under some type of observation; all fissile material production capability limited in terms of enrichment levels and isotopic ratios; no manufacturing of additional/improved weapons permitted; no testing; dominant attitude is adversarial.	All weapons in disassembled state and numbers reduced to below a dozen each; all fissile material production capability limited in terms of enrichment levels and isotopic ratios; all weapons production facilities inactive and controlled; disassembled weapons under strict control, with procedures applied to make them unusable in short time frame; dominant attitude is cooperative.
Rest of World	Universal adherence to NPT/IAEA safeguards, Comprehensive Test Ban, Chemical Weapons Convention, Biological Weapons Convention, and enhanced MTCR; dominant attitude is adversarial.	Universal adherence to greatly strengthened NPT safeguards, Comprehensive Test Ban, CWC, BWC, and MTCR; all fissile material production and handling facilities under strict international management; dominant attitude is cooperative.

in sketching in broad brush strokes what the world of virtual arsenals would look like is to be able to understand in greater detail what the real challenges would be for any verification regime.

STRESSING CONDITIONS OF INSPECTION REGIME FOR VIRTUAL ARSENALS

If virtual arsenals look like either the minimal or the optimistic worlds, what are the conditions that are most likely to stress the verification regimes that would be required to give states confidence in such worlds? Four major stressing conditions can be identified that would impact the creation of an effective inspection and verification regime. Although these conditions will impact the world of the five declared nuclear powers, the unconfirmed but known, and the rest of the world somewhat differently, there is enough in common to justify examining them as a group.

The first major stressing condition will involve establishing the *acceptable political baseline* of the world of virtual arsenals. Virtual arsenals, whether of the minimum or optimistic variety, will involve discrimination among states. Some states, the five declared nuclear powers, will be allowed to maintain a reconstitutable capacity to produce and assemble nuclear weapons. The three unconfirmed states will have their nuclear programs halted at levels significantly less than the five. In some cases, such as Israel, this would not seem to compromise its security as its likely opponents would be frozen in their current nonnuclear status. On the other hand, India might judge that given potential security concerns vis-à-vis China that it is being significantly disadvantaged. The nonnuclear states of the rest of the world will be prohibited from reaching the virtual state of either the five or the three unconfirmed states and will find themselves under significant international restrictions in pursuing alternative weapon technology. This very fact of discrimination is likely to push the inspection process in an adversarial direction.

An essential element of establishing the political baseline will involve defining and understanding the consequence of violation. It is often naively assumed that properly drafted arms-control regimes should allow the easy determination of whether states are in compliance. The actual case is that most agreements at the political level have been so unclear about the consequence of violations that the verification process is often twisted to avoid finding violations because of the uncertainty or unpalatability of political choices that would arise from confirmed violations. Examples abound of such behavior: from the historic (German violations of the arms-limitation provisions of the Treaty of Versailles were deliberately overlooked by Allied inspectors because the Allied governments were unprepared to take any actions as a consequence of violations) to the contemporary (Chinese violations of numerous nonproliferation undertakings are defined away in the face of the lack of agreement in the West about how to respond). If in a world of virtual arsenals the apparent consequence of a violation is the reassembly of nuclear weapons by others and the instability likely to follow, then the inspection regime will be under tremendous pressure to avoid finding any violations. States that feel their security to be threatened potentially by strong adversaries that might be tempted to cheat on their nuclear obligations are unlikely to draw strong comfort from the failure of a verification regime to find confirmed violations. Considerable work needs to be done on possible measures that can counteract this inherently destabilizing aspect of arms-control verification arrangements.

An essential element of the political baseline that will affect the verification mechanism is the presence or absence of effective security guarantees. At one extreme would be the situation in which every state is ultimately going to have to depend upon its own resources if an adversary decides to use force to impose its will. The other extreme would be a world in which effective collective security arrangements existed to insure against rogue aggressors. The more insecure the world, the more demanding the inspection environment. If the only recourse is for a state to fall back on its own resources when threatened, the greater its need for early warning of the violations of obligations by others and the less trusting it will be of the inspection mechanism itself. If one needs confirmation of this phenomenon, an examination of the statements of the unconfirmed but known nuclear states—India, Israel, and Pakistan—concerning their willingness to trust their security to IAEA/NPT safeguards should remove all doubt.

The extent to which political and alliance changes occur will be an important aspect of the political baseline that will impact the inspection regime. A recent example of this can be found in the collapse of the Soviet Union. The INF Treaty had been drafted in the still frosty period of the Cold War, but by the time that START I and II were being negotiated major changes in Cold War relations were clearly under way. Although START I had most of the adversarial inspection aspect of INF, many of these were never implemented, and some important aspects of START II have been implemented even without treaty ratification, much less inspection. Political changes not anticipated at the time a regime is established can have a major impact upon the inspection process. The CFE Treaty, for example, was designed to allow a mutual, stable reduction in conventional forces in Europe. The CFE Treaty, however, had been barely ratified when the Soviet Union collapsed, and the carefully crafted distribution of forces of the northern and southern flanks of the FSU no longer made sense to the Russians. The result was a Russian demand for treaty modification and the emergence of the CFE Treaty itself as an issue of political contention.

A second major stressing condition for virtual arsenals will involve establishing the agreed technical baseline. Many of the elements that are at the center of a virtual arsenal world—such as assembled or disassembled weapons, weapon alert status, de-targeting, testing, rendering weapons material unusable, time to reassemble—will have to be established in sufficient detail that inspection criteria can be established. These are concepts that are not easily open to a single, obvious definition. In some cases, different design paths taken in, for example, the design of a nuclear warhead may make one state's nuclear weapons much easier or harder to reassemble than that of another state. In such circumstances how is a level playing field to be established? Are standard nuclear weapon designs to be required? Different mixes of delivery systems will pose many of the same problems. SLBMs that are at sea without their warheads will face different constraints in re-weaponization than land-based missile delivery systems. The process of establishing an equitable framework that can be verified will not be an easy process.

If, as it almost certainly will be, an important element of virtual arsenals is to be the number of permitted weapons, then a major technical hurdle will be establishing the confidence level any given inspection regime can give with regard to verifying small numbers of weapons and detecting diversion and concealment activities. In a world of thousands of warheads, the consequence of hiding 100 warheads is probably minimal. In a world of 100 disassembled warheads the consequence of hiding 5 assembled weapons may be considerable. In this case the nature of the verification environment probably will be decisive. If it is adversarial, no inspection process will probably be adequate; if, however, the environment is cooperative, then adequate inspection procedures probably can be found. It must be recognized that this is a potentially dangerous instability.

Inspection procedures and rules crafted on the assumption that the regime is cooperative can become immediately inadequate and destabilizing if underlying political relationships turn adversarial. The rules that guide the verification process and the verification methods—rights of access, access to national intelligence data, frequency of inspection, places to be inspected—are fundamentally shaped by the verification environment and not quickly modifiable. For example, five years after the discovery of the extensive Iraqi clandestine nuclear program, the IAEA still could not get its Board of Governors to agree that it can routinely make use of environmental sampling in countries under safeguards or that it should be able routinely to use intelligence data supplied by national governments. Both methods are viewed as being too adversarial for the cooperative verification regime of the Nonproliferation Treaty. On the other hand the rejection of such methods by some IAEA members is viewed by others as evidence that they either have or may in the future engage in prohibited activities, with the result that the adequacy of the verification regime and the IAEA is doubted. It is difficult to imagine a scheme for virtual nuclear arsenals arising other than in a cooperative environment. On the other hand, history would indicate that cooperation is less than an enduring condition in international relations. Care, therefore, should be given in crafting a verification regime for a virtual nuclear arsenal world, to insure that it has methods and resources adequate to verify the performance of states under conditions much more adversarial than those that will prevail when it comes into effect. To do otherwise will only insure that the regime will not be robust enough to withstand changes in underlying political conditions.

Another difficult aspect of establishing the technical baseline will relate to defining permissible nuclear and other activities for the nonnuclear rest of the world. The individual nuclear capacity of the five declared nuclear powers today far exceeds what any other state, regardless of its financial and technical base, could hope to achieve quickly. In a virtual arsenal world, however, in which all nuclear weapons are disassembled and the numbers are in any case small, this gap will shrink. Serious technical questions will arise, for example, about whether nonnuclear states such as Japan and Germany should be permitted to maintain, even under international inspection, stocks of separated plutonium as part of their civilian nuclear program. While neither of these states today could quickly field even a modest British-sized nuclear force, the same cannot be said about their ability if the measure of merit is the very modest and disassembled forces foreseen in the virtual arsenal world. Should nonnuclear states with significant civil nuclear sectors be permitted to develop space-launched vehicles, which in most respects are functionally similar to intercontinental ballistic missiles? What about cruise-missile development? Should the inspection regime be intrusive enough to detect work on the nonnuclear parts of nuclear weapons in nonnuclear states? And what about permitted nuclear activities in states that at one time pursued nuclear weapons—South Africa, Brazil, Argentina, North Korea, Sweden? So-called rollback states, particularly those that actually developed nuclear weapons, will pose a demanding inspection challenge at virtual arsenal levels.

Even with regard to the nuclear world of the declared five and the unconfirmed three, the continuing pace of technical change will be a challenge for the inspection regime to accommodate. The very definition of testing of nuclear weapons is already undergoing a significant change as computers make it far easier to simulate in a laboratory complex physical phenomena. Whole new generations of nuclear devices may be possible without any overt testing. In the same vein, the delivery vehicles of today will in any case seem antiquated in the world of 2050. It remains to be seen whether terms such as demating, de-targeting, and prompt alert status have any meaning in the period when virtual arsenals are foreseen as possible.

A third baseline that will stress the inspection regime will be the actual verification objective that is established for virtual arsenals. Arms-control agreements, except for those of the most coercive type, have generally not sought to establish a verification requirement so rigorous as to attempt to detect all cases of noncompliance. The more common standard of the U.S.-Soviet period was to provide for the timely detection of any militarily significant violations. If the arms-control environment is adversarial and, particularly, if the arms being controlled are of great military leverage and exist in relatively small numbers, then this standard can be extremely demanding for any verification regime to meet.[4]

Other standards existed as well. For example the IAEA/NPT safeguards system, as it existed before the Gulf War, was a model of cooperative verification because safeguards were primarily intended to provide assurance to neighbors of a country's peaceful intentions and not to detect clandestine nuclear weapons programs. While one would not hold the pre–Gulf War IAEA inspection objective up as a standard worthy of emulation, it does serve to remind us that, if the verification environment changes, then the verification objective can change as well. This may be particularly important to remember when considering virtual arsenals. The very concept itself may require some fundamental changes in the relations of states if it is to be feasible at all. In terms of the banding criteria established earlier in this essay, it is worth speculating that virtual arsenals will only be possible if the optimistic conditions are achieved. The minimal condition band may simply be too stressing to achieve an acceptable verification regime. This concept needs considerably more work in the years ahead.

Determining what is "militarily significant" as it relates to establishing an arms control verification objective is influenced by a number of factors, including comparative force structures, concepts of operation, available defensive systems, the varying willingness to run risks of the states concerned, and the ease of coming up with counters to any given action. All of these have been important at various times. The Washington Naval Limitations Treaty negotiated between the two world wars limited the size of the principal capital ships of the line but did not address at all aircraft carriers or amphibious landing ships. New concepts of operations that were already emerging at the time in Japan and the United States soon resulted in these being decisive weapons systems, while the main ships of the line were left to play a largely supporting role in World War II. In the case of Israel a historic trauma of near liquidation, a lack of strategic depth, and a perception of being surrounded by only enemies have meant that it has approached all arms-control agreements with the general view that any possible cheating will be militarily significant.

As one tries to peer ahead into the uncertain world of virtual nuclear arsenals, it is impossible to say with any authority what will at that time be viewed as militarily significant in crafting an acceptable verification objective. On balance, however, it would seem that, unless nuclear weapons are devalued as a military weapon, it would be exceedingly difficult to craft an inspection objective with a detection of militarily significant violation standard that could be confidently met in an adversarial environment. If this judgment is correct, it would argue that an important aspect of research on the feasibility of virtual nuclear arsenals should be devoted to identifying those conditions that will promote the devaluing of the military utility of nuclear weapons.

Already in the work reported on in this volume one can find promising lines of inquiry. For example, Keith Payne's discussion of the role of strategic defense suggests that attention should be given to the importance of strategic defenses in devaluing the benefits of small, hard-to-detect violations of a virtual nuclear world.[5] Certain force structure postures may, as Peter Wilson argues in reference to missile-bearing submarines, make low levels of cheating less significant.[6] There indeed may be a whole range of force posture changes that will make low-level violations insignificant in terms of their ability to blunt the offensive power of other states. Nuclear weapons, to the extent that we have any real understanding of their utility, pose the greatest threat to large concentrations of military forces or fixed positions. Much of the revolution in military affairs that appears to be under way is driving toward force structures that are highly mobile and easily dispersed. To the extent that these or other strategies can lessen the military significance of low-level cheating and hence ease the required verification objective, they make a virtual nuclear arsenal agreement easier to conceive and less subject to disruption from fears about undetectable cheating.

A final general stressing condition for virtual arsenals will arise from the procedures established for actually operating the verification regime. Choices will have to be made concerning how the inspections will actually be carried out. The parties, for a variety of reasons, would probably not choose to rely entirely on national technical means, even though it would be the least intrusive and cheapest alternative. The asymmetry of NTM capability between the United States and Russia on one side and the other nuclear powers on the other would argue against reliance on this method alone. The things that must be verified—alert status, disassembly of weapons, de-targeting and demating—are all conditions in which NTM has significant limitations. To be convincing to others, the NTM would have to be shared, and this would seem to challenge a cardinal principal against divulging sources and methods of collecting intelligence. If not NTM alone, then on-site inspections would be required. But on-site inspections by whom? The five nuclear states could provide the inspectorate, but this would probably not be acceptable to either the three unconfirmed states or the nonnuclear states. On the other hand it would be hard to argue that nonprolifera-tion would be enhanced by letting Indian, Pakistani, Iranian, or Libyan inspectors, even if they were nominally in the employ of an international agency, verify the assembly status of U.S., Chinese, Russian, British, or French nuclear weapons or the operational status of special nuclear-material production facilities or any of a number of elements of the nuclear-weapons complexes that would seem to require monitoring.[7]

The formula for distributing the cost of maintaining the inspection regime will also have to be agreed upon. Historically, this has been an often contentious issue in arms-control arrangements. Very often dis-putes concerning cost-sharing arrangements are only thinly veiled attempts to limit the scope of inspections. This has certainly been the case with regard to IAEA nuclear safeguards, as was the interwar German refusal to bear the costs of the Treaty of Versailles inspections. At the negotiating stage as well the cost of inspections is often used as a bogeyman to scale back verification requirements. The cost/benefit ratio that is thought appropriate for any arms-control agreement is directly related to the nature of the verification environment. Coercive and adversarial agreements are more costly to verify than cooperative ar-rangements. Many of the more costly verification arrangements negoti-ated under START I have been quietly allowed to go unimplemented after the collapse of the Soviet Union. On-site inspection is the most costly form of verification, and the cost issue is likely to pose a significant challenge to those attempting to negotiate virtual arsenals.

Arms-control agreements generally have carefully negotiated in-spection procedures as part of the basic agreement, rather than leaving them to evolve as the technology and politics change. This reflects the origin of most arms-control arrangements in an adversarial environment in which specificity about "how" helps to determine whether "when" is ever agreed upon. The net result is that arms-control procedures are often unable to adapt to changing technology. It may have made sense to limit battleships in the Washington Naval Agreements, but this was irrelevant as aircraft carriers and submarines became more capable. The

Nonproliferation Treaty is implemented through a series of detailed facility agreements between the IAEA and the individual states that are to be inspected. These agreements spell out in considerable detail the methods to be used by the inspectors, the frequency of the inspections, and the specific location to be inspected. These agreements are static and difficult to modify but, as was shown by the case of Iraq, were drafted with reference to a nonstatic technology. It will require a considerable grant of autonomy to a verification authority by governments if the dynamic technologies involved in nuclear weapons and their delivery systems are to be effectively inspected.[8]

CENTRAL CHALLENGES

If virtual arsenals as a concept is to move from an intriguing bumper-sticker notion to the status of an idea that can appeal to governments as a way of managing the nuclear security challenge, then it will require far more rigorous work. With regard to the requirements of an effective inspection and verification regime, five central challenges need detailed investigation. These are:

1. Establishing baseline conditions with high confidence. The nuclear forces of the five declared states and of the three unconfirmed but known states differ in many important respects. While, as a first-order approximation, it is probably now possible to proceed with the required technical examination on the basis of unclassified information, this is not completely adequate. What is absolutely required is a technically rigorous discussion of this issue to identify problem areas that will require additional work.

2. Identifying strategies for coping with changing political relationships while avoiding accelerating destabilizing forces. Much of the discussion to date concerning virtual arsenals reads as if political change suddenly stops once the changes necessary to establish virtual arsenals have been achieved. There is no reason to believe that this is true. The theories of the dynamic forces that shape civilizations and social movements are as numerous as the megatheorists who propound them.

While the theories remain inadequate in their explanatory and predictive power, they are overwhelmingly convincing as a testimony to the continuity—or perhaps better described as the discontinuity—of change. Before virtual arsenals are likely to gain many adherents there will have to be convincing evidence that the concept is adaptive in the face of change and not accelerative of destructive forces. This understanding is particularly important to crafting an effective verification mechanism.

3. Coping with changing technology. Verification systems have historically been rich in detail and directed at static technologies. Both at the national and international level the record of successfully being able to regulate a dynamic technology is not encouraging. Much more work needs to be done along two fronts. First, will the creation of an effective verification regime for virtual nuclear arsenals require that nuclear weapons technology be frozen or devalued to such an extent that no one will deem it worth pursuing? If so, what are the strategies for accomplishing this objective? Second, what are the critical elements required of a verification regime that is to be adaptive and self-learning with respect to an evolving technology?

4. Understanding the impact of breakdown and breakout. Here again, much of the discussion of virtual arsenals to date assumes away the problem of cheating and regime violations. This attitude is certainly one well sanctioned by history. The typical attitude—but one not sanctioned by experience—has been that states will only join treaties with which they intend to comply. The unexamined question is what actions should arise as a consequence of violation. Avoidance of this central question is not an acceptable posture when nuclear weapons are involved and particularly when states are being asked to come down to very small levels of such weapons. The consequence of cheating becomes very serious as the number of available weapons decreases to very small numbers. Much more rigorous analysis is needed of breakdown and breakout scenarios and the implications of these for an effective verification regime.

5. Long-term operation of an effective inspection regime. Most arms-control regimes have been of relatively short duration.

While virtual arsenals may be a way station to some other state, it seems safer to assume that such a regime would not completely disappear as long as the technical knowledge to assemble nuclear weapons and the nuclear material itself continue to exist. Can such a regime be crafted? And, if so, what are the major issues that must be faced to insure that a convincing answer can be given to governments on this question? Few international institutions today seem worthy of the degree of confidence that would be required to embark on the virtual arsenal road. If this concept is to be given real bite, then the institutional underpinnings need much better definition.

NOTES

1. This is not entirely new. The Treaty of Versailles that ended World War I imposed an extremely intrusive, on-site inspection regime on Germany. See Fred Tanner, ed., *From Versailles to Baghdad: Post-War Armament Control of Defeated States* (Geneva: United Nations Institute for Disarmament Research, 1992).
2. The Strategic Arms Limitations Treaty (SALT) signed in 1972 did not require on-site verification. In the case of SALT the suspicions of the Cold War were still sharp enough to make it impractical to have inspectors of one's adversary directly probing around the strategic nuclear arsenal. The recourse was to rely on the ability of each side's intelligence capability as embodied in satellite photo reconnaissance, the so-called national technical means, to insure that mutual obligations were met.
3. If new nuclear powers, such as Iran, Iraq, or the Ukraine, were to arise as a result of the breakdown of the existing nonproliferation regime, the process of arriving at virtual nuclear arsenals would, at the least, be complicated and delayed.
4. Ratification of the Biological Weapons Convention was only possible because U.S. political and military leaders were convinced at the time that these weapons were of no military significance. On the other hand, it has proven very difficult to get the Chemical Weapons Convention (CWC) ratified by the U.S. Senate because of a fear that in the hands of rogue states chemical weapons could be militarily significant. This is true even though the CWC has the most intrusive verification provisions of any multilateral arms-control agreement, and the U.S. military no longer fields any chemical weapons of its own.
5. See Keith Payne's piece in this volume.
6. See Peter Wilson's piece in this volume.

7. The great majority of IAEA safeguard inspectors come from nonnuclear weapon states, and it would seem highly unlikely that they would be viewed as either acceptable or credible inspectors of the very heart of a military nuclear weapons program.

8. Advanced simulation and diagnostic technologies now becoming available in the United States and Japan are currently making fundamental changes in the concept of "testing." One irony in the nuclear weapons world is that the Comprehensive Test Ban Treaty, which was originally conceived of as a means of limiting the nuclear arsenals of the United States and the former Soviet Union, will, when and if it enters force, be principally relevant in limiting the nuclear arsenals of middle-level nuclear powers such as China, India, and Pakistan. The technologies for producing special nuclear materials originally required large facilities that gave off considerable amounts of heat, consumed large amounts of electricity, or required bulky facilities to separate plutonium, all of which made them difficult to hide. Gas centrifuge technology has already significantly altered this expectation, and laser enrichment technology that will soon be available will further diminish the prospect for early detection. So-called spy satellites opened up a broad range of visual, nonintrusive inspection possibilities, but, as soon as this was understood, work began on a range of countermeasures designed to limit the information that could be gleaned from this method.

RECONSTITUTION AND REASSEMBLY OF A VIRTUAL NUCLEAR ARSENAL

MICHAEL WHEELER

THE OPENING ESSAY OF THIS BOOK attempts to define a virtual nuclear arsenal (VNA). I wish to stress at the start that, while I agree that the idea of virtual arsenals is a useful tool for thinking about nuclear end-states, I also strongly believe that it is premature to be discussing VNAs as a policy option or to use analysis of VNAs as a means for advancing other arms-control schemes, for example, deep reductions beyond the levels of START II. I argued in 1992 in *The Role of Nuclear Weapons in the New World Order* (an essay I coauthored with Thomas C. Reed) that the near-term focus on deep reductions to low levels is counterproductive at this stage of international relations.[1] Since then I have encountered no persuasive reasons for changing that view. I disagree with critics of the Nuclear Posture Review (NPR) and Quadrennial Defense Review (QDR) who, like Michael Mazarr in the opening essay of this volume, contend that the review fails by default because it offers no reasonable expectation of any further progress in arms control or disarmament. In fact, the best chance for further progress arises in circumstances that first stabilize the U.S.-Russian nuclear relationship before moving on to more ambitious plans. Stabilization rests on short- and mid-term accomplishments such as finally implementing START II, deepening cooperative activities to reduce threats, and achieving some type of mutually acceptable Safeguards, Transparency, and Irreversibility (STI) regime for the nuclear warheads and fissile materials on the two sides. That is precisely the kind of arms control that is facilitated by the prudent, cautious direction of the NPR and the QDR.

But this essay is not written to rehash current policy disputes. Rather, I intend to examine a future in which one variation of a virtual-arsenal world is posited, namely, a world in which "no nuclear alerts for national forces" has become an international norm. I will examine what that norm might mean and what might be done to prevent the sorts of instabilities associated with nuclear reconstitution and reassembly that Peter Wilson and others in this volume appear to agree is a major stability dilemma for a world of VNAs.

A WORLD OF VIRTUAL NUCLEAR ARSENALS AND NO NUCLEAR ALERTS

The Cold War ended with far more grace than most expected or ever dared to hope. Academic debates on the Cold War are likely to continue for years, with few issues more hotly contested than the canonical roles nuclear weapons played in the global East/West confrontation. A full discussion of the attractiveness of the VNA concept requires an excursion into Cold War history that is beyond the scope of this essay. What is raised here are two major questions to be addressed in the following pages: first, how can an arrangement in which some possess nuclear weapons be reconciled with an international presumption against further nuclear proliferation? And, second, how can possession of and activities with nuclear weapons be made more stabilizing, especially in times of crisis?

One begins with the fact that a number of states in the post–Cold War world remain nuclear armed and are likely to remain so for the indefinite future. At least eight members of the United Nations continue to believe that nuclear weapons are needed for their security, others seek (or may in the future seek) to acquire nuclear weapons, and anyone with the proper determination and resources can find a way to join this club (probably including some nonstate actors).[2] Weapons of mass destruction continue to spread slowly, notwithstanding a substantial consensus and much activity in the international community to inhibit their proliferation through a regime of treaty agreements, export restrictions, and sanctions applied over time.

Two of the most serious long-term weaknesses in today's nuclear nonproliferation contract are: the perceived inequitable structure of the Nuclear Nonproliferation Treaty (NPT), especially if one interprets its sixth article to mean anything other than a commitment to nuclear abolition, which is an unrealistic goal; and the lack of universality for the NPT, given the seemingly intractable problem of bringing Israel, India, and Pakistan into its fold. One of the foremost uses of the concept of a virtual nuclear arsenal is that it offers the chance of shifting the terms of an increasingly sterile nonproliferation debate from one of nuclear weapons states versus nonnuclear weapons states to a prima facie more equitable situation in which *every state is seen as a virtual nuclear power.* In this altered world the conditions under which any state asserts its right to construct or reconstruct a nuclear arsenal will trigger the countervailing rights of the other states to carry out similar actions. Whether they choose to do so depends on their particular circumstances.

In a world of virtual nuclear arsenals one can envision a restructured nonproliferation bargain that includes the following:

- The NPT has been amended to allow Israel, India, and Pakistan to join as virtual nuclear powers whose status is on par with that of the United States, Russia, Britain, France, and China. This group of eight nations (hereafter referred to as the N-8) are the ones presumed to have the most advanced virtual nuclear arsenals in the world.
- The N-8 agree to: (1) have their nuclear weapons configured so they are not available for immediate use; and (2) refrain from placing nuclear weapons "on alert" without prior notification verified by outside observers.
- All states party to the NPT other than the N-8 agree not to seek nuclear weapons unless a member of the N-8 moves to place its nuclear weapons on alert status or unless they feel their security is threatened to the point that they exercise their right of withdrawal from the NPT.

- Stronger security assurances regarding nuclear aggression are put in place for all states.[3]

Monitoring and enforcing this recast regime would continue to involve a mélange of national, regional, and international actions and institutions tailored to specific challenges, some dimensions of which have been discussed by David Kay in his essay in this volume. The presumption remains against nuclear proliferation, and nothing in the recast contract prevents any member of the N-8 from deciding in the future that its security requires fewer (or even no) nuclear weapons. Nor does anything prevent them from deciding that they need more. If states other than the N-8 choose to pursue nuclear weapons (covertly or openly), the world community will have to deal with each new case on its merits, determining whether to accept or resist the activity. In the final accounting one must accept that keeping a nation from going nuclear—or convincing it to constrain, reduce, or give up nuclear weapons once it has acquired them—is a political matter that involves first-order security decisions and trade-offs likely to exact a political cost in other areas. There are no mechanical, and certainly no simple, solutions to the problems posed by nuclear weapons, and constructing a world order more receptive to the diplomacy of nonproliferation should be one of the aims of moving toward virtual nuclear arsenals.

In addition to the nonproliferation reasons, the second major argument for championing a world of virtual nuclear arsenals is to strengthen the opportunities for political processes to work constructively in times of extreme crisis. The most crucial revolution wrought by nuclear weapons is less one of absolute destruction than of compressed time for political decision, a point that Thomas Schelling eloquently summarized in 1966 by noting that the basic difference between nuclear weapons and other sorts of arms "is not in the number of people they can eventually kill but in the speed with which it can be done, in the centralization of decision, in the divorce of the war from political processes, and in computerized programs that threaten to take the war out of human hands once it begins."[4] A world of virtual nuclear arsenals may help contain nuclear anxieties early in a crisis, if those virtual nuclear arsenals are seen by their possessors as being secure and not yet necessary for dealing with the emergency.

Returning to the key definitional question, what is nuclear alert? From an operational perspective nuclear alert is one aspect of the posture that a nuclear-armed state adopts for its nuclear forces. A common image of nuclear alert involves forces poised around the clock for immediate use by the political authorities. Another image arises, however, from the more generic meaning of alert for military operations—namely, the idea of actions taken to forewarn and prepare for an impending operational mission, to increase the readiness of existing forces, or to mobilize additional forces as needed. Both these images entail specific questions such as:

- Are the nuclear weapons under the day-to-day control of the military units that will employ them if so ordered, or must they be transferred from another authority?

- How is nuclear use authorized, and what steps must be accomplished to execute, enable, and arm the nuclear weapons? What mechanical or procedural mechanisms are typically in place to guard against unauthorized or accidental use?

- Are the nuclear weapons maintained in a fully configured mode, loaded on well-serviced delivery vehicles, or must they first be assembled and/or uploaded prior to use?

- Are the nuclear force and its command and control infrastructure postured to survive a surprise, high-intensity attack, quickly retaliate under positive control, and continue to function through subsequent nuclear exchanges?

- What level of training and readiness is expected of the combat crews manning the nuclear-weapon delivery vehicles? Of the maintenance crews and other support elements?

- How often are elements of the nuclear force exercised and against what scenarios?

- How much of the force is maintained at a high level of day-to-day alert?

- Under what conditions will military personnel assigned to nuclear duties who are in peacetime training or on leave be recalled and mobilized, and when will additional nuclear forces be generated?

- Are the nuclear alerting orders passed through the channels common to all alerting orders for the nation's armed forces, or are there channels and procedures unique to nuclear alerting? Are the nuclear mechanisms kept secret from outside observers? Are they tested randomly in peacetime in ways that make it difficult for outside observers to distinguish between an exercise and an actual alert?

The different meanings of nuclear alert can be further explained by briefly reviewing selected episodes from the U.S. nuclear experience. One type of alert is that associated with bringing a force, normally in a somewhat relaxed state of readiness, to the point that it can execute a nuclear strike. There are many variations of this theme, as evidenced by the succession of postures that the U.S. nuclear strike forces had during thirteen years, from September 1944, when Col. Paul W. Tibbits was ordered to assemble and train the 509th Composite Bomb Group secretly, until late 1956, when Strategic Air Command (SAC) began testing the practice of continuous 24-hour nuclear alert. These first thirteen years (and especially the first several years after World War II) was a period more akin to the era of VNAs discussed in this essay, albeit lacking international surveillance of the actions to bring a strike force to an advanced state of readiness by assembling and/or loading nuclear weapons on strike platforms.

The second image of alert began in 1957, when SAC bombers were placed routinely on continuous 24-hour alert, to be joined over the next several years by, first, intercontinental ballistic missiles and then fleet ballistic missiles on deterrent patrols. This is the sort of alert force that is postured for very short reaction times—on the order of minutes—with mechanical systems that are maintained ready to go on an instant's notice and nuclear weapons that do not require elaborate preparations before they are used.

It is difficult for someone who has not been associated with nuclear operations to appreciate how enormously complex the vast nuclear posture of a superpower can be. It includes a number of subsystems, institutions, and procedures, many of which have nonnuclear as well as nuclear applications. When I speak of "posture," I include the following sorts of things:

- The nuclear stockpile: fissile materials, subcomponents, and assembled weapons of different "types" (designs), likely organized into various subsectors (e.g., deployed, active, reserve, retired) and possibly under control of several different authorities, all of which is maintained routinely under conditions of high security.

- The nuclear weapons design and production complex: a vast conglomerate of facilities and people devoted to designing, testing, modernizing, producing, storing, protecting, inspecting, and retiring the weapons and their fissile materials and other critical weapons requirements such as tritium.

- The military strike forces: an even more vast array of delivery vehicles (many capable of nonnuclear as well as nuclear missions), manned by trained military personnel, integrated into organizational units that draw upon a large support network to maintain and operate the systems (logistic systems, early warning and alerting systems, reconnaissance systems, planning and targeting systems, training systems, operations centers, operational inspection systems, and the like). The industrial activities that provide the hardware and software to the military strike forces also should be included in this category, and it is useful in that regard to note that there are few sectors of that industry that do not support nonnuclear as well as nuclear forces and (in some cases) commercial as well as military activities.

- The National Command Authority (NCA): a phrase denoting the officials who can order a nuclear attack. Associated with the NCA is the vast complex of procedures and actions covered by the phrase "command and control" and the industrial activities that provide the hardware and software for command and control.

As elaborate as this list is, it is worth recalling that it is imbedded in an even more elaborate and much larger standing military posture. What all this suggests is that, when we begin to speak of "reassembling and reconstituting" a nuclear force, we must be precise in our meaning—since much of what constituted a nuclear posture for the United States during the past fifty years will likely remain, even in a world of VNAs.

Before getting to the discussion of reassembly, however, it is necessary to finish the discussion of nuclear alert. The American experience during the nuclear age suggests two images of nuclear alert—one image associated with the military actions that follow decisions to develop and posture a military organization capable of delivering nuclear weapons, and the other image associated with routinely maintaining nuclear forces on continuous 24-hour alert, available for immediate use when directed by appropriate authorities. The following discussion attempts to take both images into account.

A norm of "no nuclear alert" cannot be defined operationally for an international regime unless there is some feature of nuclear alert common to all virtual nuclear powers that is reasonably visible and capable of being monitored (see David Kay's essay on inspection and verification in this volume). When one begins to examine the many different civil-military organizations around the world and their vast assortment of supporting doctrines, infrastructures, forces, and operating procedures (a task difficult in its own right, as suggested earlier, and rendered even more difficult by the many aspects of this topic that remain secret today), the problem of satisfactorily defining criteria for nuclear alert increases in difficulty.

The most promising, albeit far from risk-free, approach involves focusing on the point at which a nuclear weapon is removed from sheltered storage for loading on a delivery vehicle. Nuclear weapons are complicated mechanical devices that can use different designs to achieve the physical processes needed for nuclear and thermonuclear explosions. While some (perhaps many) of the generic aspects of nuclear-weapon design are available in open literature, the specifics (as well as the quantity of fissile material used in any particular weapon type) remain highly classified. It is the fissile material itself that is the absolutely necessary ingredient for producing a nuclear (or thermonuclear) device.[5] The fissile material may be fabricated such that it is part of a full-up (permanently assembled) nuclear weapon or as a subcomponent of a weapon to be assembled at the last moment.

The simplest procedure that lends itself to an operational definition of no nuclear alert is for the N-8 to place all of their nuclear weapons and the fissile material for nuclear weapons into declared, secure storage facilities that are safeguarded by a perimeter-portal monitoring system manned by the International Atomic Energy Agency (IAEA) inspectors. Nothing prohibits the N-8 states from removing the fissile materials or weapons; such removal, however, should be notified and will be a matter of public record. The IAEA monitors at the declared facilities are there to insure that fissile materials or nuclear weapons are not removed surreptitiously. The monitors have no mandate to attempt to prevent or interfere in any way with removal, and it is the responsibility of the monitored state to satisfy the remainder of the world if the removal of fissile materials from a declared facility is not for the purposes of reassembling a nuclear arsenal (e.g., is for normal stockpile surveillance purposes)—or, if it is for reassembly, to declare that reassembly of its nuclear arsenal has commenced. As discussed earlier, that declaration carries significant political consequences, since it releases other states from their commitments not to seek nuclear weapons.

This arrangement would be associated with a broader international regime for transparency of all fissile materials, since access to and control of fissile materials is the major challenge for those states other than the N-8 contemplating pursuing nuclear weapons. Moreover, this arrangement could be associated with a proposal that has been under consideration for almost forty years, namely, seeking a production ban on new fissile materials for weapons purposes.[6]

When all the separate strands are brought together, what transpires is a broad, worldwide transparency regime for nuclear weapons and fissile materials, including all civilian and military nuclear programs—a move consistent with dealing with the overall problem posed by the vast and increasing global inventory of civilian fissile materials that, if unsafeguarded, could be diverted to nuclear weapons programs.[7]

States would continue to use their national intelligence capabilities to supplement IAEA monitoring of fissile material status, and any state suspecting evasion of the rules is free to exercise its political choices— including the powerful but exceptional weapon of withdrawal from the NPT—and to enter into whatever arrangements it wants to secure itself in the international system, consistent with the Charter of the United Nations. It is readily apparent that the no nuclear alert scheme just described is an essentially political arrangement and is premised upon the expectation that no virtual nuclear power will routinely deploy its nuclear weapons on delivery vehicles solely under its control.

This analysis further assumes that the international system relevant to the analysis herein is one not significantly different than today's. The international community consists of some 200 or so sovereign states representing a world population that was 2.5 billion when the United

Nations was created, is approaching 6 billion today, and may reach 10 to 12 billion by the middle of the next century. These states are joined together loosely by the United Nations charter. Whatever the charter's weaknesses in setting up mechanisms for coordinating political action, it has the premier virtue of serving as a norm-creating instrument that establishes specific rules to regulate state behavior, especially regarding the use of force in state relations, which is prohibited except for: (1) force used in self-defense; (2) force authorized by the United Nations Security Council; or, arguably, (3) force undertaken collectively by the permanent members of the Security Council when formal procedures for the Security Council to act have not yet been established.[8]

On the vital questions of war and peace, this essay presumes that the future world will contain more than enough sources of tension and friction to allow one to envision armed conflict in ways not dissimilar to that of the past century (or at least of the nuclear age). Bullies, thugs, psychopaths, and the like certainly may still achieve near-total control of some governments in the system or of organized nongovernmental groups that can threaten peace and security. The sorts of ethnic and theocratic emotions that have fueled some of the cruelest wars in the past will not disappear, and, when one adds to the equation the massive growth in world population projected over the next several decades and the strain this growth will place on resources, institutions, and political processes worldwide, it is prudent to assume that the world of virtual nuclear arsenals, if it is to come about in the next several decades, must coexist with a world of armed conflicts.

Each state has its own peculiar security concerns and approach to coping with those concerns. States that feel threatened by the presence of nuclear weapons in any or all of the N-8 states today may still feel threatened in the future. Moving to virtual nuclear arsenals might change the threat dynamics somewhat but will not remove their root causes. New states may seek to join the N-8 through covert activities that are widely suspected but not established to everyone's satisfaction (as is the case, for example, in the nuclear activities of Iran). A world of virtual nuclear arsenals will not fundamentally remove those sorts of worries. Moreover, in a world of virtual nuclear arsenals, the concerns raised in quiet discussions in defense ministries and between senior security advisors and their heads of government will expand to include what I believe will be three especially disturbing themes during times of crisis:

1. It will be impossible to verify with high confidence that all nuclear weapons and fissile materials are in monitored storage.[9]
2. Reassembly of a nuclear arsenal, even if well publicized, can proceed relatively quickly if a nation decides that it must proceed down that path. (More will be said of this in the next section.)
3. Nuclear weapons in monitored storage will be more vulnerable than nuclear weapons that are operationally dispersed.

States may decide in this future world that they need nuclear weapons deployed and ready on short notice—weapons under their control or in the form of a nuclear umbrella provided by an ally—to give a degree of deterrent influence otherwise missing in the security equation. If the weapons are taken out of monitored storage and a sense of impending use is communicated, the conditions for a new set of arms races will have been re-created.

Dealing with the concerns discussed here and seeking a way of managing virtual nuclear arsenals so as to strengthen the security assurances associated with the NPT lead one to look for some reasonable sorts of safeguards. Reassembly and reconstitution of national nuclear arsenals is one such safeguard. That is the topic to which this analysis now turns.

THE MECHANICS OF REASSEMBLING NUCLEAR ARSENALS

I use the phrases *reassembling, reconstituting,* and *rebuilding* interchangeably in this essay, notwithstanding the different technical meanings such terms may have in other nuclear strategy and arms control contexts. A nation that wishes to rebuild its nuclear arsenal obviously can draw on its earlier experiences and perhaps on the experiences of others. There are as many paths to reassembly as there were to assembly in the first place, and how quickly and effectively a nation proceeds depends on its skill, resources, and the context within which reassembly begins. It is worth recalling, as discussed earlier, that a nuclear arsenal includes much more than the nuclear weapons themselves. It includes delivery systems, planning and targeting systems, reconnaissance systems, communications systems, procurement systems, maintenance and logistics support systems, highly trained personnel, and the like. Recent studies suggesting that the U.S. nuclear arsenal cost about $4 trillion are seriously misleading because, in attributing all of the system costs to the nuclear arsenal, the suggestion is that these (or even greater) costs would not have been incurred if the nuclear arsenal had not been assembled.[10] Most of the military infrastructure within which nuclear forces fit are likely to be there in the absence of nuclear weapons—bombers, for instance, missiles, satellites devoted to reconnaissance, elaborate communications and planning systems, and the like. In the absence of nuclear weapons there is reason to suspect that some parts of the infrastructure (e.g., the size and requisite capabilities of the bomber force) may be even more expensive.

How quickly a nation can reassemble its nuclear arsenal largely depends on how much of this wider infrastructure has been maintained, what plans have been devised ahead of time for reassembly, and whether these plans are regularly exercised and updated. The following analysis suggests some of the directions this reassembly can take, in terms of the different aspects of a nuclear posture discussed earlier: the nuclear stockpile, the nuclear weapons design and production complex, the military strike forces, and the National Command Authority.

THE NUCLEAR STOCKPILE AND NUCLEAR WEAPONS DESIGN AND PRODUCTION COMPLEX

Requirements for a nuclear stockpile have been set in the United States by an interaction between military planners and civilian authorities, culminating in approval at the presidential level. If the United States enters into a VNA world, presumably it will do so with a sense of requirements that draws upon this process. In other words, the VNA must satisfy many of the same sorts of criteria that are important today, which include such things as safety, reliability, security, and military effectiveness. Safety refers to the ability to maintain highly toxic and dangerous materials in a steady-state configuration that has a low risk of accident. Special handling procedures for fissile materials and nuclear weapons, limited personnel access, explosive containment, and similar concerns will continue to be part of the VNA world. Almost all, if not all, of the specialized procedures that are associated with the safety of the current nuclear stockpile would continue to obtain with a virtual nuclear stockpile.

Reliability refers to the reasonable expectation that nuclear weapons will perform as designed, if and when used. Today the United States is transitioning to a condition in which reliability is assessed without the traditional tool of nuclear testing. While I do not intend to reopen the question of the wisdom of the nuclear testing ban, I would note the caution with which the United States is approaching the new world of so-called science-based stockpile stewardship, in which advanced computational capabilities and new experimental capabilities are intended to give today's and future generations of nuclear designers the sort of confidence that nuclear testing gave prior generations, when it comes to answering the question of whether a nuclear weapon will work. The art of nuclear weapons design remains a highly conjectural art, with as many unknowns as knowns looming in the future. I presume in this analysis that the sorts of factors that led the Clinton administration to endorse a set of safeguards that requires annual certification of nuclear weapons by type will continue to obtain in a world of VNA. That would be part of the day-to-day aspects of a VNA world, not part of the reassembly equation.

As for the nuclear weapons themselves, maintaining them means replacing them over time, which leads to the requirement of having a nuclear weapons production complex that includes the capability for refurbishing and remanufacturing nuclear weapons. This includes such things as plutonium handling and fabrication facilities, tritium production, specialized and highly standardized manufacturing processes (a factor even more important in a world of no nuclear testing), and the like. The pace and scope of maintaining and replacing nuclear weapons is independent of whether they are located in storage or on alert and to a surprisingly large extent will probably prove independent of the questions of whether one is continually introducing new designs into the inventory (the experience of the past fifty years) or is refurbishing and remanufacturing already existing designs (presumably the experience of the next fifty). The wisdom of having two design laboratories, for instance, is the same if you have only a few nuclear weapon designs in the stockpile with no new designs on the drawing board as it is if you have many designs, constantly being updating. Obviously, if reconstitution takes place in the context of a dramatic breakdown of the international system that ignites a new nuclear armaments race, one would expect the nuclear design and production complex to expand. But the point made in this analysis is that, even if the issue is not one of increasing numbers of nuclear weapons but simply one of placing nuclear weapons back on alert and dispersing their alert forces, the need for a robust science and production complex is present in both cases. In other words, the ability to reconstitute a larger nuclear stockpile from a starting point defined by a VNA world may not differ significantly from that of a non-VNA world.

Finally, in terms of the numbers of types of designs, and numbers of weapons themselves, maintained in the stockpile and concerns for their effectiveness if used, that too is largely independent of whether the context is a VNA or a non-VNA world. There is no a priori reason to assume (although many authors in this book do) that a VNA world automatically equates to a world of very low nuclear stockpiles. The requirement for numbers of nuclear weapons and their desired effects continues to be driven by national assessments of roles, missions, and needs. Requirements turn in part on the question of whether there are nonnuclear options for achieving the same results. For a large country like the United States this involves a calculation of how many nuclear weapons are needed to deter other large nuclear powers and whether nuclear weapons are relevant to deterring threats other than nuclear weapons. In the past the NATO requirement to deter a large, Soviet-dominated threat to Central Europe was a large part of this equation. In the future the need to deter certain kinds of aggression by regional powers with biological weapons may be equally compelling. For a regional power like Israel, setting requirements involves judgments on how much is enough ultimately to guarantee the survival of the country in terms of its regional enemies.

The question of requirements is a complex, controversial subject whose full discussion clearly is beyond the scope of this essay. The point to be made here is that the requirements for numbers and weapons effectiveness associated with a VNA may not differ significantly from those associated with a non-VNA world, from the point of view of maintaining the nuclear stockpile. How much to hedge against breakout or cheating is a question of risk, which turns upon political judgments on the likelihood of the threat transpiring; on military advice about what should be done if the threat transpires; and on intelligence judgments on the ability to give warning of a threat in time to take effective action. Factors like the presence of advance ballistic missile defenses in the hands of enemies also would affect this calculation. Returning to the general point, however, there is strong reason to believe that the *mechanics* of reassembling a nuclear stockpile in a VNA world are likely to resemble those of a non-VNA world. What will differ are the political circumstances and consequences (a topic discussed in the next section).

THE MILITARY STRIKE FORCES AND THE NATIONAL COMMAND AUTHORITY

The concept of a VNA allows one to maintain precisely the same military strike force, with all that portends—operating forces, support forces, procedures, and so forth—as in a non-VNA world, with one exception: nuclear weapons are not routinely on alert. Maintaining a skilled, highly proficient, modernized, ready nuclear strike force does not require having nuclear weapons on actual alert. One can train, practice, exercise, and operationally evaluate this force with the use of ballistic shapes to simulate nuclear weapons while leaving the weapons in monitored storage. How well this force is maintained and trained in a VNA world is a function of how seriously the government and military take the need to possibly return nuclear weapons to alert. If nuclear weapons are marginalized in national strategy (and by that I mean that few in positions of authority in the government and military take seriously the need for nuclear weapons), then readiness will suffer. Dollars will be diverted elsewhere, exercises and training will be delayed or rendered unrealistic, assignment to nuclear forces will be seen as a dead-end career move and the quality of assigned personnel will decline, and so forth. All of this—which constitutes the baseline for reassembling a nuclear arsenal, from the point of view of the military strike forces— is independent of whether one starts in a VNA or non-VNA world.

What more accurately determines the capability for reassembly and reconstitution are other factors such as extant arms-control agreements that limit delivery systems and operations (such as the array of U.S.-Russian agreements on intermediate and strategic nuclear arms); the capacity of the industrial base to support a surge of expansion in production of delivery systems; the numbers of personnel trained in nuclear operations (specialized launch and maintenance personnel, specialized nuclear planners) and the ability of a training base to turn out increased numbers of new personnel quickly; and the like. In terms of training it also is worth noting that there already are trends under way—for instance, the availability of advanced simulators and planning tools shared by nuclear and nonnuclear planners—that will likely make it easier to reassemble a VNA if needed than to increase the size of the nuclear force dramatically today.

How long it takes to put the first nuclear weapon back on alert depends on the agreed-upon constraints for any VNA arrangement (for example, how close the weapons depots can be to military forces) and on the investment a military makes in plans and practice for accomplishing this task. The time can vary from minutes to days. Similarly, placing an entire military force back on alert depends on the readiness of that force to activate, reload, disperse (as necessary), and posture the nuclear delivery systems. This depends on actions that reflect the perceived need—maintaining a requisite number of trained loading teams on standby, for example. Obviously, sustaining an ability to reassemble a larger nuclear strike force quickly can be a source of instability in a world of VNA adversaries

Finally, as to the National Command Authority and the supporting infrastructure and procedures for commanding and controlling nuclear forces, this too is largely independent of whether one is in a VNA or non-VNA world. How robust the procedures are, how resistant to disruption or denial by an enemy, how well trained and exercised, and so forth are questions reflecting the perceived threats and the political and military actions taken as a consequence—not the simple fact that one is in a VNA world.

THE POLITICS OF REASSEMBLING NUCLEAR ARSENALS

As important to this analysis as the mechanics of reassembly is the political context within which reassembly proceeds. If reassembly is viewed as a purely national process triggered by each nation's perceptions of its own security needs, the likely result is an environment in which everyone hedges against the chances (however remote) that one's potential enemies might launch and win a reassembly race. While a significant element of the reassembly question remains one of sovereign choice, what is needed is some arrangement for giving different nations, especially the major virtual nuclear powers, a sense of cooperation in sustaining the stability of the system. In the past, nations that were bitter enemies have been brought together over time by engaging them in cooperative endeavors, as one can witness today, for instance, in the cases of Germany and France. Cooperation of this sort works best, of course, when there is some shared perception of a common threat or challenge. How might that be adapted to the world of virtual nuclear arsenals?

Those nations that today have acknowledged nuclear forces (coincidentally, the five permanent members of the UN Security Council, hereafter referred to as the N-5) have a shared interest in at least the following areas:

- Avoiding a new round of nuclear arms races among members of the N-5, fueled by misperceptions or suspicions of future action or intent.
- Sustaining an ability to reconstitute a nuclear arsenal if necessary but not in such a way as to fuel unnecessary suspicions of their intentions.
- Maintaining their virtual nuclear arsenals in a safe and secure fashion.
- Assuring that states that currently are nonnuclear do not choose to become nuclear because they feel their security cannot be assured otherwise.
- Keeping regional conflicts from escalating to nuclear war that draws in the remainder of the globe.

The N-5 united in early 1995 in supporting UN Security Council Resolution 984, which provided assurances to nonnuclear weapons states party to the NPT "that the Security Council, *and above all its nuclear weapon state permanent members,* will act immediately in accordance with the relevant provisions of the Charter of the United Nations, in the event that such States are the victim of an act, or object of a threat of, aggression in which nuclear weapons are used." The nature of action was not specified.

A MULTINATIONAL NUCLEAR FORCE

One model worth revisiting in light of the current discussion is the U.S. proposal in 1960 to create a multilateral nuclear force (MLF) for NATO. This proposal arose because of concern in NATO that leaving nuclear weapons decisions solely up to the United States did not adequately meet NATO's security needs and a concern in the United States that more members of the alliance would choose to develop their own nuclear options. As the author of the MLF proposal, Robert R. Bowie, later wrote: "The MLF proposal had several purposes: (1) to involve and reassure the allies; (2) to discourage national nuclear forces; (3) to meet the stated military need for MRBMs (medium-range ballistic missiles) while avoiding the problems of land-based missiles; (4) to encourage European integration by the prospect that the MLF might eventually become a European force as the European Community developed into an effective political entity."[11] President Eisenhower embraced the concept and discussed it with Henri Spaak, then secretary-general of NATO, who welcomed the proposal and championed it in Europe. Although the MLF did not transpire (in part because the Soviets made achievement of the NPT hostage to the United States giving up the MLF concept),[12] it served a valuable political purpose in the early 1960s by reinforcing NATO solidarity at a time of severe crisis. And it is worth revisiting in this discussion of virtual nuclear arsenals, modified as follows.

Assume that the N-5 agree to a cooperative arrangement in which a small element of each nation's nuclear force retains nuclear weapons on alert but weapons that cannot be armed unless each of the N-5 authorizes the action. There are well-developed electromechanical unlocking devices adaptable to this purpose, in which five separate coded messages—each generated by different authorities within the N-5—are needed to enable the nuclear weapons in this part of the otherwise nationally controlled nuclear forces. Further assume that arrangements are agreed upon for some degree of cooperative action in the day-to-day operations of the N-5 nuclear forces—example, liaison officers from the other N-4 being assigned to the alert force components of the fifth. The primary purpose of the alert forces (hereafter referred to as the five-nation alert force [FNAF]) is to provide a ready nuclear deterrent mechanism on those occasions that the United Nations Security Council convenes to consider a case brought to its attention under the auspices of Resolution 984. A secondary purpose is to provide each of the N-5 with a mechanism for more realistically training its nuclear weapons personnel in the vast array of operational procedures that sustain a ready base for nuclear reassembly and reconstitution.

The FNAF presumably will be operated and sustained in a fashion that secures it from surprise attack, whatever the source. It will seek the highest levels of professionalism, safety, and overall security in its daily operations and may give rise to creating a political forum for the N-5 to coordinate their joint military activities. It might also have attached to it a planning arm, serving some functions akin to those that the Nuclear Planning Group (NPG) served for NATO. And it may mature over time into a wider set of agreements that engage the N-5 in cooperatively defining further confidence- and security-building measures to strengthen common action.

The FNAF arrangement is not intended to replace the system of security alliances and bilateral arrangements that exists today. It is possible, of course, that a member of the N-5 may itself be the perceived aggressor in a specific instance and that important nations outside the N-5 (e.g., Germany or Japan) will need to rely upon their security agreements with others to protect their interests. For those nations that do not today have a security pact with a major nuclear power, the arrangement discussed in this essay makes them no less secure and, developed properly over time, may enhance their security. As for the N-5 themselves, each retains the ability to reconstitute its virtual nuclear arsenal without the veto of the other N-5 members and can invest in sustaining that capability to the extent it believes its security interests demand.

To summarize, while the FNAF proposal does not account for all security needs in the future international system, it does offer an institutional base from which to develop a maturing sense of mutual advantage and shared expectations that can help stabilize the world of virtual nuclear arsenals. One cannot prevent the possibility that this or any future international system may collapse catastrophically, in which case it is difficult to conceive of any institutional safeguards other than a massive general rearmament that will serve the interests of the different members. A world of virtual nuclear arsenals will not change the fundamentals of international politics. That requires a much more ambitious agenda.

NOTES

1. Thomas C. Reed and Michael O. Wheeler, *The Role of Nuclear Weapons in the New World Order;* reprinted in Committee on the Armed Services, *Threat Assessment, Military Strategy, and Defense Planning* (Washington, D.C.: US GPO, 1992): 156-213.

2. The Nuclear Nonproliferation Treaty (NPT) recognizes five states as nuclear weapons nations: the United States, Russia (as successor to the USSR), Britain, France, and China. Three other states are commonly accepted as having acquired nuclear weapons capability—Israel, India, and Pakistan—but are not members of the NPT. As now is well-known, Iraq was well along toward acquiring nuclear weapons by the time of the Gulf War, despite its NPT commitments, and many believe it could (and would) effectively resume the quest if current United Nations sanctions are lifted. South Africa had and gave up nuclear weapons but presumably retains a considerable knowledge of how to construct them. North Korea was pursuing nuclear weapons; so is Iran. With money and opportunity even the smaller countries such as Libya (or subnational groups, for that matter) may find it possible to purchase nuclear weapons. Any major industrial power can go nuclear militarily, probably in less time than many believe, if it has the will to do so.

3. For background on security assurances as they relate to UN Security Council Resolution 984 (1995) and its predecessor, Resolution 255 (1968), see: Michael O. Wheeler, *Positive and Negative Security Assurances* (PRAC Paper no. 9, Center for International and Security Studies at Maryland, February 1994); and Virginia I Foran, ed., *Missed Opportunities? The Role of Security Assurances in Nuclear Non-Proliferation Policy* (Washington, D.C.: Carnegie Endowment for International Peace, 1996).

4. Thomas C. Schelling, *Arms and Influence* (New Haven: Yale University Press, 1966): 20. A vast literature has been devoted to the theme of the crisis dynamic that arises when leaders have at their disposal nuclear weapons that have been alerted for immediate use.

5. This essay uses the following definition of *fissile material:* "An element or isotope that can undergo nuclei being split or divided by the absorption of thermal neutrons. The most common fissile materials are U-233, U-235, and Pu-239. Neither natural nor depleted material is fissile material." Office of Fissile Materials Disposition, United States Department of Energy, *Fact Sheet: Glossary of Technical Terms* (Washington, D.C.: USGPO, n.d.).

6. The idea for a production ban on fissile materials for weapons has been under consideration for more than thirty years. See, for instance, the declassified top-secret "Report of the Panel on the Cutoff of the Production of Fissionable Materials for Weapons," Washington, April 1, 1961, *FRUS,* 1961-63, vol. 7: *Arms Control and Disarmament* (1995): 30-31. On September 27, 1993 the Clinton administration formally proposed a global convention banning production of fissile materials for weapons, and in December of the same year

the General Assembly endorsed this endeavor. Discussions have stalled in Geneva at the Conference on Disarmament, however, in part because the existing nuclear weapons establishments would not be subject to the proposed regime, and in part because of calls for a negotiated timetable for complete nuclear disarmament.

7. See *Management and Disposition of Excess Weapons Plutonium* (Washington, D.C.: National Academy of Sciences Press, 1993).

8. See Anthony Clark Arend and Robert J. Beck, *International Law and the Use of Force: Beyond the UN Charter Paradigm* (London: Routledge, 1993): 31-32. Clark and Beck state that self-defense and force authorized by the Security Council are the only applicable exceptions to the Article 2(4) prohibition on the use of force in the charter, but they also point out that Article 106 provides that pending the coming into force of special agreements referred to in Article 43 (making elements of national military forces available to the Security Council for enforcement action), Article 106 allows the transitional security arrangement of action undertaken by the permanent members. Whether the charter paradigm will be extended to allow humanitarian intervention is not relevant to the central arguments in this essay.

9. This conclusion has been reached by every high-level study I am aware of, starting with those during the Truman years and extending to today. The major stumbling block to high-confidence verification is the so-called baseline problem; that is, accounting for all fissile materials that have been produced prior to the onset of the international monitoring regime.

10. See *Atomic Audit: What the US Nuclear Arsenal Really Cost,* ed. Stephen I. Schwartz (Washington, D.C.: U.S. Nuclear Cost Study Project, July 11, 1995).

11. Robert R. Bowie, *The North Atlantic Nations Tasks for the 1960's: A Report to the Secretary of State, August 1960* (Center for International Security Studies at Maryland, Nuclear History Program, Occasional Paper no. 7, 1991): v.

12. See George Bunn, *Arms Control by Committee: Managing Negotiations with the Russians* (Stanford: Stanford University Press, 1992): 66-72.

SEVEN

STRATEGIC DEFENSES AND VIRTUAL NUCLEAR ARSENALS

KEITH PAYNE

THE RELATIONSHIP OF ACTIVE STRATEGIC DEFENSES to the potential for severely reducing or effectively eliminating nuclear weapons has been a subject of considerable debate since the mid-1960s.[1] This debate has never concluded: it simply has waxed and waned as the prominence of ballistic missile defense (BMD) and strategic arms control has waxed and waned on the national political agenda. The relationship between strategic defense and deep offensive reductions, such as that envisaged in the concept of virtual nuclear arsenals (VNA), could be critical to the plausibility and acceptability of VNAs.

A brief review of the past and current debate concerning the relationship between strategic defense and offensive reductions should facilitate consideration of the potential relationship between strategic defense and VNA. For example, from the late 1960s through the early 1970s the debate on SALT I and the ABM Treaty focused considerable attention on the offense-defense relationship. The subject seemed to be closed with ratification of the ABM Treaty in 1972; the treaty was established on the belief that the reduction of strategic offensive forces would be made possible *only* with the capping of strategic defense, particularly BMD.[2] Over a decade passed until, in 1983, Ronald Reagan introduced the Strategic Defense Initiative (SDI). For the subsequent five years the vigorous SDI debate turned to a considerable extent on competing expectations about the offense-defense relationship, that is, on competing expectations of how the Soviet Union would respond to U.S. BMD deployment.

Concern and debate about the offense/defense relationship once again is on the rise as part of the current national debate on missile defense (this time with considerable attention devoted also to defense against cruise missiles). Renewed attention to the issue is the result of the increasing prominence of two issues, missile proliferation and START II. This renewed interest is particularly evident in congressional support for the Missile Defense Act of 1995 and the Defend America Act of 1996.

An important difference between this current debate and that of the 1960s and 1970s involves the objectives for strategic defense. Past debates focused largely on BMD scoped to address the Soviet ballistic missile threat—either to provide actual societal protection against that threat or to reduce any prospective Soviet confidence in first-strike, counterforce targeting options. In contrast, the current discussion of strategic missile defense goals focuses on protection against the limited missile threats posed by "rogue" states to U.S. territory—possibly involving up to several dozen missiles or warheads. The goal of protecting against such limited missile threats may be akin to the type of strategic defenses that would be considered useful, perhaps essential, to a VNA regime.

With regard to consideration of the offense-defense relationship in the current debate, of immediate concern is how U.S. missile defense deployment in response to proliferation might affect Third Party incentives for WMD and missile acquisition and how it might affect the prospects for Russian ratification of START II. As might be expected, critics and proponents of missile defense present competing estimates of the offense-defense relationship.

Opponents of missile defense contend that the Russian Federation will abandon START II in response to U.S. strategic defenses, because even limited U.S. strategic defenses would compel Russia to "protect its deterrent" by rejecting START II offensive reductions.

This "action-reaction" argument, of course, harkens back to the hypothesis concerning the effect of missile defense on arms control that was a centerpiece of the SALT I debate and the subsequent arms-control critique of the SDI: movement on strategic defenses and arms control are incompatible because the deployment of defenses must increase the requirement for offensive forces to penetrate the defenses.[3] The corollary of this anticipated "action-reaction" relationship is the hypothesis that the limitation of strategic defenses establishes the necessary basis for offensive limitations.[4]

These complementary hypotheses concerning the offense-defense relationship were the heart of the U.S. rationale for the ABM Treaty.[5] In the current third round of the debate, added is the notion that the same offense-defense, action-reaction dynamic will affect proliferant states—with missile defenses increasing their drive for offensive missiles and undermining efforts to control missile proliferation.

Not surprisingly, missile defense proponents hypothesize a different offense-defense linkage. They contend that the deployment of missile defenses would "devalue" offensive missiles and, to a lesser extent, WMD, by undermining their prospective value as instruments of combat or terror. This devaluation would reduce their demand and thereby contribute to nonproliferation efforts. The contention is that the deployment of missile defense will be the initial move in an "action-inaction" cycle instead of the action-reaction cycle predicted in the past. If an action-inaction cycle can, in fact, be expected, moving forward with strategic defenses could in principle help facilitate a VNA regime by reducing the incentives to develop, market, deploy, or maintain missile arsenals.

As an element in U.S. counterproliferation efforts, BMD proponents point to the need for theater missile defense (TMD) and national missile defense (NMD). With regard to NMD, proponents claim that the limited NMD necessary to address the foreseeable missile proliferation threat would be incapable of undermining the Russian strategic deterrent, even at START II offensive force levels. Missile defense, thus, need not stimulate Russian moves to augment its strategic deterrent; and, if the Russians do in fact reject START II, it will be for reasons independent of U.S. movement on missile defense.[6] Consequently, the NMD capability necessitated by proliferation should not be destabilizing in strategic deterrence or arms-control terms.

This particular hypothesis concerning a defensive capability sufficient to help address the threat from third parties but insufficient to undermine the U.S.-Russian strategic deterrence and arms-control relationship also has a lineage stretching back to the early SALT I debate. For example, in 1969 Harold Brown, having just finished his tenure as secretary of the air force in the Johnson administration, proposed that the level of BMD deployment that should be considered would include that number of interceptors able to protect against limited "third-country attacks" but incapable of undermining the Soviet deterrent and thereby destabilizing strategic deterrence. Brown identified that number of interceptors at "a figure between 100 and 1000 . . . in the neighborhood of several hundred [BMD] launchers."[7] At the time, the Soviet Union had fewer than 1,700 strategic ballistic missile warheads—more than now is envisaged under a virtual nuclear arsenal regime but about half the number allowed under START II. The requirements for strategic defense identified by NMD proponents today are well within the scope identified by Brown in 1969.

While the near-term goal is counterproliferation, the long-term goal declared by many missile defense proponents in the current debate is more comparable to the reductions envisaged in the VNA proposal. Their expressed goal is to bring an end to the strategic deterrence relationship based on mutual vulnerability to prompt and severe nuclear retaliatory threats. This would be accomplished through a combination of strategic nuclear force reductions and strategic defenses. This goal rejects the SALT I hypothesis of an unbeatable and mechanistic offense-defense, action-reaction cycle. Rather, it identifies an action-inaction process involving the deployment of strategic defenses while moving forward with deep offensive limitations. This clearly draws from the original concept of the Strategic Defense Initiative, and such a process obviously could prove beneficial to the prospects for U.S.-Russian acceptance of deep offensive reductions. Senate language in the START II Treaty Resolution of Ratification reflects this thinking:

> The long-term perpetuation of deterrence based on mutual and severe offensive nuclear threats would be outdated in a strategic environment in which the United States and the Russian Federation are seeking to put aside their past adversarial relationship and instead build a relationship based upon trust rather than fear. . . . these governments [should] promptly undertake discussions based on the Joint Statement to move forward

cooperatively in the development and deployment of defenses against ballistic missiles.[8]

This proposed goal, similar in significant ways to a combination of virtual nuclear arsenals and strategic defense, also has considerable lineage—harkening back to Don Brennan's early arms-control proposals and President Reagan's 1983 introduction of the Strategic Defense Initiative.[9] Jonathan Schell, a noted advocate of the "abolition" of nuclear weapons, captured the ethos of this defense-emphasis proposal for offensive reductions:

> Building defenses, depending on what else you do, could make it a lot easier to achieve the abolition [of nuclear weapons]. I think what arms control people are afraid of is that Star Wars is a shield that will allow Reagan to fight a nuclear war. But what if, while you build up the defenses, you reduce the offenses. . . . Then Star Wars isn't a threat at all. If you're afraid of the sword and the shield, OK. But then you should attack the sword—not the shield.[10]

The available historical record is not revealing with regard to the offense-defense relationship. Almost two decades following the ABM Treaty the number of strategic ballistic missile warheads increased dramatically. This record demonstrates fairly convincingly that one of the SALT I hypotheses was in error: banning serious strategic missile defense did not lead to the promised subsequent offensive reductions.

Nevertheless, the historical record does not demonstrate that deep offensive reductions and strategic defenses can proceed in tandem. There was a glimmer of hope in 1992. This concept came to the fore at the June 1992 Bush-Yeltsin Summit in Washington, when the U.S. and Russian leaders agreed to pursue strategic missile defenses cooperatively while simultaneously pursuing deep offensive reductions in START.[11] This mandate followed President Yeltsin's January 1992 initiative for a "Global Protection System" that would provide the basis for cooperation on missile defenses while simultaneously pursuing START reductions. It seemed to demonstrate that the SALT I–era hypotheses were invalid and that offensive reductions and strategic defenses could proceed simultaneously. Movement in this direction, ultimately short-lived, showed significant promise following the June summit, but the initiative collapsed following the U.S. November 1992 election and the Clinton administration's return to the previous SALT I–era concepts of arms control.[12]

Consequently, there is little direct historical precedent to call on when considering the potential offense-defense relationship under a VNA regime. The benefit of this situation is that it provides a freedom for open speculation about that prospective relationship that goes beyond the traditional hypotheses generated in the 1960s.

The advantages for the defense provided by a deep offensive reductions regime could be powerful. At very high offensive force levels, particularly involving nuclear weapons and advanced delivery systems, strategic defense sufficient to protect population and industry are at best a significant technical challenge and expensive for the United States. Deep offensive reductions may help to make very high levels of defense effectiveness both more easily achieved and more affordable.

The advantage that strategic defense brings to a deep offensive reductions regime also is powerful. Because a relatively small number of nuclear weapons, if targeted properly, essentially can destroy an organized society, actually providing the United States with safety against nuclear attack through arms reductions alone either is impossible or impracticable. In the absence of strategic defenses a relatively very small number of either covert or rapidly deployed nuclear weapons targeted against urban centers could annihilate much of the U.S. population and industrial infrastructure.[13]

The combination of strategic defense and deep offensive reductions offers the potential benefit, at least in theory, of both easing the burden on strategic defense to the point of affordability and effectiveness and giving meaning to offensive reductions in terms of directly contributing to the security of society against nuclear threats. The problem with this scenario, of course, is the problem confronting deep offensive reduction proposals alone: it requires a considerable level of cooperative interaction among or between states that may have high levels of mutual animosity and low levels of mutual trust.[14] A question of interest is whether the addition of strategic defenses to proposals for deep offensive reductions, such as a virtual nuclear arsenal regime, could provide the necessary level of "reassurance" for such a regime to become practicable.

THE OFFENSE-DEFENSE RELATIONSHIP
IN A NEW CONTEXT

It is important to note that the context for the offense-defense relationship in a virtual nuclear arsenals regime would be significantly different from the context pertaining to the earlier offense-defense debates that juxtaposed arms control and strategic defense. This difference in context is likely to affect expectations of the offense-defense relationship and, more generally, the value of strategic defense in a regime of deep offensive reductions.

For example, past competing hypotheses concerning the offense-defense relationship largely assumed a bilateral U.S.-Soviet relationship. In this case the value of active strategic defenses was inversely linked to the level of confidence placed in Cold War policies of strategic deterrence. And by the mid-1960s the U.S. defense and foreign policy community was extremely confident in the stability of strategic deterrence.[15] To the extent that U.S. decisionmakers were comfortable with the reliability of strategic deterrence in U.S.-Soviet relations, strategic defenses were judged unnecessary at best and possibly damaging because they might "destabilize" the trusted deterrence relationship.

Because confidence in strategic deterrence was very high with regard to U.S.-Soviet relations and the dominant strategic-deterrence paradigm identified relatively modest offensive force requirements as sufficient for deterrence,[16] essentially eliminating strategic defenses (other than ASW and passive defenses for retaliatory forces) and moving to modest offensive force levels were judged as posing little risk. And, because rejecting strategic BMD was considered the necessary prelude to achieving limitations on destabilizing offensive forces, as the action-reaction hypothesis suggested, eliminating strategic defenses was said to promise great value.

In short, Cold War–era arms-control and deterrence concepts were elaborated in a bilateral context. They offered an avenue, at least in principle, to a strategic regime compatible with very low levels of strategic offensive forces. The levels of offensive forces adequate for deterrence in this regime were, by some accounts, quite similar to a mature, if not final, stage of a virtual nuclear arsenals regime.[17] A stringent cap on active strategic defense was, however, considered an essential part of the equation.

In contrast to the essentially bilateral context of the SALT-era action-reaction hypothesis, the context for a virtual nuclear arsenals regime is much more multilateral, both in terms of the character of the proposed regime and in U.S. post–Cold War security concerns: the regime itself is similar to the NPT in that it is intended to be global in scope; and there is a general perception—following the Gulf War, the crisis with North Korea, and U.S. deployments to Haiti, Somalia, and Bosnia—that U.S. security concerns in the post–Cold War era will focus on regional rogue states.[18] In such a multilateral context, active strategic defenses are likely to be considered much more important, because, as will be discussed, confidence in deterrence is reduced.

In addition, in a multilateral context the anticipated "cost" of missile defense, as envisaged by the action-reaction hypothesis, may not be considered pertinent. It was possible to contend that the Soviet Union could, in principle, improve its strategic ballistic missile force in response to U.S. defensive capabilities, thus nullifying the value of a given level of defense, and do so at less cost than would be required to restore the defense.[19]

It will be more difficult to make the same claims to this effect with regard to Iraq, Syria, Iran, North Korea, or other potential rogues. The overall resources available to these states to devote to an offensive-defensive competition are simply so much smaller that the action-reaction hypothesis must be reconsidered. The putative offensive advantage that may have rendered effective active defense ultimately unaffordable in U.S.-Soviet relations will not necessarily be operative in U.S. relations with challengers in the post–Cold War context. Consequently, the anticipated value of limited active strategic defense for the United States may be higher in the context in which a virtual nuclear arsenals regime would be elaborated, and the potential costs, in terms previously anticipated, may be lower.

DETERRENCE AND THE POTENTIAL ROLE FOR STRATEGIC DEFENSE IN A VIRTUAL NUCLEAR ARSENALS REGIME

Both the multilateral milieu of a virtual nuclear arsenals regime and the regime itself will increase the perceived value of strategic defenses for the United States. For example, one reason for the increased interest in active strategic defense is tied directly to a reduced confidence in policies of deterrence. This is in direct contradiction to the SALT/START-era rejection of strategic missile defense, which in large measure ultimately was a reflection of the widespread U.S. confidence in nuclear deterrence policies.[20]

As the result of the proliferation of missiles and WMD to regional rogue powers, U.S. officials are beginning to express uncertainty with regard to the level of confidence that may be placed in deterrence and have tied a new interest in active strategic defenses to that uncertainty. The Senate, for example, included the following language in its START II Treaty Resolution of Ratification: "Because deterrence may be inadequate to protect United States forces and allies abroad, theater missile defense is necessary. . . . Similarly, because deterrence may be inadequate to protect the United States against long-range missile threats, missile defenses are a necessary part of new deterrent strategies."[21]

The Clinton administration has expressed similar concerns about the future reliability of deterrence in relations with proliferant states. For example, the 1994 Department of Defense annual report observes: "Deterrence approaches designed for the Soviet Union might not be effective against new possessors of WMD . . . new proliferators might not be susceptible to basic deterrence as practiced during the Cold War. New deterrent approaches are needed as well as new strategies should deterrence fail."[22] Similarly, Secretary of Defense Perry observed in March 1995: "The bad news is that in this era, deterrence may not provide even the cold comfort it did during the Cold War. We may be facing terrorists or rogue regimes with ballistic missiles and nuclear weapons at the same time in the future, and they may not buy into our deterrence theory. Indeed, they may be madder than 'MAD.'"[23]

Even assuming a successful virtual nuclear arsenals regime, the United States will likely face regional challengers armed with chemical and biological weapons, and their delivery means, and the possibility of covert nuclear capabilities and/or a "breakout" from the regime. The United States clearly will need to address such threats that will remain even in the context of a successful virtual nuclear arsenals regime.

Concern about WMD and missile proliferation clearly is driving interest in accelerated deployment of defenses against short- and medium-range ballistic and cruise missiles; it also is driving interest in strategic defenses, although congressional support for the latter far exceeds that of the Clinton administration. Nevertheless, senior officials in the Clinton administration and Congress essentially have agreed that the proliferation of missiles and weapons of mass destruction (WMD) renders defenses against short- and medium-range missiles, both ballistic and cruise, a necessary element in U.S. power projection capabilities. They also agree that proliferation either currently necessitates pursuing limited missile defense for the United States (as seen in Congress) or will, if a long-range threat matures (as seen by the Clinton administration).[24]

Reservations concerning the reliability of deterrence in the regional conflicts of the post–Cold War environment are not limited to U.S. officials. A prominent Russian military expert, General Mikhail Vinogradov, recently observed: "The events in the Persian Gulf have shown that the presence of totalitarian regimes in certain countries, ethnic and religious strife both between the peoples of several states as well as inside them can lead and have already led to armed conflict and even war. Wars of such a nature belong to the category of unpreventable because in these cases the system of global nuclear deterrence does not work".[25]

Expectations of an emerging long-range missile threat and the lack of deterrence reliability are likely to increase support for missile defense, including strategic missile defense, particularly if the North Korean Taepo–Dong II missile moves toward an operational capability. There are several reasons why the growing skepticism concerning deterrence in the post–Cold War strategic environment is warranted.

First, because some regional leaders and their regimes are largely unfamiliar to the United States,[26] their behavior is likely to be relatively unpredictable. For deterrence to function requires that the challenger be a rational decisionmaker. For deterrence to function predictably for the defender also requires that the defender has at least a general understanding of the key factors likely to contribute significantly to the challenger's decision making. Only upon such an understanding can the defender establish policies of deterrence with confidence.

Establishing deterrence policies on the assumption that the challenger's behavior will be predictable, because it will be both rational and sensible as understood by U.S. leaders, may have been appropriate during the Cold War. It probably will not be in the multilateral environment of the post–Cold War period. This is not to suggest that the leadership of regional rogue states will behave irrationally. Rather, a variety of factors may be significant in their decision making, and, if the U.S. policymakers are ignorant of these factors, they are less likely to know how to establish a reliable deterrence policy vis-à-vis the challenger.[27]

For example, to establish confident policies of deterrence, it will be important to know something about the challenger—who are the decisionmakers? What is their general value hierarchy? Are they driven by perceived need or opportunity? Are they risk prone or tolerant? Are they informed generally about the U.S. threat and the attached conditions?—and whether U.S. threats are considered credible.

Answering such questions may be critical to the effectiveness of deterrence. It may also be quite difficult vis-à-vis regional rogue leaderships and regimes with whom there has been relatively little contact and/or are closed and secretive.

Second, in the U.S.-Soviet strategic deterrence relationship, the deterrence commitments made by the United States were generally recognized as "intrinsic" interests. That is, they were interests that clearly were at the very top of the U.S. value hierarchy, such as the physical security of society and the security of Western Europe. The United States has for decades demonstrated by word and deed the extreme value it places on these interests. Consequently, the U.S. deterrent commitments on behalf of these values were assumed to be sufficiently credible for deterrence to function reliably.[28] Because the Soviet Union was assumed to be rational and sensible and the U.S. deterrence threat credible enough, analysts focused almost exclusively on the character of the strategic balance to judge the likely effectiveness of deterrence, its stability.

In contrast, the U.S. interests in many, perhaps most, of the prospective challenges by regional rogues will not involve intrinsic interests for the United States but may well involve such interests for the challenger. The national and official skepticism toward the U.S. deployment of forces to Somalia and Bosnia demonstrates the point. Consequently, it will not be reasonable simply to assume the credibility of U.S. deterrence commitments on behalf of those interests. And, as historically based analyses of deterrence conclude, establishing deterrence credibility for interests that are not intrinsic can be very difficult.[29] Indeed, it may require the manifest willingness to go to war over the interest in question.[30] The U.S. capacity to demonstrate such a willingness clearly is limited.

In short, the reduced confidence in the reliability of U.S. deterrence policies probably is warranted in the multilateral environment of the post–Cold War period. The combination of expectations that long-range missiles will, sooner or later, make their way into the arsenals of proliferant states and that crises involving regional powers will not reliably be amenable to U.S. deterrence pressure has increased the perceived value of and requirement for strategic defenses. Because a virtual nuclear arsenals regime, as envisaged, does not address missiles or WMD other than nuclear, it should not be viewed as a superior alternative to strategic defenses, as the combination of deterrence and arms control was during the Cold War.

There are several reasons why a virtual nuclear arsenals regime itself may contribute to a decrease in the reliability that can reasonably be placed on U.S. policies of deterrence, and therefore increase the value of strategic defense under such a regime. First, a virtual nuclear arsenals regime would appear to place a greater burden on conventional power projection forces as the basis for U.S. deterrence threats. The regime would reduce the promise of any U.S. nuclear deterrent threat at least for the period necessary for reconstitution, which is postulated variously at weeks to months.[31] That time frame, if accurate, could remove nuclear weapons from consideration for the entire duration of a crisis. Or it could provide a challenger with a "window" during which it could have confidence that the United States would not have an operational nuclear threat—permitting the possibility that a risk-tolerant challenger would exploit the potential for a fait accompli. Some analyses of deterrence using historical case studies suggest that deterrence failure "is likely" if the challenger believes that it can accomplish a fait accompli.[32]

In addition, U.S. sponsorship of a virtual nuclear arsenals regime also would seem to put nuclear weapons further into the "background" as a basis for U.S. deterrence threats; indeed, that appears to be one of the objectives of the regime. The very act of establishing the regime would likely contribute to doubts about U.S. nuclear deterrence commitments and to placing more emphasis on conventional forces for deterrence commitments.

A challenger might, of course, completely dismiss U.S. commitments under a virtual nuclear arsenals regime concerning the necessity for a "cushion" of time to reconstitute an operational nuclear capability. Or, to retain nuclear deterrence leverage, U.S. leaders could try to eliminate doubt on the matter by simply declaring their intention and capacity to reconstitute operational nuclear forces very rapidly in the event of a brewing crisis, particularly one involving the potential for WMD use by the challenger.[33]

To the extent, however, that there is no confidence in this temporal cushion for reconstitution of nuclear arsenals, or U.S. leaders essentially declare that no such cushion exists, an important element in the overall rationale for a virtual nuclear arsenals regime would be removed. In the latter case the proposed regime would constitute little more than an overly complicated form of minimum deterrence, at least for the United States; presumably, the regime is intended to be more than that.

The concerns that emerge from this emphasis on conventional deterrence of the virtual nuclear arsenals proposal are whether conventional forces can provide confidence in U.S. deterrence policies comparable to that provided by nuclear weapons, and the relationship of strategic defense to U.S. deterrence policies based on conventional threats.

First, although the claim that conventional forces are to be preferred over nuclear as the basis for reliable deterrence policies has become popular,[34] there are some reasons to be skeptical. For example, a question following the Gulf War was why Saddam Hussein decided against the use of the bombs and warheads armed with chemical and biological weapons that were available to him. Various answers have been proposed. In August 1995, however, Iraqi Foreign Minister Tariq Aziz reported to Ambassador Rolf Ekeus, of the United Nations Special Commission for the Disarmament of Iraq (UNSCOM), that Iraq refrained from using its WMD because the Iraqi leadership had interpreted Washington's explicit threats of grievous retaliation to Iraqi WMD use as meaning *nuclear* retaliation.[35] This explanation of Iraqi restraint as a result of the U.S. nuclear deterrent has been corroborated by a very senior Iraqi defector, General Wafic Al Sammarai, former head of Iraqi military intelligence. He has confirmed that chemical weapons were not used during the Gulf War, "because the warning was quite severe, and quite effective. The allied troops were certain to use nuclear arms and the price will be too dear and too high."[36]

The prospect of conventional battle with the United States clearly was insufficient to deter or coerce Saddam Hussein. This account by Aziz, and others, however, suggests that the Iraqi perception of a nuclear threat was the basis for deterring Iraq's use of WMD. Here is at least one "real-world" reference in response to those who suggest that nuclear deterrence may have worked vis-à-vis the Soviet Union and China, but "it is a leap of faith to assume that the existence of nuclear weapons will produce similar restraint in much more volatile regional settings."[37] In the case of Iraq's WMD threat during the Gulf War it appears that nuclear weapons were the basis of U.S. deterrence success.

Second, as previously discussed, historically based analyses of deterrence suggest that establishing the credibility of deterrence threats for nonintrinsic interests is quite difficult. Unless there is a long history of manifest linkages to an area and an apparent willingness to go to war over an interest, a challenger is unlikely to find verbal declarations of commitment persuasive.

Unfortunately, regional challenges to the United States in the post–Cold War period are likely to involve areas where the United States must deter (particularly as U.S. conventional power projection capabilities are reduced) but where it has scant hope of convincing a challenger of the credibility of the U.S. commitment by virtue of the intrinsic interests involved, past practice, and/or present conventional capabilities in the region.

Fortunately, "fearsome" military threats can, to some extent, compensate for questions of intent in the creation of a credible deterrent threat.[38] Some suggest that nuclear weapons are largely incredible for regional deterrence missions. Their capacity to compensate for doubts about U.S. will, however, appears to help explain why Saddam Hussein, who was very dubious of U.S. will,[39] nevertheless was deterred from WMD use during Desert Storm.[40]

The problem, of course, is that in a fast-paced crisis the conventional orientation of deterrence that would result from a virtual nuclear arsenals regime would reduce or eliminate the U.S. capability to use implicit or explicit nuclear threats to provide the compensation of a fearsome military capability necessary when the U.S. deterrence commitment is questioned by the challenger.

How much of a limitation will this place on the U.S. capability to deter in future crises? How effective will policies of deterrence based on conventional threats prove to be, and how often might the potential difficulty in establishing a credible regional deterrence commitment necessitate the compensation of a nuclear threat? And to what extent would that potential for nuclear compensation be degraded by virtual nuclear arsenals?

A problem for U.S. participation in such a regime is that the answers to these questions probably cannot be generalized; they will be determined by the character of the particular challenger and the context. Confident generalizations that conventional forces will or will not be adequate for deterrence are unwarranted. U.S. leaders may not know as a crisis unfolds what level of credibility the challenger attributes to U.S. deterrence commitments and whether nuclear threats will be critical for deterrence effectiveness, as they appear to have been in preventing Iraqi use of WMD.

How is this discussion of deterrence in the post–Cold War environment and under a virtual nuclear arsenals regime related to strategic defenses? Clearly, under the regime U.S. leaders will want the readily available conventional deterrent threat to be as credible as possible. That conventional threat presumably would be built around the substantial advantage the United States has in advanced power-projection capabilities.[41] Secretary of Defense Perry has identified this potential for advanced conventional forces to serve as the basis for regional deterrence duties:

> This new [U.S.] conventional military capability adds a powerful dimension to the ability of the United States to deter war. While it is certainly not as powerful as nuclear weapons, it is a more credible deterrent, particularly in regional conflicts vital to U.S. national interests. . . . The new [conventional] military capability can also serve as a credible deterrent to a regional power's use of chemical weapons.[42]

In theory the credibility of a deterrence commitment is shaped by the challenger's perception of the intent and capability of the defender.[43] In the foreseeable future the credibility of a U.S. regional conventional-emphasis deterrence policy may require both strategic and theatre defenses: theatre defenses to protect the U.S. and allied *capability* for conventional power-projection forces from the possibility of regional WMD; and strategic defenses to strengthen U.S. and allied *will* (and the perception of that will) to employ conventional expeditionary forces against a challenger armed with WMD and long-range delivery systems, including cruise and ballistic missiles.[44]

A regional challenger able to hold U.S. urban areas hostage almost certainly will be able to affect U.S. decision making significantly with regard to the projection of conventional power against the challenger in theatre—in which the interests involved are likely to be intrinsic for the regional challenger. Indeed, the attractiveness of acquiring such a deterrence capability vis-à-vis the United States is a primary reason for some proliferant states to acquire WMD and long-range delivery systems.[45]

In short, to preserve U.S. freedom to project its superior conventional forces against a challenger in theater and the credibility of a deterrence regime based on such a threat will necessitate the U.S. capability to deny regional challengers their deterrent.[46] In crises involving challengers armed with WMD and long-range delivery systems, strategic defenses could be a key to that credibility. Again, the success of a virtual nuclear arsenals regime by itself would not provide an arms-control alternative to strategic defenses in this case because the regime does not address regional chemical or biological weapons or long-range delivery systems.

In addition, strategic defenses, including active and passive strategic defenses, could contribute in significant ways to the credibility of the delayed nuclear threats possible under a virtual nuclear arsenals regime following reconstitution. For example, strategic defenses could help to protect those assets necessary for U.S. nuclear reconstitution from a challenger's conventional, biological, or chemical strikes. In the absence of active and passive defenses even a challenger participating in the regime could consider offensive strikes to disrupt or delay U.S. reconstitution, thereby gaining the deterrence or coercive advantage, however temporary, of alone having operational nuclear forces.

This discussion has focused on the relationship among a virtual nuclear arsenals regime, likely U.S. deterrence policies of the post–Cold War period, and the related need for strategic defenses. It has suggested that in the post–Cold War period strategic defenses will be perceived as of greater value than was the case during the Cold War era and that a virtual nuclear arsenals regime would further increase the value of strategic defenses for reasons related to deterrence requirements.

ADDITIONAL POSSIBLE ADVANTAGES AND SOME POSSIBLE DISADVANTAGES OF STRATEGIC DEFENSES UNDER A VIRTUAL NUCLEAR ARSENALS REGIME

U.S. leaders are likely to place increased value on strategic defenses under any prospective virtual nuclear arsenals regime for reasons separate from their potential contribution to deterrence effectiveness under such a regime. For example, in the context of an arms-control regime that evolves a departure from the traditional nuclear-threat basis for deterrence policies, strategic defense is likely to be judged of increased value for its contribution to direct societal protection.

In the absence of any basis for confidence that such a regime will have a benign or beneficial effect on U.S. capabilities for deterrence (and some reason to suspect the contrary) or directly address the potential for long-range WMD threats itself, the value of strategic defenses for its basic function of societal protection will be of greater import. Such protection could be particularly important vis-à-vis challengers who remain outside of the regime, and vis-à-vis the remaining CW, and BW capabilities of challengers committed to the regime .

For those allies continuing their dependence on U.S. deterrence commitments, possibly including Japan, South Korea, and Germany, the societal protection afforded to those allies and to the United States by strategic defenses could help alleviate concerns about the effect that a virtual nuclear arsenals regime could have on the credibility of U.S. extended deterrence commitments.

Strategic defenses also could reduce the potential for coercion and deterrence that could be available to those countries willing to engage in noncompliance, surprise breakout, or a declared nuclear rearmament program and thereby acquire a unique, if temporary, nuclear advantage. In the absence of defenses, exploitable leverage could indeed be available for a period to challengers willing and able to engage in covert noncompliance or competitive nuclear reconstitution and thereby hold U.S. society uniquely hostage to nuclear threats for a period. During that period strategic defenses could limit the exploitable advantage of noncompliance or breakout by reducing that societal vulnerability.

Perhaps more important, strategic defenses also could reduce the incentives to engage in covert noncompliance or competitive nuclear reconstitution by raising the threshold of offensive nuclear capabilities necessary to establish any exploitable deterrence or coercive advantage via violating or breaking out of the regime. Defenses could reduce those incentives both by raising the threshold and by helping to protect those U.S. reconstitution assets necessary for reestablishing a U.S. nuclear capability. In the absence of strategic defenses a challenger might anticipate an exploitable advantage by virtue of its unique operational nuclear capabilities and the vulnerability of U.S. facilities and assets necessary to reconstitute U.S. forces—holding out the possibility of extending its unique nuclear capability via selective strikes against U.S. reconstitution targets. Again, this same potential benefit from strategic defenses in a virtual nuclear arsenals regime could be important to U.S. allies, especially those continuing their dependence on a U.S. extended deterrence commitment.

Another advantage of strategic defenses in a virtual nuclear arsenals regime involves one of the stated goals of such a regime, controlling nuclear proliferation. An unintended consequence of the regime could actually be to increase the incentives for proliferant states to acquire WMD and their means of delivery. It could have such an effect for three reasons.

First, the regime, for reasons already discussed, could offer an opening in U.S. deterrence policies to be exploited by those countries possessing WMD and appropriate delivery systems. It simply is unknown, and probably unknowable, whether U.S. conventional forces backed by a threat of nuclear reconstitution can provide the basis for effective U.S. regional deterrence policies, especially against challengers armed with WMD. The possibility of such an opportunity for regional challengers could encourage proliferation among rogues that already have declared their desire for WMD and long-range delivery systems to counter U.S. power projection capabilities. The apparent successful example of U.S. nuclear deterrence in the Gulf War and the lack of a similar U.S. threat under a virtual nuclear arsenals regime in the next regional crisis illustrate the likely attraction of WMD for regional rogues in the context of the regime.

Second, a virtual nuclear arsenals regime would present at least the possibility of dramatically lowering the ceiling for developing countries wanting to achieve a WMD capability comparable or superior to those of the UN Security Council members. Acquiring such a capability could be valued simply as a matter of prestige or for the political and military advantages available to the proliferant state under a virtual nuclear arsenals regime.

Finally, the regime clearly is intended to place nuclear weapons further into the background and help to move members toward conventional forces. This should be an attraction for the United States, given its unquestioned superiority in advanced conventional forces. The problem, of course, is that the U.S. advantage of moving toward a conventional playing field is properly seen as a potential disadvantage for some proliferant states. There will be little incentive for regional challengers to stay on a playing field that provides the United States with such an insuperable war-fighting advantage.

Again, one of the self-declared motives of proliferant states to acquire WMD and long-range delivery means is to trump the developed world's obvious advantage in advanced conventional weapons for purposes of deterrence and coercion. WMDs represent their "Revolution In Military Affairs" and are seen by some as particularly essential because of the U.S. conventional force advantage. A virtual nuclear arsenals regime could, consequently, exacerbate this incentive for proliferation by promising at least a period in which the U.S. could wield only conventional deterrence threats and power projection capabilities. If such a period were not part of a virtual nuclear arsenals regime, it would appear to have little meaning.

The potential value of strategic and theater defenses in helping to address the incentives for proliferation identified above could be significant: by reducing the vulnerability of societal targets, and consequently the value of WMD and long-range delivery means for deterrence and coercion purposes, strategic and theater defenses could contribute to reducing those potential incentives to proliferate stimulated or magnified by a virtual nuclear arsenals regime. They also, of course, could help ease U.S. concerns about the proliferation that could be expected to occur under the regime.

SUMMARY AND CONCLUSION

The very idea of moving simultaneously toward strategic defenses and deep offensive force reductions typically has been regarded as impractical—a violation of standard Cold War hypotheses about the offense-defense relationship. Nevertheless, the goal in this discussion was to place traditional thinking aside for a moment, with regard to both the possibility for very deep offensive reductions and the potential role for strategic defenses in such a regime. The resultant examination of the possible offense-defense relationship under virtual nuclear arsenals is by its nature speculative and hypothetical—holding aside important questions of cost and feasibility.

Nevertheless, it appears with this initial look that strategic defenses could play an important role in providing U.S. leaders with a margin of comfort and reassurance, a margin that could be essential to the prospects for U.S. and allied acceptance of such deep offensive reductions. In the absence of effective strategic defenses the potential risks of a virtual nuclear arsenals regime could appear unacceptably high to U.S. and allied leaders. As Paul Huth notes from his examination of leadership behavior drawn from case studies, "The costs of unreciprocated cooperation in security affairs are potentially so high (military defeat, loss of territory, political blackmail) that the potential gains are often discounted."[47] If effective strategic defenses are assumed, risks would remain but could possibly be reduced to tolerable levels for some political leaders.

The flip side of that coin, however, is that the comfort and reassurance so provided to U.S. and allied leaders by effective strategic defenses could cause a comparable level of discomfort and concern to others. Would countries unlikely to enjoy the benefits of strategic defense in a VNA regime nevertheless be willing to accept such a regime? They could, obviously, be at a disadvantage if others had even a modest level of strategic defense, because such defenses could, in principle, be quite significant in any "reconstitution race." It is difficult to conceive of effective strategic defenses being available to all members of a VNA regime, unless such capabilities essentially were made available to members by the United States. This, of course, could be a powerful drawing card for movement toward VNA if the United States decided to pursue such an objective.

Ironically perhaps, the advantages of possessing strategic defense in a VNA regime could be essential to the creation of any sympathy among the United States and its allies for such a regime. Yet the likely asymmetries in defensive capabilities among prospective members of a

VNA regime could also reduce the likelihood that those destined to be without strategic defenses could find such a regime tolerable.

NOTES

This essay with permission draws from Keith Payne, *Deterrence in the Second Nuclear Age* (Lexington: University Press of Kentucky, 1996).

1. The two early presentations setting the framework for this debate were Abram Chayes and Jerome Wiesner, eds., *ABM* (New York: Harper and Row, 1969); and Johan Holst and William Schneider Jr., *Why ABM?* (New York: Pergamon Press, 1969).

2. An influential summary of this hypothesis was presented in McGeorge Bundy, "To Cap the Volcano," *Foreign Affairs* 48, no. 1 (October 1969): 10.

3. A concise summary of this argument is presented in McGeorge Bundy, and George Kennan, Robert McNamara, and Gerard Smith, "The President's Choice: Star Wars or Arms Control," *Foreign Affairs* 63, no. 2 (Winter 1984-85): 264-78.

4. For the most recent reissuing of these SALT I–era hypotheses, see Jack Mendelsohn, "The ABM Treaty Is in Danger," *Bulletin of the Atomic Scientists* 52, no. 1 (January-February 1996): 28.

5. It should be noted that very recent discussions of this issue by Russians involved in Soviet arms control suggest that at least initial Soviet interest in an agreement limiting strategic BMD was not generated by the same set of hypotheses. Rather, the Soviet Union saw little technical prospect for its own missile defense and thus saw value in curtailing U.S. movement in the area. See Aleksandr' Savel'yev and Nikolay Detinov, *The Big Five: Arms Control Decision-Making in the Soviet Union* (Westport, Conn.: Praeger, 1995): 21-23.

6. See the discussion in Sidney Graybeal and Keith Payne, "New Era for Missile Defense," *Defense News,* August 21-27, 1995, 19.

7. See Harold Brown, "Strategic Weapons: Security through Limitations," *Foreign Affairs* 36, no. 4 (April 1969): 430.

8. *Congressional Record—Senate,* S 19264.

9. For the framework of Brennan's defense-emphasis approach to arms control, see D. G. Brennan, "The Case for Missile Defense," *Foreign Affairs* 47, no. 3 (April 1969): 433-48; and Donald G. Brennan, "The Case for Population Defense," in Holst and Schneider, 107-17.

10. Quoted in Gregory Fossedal, "A Star Wars Caucus in the Freeze Movement," *Wall Street Journal,* February 14, 1985, 30.

11. For a discussion of this dramatic but little recognized effort by Russian and U. S. leaders to move forward simultaneously with offensive reductions and cooperative strategic defenses, see Stephen Hadley, "Global Protection System: Concept and Progress," *Comparative Strategy* 12, no. 1 (January-

March 1992): 3-6. See also Robert Joseph and Keith Payne, *Ballistic Missile Defense: The Need for a National Debate,* (Strategic Forum, Institute For National Strategic Studies, National Defense University, no. 37, July 1995): 3.

12. As late as November 1993, the Russian government expressed an interest in pursuing a "Global Protection System" simultaneously with deep offensive reductions.

13. In a 1985 *Foreign Affairs* article by Thomas Schelling the point is made that the value of arms control is in codifying deterrence via mutual vulnerability, not the potential for directly reducing societal vulnerability. In fact, Schelling asks "who needs arms control" if secure retaliatory capabilities are readily available. See Thomas Schelling, "What Went Wrong with Arms Control," *Foreign Affairs* 64, no. 2 (Winter 1985-86): 229.

14. Colin Gray, on the basis of historical case studies, identifies this problem as the fundamental hole in any arms reduction scheme that promises a significant impact on useful and desired military capabilities: such agreements among friends are easy to achieve and not very significant, such agreements among hostile states could be significant but are not possible to achieve because the states are hostile. See *House of Cards: Why Arms Control Must Fail* (Ithaca, N.Y.: Cornell University Press, 1992).

15. As Fred Iklé has recently observed, "Deterrence came to be seen as guaranteeing nonuse, and continued nonuse became the proof of successful deterrence" ("Facing Nuclear Reality," *Wall Street Journal,* January 2, 1996,8).

16. Systems analysis in the McNamara DoD concluded that 400 one-megaton survivable weapons would be sufficient for an "assured destruction" threat and that increasing the force beyond that level would provide rapidly diminishing marginal returns. See, for example, Alain Enthoven and Wayne K. Smith, *How Much Is Enough? Shaping the Defense Program, 1961–1969* (New York: Harper and Row, 1971), esp. chaps. 5-6.

17. McGeorge Bundy's classic 1969 statement in *Foreign Affairs* best captures the ethos of minimum deterrence: "Think-tank analysts can set levels of 'acceptable' damage well up in the tens of millions of lives. They can assume that the loss of dozens of great cities is somehow a real choice for sane men. They are in an unreal world. In the real world of real political leaders—whether here or in the Soviet Union—a decision that would bring even one hydrogen bomb on one city of one's own country would be recognized in advance as a catastrophic blunder; ten bombs on ten cities would be a disaster beyond history; and a hundred bombs on a hundred cities are unthinkable" (Bundy, 10).

18. As Edward Luttwak observes in this regard, "Now that the Cold War no longer suppresses hot wars, the entire culture of disciplined restraint in the use of force is in dissolution." See "Toward Post-Heroic Warfare," *Foreign Affairs* 74, no. 3 (May-June 1995): 109-22.

19. This was the fundamental conclusion of the McNamara Pentagon. See Alain Enthoven and K. Wayne Smith, *How Much Is Enough?* (New York: Harper and Row, 1971), 187-90.

20. As discussed at length in David Denoon, *Ballistic Missile Defense in the Post–Cold War Era* (Boulder, Colo.: Westview Press, 1995): 1-51; and Keith B. Payne, *Nuclear Deterrence in U.S.-Soviet Relations* (Boulder, Colo.: Westview Press, 1982): 11-47.

21. In U.S. Senate, *Congressional Record—Senate* 141, no. 207 (December 22, 1995): S 19264.

22. Les Aspin, *Department of Defense Annual Report to the President and the Congress* (Washington, D.C.: USGPO, 1994): 35.

23. Secretary of Defense William J. Perry, *On Ballistic Missile Defense, Excerpt from a Speech to the Chicago Council on Foreign Relations* (photocopy, March 8, 1995): 1.

24. The vetoed Missile Defense Act of 1995 called for the deployment of NMD for the United States by 2003. Secretary of Defense Perry has criticized this time frame, but agreed on the eventual need for NMD: "[NMD] is the area where the Congress has made a several hundred million dollar addition to the program we requested. The only difference between us and the Congress is an issue of timing. I do not see that threat as on the horizon today, and so I think we'll move the program along systematically. . . . So there's not a philosophical or technical difference between us, it's a matter of judgement on the timing of how quickly we have to move to meet this threat." See William Perry, *Remarks by Secretary of Defense William Perry at the Regional Commerce and Growth Association of St. Louis* (photocopy, September 28, 1995): 12.

25. M. S. Vinogradov, *Report by the Coordinator of the 1st Section at the Plenary Session of the Conference on the Problems of the Global System of Protection* (photocopy, November 22, 1993, Moscow): 3.

26. For example, U.S. Assistant Secretary of Defense Ashton Carter has noted with regard to the North Korean leadership: "We don't know how they work all that well. Even if we had more interaction with them, they are an extremely secretive regime" (qtd. in Bill Gertz, "N. Korea Nears Big Jump in Effort for Nuclear Bomb," *Washington Times,* April 8, 1994, 3). Or, as Ambassador April Glaspie observed when addressing how it was that Saddam Hussein's behavior could have surprised U.S. leaders, "We didn't understand Saddam Hussein" (qtd. in Don Oberdorfer, "Glaspie Says Saddam Guilty of Deception," *Washington Post,* March 21, 1991, A23).

27. As Craig and George observe: "Inherent in the calculus of deterrence lies the assumption of a rational opponent, one who can be deterred from a given course of action if the costs of pursuing it clearly outweigh the benefits to be gained thereby. While it is not the purpose here to explore all the ramifications of this assumption, it can be said that in making it, a grave and often fatal error may be committed. Not all actors in international politics calculate utility in making decisions in the same way. Differences in values, culture, attitudes toward risk-taking, and so on vary greatly. There is no substitute for knowledge of the adversary's mind-set and behavioral style, and this is often difficult to obtain or to apply correctly in assessing intentions or *predicting responses* (Craig

and George, *Force and Statecraft: Diplomatic Problems of Our Time,* 3rd ed. [New York: Oxford University Press, 1995], 188; emph. added).

28. Thomas Schelling, for example, observed that threats intended to protect the homeland, an "intrinsic" interest, are "inherently credible, even if unspoken." See *Arms and Influence* (New Haven: Yale University Press, 1966): 36.

29. See, for example, the discussions in Kenneth Watman and Dean Wilkening, *U.S. Regional Deterrence Strategies* (Santa Monica, Calif.: RAND, 1995): 57-64; and Eli Lieberman, *Deterrence Theory: Success or Failure in Arab-Israeli Wars?* McNair Paper no. 45 (Washington, D.C.: National Defense University, Institute for National Strategic Studies, 1995): 2-3, 64-65.

30. Lieberman, *Deterrence Theory,* 64-65.

31. See Michael Mazarr, "Virtual Nuclear Arsenals," *Survival* 37, no. 3 (Autumn 1995): 14, 16.

32. See, for example, Paul Huth, *Extended Deterrence and the Prevention of War* (New Haven: Yale University Press, 1988): 86.

33. As suggested in Mazarr, "Virtual Nuclear Arsenals," 21.

34. This suggestion has become fairly common. See, for example, Seth Cropsey, "The Only Credible Deterrent," *Foreign Affairs* 73, no. 2 (March-April 1994): 14-20.

35. Presented in R. Jeffrey Smith, "U.N. Says Iraqis Prepared Germ Weapons in Gulf War," *Washington Post,* August 26, 1995, p. A19.

36. For a detailed discussion, see Payne, *Deterrence in the Second Nuclear Age,* 82-87.

37. See Ted Galen Carpenter, "Closing the Nuclear Umbrella," *Foreign Affairs* 73, no. 2 (March-April, 1994): 13.

38. As Watman and Wilkening conclude, based on their empirical investigation: "The communication of a strong will to act can compensate to some extent for a less certain military capability. Similarly, a fearsome military capability can compensate for some uncertainty the adversary may feel about the U.S. will to act" (U.S. Regional Deterrence Strategies, 57).

39. For an excellent discussion of this perception of the United States by Saddam Hussein and its importance as a dynamic behind the Iraqi invasion of Kuwait, see Jeffrey Record, "Defeating Desert Storm (and Why Saddam Didn't)," *Comparative Strategy* 12, no. 2 (April-June 1993): 126-28.

40. U.S. nuclear threats were near explicit with regard to the U.S. response to Iraqi WMD use during Desert Storm.

41. The power of conventional deterrence built around U.S. advanced conventional capabilities, especially reconnaissance strike forces, is at the heart of the proposal for a cooperative security regime by Ashton Carter, William Perry, and John Steinbruner (*A New Concept of Cooperative Security* [Washington, D.C.: Brookings Institution, 1992], 24-27).

42. William Perry, "Desert Storm and Deterrence," *Foreign Affairs* 70, no. 4 (Fall 1991): 66.

43. See, for example, the discussion in Richard Lebow and Janice Stein, *When*

Does Deterrence Succeed and How Do We Know? (Ottowa: Canadian Institute for International Peace and Security, 1990): 60-61; see also Huth, *Extended Deterrence,* 4-5.

44. For a detailed discussion of the relationship between U.S. conventional deterrence threats and the related requirement for theater and strategic defenses, see Keith B. Payne, *Missile Defense in the 21ˢᵗ Century* (Boulder, Colo.: Westview Press, 1991); and Denoon, *Ballistic Missile Defense.*

45. See the discussion in William Odom et al., *The Emerging Ballistic Missile Threat to the United States* (Washington, D.C.: National Institute for Public Policy, 1993).

46. Paul Nitze introduced this concept of "denying" a challenger its deterrent in terms of U.S.-Soviet relations ("Deterring Our Deterrent," *Foreign Policy* [Winter 1976-77]: 195-210).

47. Huth, *Extended Deterrence,* 7.

PART THREE

CASE STUDIES

EIGHT

THE ESTABLISHED NUCLEAR POWERS AND VIRTUAL ARSENALS

MICHAEL J. MAZARR

PERHAPS THE MOST IMPORTANT VARIABLE influencing the fate of virtual nuclear arsenals (VNAs) is their reception by the established nuclear powers. As the masters of virtually all nuclear weapons on earth, these five nations—the United States, Russia, China, France, and the United Kingdom—possess the dominant voice on matters nuclear. Strong opposition from a majority of these nations will in all likelihood prevent any nuclear initiative from seeing the light of day; significant interest or support from two or more members of the nuclear club could transform a vague idea into a detailed and important policy option.

This essay therefore examines the likely perspectives of the five declared nuclear powers on the idea of virtual nuclear arsenals. It is an exercise in forecasting as much as anything else, because no government or other body has formally proposed VNAs in a manner that has required these states to render a formal opinion. And, even if they had done so, opinions can change; especially because VNAs will not be implemented for well over a decade, any analysis of nuclear power reactions must focus not on the present but on the future. The task is further complicated by the fact that each of the declared nuclear powers views nuclear weapons in a different way, and their reactions to VNAs are likely to differ in similar fashion.

To tackle this demanding task, I examine the five declared nuclear powers in turn. In each case I discuss their missions for nuclear forces and the resulting reasons why each might favor or oppose VNAs. In every case the Cold War lent each of the five powerful reasons for desiring operational nuclear forces, and it is clear that the transition to VNAs would require a revolution in defense thinking and planning. I am assisted by the short essays that follow this one, each offering the thoughts of a regional or country expert on a specific member of the nuclear club, and by several of the essays in the volume's "Reactions" section, which also focus on particular countries. Despite the value and expertise of these case studies, a comprehensive look at the five powers and VNA seemed appropriate; it is only when the five are considered together that one sees how the very reasons for one to favor VNAs offer equally powerful reasons for another to oppose them. The case studies, moreover, focus on the reactions within these various countries to the idea of VNAs; here I aim at a more objective strategic assessment.

The essay does not discuss one contextual issue that relates to the future perspectives of all five declared powers: the future of international relations. As noted in the introductory essay, the broad level of relations enjoyed by the five declared powers (and other great and medium powers in world politics) will help determine the status of arms-control proposals such as VNAs. A world of hostile or highly suspicious powers will be far less amenable to dramatic cooperative proposals like VNAs than a world in which European integration continues apace and Russia and China are more fully integrated into the community of democratic, free-market states. As with the volume as a whole, however, this essay will make no predictions or assumptions about the state of international relations ten or twenty years hence. It simply recognizes that this result will make an enormous difference for the feasibility of VNAs.

THE UNITED STATES

The nuclear forces of the United States are unique among the five declared nuclear powers in their missions, requirements, and capabilities. Given the collapse of the Russian nuclear infrastructure, the U.S.

nuclear force is rapidly becoming unique in the category of numbers as well. During the Cold War U.S. governments assigned a host of different roles to their nuclear forces, ranging from deterrence of direct nuclear attack on the United States to forestalling conventional invasions of distant U.S. allies.[1] During the Cold War, therefore, the United States would have been the least likely of any of the five declared powers to endorse the concept of VNAs.

Then the Cold War ended, and everything changed—at least in objective circumstances, if not in actual U.S. nuclear doctrine. Of the five nuclear powers the United States is today the one with the most unambiguous interest in a denuclearized world. Apart from traditional concerns attaching to any arms-control scheme, issues like verification and stability, the United States arguably stands to gain more from the transition to a virtual nuclear world than any other major power.

During the Cold War U.S. presidents employed their nuclear forces to counterbalance Soviet conventional strength and to shore up allied solidarity. As a result, those nuclear forces acquired a range of missions unparalleled by any other nuclear power. The question now is how many of those missions remain valid and how many could be satisfied by VNAs.

The simplest and most straightforward mission is also the least demanding: deterring direct attack against the U.S. homeland. I do not discriminate here between nuclear, chemical or biological, or conventional attacks, because I presume that any direct threat to the territorial integrity of the United States or the well-being of its citizens will be met by whatever level of force is required. This mission would demand only the ability to inflict fatal damage on the military forces or homeland of the aggressor—a few hundred survivable nuclear weapons.[2]

U.S. nuclear forces also serve as a shield covering U.S. military forces in combat. An enemy thinking of employing nuclear weapons against U.S. troops abroad must respect the risk of retaliation in kind. A state toying with the idea of using biological or even chemical weapons against U.S. troops must weigh the chances of a nuclear retaliation as well, as Saddam Hussein and his generals discovered in the Persian Gulf War. An accomplished or aspiring proliferant whose weapons or facilities are impervious to conventional attack might even have to reckon on a U.S. preemptive nuclear blow—an option occasionally mentioned, for example, in connection with North Korea. In the situation that poses perhaps the most wrenching decision of all, a U.S. president who had ordered an advance party of U.S. troops into battle before its support could arrive—the 82d Airborne Division, perhaps, thrown in front of Saddam Hussein's armies in a more sinister version of the events of 1990—might be forced with a decision of using nuclear weapons to prevent U.S. conventional forces from being overrun.

Finally, U.S. nuclear weapons have served a similar shielding function over U.S. allies. To achieve two simultaneous purposes— deterring Soviet attacks against allied nations and forestalling those nations from developing their own nuclear forces—the United States during the Cold War extended its nuclear deterrent to cover a variety of nations, most notably Germany, Japan, and South Korea. In all three cases U.S. presidents at least indirectly threatened nuclear war if Moscow or its proxies launched conventional invasions of the allies; in all three cases U.S. tactical nuclear weapons were stationed on or around the allies to bolster the credibility of that somewhat irrational promise.

These last two sets of missions call for a much more flexible, and more numerous, nuclear force than simple homeland defense. Many of these missions demand focused, limited uses of nuclear weapons, as much for symbolic reasons as any other. They therefore require smaller and more tailored weapons to go along with the city-busters suitable for homeland defense. And most important of all, if U.S. leaders are to contemplate nuclear first use against nuclear-armed opponents, they may want—during the Cold War they did want—at least a theoretical capacity for a disarming first strike. If one is planning to fight a nuclear war, so the reasoning went, one might as well plan to win it, even if "victory" in the nuclear age looks like a rather hollow enterprise.

Here, in fact, amid the arcana of strategic analysis, we find perhaps the most powerful engine of the Cold War's terrible nuclear arms race. For in order to make these last two categories of missions credible—in order to convince allies and adversaries that it actually would use nuclear weapons first—the United States developed far-reaching targeting strategies that offered the theoretical (to critics, mythical) opportunity to fight and win a nuclear war.[3] These targeting strategies, known by various names including counterforce and countermilitary, called for enough weapons to wipe out an enemy's entire nuclear infrastructure, and much else, in the initial blow. This obviously demanded hundreds of warheads to begin with and, as the enemy proliferated its own arsenal (as Soviet war planners thought similar things), the hundreds became thousands.

One major question facing U.S. planners is why, with the Cold War now over for nearly a decade, they still see the need for counterforce targeting when the war-winning nuclear plans it supported are no longer necessary. Today U.S. conventional forces have the advantage over any conceivable foe; Russia's army is in decline and disrepair, and, with Eastern Europe freed from Soviet control, Europe could more than hold its own in a conventional war with Russia even without U.S. support. Counterbalancing a Russian conventional advantage need no longer be the core mission of U.S. nuclear forces, but the Defense Department, in rejecting proposals for deeper nuclear reductions, behaves as if it must.[4]

Here we find the first, least tangible, but arguably most powerful reason why the United States might oppose VNAs: the logic of the "nuclear security blanket." Nuclear weapons have provided a catch-all answer to a host of threats for the last half-century, and U.S. planners will be loathe to surrender them, even if they are only asked to give up their day-to-day operational status. They will argue (as a few U.S. officials have already argued at conferences at which the VNA idea has been broached) that, once nuclear weapons are disassembled, any president who tries to assemble them in a crisis will face implacable opposition from many quarters—the public, the press, perhaps even the Congress. Like the fable character Humpty Dumpty, many U.S. officials believe, once the weapons are taken apart, they will never be put together again, and this will deprive the United States of a powerful psychological deterrent to all forms of nefarious acts in world politics.

Two more concrete bases for the United States to retain a firm skepticism of VNAs relate to verification and extended deterrence. Concerns about the verifiability of arms-control proposals always occupy center stage in U.S. debates on the issue, with the worsening fate of the proposed Chemical Weapons Convention (CWC) only the latest example. It may be difficult to assemble a set of verification procedures that are both acceptable to all declared nuclear powers and intrusive enough to satisfy skeptics in Washington. Indeed, the United States is already on the verge of the somewhat embarrassing position of becoming a verification holdout, arguing that some proposed treaties can only be enforced by a level of verification that the United States itself will not allow.

American allies that rely on U.S. nuclear guarantees may also be profoundly skeptical of how well VNAs would safeguard their security, a skepticism that will then be conveyed to Washington. Although in theory the deterrent process could work as before—with the United States promising to go to war for Germany or Japan and the attendant expectation that the U.S. virtual arsenal could be assembled and used in such a war—U.S. allies might fear that an aggressor would calculate the risks differently than if the United States had operational bombs. One can question whether international politics will produce any aggressors who would make that calculation and whether the dismantling of U.S. nuclear weapons would make any difference to them. Nonetheless, countries that have relied on a tangible U.S. nuclear guarantee for forty years will take some time to accustom themselves to a very different kind of guarantee.

In stark contrast to these reasons for skepticism, however, are some very powerful grounds for the United States to favor the marginalization of nuclear weapons in world politics, reasons that may, with the passage of time, overtake the opposition and turn the United States into a major advocate of VNAs and other radical arms-control proposals. These reasons relate not to vague dreams of a nonnuclear world but to hard-headed calculations of U.S. national interests.

The introductory essay cited a number of analyses that have recently made this argument. Their case for a lower nuclear profile in world politics—which may (or, to the authors, may not) offer reasons for the United States to support VNAs—includes four main components: maximizing U.S. conventional advantages; controlling Russian nuclear weapons; avoiding a new Cold War with Russia; and forestalling nuclear proliferation.

Probably the most powerful basis for the United States to seek a less nuclear world is because of the growing, indeed dominant, strength of its conventional forces. The emerging Revolution in Military Affairs holds the potential to remake the modern battlefield, and the U.S. military is well out in the lead in employing and developing the revolutionary technologies of long-range precision and information warfare. In the 1960s nuclear weapons helped the United States offset Soviet conventional advantages; today they help U.S. adversaries offset U.S. superiority. A world in which nuclear weapons had been marginalized would therefore theoretically be one in which U.S. power would grow.

Further progress in strategic arms control might also provide for better international monitoring and enhanced control of Russia's disparate—and, some worry, haphazardly guarded—nuclear arsenal. Scenarios of the illicit use or sale of Russian nuclear weapons are among the most plausible means of imagining a nuclear strike against the United States and its allies, and any step that reduced this danger would benefit U.S. security.

At the same time, the maintenance of large, operational nuclear forces carries the risk of renewing hostility between the United States and Russia. For each country, large nuclear forces capable of counterforce strikes make sense only in the context of an adversarial relationship between them, for no other country's arsenal is large enough to pose the same targeting challenge. If large arsenals remain in place, at some point decisionmakers in Washington and Moscow will begin to question the intentions of the other side. Debates over START II, and Moscow's inability to maintain the force sizes allowed by that agreement, may put the first match to this tinderbox of potential mistrust and hostility.

Finally, a number of commentators have argued that a major U.S. campaign to diminish the profile of nuclear weapons in international relations would benefit U.S. nonproliferation goals. Especially in the wake of the 1995 extension conference of the Nuclear Nonproliferation Treaty (NPT), U.S. arms-control initiatives would help cement the transition to a less nuclear world and perhaps help convince a number of potential proliferants that nuclear weapons are a declining stock. New arms-control accords might also provide U.S. and international inspectors with more leverage, and legal basis, to demand tight verification of proliferants such as North Korea, Iran, and Iraq.[5]

A transition to a world of virtual nuclear arsenals might promote these various interests by working to marginalize nuclear weapons in world affairs, make their use against U.S. conventional forces less likely, and gain greater control of Russian nuclear weapons. In theory, then, the United States has some very important reasons to be interested, on the grounds of national interests, in a VNA scheme.

RUSSIA

If the end of the Cold War offers the United States reasons to favor arms control, it has had the opposite effect in Russia. Its economy in a tailspin;

its conventional military collapsing, unable even to suppress a rebellion in Chechnya; its national boundaries laid bare by the collapse of the former Soviet Union—all in all, Russia is not a country whose leaders can feel very confident about defense planning. Much like the United States during the Cold War, Russia today faces a range of possible threats for which its only persuasive answer may be a nuclear fist into the aggressor's teeth. As a result, "the role of nuclear weapons in Russian doctrine has not declined; they continue to play a key role and their missions have in some respects even been extended."[6] This point is discussed at length in Konstantin Sorokin's case study, and Alexei Arbatov points out in his essay that it is particularly true vis-à-vis China, whose massive armies give Moscow pause—and a clear role for nuclear deterrence.

Today, too, Russia must see some political value in its large nuclear arsenal, confirming its role as a superpower at a time when its economy and society are faltering. With the end of the Cold War, notes Sergei Rogov, "the Soviet Union was said to be an Upper Volta with missiles; and there is now no desire on the part of Russia to become an Upper Volta without missiles."[7] Arbatov makes this same point in his chapter when he discusses the importance of nuclear weapons as a legacy of the former Soviet Union's status and influence.

As documented by both Arbatov and Sorokin, then, given Russia's newfound security fears and the notable nationalistic drift in its politics, the tenor of thinking in Moscow is running very much against an idea like virtual nuclear arsenals.[8] But not all Russians are opposed to arms control; even some nationalists might prefer a balance at half START II's ceilings to one in which the United States had a large numerical advantage because Russia cannot afford to field a force larger than perhaps 2,000 warheads;[9] and in the longrun, the political and security winds might change, especially if Russia and an increasingly unified Europe develop a good working relationship of long standing. In a more theoretical sense, then, a decade or more from now, what might a democratic, largely secure Russia think of VNAs?

It would likely think a variety of things, not all of them good. For, even putting aside the current sour mood on security questions in Moscow, Russia may see serious dangers in VNAs. Many of them have to do with Russia's relative position vis-à-vis other nuclear powers.

For one thing, Russia, as much as any of the five declared nuclear powers, might be unwilling to accept the kind of verification demanded by a VNA agreement. Its national security establishment may see such measures as an attempt by the West to gain military secrets. The strength of this possible objection will depend heavily on the level of cooperation between Russia and the West; even if that cooperation is good, however, given the likely Russian dependence on nuclear weapons as an ultimate deterrent, officials in Moscow may be hesitant to share critical information even with countries considered friendly.

In a strategic sense, too, Russian leaders may believe that VNAs place them at a relative disadvantage to the West compared to the current situation. From the starting point of virtual arsenals, it is possible that Britain and France, because of their superior technology and defense industrial base, would win a rearmament race, reconstituting (or building) nuclear weapons too quickly for Russia to keep pace. Some Russian officials might therefore fear that, in moving to a virtual nuclear world, they would trade their current nuclear superiority in Europe for inferiority. The Russian nuclear arsenal is today in bad shape—poor morale, falling budgets, lack of trained personnel—and its situation would not inspire confidence in Moscow that a dismantled nuclear force could be rapidly regenerated. These concerns relate to the notion of "virtual proliferation": the risk that currently nonnuclear powers (such as, from the Russian perspective, Germany or Ukraine) would choose, in a VNA world, to enhance their nuclear weapons capabilities almost to the level of the established nuclear powers—in other words, to bring themselves to the starting line of a reconstitution race.

There are a number of responses to this problem. At issue is the specific nature of the VNA agreement. If it permitted the United States and Russia to maintain as many as 1,000 weapons in relatively easily reconstitutable form, while France and Britain each had only 100 or so in that status, then Moscow might have little to fear from Europe—it would retain superiority at last in the early phases of reconstitution, which might be enough to satisfy its concerns. Moreover, Britain and France (and certainly potential virtual proliferants such as Germany and Ukraine) have relatively small nuclear weapons infrastructures, probably incapable of quickly churning out large numbers of weapons. In his case study of Britain in this volume, Stuart Croft argues that London might not be able to retain its nuclear infrastructure at all under a VNA regime—and indeed argues that British officials would see a Russian rearmament advantage in the scheme. Whether these arguments would be persuasive to Russian leaders, however, is open to question.

Russian officials might also worry in a more general sense about losing a long-term rearmament competition. If the U.S. nuclear infrastructure were added to the equation, Russia might be left far behind after the initial reconstitution. The same people who sat in the Kremlin counting targets during the Cold War will inevitably turn out thick studies contending that, within eight or nine or fifteen months after a reconstitution competition began, the West would have achieved a "first-strike capable advantage" or something of the sort.

Here, too, one can find obvious answers to the concern, but here, too, good analysis may not be enough to persuade Russian officials to abandon operational nuclear forces. In this case the same danger of unequal reconstitution would exist even in a world of small but operational nuclear forces, because (unlikely as the prospect now seems) a new Cold War could cause the West to rebuild or expand its arsenals quickly.[10] And operational weapons offer no unique means of cushioning this risk, because even under VNAs Russia would be able quickly to reassemble 200 or 500 or 1,000 weapons. The question is what happens in the reconstitution race after that time, but that same question would apply even if those readily reconstitutable forces were held in an operational status to begin with.

All of this raises critical questions to be answered by any VNA agreement: What stance would it take on nuclear infrastructures? Would countries be constrained from preserving in an operational mode the facilities for handling fissile material, for warhead assembly, for missile construction? The Russian example further demonstrates that these questions are not as simple as they appear. It would seem logical to take as many steps as possible to prevent a rearmament race from happening: put excess fissile material under international control (perhaps even shipping it completely out of the nuclear powers' territory); mandate the closing and destruction of nuclear weapons production facilities; closely monitor the construction of delivery vehicles like intercontinental missiles; and so on. But for some countries, perhaps including Russia, keeping those things might be a basic precondition for agreeing to VNAs, because they would provide some assurance of an ability to reconstitute a large force if the strategic environment dictated such a step. Much may depend on the nature and intrusiveness of verification: Russia might prefer a total ban on reconstitution, which would avoid some of the rearmament disadvantages previously outlined, but only if it had confidence in the monitoring scheme developed to enforce such an accord.

Even more complicated is the relationship between nuclear and conventional forces. Alexei Arbatov, in his reaction essay in this volume, contends that Russia might fear that advanced Western conventional weapons could be used to launch counterforce strikes against the dismantled Russian virtual nuclear arsenal. This is a very real issue—not only for Russia, but for all the nuclear powers. For the overall system to be stable, the components of a VNA must presumably be survivable against long-range conventional attack—a daunting requirement in the age of the Revolution in Military Affairs.

A final reason for Russian leaders to be skeptical of VNAs involves a very different sort of military competition—one in strategic defenses. U.S. technology in missile defenses appears to be much more advanced than Russia's, and officials in Moscow might fear that the United States could assemble the elements of a strategic defense quickly enough to provide a reliable shield against Russia's reconstitutable arsenal. Paradoxically, this perception might be heightened by precisely the restrictions on rearmament that would help assuage Russian fears about a weapons reconstitution race: a Russian arsenal with only a few hundred reconstitutable weapons and no capability to build more would pose a far more manageable challenge to a U.S. strategic defense than Russia's current nuclear force. These risks would appear to call for a VNA agreement that either strictly banned strategic defenses or allowed them for all parties, a point examined in Keith Payne's essay earlier in the volume.

Russia's leaders ten or twenty years hence may therefore have some powerful reasons for opposing VNAs. Yet, like all the nuclear powers, they might also find reasons to like the idea—reasons just as persuasive as the ones dictating skepticism.

It is worth recalling, to begin with, that Russia essentially had virtual arsenals for the first two decades of the nuclear era. As Bruce Blair has documented, Russian missiles required various launching and fueling procedures that would have taken many hours, if not days, before they could be employed.[11] The presumption in Moscow apparently was that they would have adequate strategic warning to have their weapons operational in a crisis. A country willing to trust its security to virtual arsenals during the depths of the Cold War might do so again, if strategic considerations favored such a step, and there are several reasons why Russia might favor VNAs.

First, notwithstanding the concerns discussed earlier about relative strengths during and after rearmament races, Russian leaders must also be concerned with a more prosaic nuclear balance: the existing one. Here, with the decline of its nuclear infrastructure and its plummeting defense budget, Moscow has very real reasons to worry. Many experts now believe that Russia will be unable to maintain its allowed START II force level of 3,000 to 3,500 warheads; in fact it might be able to field and maintain only about 2,000, and that at high cost. Meanwhile, U.S., European, and Asian technological advances in relevant areas such as precision weapons and missile defenses continue apace. It may not be too long, then, before at least a few senior Russian officials begin to worry about "losing" a very quiet post–Cold War "arms race" of sorts and see VNAs as a way to level the playing field among the five declared nuclear powers.

Similarly, some in Russia might see in VNAs an opportunity to head off possible future threats. It is not too difficult to imagine a series of events that would lead Germany, Japan, some Eastern European countries, and perhaps other states to seek independent nuclear deterrents. For obvious reasons proliferation on the part of many of these countries would pose a direct threat to Russian interests, and officials in Moscow might see VNAs as a way to lock these countries out of the nuclear business forever.

At the same time, Moscow can be no more sanguine about the risk of out-of-control nuclear weapons from its own inventory than other countries. Indeed, an accidental or unauthorized use of a Russian nuclear weapon is as likely to land on Russian soil as anywhere else— probably more so. If VNAs and their attendant verification arrangements offered an opportunity for Moscow to gain greater control over its crumbling nuclear arsenal, this would constitute a reason, just as it does for other states, for Russia itself to favor VNAs.

Finally, as the case studies by François Heisbourg and Stuart Croft both suggest, there is a chance that the transition to VNAs would weaken U.S.–European Union (EU) cooperation by diminishing, or even breaking, the transatlantic nuclear bond of U.S. extended deterrence. As disturbing a possibility as this is for the United States and its allies, Russia might welcome this development and, hence, favor the nuclear arrangement that some in Moscow might hope would bring it about.

In sum, then, the Russian case is as complex as any of the five declared nuclear powers. Russia is a great power passing through a temporary period of rather extreme weakness. Whether its recovery makes it more or less amenable to dramatic nuclear arms control, whether echoes of its weakness last only a few years or persist for decades, and how its officials perceive the likely results of VNAs will all exercise a profound effect on Russia's opinion of the idea.

CHINA

China is perhaps the one declared nuclear power most likely to support VNAs, both rhetorically and in reality. With an enormous territory, a huge conventional army, a growing economy, and a millennial perspective of the ebb and flow of history, China is the least reliant on nuclear weapons of any of the five. As Taeho Kim explains in his case study, it is also the loudest champion of nuclear arms control and disarmament. While Beijing would undoubtedly have some problems with the strategic implications of VNAs, on the whole its reasons to favor this scheme (or something like it) seem preponderant.

Partly this is because China has assigned only very limited missions to its nuclear forces—essentially a last-ditch form of homeland defense, a way to ward off nuclear attacks from the United States or other potential adversaries, and a limited adjunct to conventional war-fighting strategies. In many ways these same purposes could be served by a Chinese VNA, and, if in the process China could achieve the complete dismantling of the very large U.S. and Russian standing nuclear forces, the bargain might well be one Beijing would take.

This might be true, first of all, because a transition to VNAs would equalize the nuclear playing field from Beijing's point of view. At least in an operational sense the United States and Russia would lose their vast nuclear superiority over China, whose perceived power and influence might therefore grow.

Like the United States, too, though for very different reasons, China might benefit in a military sense from a denuclearized world. The vast size of its territory and military provide it with an edge in conventional war similar to that provided by advanced U.S. technology. Chinese officials might believe, for example, that the Russo-

Chinese military balance is more equal (or even favors China) in the conventional sphere. This perception might be heightened by China's rapidly growing economy, which will slowly but surely produce advanced military technology to go along with Beijing's huge numerical edge. In short, particularly on a regional basis, China's leaders may well believe that within two or three decades their conventional military strength will be unmatched and that a transition to VNAs would dilute to counterbalancing effects of nuclear weapons.

And, also like the United States, China might see in VNAs a way for the international community to insure greater control of Russian nuclear forces. With its long common border with Russia, China may be concerned that stolen Russian weapons could find their way into its territory or that accidental denotations could occur that would affect the Chinese people.

Like Russia, China may welcome what its leaders may see as the disruptive effects of VNAs on U.S. alliance structures. In Asia, as in Europe, U.S. extended nuclear deterrence has played a critical role in preserving American alliances. Without operational U.S. nuclear weapons to undergird such deterrence, it, and the alliances it serves, may weaken over time. China might well applaud such a development.

Also like Russia, as Taeho Kim suggests, China might hope to use VNAs to keep possible future rivals out of the nuclear business. If nuclear arms control made no further progress, and if China eventually felt the need to bolster its own deterrent to match more closely those of the United States and Russia, then countries like Japan, Taiwan, South Korea (or a unified Korea), Indonesia, and perhaps even Vietnam might be forced to rethink their nonnuclear status. India might believe it had to deploy an operational, survivable nuclear force, a step Pakistan would surely feel the need to match. In other words, officials in Beijing might see as the alternative to something like VNAs a regional nuclear arms race that would result in a security context far less favorable to Chinese interests.

Like all the declared powers, China would also have reasons to be skeptical of VNAs. Like Russia, it might fear that it would lose a rearmament race, either in offensive nuclear weapons or in strategic defenses (or both). Moreover, as Harvard's Iain Johnston has suggested,[12] the tough and aggressive realpolitik that characterizes Chinese strategic thought may have produced a substantial program to modernize and expand Beijing's nuclear arsenal. Notwithstanding his crafty public statements in the 1950s about the irrelevance of nuclear weapons, Mao Zedong well understood their significance, and early Chinese thinking on the question betrays much the same recognition as the other great powers of the time: that nuclear weapons constitute a necessary, if not sufficient, precondition for great power status.

Johnston draws on recent Chinese strategic writings to argue that Beijing is moving in the direction of "limited deterrence," a doctrine much more ambitious than the traditionally assumed Chinese approach of minimum deterrence. Limited deterrence essentially involves restricted nuclear war fighting and calls for a large number of advanced nuclear weapons, missile defenses, space-based warning and command and control systems, and so on. China is therefore moving slowly along the same dangerous road that the United States and Russia have already traveled, and is unlikely to be interested in multilateral arms-control regimes that divert it from this path, unless those regimes promise comparable benefits.

Like Russia, China might also have concerns about the risk of virtual proliferation (which Taeho Kim calls "veiled proliferation"). Japan is already well along the road toward some definition of a virtual nuclear arsenal, and, if China scaled its own force down to virtual status, other countries in the region—notably Taiwan—might see an easy opportunity to rise to a similar level. The result, China might fear, would be more states in the starting blocks of an Asian rearmament race.

But perhaps the biggest barrier to full Chinese acceptance of a VNA agreement would be its verification provisions. As a closed, totalitarian system, Beijing is unlikely to accept the sort of intrusive-challenge inspection regime that would undoubtedly be required to verify a shift in the nuclear balance as dramatic and fundamental as VNAs. Chinese leaders might believe that the strategic value of VNAs outweighs the risk of surrendering secrets through inspections, especially if China's system continues to evolve slowly in the direction of reform and openness. But the decision will likely not be an easy one for any Chinese government in the foreseeable future. For the question is not simply one of democracy but also one of security concerns relevant to any nation; as previously argued, even some officials in the United States are objecting to the verification provisions of existing arms-control accords. Magnified by China's traditional insularity, mistrust of outsiders, and possible continuing autocratic

rule, these broad reasons for opposing a VNA verification regime might
become crippling.

China would therefore appear to enjoy important strategic benefits
from VNAs, benefits that would improve its security relative to all of its
possible regional and global adversaries. But it is open to question
whether a Chinese government would be willing to pay the price of such
a transition—a rigorous and intrusive process of verification. And the
elements in the Chinese military now arguing for a massive and
sustained nuclear modernization might not be tempted by the theoretical advantages of a virtual nuclear world.

FRANCE

As Philip Gordon and François Heisbourg convey in their case studies,
France is perhaps among the least likely of the declared nuclear powers
to support VNAs. The reason is simple: France has used nuclear
weapons to gain and preserve its access to the ranks of the great powers.
This important symbolic value transcends narrow security concerns and
imbues the nuclear debate in France with enormous power and complexity. Edward Kolodzeij describes very well the symbolic role of
nuclear weapons in French security policy: "French possession of nuclear
weapons does not depend finally on the existence of a clear and present
foreign threat. The acquisition of nuclear weapons was portrayed from
the start of the Fifth Republic as endowing France with a unique
international standing—grandeur—and as confirming its status as a
victorious power in World War I, its privileged position as a permanent
member of the UN Security Council, and its glorious history and
accomplishments as a modern, scientific state."[13] David Yost agrees that,
apart from their actual deterrent power, French nuclear weapons have
become associated "with de Gaulle's successful efforts to restore France's
honor and international status."[14]

This broad perception of nuclear weapons as the admission card to
the "Club of Five" permanent members of the United Nations Security
Council is perhaps the most powerful reason for French leaders to resist
the transition to VNAs, but there are others. One is that France, like
many current nuclear powers, may fear a process of virtual proliferation.
Having reduced the readiness level of their own nuclear force, French

officials might believe, other states in Europe or the Middle East might enhance the status of their nuclear weapons capabilities—stopping well short of deployed weapons but more closely matching French nuclear potential. The result might be a diminution of relative French power and influence.

Like the United States, France also conceives fairly broad roles for its nuclear weapons, roles that might be disrupted by a transition to VNAs. Deterring chemical or biological attack on French forces or developing a capability to destroy incipient nuclear forces in hostile developing nations are two such missions.[15] French officials have also been more and more receptive, in the context of European integration, to the idea of a French extended deterrent covering at least Germany and perhaps eventually, in combination with Britain's, the whole of the European Union.[16] Such an extended deterrent, which might establish a unique and important role for France in the EU, might not be as necessary, important, or credible in a world of VNAs. More broadly, the experience of two world wars has imbued many French strategists with a deep mistrust of traditional conventional deterrence, which magnifies Paris's reliance on a nuclear option of last resort—an option that, while arguably still in place with VNAs, would appear to some in France as less effective.

Like all the other nuclear powers, too—as Philip Gordon notes in his essay—France will bridle at the verification requirements of a VNA regime. Quite apart from the objective risks of the loss of military secrets, French officials who will struggle for decades with the public opinion costs of European integration may have little political capital left for a nuclear arms-control enterprise that demands further perceived slights to France's already well-trammeled sovereignty.

Heisbourg also notes that the French deterrent is evolving in the direction of a submarine-only force, or at least a force dominated by submarine-based nuclear weapons. As several of the technical chapters in this volume have suggested, submarines are by far the most challenging form of weapon to integrate into a VNA regime: they depend for their survival on their undetectability, but that very quality makes their status difficult to verify. There may be ways of resolving this problem, but its very complexity—and the fact that any verification regime will inevitably reduce the survivability of nuclear missile submarines to some degree—means that nations depending largely on this form of deterrence may be discouraged from participating in the VNA regime.

Finally, France may be concerned that a transition to VNAs would weaken the transatlantic security link—the same development Russia might welcome in Europe, and China in Asia. And, while Paris's attitude toward the U.S. role in Europe is complex, French leaders would almost certainly not welcome a severe loss of credibility of the U.S. extended deterrent (though this attitude is not immutable). Even emergent French thinking about a Paris-based extended deterrence regime within Europe have not dampened this concern: On September 7, 1995, for example, French Prime Minister Alain Juppé gave a foreign-policy speech that, in part, "was at pains to make clear that the French nuclear security initiative vis-à-vis Europe was not an effort to supplant the United States role as guarantor of European security."[17]

Thus, the atmospherics and traditions of French security policy suggest a hostile reception for the concept of virtual nuclear arsenals. When looked at more objectively, however, France has a good deal to gain from the option.

For one thing, in an objective sense, the purposes of French nuclear forces are becoming less obvious. Nuclear weapons, writes Edward Kolodziej, "are losing their centrality in French strategic thinking, military doctrine, and operational strategy. For the first time since the creation of the *force de dissuasion,* France has nuclear weapons searching for a role."[18] Although the perception is far from universal in Paris, France and its EU allies (even setting the United States aside) do not need nuclear weapons to deter even a resurgent Russia. They may want nuclear weapons for that purpose, believing that nuclear deterrence is more airtight than its conventional counterpart, but VNAs arguably preserve this last-ditch nuclear option. Beyond this general appreciation of France's changed strategic context, however, Paris stands to gain a number of specific benefits from a transition to virtual arsenals.

The first category of benefits relates to the Russian nuclear arsenal. Like the United States, France would certainly benefit from any system promising greater control over Russian nuclear weapons. And, also like the United States, France's strategic situation vis-à-vis Russia might be substantially enhanced in a world of VNAs: at one stroke, Russia's massive nuclear superiority in Europe would be wiped away, and it is possible that, as Russian leaders must fear, France's technological superiority would make it a winner in a long-term rearmament race against a newly aggressive Russia. Even if that cannot be guaranteed, the symbolic benefits of abolishing the operational Russian nuclear force are hardly minor.

As Heisbourg implies, too, VNAs might energize a new and advantageous degree of EU cooperation on nuclear matters, with France leading the process. French discussions of a Europeanized deterrent began in recent years in July 1990 with the proposal of then Defense Minister Jean-Pierre Chevenement for a West European nuclear umbrella covering Germany. In 1992 former President Mitterand made similar comments, and in 1995 Prime Minister Juppé again suggested a French extended deterrent over Germany.[19] Collaboration on the elements of virtual nuclear preparedness might be less politically risky than cooperation on deployed nuclear forces. As a result—and contrary to the idea noted earlier that arms-control schemes would reduce the feasibility of a French extended deterrent—VNAs might allow the EU to broaden and deepen its nuclear integration in a less controversial way than it could with operational nuclear forces, thus strengthening intra-European defense cooperation.

The end of the Cold War has complicated implications for French nuclear policy, some favoring French support for VNAs and some not. French nuclear policy is evolving: "deterrence of the weak by the strong," the classic formulation of the French minimum deterrent policy aimed at Russia, has given way to a policy of "diversified nuclear options," which recognizes the potential for threats from other quarters. But, as Philip Gordon makes clear, this trend is not necessarily a good one for VNAs: as French thinking drifts more and more to unpredictable proliferants in the developing world, its Cold War thinking on nuclear issues, now largely discredited, may be replaced by a new series of justifications for operational nuclear forces.[20]

Thus, the reality today is that France, given its history and strategic context, is unlikely to favor VNAs. In the long run, however, if some of its rationale for desiring an operational arsenal were to decline—if it found, for example, other means to reaffirm the justice of its position on the Security Council—and an appreciation of the strategic benefits of VNAs for France were to grow, the attitude of French leaders could change. Ultimately, the real questions for Paris are the same ones confronted by all the declared nuclear powers: What missions will it assign to nuclear weapons? And are those missions compatible with less numerous and less operationally ready nuclear forces, including VNAs?

For David Yost, the consensus underlying French nuclear weapons may actually be "superficial and fragile" and may decline if French conventional forces prove their mettle in coming conflicts and if a test ban regime undermines the reliability of French nuclear weapons.[21] At such a moment advocates of arms control—including schemes such as VNAs—might have an opportunity to strike.

THE UNITED KINGDOM

As Stuart Croft implies in his case study, British perceptions of VNAs are likely to mirror those of the French in many ways, with two additional complications: Britain's greater interest in nuclear cooperation with the United States and the extreme secrecy that has surrounded British nuclear planning.[22]

Many of the disadvantages to VNAs seen by France and other nuclear powers would also be noticed by Britain. British officials would undoubtedly fear virtual proliferation on the part of second-tier powers that would match the British nuclear capability. They might worry about a loss of credibility for the last-resort nuclear option that has been a major element of British defense planning for decades; one recent British official statement concluded, for example, "Our independent nuclear forces continue to provide the ultimate safeguard of our security and make an important contribution to NATO's strategy of war prevention."[23] Even more than the French arsenal the British deterrent now relies entirely on submarines, and the problems inherent in integrating them into a VNA regime may further discourage British support for such an enterprise. British leaders might be concerned that, contrary to the argument made earlier, Russia, with its vastly larger nuclear weapons infrastructure, would win a rearmament race in a big way, and they may want operational nuclear weapons to deter rogue states in the developing world that threaten Britain.

As a result of these and other factors, "Britain is moving toward a minimum deterrent with a minimum rationale," writes Lawrence Freedman, "and thus a minimal interest in arms control." Looking to the future, Freedman concludes: "For three decades Britain has kept its national nuclear force apart from arms control. There is no reason to expect this policy to change now."[24] In this context two concerns are likely to be of special importance to British perceptions of a proposal for VNAs: their likely effect on British-American security ties and the level of verification required to implement them.

Stuart Croft's case study admirably points up the enormous significance assigned in London to the British-American security alliance, especially on the nuclear side. Above and beyond U.S.-UK links through NATO, the "special relationship" between the two has been a major assumption—and goal—of British national security policy since World War II. Britain views itself as something of a middleman between Europe and America; it is the closest to the United States of any EU power, and the most resistant to European integration. For Britain, then, anything that would threaten the future of its military and political ties to the United States must appear as a substantial threat. And many British officials will undoubtedly see VNAs—which would dismantle the U.S. nuclear weapons that have symbolized the transatlantic extended deterrence link—as precisely such a threat.

Britain may also end up having a severe allergy to the sort of intrusive monitoring that a VNA accord will bring. Britain has long maintained a tight shroud of secrecy around its nuclear program, arguably as much as or more than any other nuclear power, and it may not welcome the openness required to implement a VNA agreement. Britain, then, along with France, emerges as one of the most likely holdouts against dramatic arms control among the five declared nuclear powers. It has reasons to oppose VNAs that go beyond many of the other nuclear powers.

And yet, as with all the other declared powers, one can also find reasons for an objective British interest in virtual arsenals. Eliminating the operational Russian nuclear forces, gaining additional safeguards against loose Russian nuclear weapons, and opening the possibility that the European Union would win a rearmament race against Russia—all these possible benefits of VNAs should appeal to Britain as much as they do France. Over time, too, the credibility of a potential independent European deterrent should increase along with the process of integration, so that an EU deterrent based around French and British forces, perhaps virtual forces, may be seen as sufficient for security. Moreover, as Lawrence Freedman points out:

Britain has always been more sympathetic to proposals for confidence-building measures that do not impinge directly on force structure. Thus London has its own "hot-line" with Moscow, and there has been considerable sympathy for the American effort to add to the locks and safety catches safeguarding nuclear arsenals by strengthening command-and-control procedures, the end of quick-reaction alerts, dismantling of warheads, and the separation of nuclear weapons from general purpose forces.[25]

If the trend toward VNAs began with more elaborate reductions in alert levels, as it inevitably must, Britain might therefore find itself on board the train for the first few stops. And as the process continued, gaining political momentum and the credibility of inspection regimes and formal accords, British leaders, like those of all the declared nuclear weapons states, might find themselves hard-pressed to get off.

"For Britain," Lawrence Freedman concludes, "nuclear weapons remain little more than a hedge against an uncertain future."[26] If that future became a little less uncertain, with Russian reform cemented in place a decade or so from now; if nuclear alert rates in all the declared powers continued to fall, accustoming their officials to such a world; and if the central advantage of VNAs became widely accepted, then it is possible to see London becoming an advocate of virtual nuclear arsenals. Indeed, one can see the first tentative steps in this direction in the first statements on nuclear policy by Tony Blair's Labor government.

CONCLUSION:
A COMPLEX WEB OF MOTIVATIONS

It should be apparent by now that the reactions of the declared nuclear powers to VNAs are complex and interrelated. Because their security interests are not identical, and indeed in some cases conflicting, any given reason for one state to favor the proposal might serve as an equally powerful reason for another state to oppose it. And, because a guiding assumption of this volume is that such conflicting national interests are a staple of international relations and will not disappear any time soon, this situation is unlikely to change.

But it can be argued that, on the whole, many of the reasons why the nuclear powers might oppose VNAs fall into one of two categories: they are either a residue of the Cold War, or they are based on misperceptions of the nature of VNAs and nuclear deterrence. The continuing French and British fixation on an immediate and credible U.S. extended deterrent guarantee, for example, may fade somewhat if Russian reform (or collapse) produces a state that poses little or no threat to Europe. Similarly, the general perception that VNAs would undercut the role of nuclear weapons in homeland defense seems to ignore the central advantage of the arrangement: precisely because weapons could be reassembled relatively quickly, such a last-ditch nuclear deterrent would remain in place.

The reasons why these five states might see value in VNAs, on the other hand, appear to be based on a more objective analysis of the proposal and the strategic situation in which the five states may find themselves a decade or two from now. The United States, as a number of far sighted analysts have recognized, would benefit from a process of nuclear marginalization. Russia could avoid nuclear inferiority while preserving the potential for last-ditch homeland defense. China could equalize a nuclear balance long highly unfavorable to it, while Britain and France could keep the potential for ultimate deterrence while gaining additional controls on and reductions in the Russian force.

To be sure, the exact details of a VNA proposal will exercise a major effect on the perceptions of states confronted with it. To cite just one example, because at least two nuclear powers (France and Britain) will soon rely solely or largely on submarines for their deterrent, and another (the United States) will depend on them for its survivable deterrent, how a VNA regime deals with the thorny issue of reducing alert rates on submarines will also make an enormous difference in determining the reactions of the declared nuclear powers.

Clearly, the issue of VNAs is enormously complex. Nuclear weapons are firmly woven into the tapestry of international relations, and changes in nuclear balances or the role of nuclear weapons will affect world politics in fundamental ways. But I believe a strong argument can be made that virtual nuclear arsenals would, on balance, enhance the security of all five declared nuclear powers. All of those countries will be extremely skeptical of the idea at first, but the potential of VNAs to revolutionize the strategic environment in a way that benefits all the major powers suggests that the concept deserves further thought and study.

NOTES

1. See, for example, Lawrence Freedman, *The Evolution of Nuclear Strategy* (New York: St. Martin's Press, 1983): 1-224; and chapters by David Allan Rosenberg and Desmond Ball in *Strategic Nuclear Targeting,* eds. Ball and Jeffrey Richelson (Ithaca: Cornell University Press, 1986): 35-86.

2. For calculations supporting the figure of 200 warheads in the context of a conflict with Russia, see my essay "Military Targets for a Minimum Deterrent: After the Cold War, How Much is Enough?" in *Toward a Nuclear Peace,* eds. Mazarr and Alex Lennon (New York: St. Martin's Press, 1994): 113-41.

3. Advocacy of this doctrine can be found in Colin Gray, "Nuclear Strategy and the Case for a Theory of Victory," *International Security* 4, no. 1 (Summer 1979); and Michael May, "Some Advantages of a Counterforce Deterrent," *Orbis* 14 (Summer 1970).

4. See William Arkin and Michael J. Mazarr, "The Clinton Administration and Nuclear Weapons," in *Clinton and Post-Cold War Defense,* ed. Stephen J. Cimbala (Westport, Conn.: Praeger, 1996): 49-69.

5. This advantage may actually prove most important in relation to a country few number among the world's proliferation risks—China. Recent indications (as I will suggest, and as Taeho Kim makes clear in his case study in this volume) are that Beijing is intent on expanding its nuclear arsenal. It may now have a full-fledged doctrine of nuclear war fighting, and within a decade may be poised to achieve the sort of destabilizing, first-strike capable nuclear posture previously reserved to the United States and Russia. Such a development would obviously have profoundly negative consequences for U.S. security, and implementing a VNA agreement may provide one means of forestalling it in a stabilizing fashion.

6. John W. R. Lepingwell, "START II and the Politics of Arms Control in Russia," *International Security* 20, no. 2 (Fall 1995): 73.

7. Sergei Rogov, "Russian Views of Nuclear Weapons," in *Toward a Nuclear Peace,* eds. Michael J. Mazarr and Alex Lennon (New York: St. Martin's Press, 1994): 206.

8. See, for example, the comments in Lepingwell, "START II and the Politics of Arms Control in Russia," 63-64.

9. See Konstantin E. Sorokin, "Russia after the Crisis: The Nuclear Strategy Debate," *Orbis* 38, no. 1 (Winter 1994): 35-40.

10. START counting rules magnify this risk by allowing both sides a vast reserve of reconstitutable weapons in case of new hostilities. As Bruce Blair points out in his essay in this volume, for example, the United States is planning to keep, in addition to 3,500 strategic and 1,500 tactical nuclear weapons in an operational mode, 5,000 dismantled but rapidly reassemble-able weapons and 9,000 nuclear "pits" of fissile material.

11. Bruce G. Blair, *Global Zero Alert for Nuclear Forces* (Washington, D.C.: Brookings Institution, 1995): 96-97.

12. See, for example, Alastair Iain Johnston, "China's New 'Old Thinking': The Concept of Limited Deterrence," *International Security* 20, no. 3 (Winter 1995-1996).

13. Edward A. Kolodziej, "French Nuclear Policy: Adapting the Gaullist Legacy to the Post-Cold War World," in *Toward a Nuclear Peace,* eds. Mazarr and Lennon, 176.

14. David S. Yost, "France's Nuclear Dilemmas," *Foreign Affairs* 75, no. 1 (January-February 1996): 118.

15. France, as Heisbourg points out, is the only country besides the United States to have hosted a debate on the potential merits of low-yield nuclear weapons (so-called mininukes). And although a recent speech on defense issues by Prime Minister Juppé rejected their use in fighting proliferation in the developing world—"France has ruled out the development of miniaturized [nuclear] weapons for employment," Juppé said, weapons "which would furnish a pretext for clandestine nuclear programs"—nonetheless there is a school of thought in Paris pressing for more varied and flexible nuclear options (cited in Yost, "France's Nuclear Dilemmas," 115); on the school calling for flexible options, see 115-16.

16. For the complications attendant to such an idea, see Yost, "France's Nuclear Dilemmas," 111-14.

17. Leon Sloss, "Recent Observation[s] on the French and British Nuclear Weapons Programs" (summary of a presentation) in *Implications of the Nuclear Policies, Forces and Doctrines of France and Great Britain: Final Report* (McLean, Virg.: Science Applications International Corporation [SAIC], October 1995), 4. France's ambiguous attitude toward the U.S. role in Europe, and its implications for French nuclear policy, is examined by Kolodziej, "French Nuclear Policy," 170.

18. Kolodziej, "French Nuclear Policy," 168.

19. Jessica Kaplan, "Implications of the Nuclear Policies, Forces and Doctrines in France and Great Britain for Future Reductions," in *Implications of the Nuclear Policies* (SAIC), 14-16.

20. See Kolodziej, "French Nuclear Policy," 176-77.

21. Yost, "France's Nuclear Dilemmas," 118.

22. For general information on the British deterrent, see Nicholas Whitney, *The British Nuclear Deterrent after the Cold War* (Santa Monica, Calif.: RAND Corporation, 1995).

23. "British Nuclear Forces, Doctrine and Policy," in *Implications of the Nuclear Policies,* Table E, 1.

24. Lawrence Freedman, "Britain, Nuclear Weapons, and the Future of Arms Control," in Mazarr and Lennon, *Toward a Nuclear Peace,* 146, 160.

25. Ibid., 159.

26. Ibid., 160.

NINE

VIRTUAL NUCLEAR ARSENALS: A VIEW FROM MOSCOW

KONSTANTIN SOROKIN

THE CONCEPT OF VIRTUAL NUCLEAR ARSENALS (VNA) provides badly needed guidelines about how nuclear arms control should proceed at its crucial and sensitive closing stages. But, like any novel approach, this one is to be closely examined to determine its merits and possible drawbacks and to assess prospects for its implementation.

Undoubtedly, the VNA idea injects fresh blood into traditional nuclear arms-control thinking at a time when regular approaches seem to have outlived their utility. The VNA concept's unquestionable virtue is that it offers a clear vision of how to bridge a gap between reduced levels of nuclear weapons and zero (assembled) nuclear arsenals and successfully challenges the gloom of the "nuclear weapons cannot be disinvented" dictum. In this respect the VNA proposal goes far beyond the disarmament initiatives of the 1950s and even the latest Gorbachev "non-nuclear and non-violent world" plan of December 1988. Still, on the positive side, the VNA debate addresses a much wider range of issues associated with the process of nuclear disarmament than any discussion of this kind so far. Finally, proponents of the VNA idea are determined to go on refining their proposal, which makes it highly probable that eventually they will come up with a theoretically impeccable and technically viable arrangement.

In my appraisal of the concept I will avoid going into technical details, however important they may be, for two reasons. First, in arms control, as in many other fields of international activity, technical aspects are second to the expressed political will of the sides involved, and pass from declarations of intention to practical actions. Second, personal participation in elaborating a unique verification scheme for the INF agreement (in which arms control on-site inspections were envisioned for the first time ever) persuaded me that if there is a (political) will, there is a (technical) way.

Instead, I will concentrate on the primary issue of political feasibility of the VNA concept. To give the authors of the VNA idea their due, they anticipate that "views of the major powers" may cut across their proposals.[1] But it looks as though they underrate the scale of problems facing them. Indeed, by definition the VNA scheme is a global cooperative arrangement and, as such, requires uninterrupted collaboration of all those concerned based on their undiminished political goodwill. Should one or more nuclear/threshold nations opt out, transition to the VNA regime would be stalled or derailed. But it is doubtful that the right amount of cooperation is readily available in what is vaguely and cautiously defined as the "post–Cold War era." While it is probably too much to claim the collapse of liberal values,[2] or revert to unbridled realism to describe the current situation,[3] it is becoming increasingly clear that close international cooperation will go hand in hand with bitter rivalry between major powers and/or established and emerging geopolitical alliances.[4] Such a dual nature of international relations still demands sustained (or, better, increased) levels of power and influence from all major international players and is not very conducive to radical nuclear arms cuts and denuclearization.

For example, maturity of the VNA scheme will almost certainly coincide with the "post-Deng" period in Chinese history widely expected to be stormy and leading to China's weaker stance in international affairs. And Beijing may place a higher emphasis on nuclear weapons to compensate for real or imagined losses in security, influence, and prestige and thus sabotage the VNA arrangement.

But, probably, Russia's attitudes will be the greatest stumbling block. Even under the nominally liberal Boris Yeltsin, Moscow has registered two conflicting lines of behavior in nuclear matters. One may be defined as an "arms control spill-over" from the Soviet Gorbachev time. Its momentum, initially higher (exemplified by the exchange of unilateral disarmament initiatives between Yeltsin and President Bush in early 1992, conclusion of the START II agreement, de-targeting nuclear missiles), has been slowing down over the past few years with the START II agreement (irreversibly?) stranded in the state Duma and increasingly under attack from many quarters (this, of course, leaves little ground for START III or any other arms-control scheme).

On the contrary, pro-nuclear bias has been growing in intensity over the last three years, meaning that nuclear arms control runs into mounting opposition even in the current leadership recognized as democratic by the West. Resumption of the nuclear first-use stance announced by a new version of the Russian military doctrine (in late 1993) almost coincided with a remark by the commander of the Russian Land Force, General Semenov, who said in a newspaper interview that a new Army lever tactical ballistic missile was on the drawing board. Slated to offset the loss of the "Oka" missile destroyed under the INF agreement, the new weapon was tested in October 1995.[5] While it is credited with accuracy high enough (CEP = 10-15 m) to be fitted with conventional warhead, some unconfirmed reports indicate that this missile is also nuclear capable, as is practically any modern missile system (a lighter nuclear warhead, among other things, will enable the newcomer to fly beyond the officially declared range of 400 km). On the strategic nuclear level, in 1995 Russia tested "Topol-M" (SS-25M) ICBMs for silo deployment. Additionally, it extended service life for SS-19 ICBMs from 15 to 21 years, with plans for further extension up to 25 years. Russia also bought 16 freshly produced SS-19s from Ukraine (in late November 1995 Russia and Ukraine agreed that Moscow would purchase 32 additional SS-19s as well as 10 Tu-160 and 15 Tu-95 heavy bombers). In a more serious development, Russian "ICBM generals" are reported to have threatened massive deployment of small-sized cheap "Kourier" ICBMs to complement SS-25s if Washington quits the ABM agreement and/or refuses to reconsider some of the START II provisions.[6] At the same time, on September 15, 1995 the Russian Defense Ministry was relieved of civilian control over its nuclear operations (in June 1992 Gosatomnadzor, a federal commission, was authorized to monitor safety and security situations at military nuclear-related installations, but in principle it could also detect and report any unauthorized activity by the military). There are also more calls for resumption of nuclear testing.[7] Chinese and especially French nuclear explosions in 1995 came as a welcome boost to this position.[8] The official Russian Armed Forces periodical even went to the extreme of reprinting an interview by the French defense minister in which he produced a list of arguments in support of the French testing program.[9] Finally, it is probably no coincidence that, after a period of passivity, Russian nuclear scientists chose 1995 to resume their lobbying activities to expand the research into smaller but safer and more accurate strategic weapons and to reintroduce tactical "nukes" for regional deterrent purposes.[10]

These tentative moves toward re-nuclearization are accompanied and, apparently, encouraged by a new pro-nuclear mood among the rising number of Russian civilian experts in security matters. Even many recent advocates of deep nuclear cuts now seem to be preoccupied with upholding and modernizing Russia's nuclear potential.[11] As for less-committed analysts, even they have broken the taboo of the last several years in calling for Russia's full-scale nuclear rearmament.[12] They caution that, in the present volatile political and security situation around Russia, nuclear arms-control reductions may increase rather than decrease the threat of nuclear war, and they argue that nuclear weapons are not that bad.[13] This is not to say that supporters of START II and further drastic moves on strategic arms control have disappeared altogether, but their ranks have thinned considerably.

The renewed infatuation with nuclear weapons can best be explained by the widely perceived gap between: (1) geopolitical and security challenges and dangers facing modern Russia (the situation around Russia is usually described as considerably worse compared to that around the former USSR); and (2) Russia's capability to protect its vital interests beyond and even within its national borders (Moscow's real resources are rated far below that of the Soviet Union).

In more concrete terms, unwelcome geopolitical and security developments include: the abysmal loss of allies and buffer zones along the national proper (some calculations indicate that in the Soviet era Russia had at least 24 allies worldwide, while the opposing coalition numbered around 70 states; at present Moscow does not have reliable allies even within the CIS); rising indifference and even hostility by Western nations, the enlargement of NATO being the most telling symptom of the new Western mood; continued nuclear modernization by official nuclear nations; the massive introduction of high-tech conventional weapons (which can accomplish strategic missions) into arsenals of (semi) industrialized nations; impending "adjustment" of the ABM treaty (and, possibly, U. S. unilateral withdrawal from this treaty); the long-term unpredictability of the Chinese colossus; an upsurge of Muslim fundamentalism in the south; the unstoppable spread of weapons of mass destruction in close proximity to the country's southern borders; and the projected creation of nuclear weapons infrastructure in East European nations if and when they join NATO.[14]

At the same time, Russia's resources are depleted by: steep reductions in the overall economic potential due to the "detachment" of fourteen constituent Soviet republics; a deep and persistent economic crisis; atrophy of the military-industrial complex, which in some areas is irreversible; disintegration of the armed forces as a state institution; degeneration of the strategic early warning system; and a demographic crisis resulting in a growing deficit of potential conscripts.

The existing gap, the argument goes, can be bridged with greater reliance on nuclear weapons, which is the only affordable, cost-effective, dependable, and long-lasting solution. No less important is that the nuclear capable part of the Russian army has been least hit by undiscipline and disarray and that the nuclear section of the military-industrial complex has been least damaged by poorly conducted conversion. Both need relatively little refurbishment to be back in good shape.

This reasoning was initially advanced by the military and civilian experts on security matters. Later it was borrowed by opposition political forces ranging from neocommunists to nationalists. Also, as previously indicated, pro-nuclear logic has recruited supporters even in the current administration. It appears that re-nuclearization has not yet started in earnest due to resistance offered by a few Western-style democrats still in the government and by the president himself. To put it differently, in order to keep the nuclear arms–control process going on the Russian side (meaning ratification of START II, conclusion and ratification of START III, and/or wholehearted adoption of the VNA approach), its genuine supporters (which are mostly Western-style democrats) first have to convincingly win the Duma elections on December 17, 1995 (which is hardly probable but also not crucially important, as the Duma is not the seat of real power in Russia) and, second, to get a president sympathetic to their aspirations in the summer elections next year. Even if reelected (which is by no means certain), Yeltsin can hardly be expected to serve the whole new term, due to his poor health. And there are no unshakably committed arms controllers among alternative candidates to the presidential post.[15]

To wind up, it appears that the VNA concept arrives at a time when the first "Russian train" has already left. This concept would have been warmly welcomed in Moscow several years ago at the height of the Soviet/Russian–American/Western "love story." At present and in the foreseeable future, when political relations are getting more sober to the extent of becoming cool, it will not fall on fertile ground. Even if the next leadership pays some lip service to VNA basic ideas, most likely it will not address them seriously.

This is not to say that the VNA concept has no future in Russia. But it will take some time for a new Russian train to arrive. Today Russia is being overwhelmed by an understandable psychological rejection of the reformers' clumsy attempt to accomplish too much too soon (and too recklessly) and of their inability to establish new Russia's identity, find it a right place in the world, and elaborate viable foreign and security policies. This has forced the pendulum to the counter-reformist extreme in domestic and foreign (including nuclear arms control) domains. But slowing down or stopping the reforms will do nothing to solve Russia's entrenched problems. New attempts to "update" Russia will have to be made, this time in a more balanced and cautious way. It is hoped that the next round of modernization will occur in a more benign international climate, when trust between Russian and Western nations returns to the level that existed in the late 1980s and early 1990s, or exceed it, and when real security partnership is forged between Russia and the West. That would be the right time and circumstances for the VNA concept to be realized by joint efforts of all sides concerned, including Russia.

NOTES

1. M. Mazarr, "Virtual Nuclear Arsenals," *Survival* 37, no. 3 (Autumn 1995): 17.
2. See S. Hoffmann "The Crisis of Liberal Internationalism," *Foreign Policy,* no.

98 (Spring 1995): 159-77.

3. As one distinguished professor put it recently: "so long as security depends ultimately on rival goods, goods that have to be competed for, such as territory, alliances, access to scarce resources, then more security for one state will mean ultimately less for the other" (M. May "Fearsome Security: The Role of Nuclear Weapons," *The Brookings Review* 3, no. 3 (Summer 1995): 26.

4. See the author's views on the merging global geopolitical situation in K. Sorokin, *Geopolitika sovremennogo mira i Rossia* (Geopolitics of the Modern World and Russia).

5. *Izvestia,* November 17, 1995.

6. *Segodnia,* November 18, 1995.

7. See interview with General E. Maslin, head of the 12th Department of the Defense Ministry responsible for handling nuclear warheads, in *Moskovskie novosti,* June 25–July 2, 1995, 14. In an earlier interview V. Mikhailov, head of the Russian Atomic Energy Industry, also supported the resumption of nuclear testing as well as explosions for peaceful purposes. He added that attacks on the nuclear industry were organized by Russian exporters of oil and gas, which was a clear hint at Prime Minister V. Chernomirdin and his team (*Moskovskie novosti,* February 5-12, 1995, 14).

8. It is interesting to note how the issue of French nuclear testing was inflated to add up to the urgency of Russia's nuclear rearmament. One report said that Paris was widely sharing information resulting from nuclear explosions with Washington and London (*Krasnaia zvezda,* September 26, 1995). Another report claimed that Paris offered to cover Germany with a French nuclear umbrella to protect it from dangerous Russia (*Izvestia,* September 13, 1995). This liberal newspaper also alleged that the United States was just looking for an excuse to resume small-sized nuclear testing of its own (*Izvestia,* June 21, 1995).

9. *Krasnaia zvezda,* September 19, 1995.

10. See a report on the pro-nuclear crusade launched by Arzamas, a group of sixteen scientists, in *Segodnia,* June 15, 1995.

11. For instance, Andrei Kokoshi, former deputy director of the American and Canadian Studies Institute in Moscow and one of the authors of the Soviet "radical nuclear arms cuts" concept (he was in charge of devising ways to insure strategic stability during and after such cuts), in his current capacity as deputy defense minister is fighting hard to sustain production of SLBMs and resume R & D in this field (note the deep gratitude expressed to him by the director of the Krasnoyarsk SLBM plant, in *Krasnaia zvezda,* April 15, 1995). Another prominent arms controller, Alexei Arbatov, takes care of the ICBM leg of the triad. As deputy of the state Duma, he unites his efforts with other politicians to lobby for financial needs of this service. See, for instance, a report on the meeting of RVSN Commander General I. Sergeev with A. Arbatov, V. Zhirinovskii, V. Lukin, and others, in *Nezavisimaia gazeta* (Military Survey no. 3), November 11, 1995.

12. For instance, one expert agitated by the NATO enlargement issue claimed that "only the resumption of the [Russian] nuclear threat can force the self-conceited West to notice Russia's concern over European security, and extract some concessions [from Western nations]" (*Nezavisimaia gazeta,* November 18, 1995).

13. Dispelling "myths" about nuclear weapons, one expert asserts that these weapons cannot be called immoral (because so far many more people have been killed with Kalashnikov submachine guns than with nuclear explosions) and that it is wrong to believe that nuclear weapons are unusable on ecological grounds (because hundreds of nuclear tests and two actual bombings failed to cause a global catastrophe) (V. Zakharov "Ostavatsia li Rossii iadernoi?" [Should Russia Stay Nuclear?] *Nezavisimaia gazeta,* October 12, 1995).

14. *Segodnia,* September 22, 1995; *Izvestia,* October 5, 1995.

This chapter was written in November, 1995, before the outcome of the Russian elections was known.

CHINA AND VIRTUAL NUCLEAR ARSENALS

BALANCING THEIR POTENTIAL RISKS AND BENEFITS

TAEHO KIM

WHILE THE "CHINA FACTOR" has long been salient in global and superpower arms-control negotiations, its importance has taken on a new relevance in the post–Cold War era in light of the renewed clarion call for dramatic nuclear disarmament and China's growing regional and international profile. For one thing, China's cooperation in such global arms-control and disarmament (ACD) talks as the Nuclear Nonproliferation Treaty, the Comprehensive Test Ban Treaty, and the Fissile Material Production Cut-off Convention will remain critical to their effective and full implementation. For another, further progress in U.S. and Russian ACD negotiations in strategic weapons increasingly hinges on the level of participation by the medium-sized nuclear weapon states; China's stance will particularly affect the position of the United Kingdom and France. For still another, now that nonproliferation concerns supersede the Cold War containment policy, at least in the U.S. view, China's propensity to export nuclear and missile components and technologies guarantees that it is a major factor in both regional and global security.

To current and future Chinese leaders, on the other hand, few arms-control proposals would seem as comprehensive and bold as the concept of virtual nuclear arsenals (VNAs). During the Cold War not only did China fervently advocate the drastic reduction of superpower nuclear arsenals, but it also called for the total destruction of nuclear weapons, due primarily to its own strategic weakness vis-à-vis the superpowers and also to the low probability that its proposals would be realized. Since the late 1980s and continuing in the 1990s, however, the kaleidoscopic changes in the relative national power of the United States, the Soviet Union/Russia, and China and the ensuing changes in the nature of their old triangular relationship have not only made China's ACD position untenable but have led Chinese leaders to rethink the actual and potential benefits of the ACD talks for China's interests. It is in this changing national and global context that China's prospective stand on VNAs should be examined.

To assess what positions China might take in the VNAs proposal and what conditions would make the proposal palatable to current and future Chinese leaders, this essay has the opportunity to take stock briefly of the Chinese views on its post–Cold War security, the role of nuclear force, and ACD talks. It then specifically addresses what incentives and disincentives VNAs might offer to China and how China would react to the question of stability in the transitional period leading to the end-state of VNAs. Provided China's capability to close the nuclear technological gap between itself and advanced Western countries, finally, it concludes that China has strong potential incentives to support and even actively participate in the VNA process in the twenty-first century. The overall conclusion is partly supported by interviews with Chinese strategists associated with the People's Liberation Army (PLA).

NUCLEAR WEAPONS AND CHINA'S POST–COLD WAR SECURITY

In Beijing's view the end of the Cold War has been a mixed blessing for China's security. It resulted in a significant reduction of conventional land threats to China, especially those emanating from Russia, India, and Vietnam. A peaceful external environment, as Chinese leaders often remind the foreign audience, is critical to the success of the Four Modernizations drive. Thus, it is not uncommon to hear Chinese leaders and strategists say that its present security environment is the "best since 1949," the year the People's Republic was founded.[1]

It is perhaps ironic to note that under such an unprecedented peaceful environment came a sharp and sustained increase in China's defense budget and weapons acquisitions from abroad, especially from Russia.[2] While there are no simple explanations to this seemingly contradictory trend, Chinese strategists maintain that the passing of the Cold War opened up old rivalries and that, given its extensive involvement in Asia's major sources of tension, from territorial disputes to arms buildup and from the Korean peninsula to the South China Sea, China will be hard-pressed to safeguard its extensive borders.

Given its vast landmass, with expanding maritime interests, China doubtless has a legitimate security need to maintain a large military, currently at three million, with diversified defense assets. Given also its huge but outdated weapons inventory, which can be likened to the world's largest open-air museum of old weaponry and equipment, it is quite understandable that China needs to improve its defense capability, especially its naval and air assets.

China's recent growth in economic and military capability has not been followed, however, by its efforts to assuage the fear of its neighbors. On the contrary, the Chinese authorities have not only closely guarded major defense aspects such as budget, strategy, and modernization programs but have often accused foreign governments and scholars of spreading "totally groundless" allegations against China, such as the "China threat thesis."[3] One combined effect of Beijing's lack of military transparency and studied ambiguity has been a considerable level of apprehension over China's future and particularly its military behavior.

Amid the pervasive discussions over China's military modernization, the nuclear weapons issue is conspicuous for its absence. In a litchi nutshell the value of nuclear weapons for China has been remarkably consistent: deterrence and prestige. They helped deter superpower nuclear blackmail and use against China during the Cold War and will continue to serve this purpose, even if the chance of nuclear threat to China is now very low. In the unlikely event of a nuclear war, China's nuclear forces could function as a firebreak against escalation. They also provide China with international status and prestige to which China, as a major power, should be entitled.

Most Western PLA specialists concur that China's nuclear force of approximately 300 deployed nuclear warheads is primarily dedicated to the strategy of minimum deterrence, which can be inferred from its relatively modest size, the technology-driven countervalue strategy, and China's no-first-use pledge. This observation is also partly reinforced by China's apparent decision not to increase the size of its nuclear arsenal for the last ten years, despite its clear capability to do so.

Yet there is little indication that the role of nuclear weapons in overall Chinese security has declined in the post–Cold War era. The Chinese have, instead, vigorously pursued the nuclear modernization program to improve the survivability, reliability, and safety of its nuclear arsenal in conjunction with its conventional military modernization. China's ongoing major nuclear modernization program, which predates the post–Cold War, includes:

- Land-based systems: continued improvement and new development of its Dongfeng (DF) series such as DF-31 (flight-tested in May 1995) and DF-41; mastering such diverse technologies as accuracy, solid propellant, MIRVing, and basing modes;
- Seaborne systems: continuing development of the second-generation SLBM, Julang (JL)-2, which is the seaborne version of the DF-31; and
- Bomber forces: near-completion of the Jianhong (JH, H, or B)-7 bomber;[4] acquisition and possible license production of nuclear-capable aircraft such as the Su-27.

China's future improvement in its nuclear capability would reinforce nuclear weapons' minimum deterrent value and may even facilitate the burgeoning nuclear doctrinal shift to "limited deterrence."[5] As long as China aims at achieving the technological sophistication of its nuclear arsenal to the level of advanced Western nations, it may well be reluctant to join the ACD processes, which would impose external constraints on its nuclear modernization program.

CHINA'S EVOLVING ATTITUDE TOWARD NUCLEAR ARMS CONTROL

China's calculus toward nuclear ACD consists of a complex web of internal and external factors. China is not different from other nuclear powers that seek to enhance their relative security through ACD processes. It is, however, considerably different from others when it comes to the question of external constraints on its nuclear arsenal, which largely stems from its leaders' hard-core realpolitik worldview, nuclear inferiority compared to the United States and Russia, and the lack of military transparency.

While the security factor has been most prominent in formulating China's arms-control policy, it is often moderated by other factors as well. In particular, domestic political and external considerations have been most significant. China's unusually active participation (if not cooperation) in the global ACD talks since the early 1980s, for example, has been informed by its domestic economic imperative and the gradual but discernible reduction of the Soviet threat to China. Additionally, China's reform agenda has not only required a peaceful environment conducive to its economic development, but it has meant that China has to pay more attention to world opinion about China than in the past.

Among a host of internal and external factors affecting China's nuclear modernization, as Alastair Johnston has convincingly argued, multilateral ACD processes will put the maximum constraint on its future development.[6] The underlying rationale is the invocation of the so-called image cost of a China copping out of the ACD processes, which would put real constraints on capability of the declared and undeclared nuclear powers, thus deemed important by the international community. Lisbeth Gronlund and others have made a similar point regarding China's stance on the CTBT. Signing the CTBT will not serve the PLA's interests, they argue, but Chinese leaders have to factor in larger political benefits, so that "it wants to sign [the CTBT] for image reasons, but wants to delay [the CTBT] for military reasons."[7] A logical extension of these arguments can be made in regard to China's position on the indefinite extension of the NPT, a cut off convention, and VNAs.

No matter how plausible the dichotomy of Chinese military and political interests may be, the apparent contradiction between China's defiance of the U.S. test moratorium in September 1992 and its repeated assurance that it will sign the CTBT when the latter *comes into effect* needs further explanation. Would the signing of those ACD agreements be detrimental to the Chinese military interests but beneficial to political interests? In any case this line of logic will collapse if political and military interests in China are not as divergent as they have argued, an assumption many Western PLA specialists share.

Then, if the same cause (competing political and military interests) can produce different effects (different ACD policies) over time and the same effect can be attributable to different causes (image, cost), then no singular relationship can be established, and the analyst must specify which variables are more important at different times and under what conditions.

A more plausible explanation of China's contradictory behavior in its defiance of the U.S. moratorium and the anticipated signing of the CTBT might be the treaty's technological and testing schedule requirements. Not only has China been in the middle of modernizing its nuclear arsenal, but the testing schedule would not have allowed it to be more flexible concerning the U.S. moratorium. Therefore, China might have simply wanted to buy enough time to complete its testing schedule and, by the time it signs the CTBT, expects to find other ways to insure the reliability of its nuclear arsenal. While incorporating the findings of other analysts on China's ACD attitude, this time-specific, holistic approach would make for a better understanding of China's perspective stance on VNAs.

INCENTIVES AND DISINCENTIVES OF VNAs

China's stance on VNAs will, first and foremost, depend upon their impact on China's overall national interests, of which security concerns are an integral part. Perhaps the strongest incentive China might have in joining the VNA process is the removal of a direct nuclear threat to China. Though the VNAs may still pose subtle and indirect threats, they are not equal to the world of massive nuclear stockpiles that has existed since 1945. As the only nation that was subject to both superpowers' nuclear blackmail, China is highly likely to see VNAs in this light, especially if the process begins after its completion of the nuclear modernization program.

Second, VNAs are congruent with China's rhetorical but principled nuclear stance, which it has held since 1964: the complete prohibition and thorough destruction of nuclear weapons. While the debate on

China's gap in declaratory and operational policy is an inconclusive one, VNAs nonetheless offer a venue for the nuclear superpowers to "take the lead" in making deeper cuts and for all nuclear and nonnuclear states to discuss disarmament "on an equal footing," both of which China has long demanded. A PLA colonel, when "exposed" to the notion of VNAs, has also emphasized that VNAs come closest to the Chinese long-standing proposal of total nuclear disarmament.[8]

Third, while not as compelling as the first two, VNAs might well retard the qualitative competition among the nuclear states, thus complementing China's relative security. Not only has China long found the technological competition with the United States and Russia difficult to match, but the competition itself is destabilizing. Notwith-standing its incipient limited nuclear deterrence, China has been and is likely to be content with minimum deterrence for the foreseeable future.

Fourth, China's economic benefits accruing from a VNAs end-state should not be underestimated. China's nuclear establishment consists of the 90,000-strong Second Artillery Force, the missile bureaucracy, and numerous facilities and research institutes around the country. Not only does China spend large sums each year to operate its nuclear force, but it invests substantial human and material resources on various new projects, only parts of which are known to the outside world.

On the other hand, VNAs in their present form would create quite a few questions whose answers may be found a decade or more down the road. Some of the more discernible are as follows: the most immediate and current fear of the VNAs proposal seems to be that it may freeze China's nuclear modernization program at a level that is well below that of advanced Western countries. Several PLA strategists and officers interviewed have all asked, directly or indirectly, about the time frame under which VNAs will be pursued. When assured of its long-term nature, extending ten or twenty years or longer, they forecast that the Chinese government would support the idea.[9] In all likelihood VNAs' potential impact on China's nuclear modernization program remains the gravest concern for the current and future Chinese leadership.

An equally disturbing prospect is VNAs' nondiscrimination be-tween nuclear and nonnuclear powers, especially at peacetime. Even if this would not deprive China of its hard-won great power status, the nondiscrimination could water down its peacetime diplomatic leverage.

Would the PLA's conventional capability be strong enough to bolster China's expanding interests, say, in the 2010s? The future trajectory of China's conventional capability would clearly have an important bearing on China's stance on VNAs.

As befits their realpolitik worldview and arguably their mirror image, current and future Chinese leaders will have to delve into the haunting possibility of clandestine nuclear development by other states. Familiar with the Cold War worst scenarios, Chinese leaders could contemplate a situation in which a longer reconstitution leads to a nuclear attack on a disarmed China. On the other hand, contrary to the prevailing view that China is afraid of the spread of the nuclear states along its borders, none of those interviewed expressed concern about the issue. At least one of them explicitly rejected such concern on the ground that any future regional proliferant would not substitute for the Soviet threat.[10]

Taken together, VNAs could well enhance China's relative security and peace-loving image when instituted after China's current technological weaknesses are more or less overcome. China's putative incentives, however, need to be balanced against the lingering doubts on technological, diplomatic, and sovereignty costs. China's ultimate decision to join the VNA process will be shaped by the course of internal and external developments during the transitional stage.

THE QUESTION OF STABILITY

Once the transition to a VNAs end-state begins, China will actively maneuver in the negotiation arena so as to carefully craft the solution to its favor. In particular, Chinese leaders and strategists would need to address each stability question originally raised by Michael Mazarr.

Veiled Proliferation. Regional proliferation of states with VNA capability will remain a concern but at a much lower level than the United States. China has made nuclear transactions only with those countries that it deemed "friendly" and traditionally focused more on the spread of advanced aircraft in the Asia-Pacific region than on missile or nuclear proliferation. China, therefore, would not press this issue as hard as Russia or Western nuclear powers.

Verification and Inspection. Given a choice, China's clear preference would be an inspection regime under the international agency, over which China can exercise some leverage, rather than the national technical means of verification. China's relative backwardness in this field would foreclose this option. In addition, China's continuing secrecy over military issues, and if an authoritarian regime remains in power, would lead it to opt for a minimum inspection regime. The level of China's participation in the VNA process and to some extent the success of VNAs themselves depend upon, albeit indirectly, the nature of the future Chinese regime.

Reconstitution and Survivability. Like the other former nuclear states, China will have to guard against cheating. In the transitional period China would not find tandem reductions particularly objectionable as long as an adequate inspection mechanism is in place; it could also retain a modest survivable force against the eventuality. At the final stage of VNAs, however, it is hard to tell whether China will be able to maintain "disassembled and invulnerable" arsenals. Or in the penultimate stage China may cop out of the VNA process, declaring that steps beyond a much reduced arsenal are not in its interests. An entire VNA scheme will then be in jeopardy.

Strategic Defense. China's traditional concern on superpower ABM capability will run deep even in a world of VNAs. Notwithstanding the alleged stabilizing role of strategic defense in a disarmed world, Chinese leaders must think hard about the worst-case scenario—what if it is attacked with nuclear weapons, for example, by an aggressor employing an effective strategic defense? In light of China's actual and perceived lack of strategic defense capability and the potential competition for space-based defense, it is a distinct possibility that China sees strategic defense as destabilizing even in a VNA world.

Nuclear Weapons and War Proneness. With no extended deterrence commitments, China will not see the need to launch "nuclear counterattack operations" (the name dictated by its no-first-use pledge) unless it is attacked by nuclear weapons. Knowing full well that its nuclear force prevented the actual and threatened use of nuclear weapons against China, its leaders cannot help but worry about alternative types of warfare in a world of virtual arsenals. A rapid reassembly of dismantled arsenals cannot possibly address the full spectrum of conflict, thus making an aggressor more likely to engage in a low-level conflict.

FUTURE PROSPECTS

China has so far resisted any ACD measures that would put real constraints on its nuclear modernization program, for technological and security reasons. But China's evolving ACD posture over time and issues strongly indicates that other major factors are at work in its ACD policy formulation. In the case of VNAs as well, the most immediate post-Deng leadership may not be too receptive to the idea, given the rising influence of the PLA amid the weak civilian lineup. Over the longer term, however, social forces rather than individual leaders will decide the character of the regime, composed of the foreign-educated elites who would appreciate more the virtue of such ACD initiatives as VNAs than their predecessors.

On balance, if all deployed nuclear arsenals are disassembled and removed from day-to-day alert, as envisioned in the VNA proposal, China's future security prospects seem brighter than at any time before. How nicely these potential benefits intersect with the future of China depends upon the different trajectories at work, but the political one will be of the utmost importance.

In the years ahead, making progress in such impending ACD processes as START II, a CTBT, and a cut off convention will be an important first step toward the long road of VNAs. To take a great leap forward, however, the United States and Russia should not only recognize China's differing yet often legitimate security requirements, but they should also make genuine efforts to build confidence with China. The future success of VNAs will increasingly hinge on how to deal with the old China factor in the new era.

NOTES

1. An excellent analysis on the changes in China's security perceptions and military doctrine is available. See Yao Yunzhu, "The Evolution of Military Doctrine of the Chinese PLA from 1985 to 1995," *Korean Journal of Defense Analysis* 7, no. 2 (Winter 1995). See also Bonnie S. Glaser, "China's Security Perceptions: Interests and Ambitions," *Asian Survey* 33, no. 3 (March 1993): 252-71.

2. For an overview of China's arms acquisitions from abroad, including Russia, see Bates Gill and Taeho Kim, *China's Arms Acquisitions from Abroad: A Quest*

for "Superb and Secret Weapons" (Oxford: Oxford University Press, 1995).

3. See, for example, Mu Huimin, "'Chinese Military Threat Theory' Is Totally Groundless," *Renmin Ribao,* April 17, 1993, 6, in *Foreign Broadcast Information Service—Daily Report: China,* April 28, 1993, 20-21.

4. "Delayed Chinese JH-7 Bomber Seen Operational," *International Defense Review* (June 1995): 6. For a brief discussion of China's ongoing nuclear modernization, see Robert S. Norris, Andrew S. Burrows, and Richard W. Fieldhouse, *British, French, and Chinese Nuclear Weapons,* Nuclear Weapons Databook vol. 5 (Boulder: Westview Press, 1994), 372-73.

5. For a fuller discussion of China's limited nuclear deterrence, see Alastair Iain Johnston, "Chinese Perspectives on Nuclear Doctrine: The Concept of Limited Deterrence," *International Security* 20, no. 3 (Winter 1995-96).

6. Alastair Iain Johnston, "Prospects for Chinese Nuclear Force Modernization: Limited Deterrence versus Multilateral Arms Control" (paper presented at a conference on "The PLA towards 2000," cosponsored by the Chinese Council of Advanced Policy Studies and *China Quarterly,* Hong Kong, July 14-15, 1995).

7. Lisbeth Gronlund, David Wright, and Yong Liu, "China and a Fissile Material Production Cut-off," *Survival* 37, no. 4 (Winter 1995-96): 162.

8. Interview with the author, January 1996. It should be noted, however, that when Chinese officials speak of total nuclear disarmament, it literally means the destruction of nuclear weapons and seldom refers to the prohibition of fissile material or nuclear research.

9. Interview with the author, February 1996.

10. Ibid.

ELEVEN

FRANCE AND VIRTUAL NUCLEAR DETERRENCE

PHILIP GORDON

FRANCE AND VIRTUAL NUCLEAR ARSENALS

THE NOTION OF DEACTIVATING NUCLEAR WEAPONS does not seem likely to become very popular in France. This is not to say that France would be able to block the development of a virtual nuclear world if the other major powers chose to pursue one or that certain changes in French domestic politics could not provoke increased interest or support in Paris. It is simply to say that France is, and is likely to remain, particularly unenthusiastic about the idea of moving toward a virtual nuclear world. Some of the same factors that make virtual deterrence potentially appealing to the United States and nonnuclear countries also apply to France, as do the technical obstacles and challenges to the scheme. But there are other factors, particular to both the French strategic situation and French strategic culture, that will make France less likely than most other countries to support virtual deterrence.

Perhaps the most telling comment about the current French attitude toward virtual nuclear deterrence is that hardly anyone in France is actively promoting the idea. This may be no more than the product of a relatively small arms-control community that has traditionally had little reason to consider schemes for moving toward a nonnuclear world; the official French nuclear community certainly does not devote time and resources to it, and the all-party consensus in support of nuclear deterrence has meant that political movements have not been interested either. But the more likely explanation is that what might be called France's "dual nuclear mythology"—that nuclear weapons make war impossible and that France's possession of them helps make France a great power—is deeply and widely held. While it would theoretically preserve the function of deterrence, a virtual nuclear scheme would be a step away from what the French believe has prevented war in Europe for fifty years (after three devastating wars in the previous eighty years), and it would eliminate one of the ways in which France has distinguished itself from other medium-sized powers for more than three decades: the possession of the bomb—an important element in France's perception of itself.

To focus on factors such as the French belief in nuclear deterrence or French self-perception is not to say that France is not, like other countries, interested in ways to reduce the risk of nuclear accidents or to contain proliferation (which virtual nuclear deterrence would allegedly do) or that it would be biased in its consideration of the technical challenges to the scheme (discussed in other essays in this volume). Rather, the point is simply that France's particular commitment to traditional deterrence will make it even more skeptical than others about the advantages of the scheme and even more attentive to the obstacles. This essay examines the reasons why France is likely to be unenthusiastic and also looks at the potential for change in French thinking, which cannot be excluded.

THE BASES OF FRENCH SKEPTICISM

FRENCH NUCLEAR WEAPONS AND NATIONAL PRESTIGE

There were a number of reasons for the original French decision to build a nuclear force: lack of confidence in the U.S. deterrent; technological benefits; the need to give a new role to the French army after Algeria; and the desire to achieve diplomatic influence. But the most important motivation was probably restoring France's diminished prestige as a great power. For General Charles de Gaulle, as for all of his successors, restoring French influence and "rank" was an essential political goal, and joining the exclusive nuclear club "at the top" was an effective way to achieve it. This factor alone seems good enough reason for France to oppose moving toward virtual disarmament. In a truly virtual nuclear world France—the great power, permanent member of the United Nations Security Council (which happens to be the same nuclear "club of five"), and country that had spent billions of francs developing its nuclear forces over the years—would be no more a "nuclear power" than Germany, Italy, Japan, and Switzerland, a difficult situation for the French to accept.

There seems little sign that France is no longer interested in pursuing the goal of great power status or that it has concluded that nuclear weapons are not an effective means to do so. Since the end of the Cold War, while pressing ahead with the modernization of its nuclear arsenals (including the deployment of a new generation of submarine and submarine-launched nuclear missiles), France has resisted moves toward the "delegitimization" of nuclear weapons, such as NATO's pledge to use them only as a "last resort" or the more recent pledge by nuclear powers to "de-target" their weapons. (France may have some of the last "targeted" nuclear weapons in the world.) France's decision in 1992 to adhere to, and then seek indefinite extension of, the 1968 Nuclear Nonproliferation Treaty was designed more to *preserve* the legitimacy of nuclear weapons than to question it, and France only agreed to sign a Comprehensive Nuclear Test Ban Treaty (CTBT) under the condition that it "not in any way envisage the elimination of nuclear weapons or seek to undermine the status of the nuclear powers."[1]

More recently, of course, France went ahead with its final series of nuclear tests in order to preserve the future credibility of its arsenal and perhaps also to make a statement about the continued legitimacy of deterrence. While it is probably true that the government underestimated the vehemence of the international reaction to the tests, it did know that it would have to pay a price for testing, and went ahead anyway.[2] The continued French commitment to remaining a great power by being a nuclear power was most recently summed up by the current defense minister, Charles Millon: "If France were to renounce nuclear weapons, it would be necessary to foresee an alternative policy, but I don't see any other, except to say that France is not a great power."[3] Not being a great power is still unacceptable to France.

NUCLEAR DETERRENCE AS WAR PREVENTION

France's commitment to nuclear deterrence is, of course, not only a function of its desire for status but also, it seems, of a genuine belief in the war prevention effect of nuclear deterrence. French strategic thinkers and officials over the years have strongly supported the logic that a "balance of terror," or indeed any second-strike nuclear capability, made war impossible in Europe, and they will therefore be very skeptical about taking any steps that move away from that status. It is hard to dissociate the sincerity of the belief in deterrence from the desire for global status (were French presidents really convinced of the bomb's war-preventing role, or was that a convenient argument in support of what they wanted for other reasons?). Yet faith in the functioning of deterrence does seem to have been widespread, and it apparently remains so.

The most recent official explanation of French strategy, the Defense White Paper of 1994, asserted the continued need for nuclear deterrence. It noted the possibility that in the next twenty years a threat of major aggression in Europe (and, in the long term, even beyond Europe) could come "from a state or coalition of states with large nuclear and conventional forces and hegemonic ambitions." In such a case France would have to depend on nuclear deterrence—with adequate nuclear and C3I capabilities—to "prevent the execution of the threat."[4] Although most French explanations of the country's need for nuclear weapons focus on other states' nuclear weapons (for example, Prime Minister Alain Juppé's comment that "so long as other countries possess nuclear weapons, so, of course, will France"[5]), conventional and nonnuclear weapons of mass destruction (WMD) threats are also seen as cause for the preservation of the French deterrent. French authorities have not adopted, and have shown little interest in, a doctrine of "no-first-use."[6] If French leaders continue to see nuclear weapons as necessary to deter nonnuclear threats (such as chemical or biological attacks against French vital interests), they are unlikely to support a virtual nuclear scheme.

For further evidence of the enduring French support for nuclear deterrence, it might be worth noting that even some of the main critics of the continued nuclear tests have not argued that the tests themselves or French deterrence was illegitimate but, on the contrary, that the tests ran the risk of contributing to nuclear delegitimization, which was to be avoided. Leading French strategic analyst François Heisbourg questioned the need for the tests in an article tellingly entitled "Too Much Nuclear Kills the Nuclear" (i.e., "too much nuclear policy undermines nuclear deterrence"), and Pascal Boniface, another nuclear expert, has opposed the tests while vigorously supporting the need to preserve the French consensus that nuclear deterrence is essential.[7] In the National Assembly the former Socialist head of the National Defense Committee, Jean-Michel Boucheron, asserted that the Socialists were "against the nuclear tests" but "for deterrence."[8] The French consensus in support of nuclear deterrence could, of course, break down, but it has not broken down yet.

LACK OF CONVENTIONAL MILITARY SUPERIORITY

One of the main reasons why the idea of virtual nuclear arsenals has recently gained momentum in the United States is that some American strategists feel increasingly confident that the United States can deal with any military threat with high-tech conventional responses and that the danger of nuclear proliferation is becoming greater than the need for nuclear deterrence.[9] Given a choice (if it is indeed the choice) between many countries having nuclear weapons and none having them, an increasing number of Americans would choose "none." Giving up deterrence would be worth it if nonproliferation were the prize.

France does not feel it has such a "luxury." To be sure, France, too, now thinks of "defense" more in terms of possible military interventions abroad than in preventing an attack on the homeland, and France, like the United States, has more powerful conventional forces than any single state with which it is likely to come into conflict. But France does not have the overwhelming conventional superiority that the United States has, and French strategists are far less willing than some Americans to rely solely on its conventional capabilities to deter attacks against France or French forces. Indeed, in somewhat defensive language the French White Paper argued that "it is illusory and dangerous to believe that [conventional] technologies could have the effect of preventing war as nuclear weapons do. . . . Nuclear weapons remain the means to compensate, if necessary, for possible insufficiencies in other areas, and allow for an avoidance of a 'conventional arms race' that would be contrary to our defense policy and unacceptable from a financial viewpoint."[10] Rather than accept the American logic whereby nuclear weapons would be delegitimized (and perhaps even abandoned) in order to pursue nonproliferation goals, many French analysts reject the American view as an attempt by the United States to remove the "equalizing power of the atom" and achieve global military supremacy.[11]

AN ABSENCE OF A "NUCLEAR ALLERGY"

Another reason why some proponents of virtual nuclear arsenals support the scheme is that they see nuclear weapons, and the nuclear industry that surrounds them, as an environmental hazard to be reduced or even banished, if possible. But France has always been rather less concerned about nuclear pollution or accidents than some of its neighbors—to the point where one commentator could conclude in 1988 that "the cloud of Chernobyl" had (figuratively) stopped at the Rhine.[12] Environmental concerns have grown in France since then and may be further aroused by the vehemence of the European reaction to the recent French nuclear tests. But the French green movement is still small compared to that of France's neighbors, and France still maintains the most extensive network of nuclear power plants in Europe (relying on nuclear power for more than 75 percent of its electricity). Even though 59 percent of the French public opposed the recent nuclear tests, just as many of the French in the same polls supported the continued possession of a French deterrent.[13] Unlike in Germany, for example, where nuclear weapons are generally associated with war, devastation, and environmental danger, in France they remain associated with power, prestige, status, and defense—and are thus unlikely to be abandoned.[14]

TECHNICAL ARGUMENTS AGAINST
VIRTUAL NUCLEAR ARSENALS

The reasons, previously outlined, that France will likely be skeptical about moving toward a virtual nuclear regime are particular to the French situation. But it should also be noted that French officials have also expressed some of the same concerns about the scheme that others, including their proponents, have expressed. In reaction to the virtual nuclear scheme as outlined in the *Survival* article by Michael Mazarr, French Ministry of Defense (MoD) officials noted the following concerns.

First, French officials argue that the example of Iraq shows that an effective verification regime would be extremely difficult to implement and, without extensive intrusion into domestic affairs at potentially great cost, would never inspire complete confidence that the rules of the regime were not being violated. Second, some French sources claimed that a virtual nuclear world would be potentially unstable, with "strong payoffs for breakout," unless the virtual nuclear powers could reconstitute their forces with security and in reasonable amounts of time. Finally, French MoD officials asserted that a virtual nuclear scheme would do little to clear up the problem of "loose nukes" in the former Soviet Union and that to believe so reflects a confusion between the symptom and the disease. "The real problem is the lack of control of the central authorities. Implementing a virtual nuclear regime would require a degree of control that does not exist; but if it did exist the loose nukes problem would disappear along with the incentive to move toward virtual nuclear arsenals."[15]

These sorts of technical difficulties are well-known to those analyzing virtual nuclear regimes; the point here is that, if France chose to oppose moving to a virtual nuclear world for reasons particular to it, it would have a number of more general arguments at its disposal.

CONCLUSIONS AND PROSPECTS FOR CHANGE

France is a conservative nuclear power. As a nuclear "rebel" in the 1960s that developed its own forces and refused to sign the NPT, France has since become a status quo nuclear power, content to maintain a world of five official "haves" and many other "have-nots." This basic nuclear conservatism does not seem to have changed significantly.

Change cannot, of course, be excluded. Just a few years ago France's support for a "zero-threshold" Comprehensive Test Ban Treaty or willingness to discuss nuclear policy with NATO would both have seemed as unlikely as French support for virtual nuclear arsenals seems today. But both have now come about. A nuclear accident, heavy pressure from the other nuclear powers or France's European partners, or much greater progress toward true, global denuclearization, including among the currently nonnuclear powers, could all push France in the direction of reconsidering the notion of virtual nuclear arsenals. If the former nuclear superpowers reduce their arsenals to levels comparable to

France's, and in the absence of a concrete WMD threat from a potential regional adversary, France may over time come to see nuclear weapons more as a problem and irritant than as a source of prestige.

More specifically, it should be noted that the combination of a rapidly changing strategic situation and political *alternance* in France (the election of a Gaullist president after 14 years of Socialist rule) create the possibility that after years of consensus nuclear weapons will again become a source of division and debate in France. The famous "consensus," after all, was itself the product of a fortuitous combination of political factors, and it could disappear as quickly as it came about.[16] The Communist Party has already gone back to its antinuclear roots, and the Socialists were vehement in their opposition to French nuclear tests. No leading Socialist (except for a very small group in the party led by Julian Dray) has come out in favor of a virtual nuclear arsenal or of scrapping nuclear deterrence altogether, but the party could conceivably come to oppose the nuclear force if it felt that public opinion was also turning against it.

Notably, former Prime Minister Michel Rocard has agreed to participate in a high-level group of "wise men" convened by Australian Prime Minister Paul Keating to examine the possibility of a world without nuclear weapons—a project based on the very same set of assumptions as those held by proponents of virtual nuclear arsenals.[17] In his willingness to consider fundamentally rethinking the role of French nuclear weapons, Rocard's thinking is consistent with the line traced out by his former advisor for strategic affairs, nuclear expert Marisol Touraine (now a professor at the Institut d'Etudes Politiques in Paris), who has for several years argued that "the fight against proliferation requires that the current nuclear powers marginalize the role that they give to nuclear weapons in their own security policies."[18]

A growing willingness to reconsider the role of nuclear weapons in French security policy can, thus, not be excluded. But given the continued French association of nuclear weapons with independence and prestige; the enduring belief in nuclear deterrence; the perceived absence of conventional options in some cases; the absence of a strong antinuclear energy movement in France; and the many technical difficulties with any virtual nuclear arsenals scheme, it seems likely that France will fight to preserve its existing deterrent, even if support for the

scheme grows elsewhere. As one French official put it, quoting the
poetry of Victor Hugo: "And if only one remains, I shall be the one!"[19]

NOTES

1. Then–Prime Minister Edouard Balladur speaking on May 10, 1994; cited in
   Yost, "Nuclear Debates in France," 131. Balladur added, "Any move in this
   direction would encounter France's opposition."
2. Even François de Rose, the former French ambassador to NATO, who can
   hardly be considered insensitive to consequences for France's diplomatic
   relations, argued in 1994 that a diplomatic crisis would be a "lesser evil" than
   the potential erosion of French nuclear credibility that would allegedly result
   from not testing. See François de Rose, "Préparer la reprise des essais
   nucléaires," *Enjeux du Monde,* no. 14 (February 1994): 15.
3. Millon, cited in *Le Figaro,* July 13, 1995.
4. See *Livre blanc sur la défense: 1994* (Paris: French Ministry of Defense, 1994):
   70-72.
5. See Alain Juppé, "La dissuasion nucléaire dans le nouveau contexte
   international" (speech given at the Institut des Hautes Etudes de Défense
   Nationale, Paris, on September 7, 1995; published in *Politique Etrangère,*
   March 1995, 746).
6. France did pledge in 1982 not to use nuclear weapons against nonnuclear
   states that had promised not to develop nuclear weapons and were not in
   alliance with another nuclear state, a pledge it reiterated at the Nuclear
   Nonproliferation Treaty Extension Conference in April 1995. Prime Minister
   Juppé, however (speaking while still foreign minister), has made it quite clear
   that France's "negative security assurances" were compatible with deterrence,
   and that "it goes without saying that [France's] deterrent covers any threat to
   [its] vital interests, whatever the means and the origin of the threat, including,
   of course, that from weapons of mass destruction produced and used despite
   the international ban on them." Analyst Pascal Boniface agrees, calling no-
   first-use "by definition incompatible with deterrence," and refers specifically
   to the potential chemical attack from a nonnuclear state as a reason for this.
   For Juppé, see his speech to the Senate Foreign Affairs, Defense and Armed
   Forces Commission of 6 April, 1995, printed as an appendix in Xavier de
   Villepin, "La lutte contre la prolifération nucléaire, enjeux et perspectives,"
   *Rapport au nom de la commission des Affaires étrangères, de la Défense et des Forces
   armées du Sénat,* no. 311, (June 1995): 17. For Boniface, see "Dissuasion et
   non-proliferation: un équilibre difficile, nécessaire mais rompu," *Politique
   étrangère,* March 1995, 715, which also discusses the 1982 negative security
   assurance. For a (minority) French view *in favor of* France's adoption of no-
   first-use, see Marisol Touraine, "Le facteur nucléaire après la guerre froide,"

Politique Etrangère, no. 2 (Summer 1992): 395-405.

7. See François Heisbourg, "Top de nucléaire tue le nucléaire," *Liberation* (September 1995) and Pascal Boniface and Françoise Thual, "Refonder le consensus sur la dissuasion nucléaire, *Le Monde,* November 24, 1995. Also see Boniface, "Dissuasion et non-proliferation."

8. Cited in "M. Balladur soutient les essais nucléaires lors d'un débat à l'Assemblée nationale," *Le Monde,* December 15, 1995.

9. See, for example, the suggestion by then chairman of the House Armed Services Committee, Les Aspin, that, "if we now had the opportunity to ban all nuclear weapons, we would" in Aspin, "From Deterrence to Denuking: A New Nuclear Policy for the 1990s," U.S. Congress, House of Representatives Committee on Armed Services, Defense Policy Panel, *Shaping Nuclear Policy for the 1990s: A Compendium of Views,* 102d Cong., 2d Sess. (Washington, D.C.: USGPO, 1992), January 21, 1992, 9. Also see the discussion in Michael J. Mazarr, "Virtual Nuclear Arsenals," *Survival* 37, no. 3 (Autumn 1995): 7-26; and Stephen A. Cambone and Patrick J. Garrity, "The Future of U.S. Nuclear Policy," *Survival* 36, no. 4 (Winter 1994-95): 73-95.

10. See *Livre Blanc,* 56-57.

11. Interviews with French officials; see also Yost, "Nuclear Debates in France," 129.

12. See Pierre Hassner, "Un chef d'oeuvre en péril: le consensus français sur la défense," *Esprit* (March-April 1988): 71-82.

13. Figures from a September 1995 poll showed 60 percent of the French in favor of preserving the French bomb and 59 percent opposing the nuclear tests. A similar poll from August 1995 showed 58 percent in favor of the bomb and 59 percent opposing the tests. For the first, see "Deux sondages confiirment l'hostilité des Français et des Japonais à là reprise des essais nucléaires," *Le Monde,* September 7, 1995; and "59 percent des Français sont hostiles à la reprise des essais nucléaires," *Le Monde,* August 21, 1995.

14. On differing French and German "strategic cultures," see Philip H. Gordon, *A Certain Idea of France: French Security Policy and the Gaullist Legacy* (Princeton, N. J.: Princeton University Press, 1993); and Philip H. Gordon, *France, Germany and the Western Alliance* (Boulder, Co: Westview Press, 1995).

15. Interviews with French officials, December 1995.

16. See Pascal Boniface, *Vive la bombe* (Paris: Edition 1, 1992): 97-107; Gordon, *Certain Idea,* 106-18; and Jolyon Howorth, "Consensus of Silence: The French Socialist Party and Defense under François Mitterrand," *International Affairs* 60, no. 4 (Autumn 1984): 579-600.

17. See Gareth Evans, "Step by Step Together toward a World without Nuclear Weapons," *International Herald Tribune,* December 5, 1995.

18. See Touraine, "Le facteur nucléaire après la guerre froide," 404.

19. "Et s'il n'en reste qu'un, je serai celui là!" (cited in David S. Yost, "Nuclear Debates in France," *Survival* 36, no. 4 [Winter 1994-95]: 139).

TWELVE

BRITAIN

STUART CROFT

THAT THE WORLD HAS BEEN TRANSFORMED would not be disputed by senior British officials; that this requires a fundamental reappraisal of the utility of nuclear weapons, however, would. There has not been a defense consensus in Britain that has ranged across the political spectrum, as arguably it has done in France. Yet there is a strong defense and nuclear consensus among policymakers, and this consensus has survived changes in government since its genesis in the late 1940s. Thus, to assess the impact of the concept of virtual nuclear arsenals on the British debate requires, first, that the British nuclear mind-set be examined and explained. That task is undertaken in the first part of this essay. From this basis it becomes clear that, from London's perspective, nuclear weapons are seen to play positive roles in international politics (although the enormous risks are fully recognized), and, thus, the virtual nuclear arsenals concept is likely to be resisted for a variety of reasons related to strategic logic and the challenge of the concept to the British nuclear mind-set. These factors are examined in the second section.

THE BRITISH NUCLEAR MIND-SET

That which may be termed the *British nuclear mind-set* has related to four main points: the nature of international relations, assumptions regarding

Soviet and Russian hostility, the centrality of the American alliance, and the general utility of nuclear deterrence and British nuclear forces.[1]

The major assumption has been that the international system is anarchic. Of course, many national traditions share this perspective, and it is at the core of major theoretical approaches. It should simply be noted, however, that London believes that Britain has had a long tradition of *policy making* based on this assumption. In the nineteenth century this was through shifting alliances. As the structured Congress system became less used in the 1820s, the British foreign secretary, George Canning, declared: "So things are getting back to a wholesome state again. Every nation for itself, and God for us all."[2] The Maud Committee, set up in 1940 to investigate the possibility of manufacturing an atomic weapon, concluded that "no nation would care to be caught without a weapon of such decisive possibilities."[3] In the post–Cold War world the British expect new patterns of hostility and confrontation to emerge as the normal pattern of international relations.

During the Cold War, Britain did not abandon its balancing policy, but, in contrast to the nineteenth century, from the 1940s London's perception was that the Soviet Union was the predominant European power, one that could not be matched by any grouping of European states: hence, there had to be an alliance with the United States.[4] Although the Soviet Union has collapsed and Russian power is comparatively much weaker, concerns about the possibility of Moscow destabilizing Europe remain, and, as a consequence, the centrality of the American relationship remains. This is not to suggest that Britain is hostile to the development of a greater European defense capability, but it is to recognize that, even in the post–Cold War world, it is still only the United States on the Western side that can bring about fundamental change, a key lesson reinforced by the Bosnia imbroglio. Therefore, it has been of great importance to the British mind-set to be able to influence the actions and attitudes of the United States: the special relationship has, consequently, been of overwhelming importance.[5] That privilege that London believes it has with Washington has been seen to be useful in both maintaining a U.S. commitment to European security and also in restraining any destabilizing impulses on the American side relating, in part, to nuclear strategy.

In this worldview nuclear weapons have two vital functions. First, the British nuclear force has been in part an investment to gain influence over U.S. nuclear strategy. Purchases of American delivery systems, initially through *Polaris,* and then *Trident,* has been seen by some as British weakness; but for British policymakers, by moving to *Polaris* the United Kingdom was able to maintain a force that was operationally independent while deepening a whole range of collaborative contacts with the United States, which offered the possibility of enhancing British influence over U.S. policy.[6] And the British, in direct contradiction to the French, were at great pains to stress that the development of a British force did not reflect negatively on the credibility of the American extended deterrent. In public presentation it was not the British who doubted the future credibility of the U.S guarantee; it was also the Soviets, and the British deterrent provided an insurance against Soviet doubts about the American will to maintain extended deterrence.[7]

The second function of nuclear weapons for the British has been to make all war inconceivable. Nuclear deterrence has been seen to be a fundamentally stabilizing innovation in an inherently unstable international system, since nuclear deterrence not only made nuclear war inviable; it also made conventional warfare impossible to contemplate, for fear of escalation to the nuclear level. As a consequence, nuclear weapons were inherently seen to be an international good. As the 1987 *Defense Estimates* put it:

> It is easy to forget that in the first half of this century the world was twice plunged into immensely destructive global conventional war, precipitated on both occasions by a state numerically weaker than the combination of states that faced it. In the last century Europe was torn asunder by several major wars. By contrast, in the 40 years since the end of the Second World War—40 years of nuclear deterrence—there has been no war in Western Europe, either conventional or nuclear, in spite of deep ideological hostility between East and West. This is a striking achievement.[8]

Thus, the nuclear order has been a nonwar order.

These fundamental approaches have, from London's perspective, not been undermined by the end of the Cold War.[9] The Soviet Union may have disappeared, but the threat of Soviet nuclear weapons has not.

As the 1992 *Defense Estimates* put it: "Uncertainties and risks remain. The massive nuclear arsenal of the former Soviet Union still exists. . . . Planned reductions will . . . take years to implement, and the residual holdings will have colossal destructive potential. . . . Russia remains the largest single military power in Europe."[10] Most starkly, "it would be foolhardy to assume that what emerges from the wreck of the Soviet communism can never again bear upon our defense needs."[11] Thus, risks and challenges from the East continue to have an impact upon British nuclear thinking. But not only is that the case, there is also a concern with newly emerging threats, which might also in turn require deterrence through the possession of nuclear forces. In 1990 Prime Minister Margaret Thatcher drew attention to the growing dangers of newly arming states, an important theme in her speech to the NATO Heads of Government meeting at Turnberry in mid-1990. As the 1992 *Statement* put it, "Outside Europe, the proliferation of ballistic missiles and weapons of mass destruction and of sophisticated conventional weapons could pose a threat to our dependencies, our allies and the United Kingdom itself."[12] Thus, in these two senses strategic nuclear deterrent forces, "the ultimate guarantee of our country's security," remain vital.[13]

RESISTANCE TO VIRTUAL NUCLEAR ARSENALS

British resistance to any moves toward virtual nuclear arsenals might, therefore, be expected. There are two levels to this opposition. The first is a strategic critique of the approach. The second draws on Britain's underlying assumptions.

In terms of a strategic critique two elements predominate.[14] First, suggesting that a virtual nuclear arsenals regime might look like the Nonproliferation Treaty might not be very attractive to London, for the NPT allows for states to withdraw unilaterally from the treaty (although there are clearly normative constraints on such a decision, as the North Koreans found). But in London there would be a rejection of the implications of this treaty, which is that major states could rely upon rearmament retaliation to respond to any state breaking out of its virtual nuclear status. The problem is one of capability. Certainly, the United States may be able to remain in a high state of readiness, able to respond to any breakout at short notice, but for the United Kingdom this is unlikely to be practicable. The breakup of design teams and other expertise is one that the British have constantly had to worry about, at least since the early 1970s and the development of the expensive Chevaline program. For Britain, nuclear weapons and status should not be made more expensive, as would be required by the ability to respond to a short-warning breakout from any virtual nuclear regime.

The second element in the strategic critique revolves around Mazarr's suggestion, in "Virtual Nuclear Arsenals," that extended deterrence would remain, as "any all-out war would lead to reassembly and thence to nuclear use."[15] This view is most certain to be rejected in London. The extended deterrence of a virtual nuclear arsenals world would be seen to be weaker than anything that NATO had previously seen. What guarantee would there be that a U.S. president would reassemble, deploy, and then use nuclear weapons? Is there not a danger of self-deterrence at each point? European NATO allies—most volubly the French but not them alone—have long feared that strategic coupling might lose its credibility. It seems very difficult to believe, from the eastern side of the Atlantic, that American-European coupling could survive in a virtual nuclear arsenals world. And even if one believed in the commitment of the United States to Western Europe, which has been questioned in the post–Cold War world, there are good strategic arguments to doubt the automaticity of the reassembly-deployment-use link. In a crisis in which one state may have reassembled its nuclear forces, for the United States to reciprocate would be to escalate the crisis dramatically. Therefore, there are good crisis management reasons to doubt the automaticity of that link.

From London's perspective, therefore, the strategic fear would be that virtual nuclear arsenals would be tantamount to structural disarmament for middle-range states like Britain, without providing the confidence that all states in the world would be similarly restrained and while promising to break strategic coupling with the United States. Ironically, a virtual nuclear arsenals regime would, from this perspective, seem to benefit superpowers at one end of the spectrum, and near-nuclear/threshold states at the other while squeezing middle-ranking countries like Britain and France. But it is important not simply to take these arguments at face value but to go deeper and to see how fundamentally the concept of virtual nuclear arsenals threatens the British nuclear mind-set.

The second level of examining British responses, therefore, requires a reevaluation of that British nuclear mind-set in the light of the virtual nuclear arsenals proposal.

In terms of Britain's "realist" worldview the proposal is most unattractive. It would reduce Britain's nuclear position to that of, say, Israel or India. In terms of status, this would be most unwelcome. But, while a good deal of the international debate about the British nuclear force has revolved around status questions, among the British elite these issues have always been secondary to security questions. And in security terms it seems that virtual nuclear arsenals would put the United States in a stronger position (it would be technically most able to respond to a breakout) but would also undermine U.S.–West European coupling. In addition, the Anglo-American special relationship would be dramatically weakened, since nuclear cooperation lies at its heart, and in a virtual nuclear arsenals world the grounds for Anglo-American nuclear cooperation would be much reduced. Thus, in sum, in a virtual nuclear world Britain would feel it necessary to rely more on the United States but would fear it would be able to influence Washington less and would also worry that the U.S. commitment to Europe would be weaker than at any time since the 1930s.

Perhaps one might argue that the British should accept such concerns for the greater prize of eliminating an operational Russian nuclear force, particularly if Moscow should move further to the political Right. There would be a fear, however, that Russia would be in a stronger breakout position than would the United Kingdom because of the size of its nuclear infrastructure and because any authoritarian regime that decided on breakout would have a greater control over government resources to direct in favor of that policy than would any British government in responding to it. Russia, in this light, appears to be more of a superpower than a middle power. Further, removing—or, at least, seriously downgrading—the role of nuclear forces would increase the relevance of conventional forces. While Britain could not reasonably expect to be the victim of Russian military aggression, this might not be so for other members of an expanding European Union. The security dimension of an enlarged EU is absolutely critical. While the problem of managing the enlargement of the EU and NATO may be handled for the first few states of the former communist world, the link may, at some point, break. Will Britain, France, and other West

European countries be left with security commitments in Central and Eastern Europe through the widening of the European Union without both U.S. forces and nuclear weapons?

France has foreseen this problem since the late 1980s and has been engaged in a process of discussions with the British over nuclear collaboration. From 1992 the question of French and British nuclear forces forming the basis of an EU nuclear deterrent has been put firmly on the agenda by Paris, reaffirmed by the notion of concerted deterrence introduced by Alain Juppé and supported by Jacques Chirac. Yet, the strategic questions to be overcome in creating such an EU force are enormous.[16] Virtual nuclear arsenals are one solution to some of the dilemmas. While this might, however, be a point in France's favor, it is unlikely to be one for the British, who have constantly sought to maintain that there are limits to European integration and that the British bomb is outside the parameters of that process.

CONCLUSION

London's hostility to virtual nuclear arsenals, certainly in private, will be deep. Indeed, how could it not be, when the proposal strikes at the heart of the British nuclear mind-set? One is put in mind of the debate over the Strategic Defense Initiative (SDI) in the mid-1980s. Although the British sought to maintain a diplomatic air over the issue, few were in doubt that the government opposed any moves toward a change in the ABM Treaty and certainly were antagonistic toward any joint Soviet-American deployment. SDI was one of those American strategic innovations that the British sought to restrain through the operation of the special relationship. One can certainly see virtual nuclear arsenals being viewed in the same way.

One should, however, not take this to be the final word. There are many in the wider policy community and among the pressure groups in the United Kingdom who would welcome serious discussion of a virtual nuclear world. Michael MccGwire has written of the need to set a target for a nuclear-free world.[17] Paul Rogers and Malcolm Dando have already argued that "the West did not respond adequately to the possibilities opened up by Gorbachev between 1985 and 1991 . . . there is a need for new political thinking in the West. Now is the time to seize the opportunity to reverse the arms race."[18] Ken Booth would certainly criticize virtual nuclear arsenals for keeping some deterrence logic, which he criticizes as being deeply dangerous.[19] In short, there would be a good deal of support in the British nuclear debate. Yet, that debate is one that has been fractured for fifty years, and thus it should not be surprising that a radical idea such as virtual nuclear arsenals should be seen in a partisan fashion by the participants in that debate.

NOTES

1. For a more detailed examination of this framework, see Stuart Croft, "Continuity and Change in British Thinking about Nuclear Weapons," *Political Studies* 42, no.2 (1994): 228-42.

2. Quoted in Kenneth Bourne, *The Foreign Policy of Victorian England, 1930-1902* (Oxford: Clarendon Press, 1970): 13.

3. Reproduced in Margaret Gowing, *Britain and Atomic Energy, 1939-45* (London: Macmillan, 1964): 394.

4. For an examination of the origin of this policy, see Stuart Croft, *The End of Superpower: Foreign Office Conceptions of a Changing World, 1945-51* (Brookfield, VT: Dartmouth, 1994).

5. As shown by the essays in Wm. Roger Louis and Hedley Bull, ed., *The Special Relationship: Anglo-American Relations since 1945* (Oxford: Clarendon Press, 1986), the special relationship related many aspects of Anglo-American relations, but for elite thinkers the core was security policy.

6. On the issue of British nuclear procurement, see, for example, John Simpson, *The Independent Nuclear State: Britain, the United States and the Military Atom* (London: Macmillan, 1986); and Peter Malone, *The British Nuclear Deterrent* (London and New York: Croom Helm and St. Martin's Press, 1984): 58-74.

7. This "second center of decision making" argument was devised in the 1960s, perhaps by Defence Secretary Denis Healey, who reportedly argued that "if you are inside an alliance you increase the deterrent to the other side enormously if there is more than one centre of decisions for first use of nuclear weapons" (B. Reed and G. Williams, *Denis Healey and the Policies of Power* [London: Sidgwick and Jackson, 1971]: 169). This argument became institutionalized in public rationales. In 1980 Defence Secretary Francis Pym explained that using nuclear force "would be a decision of a separate and independent Power . . . whose survival in freedom might be more directly and closely threatened by aggression in Europe than that of the United States" (*Hansard* 977, col. 679, January 24, 1980).

8. *Statement on the Defence Estimates: 1987* (London: HMSO 1987): 13.

9. For a particularly sophisticated justification, see Sir Michael Quinlan, "The Future of Nuclear Weapons: Policy for Western Possessors," *International*

Affairs 69, no. 3 (1993): 485-596.

10. *Statement of the Defence Estimates: 1992 Cm1981* (London: HMSO, 1992), para. 104, 7.

11. Ibid.

12. Ibid., para. 4, 8.

13. Introduction by Secretary of Defence Malcolm Rifkind, in ibid., 6.

14. These are developed from the argument in favor of virtual nuclear arsenals in Michael H. Mazarr, "Virtual Nuclear Arsenals," *Survival* 37, no. 7 (Autumn 1995): 7-26.

15. Ibid., 16.

16. For an attempt to come to terms with them, see Roberto Zadra, "European Integration and Nuclear Deterrence after the Cold War," *Chaillot Paper 5* (Paris: WEU Institute for Security Studies, 1992).

17. Michael MccGwire, "Is There a Future for Nuclear Weapons," *International Affairs* 70, no. 2 (April 1994): 211-28.

18. See Paul Rogers and Malcolm Dando, *A Violent Peace: Global Security after the Cold War* (London: Brassey's, 1992): 160, 179.

19. See Ken Booth's comments in *New Thinking about Strategy and International Security* (London: Harper Collins, 1991): 10-20.

This chapter was written before the Labour Party victory in 1997.

THIRTEEN

VIRTUAL NUCLEAR DETERRENCE AND THE OPAQUE PROLIFERANTS

DEVIN HAGERTY

THIS ESSAY will explore the role of the nuclear threshold states, or "opaque proliferants," in the global evolution of a virtual deterrence nuclear end-state (VDNES). Opaque proliferants secretly develop nuclear weapon capabilities while publicly denying any intention actually to deploy nuclear weapons.[1] For the purposes of this essay these countries include India, Israel, and Pakistan, each of which is believed to have at least the capability to assemble and deliver nuclear weapons early in a crisis. The essay's main focus will be the likely reaction of these opaque proliferants' strategic communities to movement toward a VDNES on the part of the declared nuclear weapons states—China, France, Russia, the United Kingdom, and the United States.

It will be useful at the outset to identify the main assumptions structuring this essay. First, it assumes no fundamental transformation in the nature of world politics over the two- to five-decade time frame envisioned in this project. Relations between states will continue to encompass a wide variety of interactions ranging from conflict to cooperation. In the parlance of international relations theory "realist" self-help imperatives will at times be tempered by "liberal" normative constraints. Countries will ally with one another to achieve their security goals, but a true global collective security system will not have evolved. At the "core" of the international system liberal democracy and economic interdependence will dampen tendencies toward war, while at the system's "periphery" economic underdevelopment, political authoritarianism, and ethnic conflict will combine to increase the relative likelihood of war.[2]

A second central assumption concerns the nature of the VDNES itself. The analysis that follows assumes great power agreement on a step-by-step plan to denuclearize world politics. This process will involve "de-alerting" established nuclear arsenals, dismantling all nuclear weapons, and placing their components under a verifiable international inspection regime. The essay does *not* assume that some supranational body such as the United Nations will assume control over the world's virtual nuclear arsenals; ultimate launch authority will remain in national hands. The main advantage of such a system is that it would retain deterrence between the world's nuclear weapons states while at the same time dramatically decreasing the chances of preemptive nuclear war, nuclear accidents, and the unauthorized use of nuclear weapons. A secondary advantage of a VDNES as it relates to the opaque proliferants is that it would bridge the gap between great power arms control and global nonproliferation policy, thus "consummating" one of the deals embodied in the Nuclear Nonproliferation Treaty (NPT).[3] Bringing all nuclear states into the denuclearization process would engender a sense of shared purpose and thus enhance its legitimacy.

The demands of an effective VDNES are stiff. Such a regime must: (1) retain nuclear deterrence; (2) promote enhanced security against preemptive nuclear use, nuclear accidents, and unauthorized nuclear use; (3) be technically feasible; (4) be politically feasible; and (5) promote sufficient trust to dampen each nuclear power's fear of "breakout" by adversaries. This essay will focus on three of these issues: nuclear deterrence, political feasibility, and trust. The reason for this focus is twofold: since little information is publicly available on the opaque proliferants' command and control practices, analysis of these arrangements under a VDNES would be entirely speculative; moreover, the technical feasibility of a VDNES is extensively discussed in other essays in this volume, and the assumption in this one is that, if the technical requirements for great power denuclearization can be met, then they can also be met for the opaque proliferants. Because India, Israel, and Pakistan remain embroiled in regional cold wars, the more difficult issues involve the strategic and political implications of denuclearization.

The remainder of this essay is organized as follows. The second section is a brief conceptual overview of the most important characteristics of opaque proliferants and an explanation of why this "proliferation style" has significant analytical implications for Indian, Israeli, and Pakistani denuclearization. The third section is a survey of the opaque proliferants' nuclear postures. It describes each country's capabilities, its imperatives to pursue nuclear weapons in the first place, and its public diplomatic stance concerning nonproliferation. This section also touches on the nature of nuclear deterrence in the Middle East and South Asia, by briefly assessing the nuclear dimensions of the 1990-91 Gulf War and the 1990 Indo-Pakistani crisis over Kashmir. The fourth section analyzes the opaque proliferants' likely reactions to an evolving VDNES and the most challenging obstacles to bringing India, Israel, and Pakistan into such a regime. The fifth and final section assesses the prospects for extending a VDNES to the Middle East and South Asia.

OPACITY AS AN ANALYTICAL CONCEPT

At its most fundamental level opaque proliferation is a government's covert development of nuclear weapon capabilities combined with its public diplomatic posture of nuclear restraint. As Benjamin Frankel has observed: in the "overt culture" of the five original nuclear powers, "nuclear weapons, their testing, and the means to deliver them were all on display—an integral and pronounced part of the nuclear age's politics." In the "covert culture" embraced by subsequent proliferants, nuclear weapon capabilities have been acquired secretly and often in violation of international norms and national laws against the spread of nuclear weapons. Most important from an analytical standpoint is that "this technological covertness has been accompanied by declaratory 'opaqueness.'" Leaders of the countries involved deny vigorously any involvement in weapon production[4] and even profess loyalty to the nonproliferation regime.[5] The cornerstone of nuclear opacity is this tension between what the international community believes about a country's nuclear program and that state's official public stance concerning nuclear weapons.

Opaque proliferants share several characteristics that are significant for any analysis of the prospects for denuclearization. First, as noted earlier, they deny possessing nuclear weapons, "although they acknowledge—some more so than others—their capability to build such weapons quickly."[6] Such a posture allows the opaque proliferant to derive deterrent security from its nuclear capabilities without suffering the international opprobrium that a public admission of nuclear weapon possession would spur. Second, since the opaque proliferant's adversaries cannot be sure whether he has actually deployed nuclear weapons or not, they must assume that he has. Former U.S. Central Intelligence Agency director R. James Woolsey captured the essence of this point when he told Congress in 1993 that "both India and Pakistan have the capability to assemble the components of nuclear weapons . . . within a very short period of time. . . . [T]he distinction between whether those weapons are in fact assembled or only able to be assembled within a few days is a very small distinction."[7]

Third, opaque proliferants conduct no open debate about nuclear weapons and articulate no public doctrine for their use. Unlike the overt nuclear weapons states, which have a long history of debate about nuclear policy and have subsequently made public at least the outlines of the resultant doctrines, opaque proliferants condone little by way of officially sanctioned nuclear discourse. There are, of course, important citizens in India, Israel, and Pakistan who debate the merits of openly going nuclear and of different strategic concepts. Such debates usually have one thing in common, though, and that is their nonofficial quality: "to the extent that there is a debate, it is an academic debate."[8] Fourth, opaque proliferants make no direct nuclear threats against their adversaries.[9] This is not to say that opaque proliferants do not trumpet their nuclear resolve; never alluding to one's capacity to inflict enormous damage against an enemy lessens the deterrent value of nuclear capabilities. As will be discussed in the next section, however, opaque proliferants signal their deterrent resolve in a more oblique fashion than do the overt nuclear weapons states.

What are the perceived advantages of an opaque nuclear posture? Perhaps most important, the steady legitimation of the nonproliferation norm in international politics since 1968 has sharply increased the diplomatic costs of overt nuclear weaponization. When China went nuclear in 1964, the main obstacle it faced was the possibility of preventive strikes or sabotage by its nuclear-armed adversaries; when Pakistan took the same course in the mid- to late 1970s, it too faced these possibilities but also a variety of other hurdles intended to inhibit more countries from acquiring nuclear weapons. These included the NPT and an array of U.S. laws that threatened a cut off of aid if Pakistan followed the nuclear path to security.

Several other factors may influence the decision to maintain an opaque rather than an overt nuclear posture: (1) opacity is a way to signal a country's nuclear capabilities and flex some deterrent muscle without antagonizing adversaries into like responses and igniting a destabilizing and expensive nuclear arms race; (2) opacity is much less expensive than a transparent nuclear posture, which for the overt nuclear powers has involved developing redundant and diverse nuclear forces to insure the survivability of second-strike weapons; and (3) opacity preserves the flexibility future policymakers may need to back away from nuclear weapon capabilities if security conditions change. In other words, opacity provides an avenue to denuclearize without losing face or suffering domestic discontent owing to the popularity of an open nuclear stance.[10]

Finally, what is the theoretical relationship between opaque proliferation and nuclear arms control? On one hand, the opacity threshold provides a firebreak against steady, unfettered arms racing and its attendant insecurities. Put another way, this taboo against open nuclear deployments is *itself* an arms-control measure, one negotiated not formally through detailed agreements but informally through tacit communication. On the other hand, opacity can hinder the realization of more formal agreements to contain nuclear proliferation.[11] While arms control requires a certain degree of transparency, opaque proliferants see advantages to projecting ambiguity about their exact nuclear capabilities, which would be compromised by making public to adversaries the details of their force postures. The distinctive denuclearization challenge posed by opacity is therefore to shore up arms-control arrangements that have evolved tacitly, without eroding the nuclear deterrent effect that derives its power in part from ambiguity.

THE OPAQUE PROLIFERANTS' NUCLEAR
WEAPON POSTURES

CAPABILITIES

Of the three countries covered in this essay Israel enjoys clear
superiority, quantitative and qualitative, in nuclear weapons capabilities. The Israeli arsenal has been estimated at anywhere from 50 to 300
nuclear devices. These weapons can probably be delivered by F-4, F-
15, F-16, or Kfir fighter-bombers. Israel also deploys two nuclear-
capable ballistic missile systems; the Jericho I has an estimated range
of 660 kilometers, while the Jericho II can destroy targets approximately 1,500 kilometers away.[12] Turning to South Asia, U.S. officials
estimate that India has enough fissile material for at least 20 to 25
nuclear devices, and Pakistan enough for 6 to 8.[13] Both countries
could possibly deliver these weapons via a variety of fighter-bombers,
including Pakistani F-16s and Indian Jaguars. Neither side has yet
deployed operational ballistic missiles, and there is no conclusive
evidence that either can effectively mate nuclear warheads with missile
delivery systems. American officials worry, however, that both Islamabad and New Delhi may be on the verge of deploying ballistic missiles
with ranges of roughly 240 to 320 kilometers.[14]

NUCLEAR IMPERATIVES

Like each of their nuclear predecessors, the opaque proliferants have
pursued nuclear weapons capabilities primarily for deterrent purposes.
In the mid- to late 1950s the Israeli leadership under Prime Minister
David Ben-Gurion decided that Israel should develop at least the option
to build nuclear weapons if future security circumstances warranted
them. As Avner Cohen has written, Israeli leaders viewed this as a "sacred
matter of national survival, the ultimate way to offset the fundamental
geo-political asymmetry in conventional power between Israel and an
Arab world that repeatedly threatened to destroy it." This nuclear option
became "Israel's ultimate insurance policy," one that gave it the ability to
"inflict a holocaust to prevent another Holocaust."[15]

In South Asia, New Delhi's 1974 nuclear explosive test was the
product of a national debate over nuclear weapons in the aftermath of

India's humiliating defeat in its 1962 war with China and of China's own nuclear test. In 1964, Indian Prime Minister Lal Bahadur Shastri "launched a program to reduce the time needed to build nuclear arms to six months," thereby giving "official sanction to the development of an Indian nuclear weapons option."[16] Shastri's successor, Indira Gandhi, nudged the Indian nuclear program one step further in 1972, when she decided to proceed with an Indian nuclear explosion as soon as possible. In a striking historical parallel Pakistan began its journey down the nuclear path in the wake of its loss to India in the 1971 Bangladesh war. Given the gaping asymmetry that had emerged in Indian and Pakistani military capabilities with the loss of East Pakistan, President Zulfikar Ali Bhutto ordered Pakistan's scientific community to begin developing nuclear arms in 1972. In turn, India's 1974 nuclear test intensified Islamabad's resolve to acquire nuclear capabilities. Washington judged Pakistan to be nuclear weapon–capable by the mid- to late 1980s.

Israel and Pakistan display striking similarities in the strategic realm. Both states were created in the late 1940s on the basis of religion. Israel would be a Jewish homeland, while Pakistan would provide political refuge for South Asia's Muslims, a distinct minority on a mainly Hindu subcontinent. Just as Israel's neighbors refused to recognize its very existence, Pakistan's legitimacy as a nation-state was often called into question during its early decades. Both countries have fought several wars against quantitatively superior enemies—Israel more successfully than Pakistan—and both have minimal strategic depth, severely limiting their margin for error in war. As a result of these historical and geopolitical factors, Israel and Pakistan have pursued similar national security strategies at various times in their histories. Both countries have sought to engage the United States in their regions, to help balance against adversaries' "natural" military advantages. Israel and Pakistan have also hedged against an erosion of U.S. support by pursuing a nuclear deterrent whose "last resort" quality is particularly pronounced. Indeed, these strategies are probably linked: both countries may view their nuclear status as insuring that U.S. attention remains focused on their respective regions.[17] For Israeli and Pakistani leaders, U.S. involvement makes war less likely, serves to end wars more quickly if they erupt, and therefore decreases the likelihood that they will actually have to make good on their implicit threat to use nuclear weapons in a moment of national emergency.

India's nuclear posture has more of an expressly political purpose than either Israel's or Pakistan's. Indian analysts have been concerned not only with a possible military threat from China but also by the prospect of Chinese political intimidation. The consensus has been that, when New Delhi and Beijing get around to dealing with their territorial dispute, India will fare better from a position of very rough nuclear parity with China. There is also evidence that Indian leaders over the years have viewed the acquisition of nuclear weapons capabilities in terms of enhanced prestige, not unlike French statesmen did in the 1950s and 1960s. For an Indian strategic elite committed to achieving great power status, it is no coincidence that the world's five acknowledged nuclear weapons states are also the five permanent members of the United Nations Security Council.

Several factors may eventually lessen New Delhi's appetite for nuclear weapons. First, the role of nuclear weapons in world politics is being gradually delegitimized, as evidenced by the Strategic Arms Reduction Talks (START) process and the indefinite extension of the NPT in 1995; second, if nonnuclear Germany and Japan are added to the Security Council as permanent members, this will erode the apparent correlation between great power and nuclear status; and, third, India's relations with China have warmed considerably since the end of the Cold War. India's less pronounced preoccupation with the military deterrent aspects of nuclear capabilities, relative to Israel and Pakistan, may imply a somewhat greater willingness eventually to denuclearize, although the political climate in New Delhi today militates against such a course in the immediate future.

THE NATURE OF REGIONAL DETERRENCE

Opaque proliferants try to deter aggression by manipulating the ambiguity surrounding their nuclear capabilities. Each government does so in a different way. Although Israeli leaders steadfastly claim that they will not be the first to "introduce" nuclear weapons into the Middle East, this mantra has not prevented them from indulging in some fairly obvious nuclear signaling at moments of national peril. During the Gulf War, for example, Israel "made veiled but unmistakable threats to 'go nuclear' if Saddam Hussein made good on his threats to unleash chemical weapons on Israeli population centers."[18] In early 1990, after the Iraqi leader threatened to "scorch half of Israel" with chemical weapons, Israeli Prime Minister Yitzhak Shamir warned that Israel's response to such an attack would be "ayom venora"—"awesome and dreadful."[19] Just after the Iraqi invasion of Kuwait, in August, Shamir reiterated that "elements contemplating an attack on Israel know very well they will pay a terrible price should they attempt such an attack."[20] Shamir's nuclear signaling was buttressed by Israeli military censors, who were never as "blasé on the nuclear issue" as they were in 1990-91. Indeed, the Israeli press "began to refer to the country's nuclear option with unprecedented openness" as the censors' "insistence on the use of the euphemistic disclaimers eased significantly during the crisis."[21]

These examples of Israel's nuclear signaling raise the question of whether or not Israeli nuclear deterrence was "successful" during the Gulf War. In the judgment of Shai Feldman, Saddam Hussein was "probably" deterred from attacking Israel with ballistic missiles armed with chemical weapons "not by any certainty that Israel would retaliate with nuclear weapons, but rather by his inability to rule out this possibility."[22] Yair Evron argues that this explanation is "not necessarily valid," pointing out that there may have been "physical or technical reasons" for Iraqi restraint in using unconventional weapons. Evron also notes that, whatever the deterrent effect of Israeli nuclear capabilities, Iraq's behavior was almost certainly chastened by the deterrent signaling of U.S. officials, who "warned Iraq that any use of chemical weapons against any party, including Israel, would result in dreadful punishment."[23] Space limitations preclude a full discussion of Israeli nuclear deterrence in 1990-91, but the following "first cut" explanation seems plausible: (1) Saddam Hussein calculated that Israel would not respond to conventional ballistic missile attacks with nuclear weapons; (2) for Iraqi leaders any lesser Israeli response would have been worth the benefits to be gained from splintering the allied coalition; and (3) even if Saddam had the capability to mate chemical warheads with his SCUD missiles, he was deterred from launching them by the likelihood of high Israeli casualties and the consequent possibility of Israeli nuclear retaliation.

South Asia is also home to an opaque nuclear dialog. Having demonstrated its nuclear prowess in 1974, New Delhi's nuclear signaling has been relatively restrained. As India's preeminent nuclear strategists argue, "India has been content to demonstrate [its nuclear] capability, put basic infrastructure in place, and leave deterrence implicit and somewhat ambiguous."[24] Pakistani leaders, lacking demonstrable evidence of their nuclear muscle, have had to project their capabilities more forcefully. Pakistan's first official admission that it maintains unassembled nuclear weapons came in February 1992, when Foreign Secretary Shahryar Khan told the *Washington Post* that "the capability is there." Islamabad, he continued, possesses "elements which, if put together, would become a [nuclear] device."[25] Prime Minister Benazir Bhutto conveyed the essence of Pakistan's nuclear posture during her 1995 visit to the United States: "Our nuclear program is peaceful. But if the existence of our technology and perceived capability has served as a deterrent to India—as a deterrent to a proven nuclear power that has gone to war against us three times in the last forty-eight years—I certainly have no apologies to make, not in Islamabad, not in New Delhi, and not in Washington."[26]

South Asian nuclear deterrence was put to the test in the spring of 1990, during an Indo-Pakistani crisis over the disputed territory of Jammu and Kashmir (Kashmir, for short). As Islamic separatists escalated their insurgency against New Delhi in the Indian-held portion of Kashmir, Islamabad stepped up its support for the militants. A war of words broke out between two inexperienced leaders, Bhutto in Pakistan and Prime Minister Singh in India. This rhetorical skirmishing was accompanied by military movements that intelligence agencies on both sides of the border interpreted as threatening. As pressure mounted on the Indian government to destroy the Kashmiri insurgents' sources of support in Pakistan-held Kashmir, Prime Minister Singh warned Indians to prepare for war. The U.S. ambassador to New Delhi, William Clark, recalls that Pakistani leaders made "slightly veiled threats" to the effect that: "We have something that will make you very sorry." Indian officials replied: "If something happens, we will respond in the appropriate manner." Clark says, "I know how to read that: 'we've got one too.'"[27] The crisis eased in May, after President Bush dispatched a high-level U.S. delegation to the region. I have argued elsewhere that India and Pakistan were deterred from aggression in 1990 by each side's knowledge that the other was nuclear weapons–capable and that any direct military encounter between them might have escalated to the nuclear level.[28]

NUCLEAR ARMS CONTROL: BASIC POSITIONS

By definition opaque proliferants cannot have well-developed public positions on denuclearization, since they deny even possessing nuclear weapons. Still, the outlines of the Indian, Israeli, and Pakistani views of nuclear arms control in their respective regions can be inferred from their general nonproliferation policies. For Israel the bottom line in this regard is that movement on nuclear arms control in the Middle East can come only at the end of a comprehensive process of regional political reconciliation encompassing both formal peace agreements and verifiable reductions in conventional and unconventional military threats. As Gerald M. Steinberg writes: "The Israeli nuclear capability was developed to deter threats to national survival, and as long as the threats continue, and the legitimacy and permanence of Israel is questioned, nuclear weapons will continue to be seen as the ultimate guarantor against existential threats. Israeli policy places nuclear weapons at the end of the process, and as long as the Arab-Israeli conflict continues . . . Israel is likely to maintain its nuclear deterrent."[29]

Several factors combine to render Israeli denuclearization unlikely for the foreseeable future. First, Israeli leaders view arms control with profound skepticism. They doubt the efficacy of existing verification and inspection arrangements and, indeed, of international institutions in general. Iraq's success in evading the nuclear nonproliferation regime provides Israel with a compelling illustration of the dangers inherent in relying on multilateral nuclear security mechanisms.[30] Second, a comprehensive Middle East peace settlement may have paradoxical effects on Israeli security. Any such arrangement would likely involve the withdrawal of Israeli forces from the Golan Heights, yet this very retrenchment would further erode Israel's strategic depth and thus increase its reliance on deterrence as the bedrock of national security.[31] Under these circumstances Israel would be reluctant to cancel its "ultimate insurance policy." Third, the traditional challenge of nuclear breakout—the possibility that Libya, for example, might suddenly acquire nuclear weapons and threaten a disarmed Israel's national survival—has grown even more daunting with the disintegration of the Soviet Union and the prospect of "nuclear leakage" from the former Soviet republics.[32] The greater availability of nuclear materials and know-how on international markets gives Israeli leaders yet another good reason not to forgo nuclear weapons.

Denuclearization is only slightly more imaginable in South Asia's near-term future. India and Pakistan remain embroiled in a bitter cold war whose epicenter is the disputed territory of Kashmir. In addition to its substantial human toll, the simmering insurgency in Kashmir insures that few politicians in either New Delhi or Islamabad can publicly favor Indo-Pakistani detente; instead, the smart political course is to rail incessantly against the outrageous policies pursued by unscrupulous statesmen across the border. With daily headlines blaring the news of deaths and atrocities in Kashmir, the political climate could hardly be less conducive to nuclear arms control.[33]

What have been the standard Indian and Pakistani positions on denuclearization? New Delhi has for decades advocated global nuclear disarmament. Indian leaders denounce the NPT's division of treaty signatories into nuclear weapons states and nonnuclear weapons states as a repugnant form of "nuclear apartheid." From their perspective true global arms control requires replacing the NPT's discriminatory formula with a more egalitarian framework. Furthermore, India categorically rejects international efforts to achieve regional arms control in South Asia that do not require equivalent sacrifices on the part of China. In this respect, then, the road to denuclearization in South Asia passes through Beijing. This is all the more true because Islamabad claims that it will sign the NPT the same day India does. Indian analysts scoff that Pakistan's offer is pure rhetoric, intended to claim the diplomatic high ground in the knowledge that New Delhi will never accept its terms without nuclear concessions from China. In effect, the perceived Chinese threat has given New Delhi a convenient rationale to squelch efforts at regional arms control.

THE OPAQUE PROLIFERANTS' LIKELY RESPONSES TO AN EVOLVING VDNES REGIME

Before assessing the prospects for extending a VDNES regime to the Middle East and South Asia, it will be useful to reiterate the main assumptions structuring the following discussion. First, the relevant time frame is two to five decades into the future. Second, the analysis is predicated on the established nuclear weapons states reaching a comprehensive denuclearization agreement. For purposes of analytical clarity let us assume the following progress toward a global VDNES: first, China, France, Russia, the United Kingdom, and the United States have agreed in principle to maintain residual nuclear forces of no more than 500 weapons each; second, these weapons are to be disassembled, with their component parts made subject to a verifiable multilateral inspection regime; and third, the main challenge of incorporating the opaque proliferants into the VDNES regime is to formalize arms-control arrangements that have already evolved tacitly.

ISRAEL

Given their traditional ambivalence about nuclear weapons, Israeli leaders are likely to be cautiously receptive to the idea of joining a VDNES regime. Their initial interest will only be translated into action, however, if a number of stringent preconditions are met. Absent the following developments, any discussion of Israeli nuclear arms control is purely hypothetical. First, Israel will insist on extending the ongoing regional peace process to Syria and, by extension, Lebanon. True detente with Syria is Israel's minimum condition for pursuing more ambitious regional security arrangements. Second, Israel will likely demand agreement on a comprehensive package of confidence-building measures (CBMs) with its "inner circle" of historical adversaries: Egypt, Syria, Jordan, and the Palestinian Authority (or its successor). These might include crisis "hotlines," advance notification of military exercises, and, most important, agreements on allowable conventional force ratios.[34] A lessened Israeli reliance on nuclear deterrence must be matched by a corresponding increase in reassurance concerning conventional military threats; this would be all the more imperative with the return of the Golan Heights to Syria and the evolution of the Palestinian Authority to full statehood. Third, Israel may well request a formal defense treaty with the United States that would pledge well-defined U.S. security assistance in the event of future aggression against Israel. Here defensively oriented "external balancing" would help to compensate for the anticipated erosion of Israel's internal deterrent preparedness.

What would joining a VDNES regime entail on Israel's part? The answer to this question depends on the present deployment status of

Israel's nuclear arsenal. If Israel's nuclear weapons are assembled and operational, they would have to be disassembled and made subject to the same inspection arrangements agreed to by the overt nuclear weapons states. If, on the other hand, the weapons are unassembled, Israel would simply have to declare the quantitative and qualitative nature of its arsenal's component parts and then adhere to the new inspection regime. This would, of course, require an admission by Israeli leaders that they have been dissembling about their nuclear program all along. Israeli officials are likely to be unembarrassed by this prospect. For most of its existence as a modern nation-state Israel has been surrounded by profoundly hostile countries that have not even acknowledged its existence. Indeed, it has been repeatedly attacked by its adversaries, either singly or in various combinations. Moreover, the Holocaust provides Israeli leaders with sufficient evidence of man's inhumanity to man that they would have been imprudent not to have provided their nation with the ultimate insurance policy. Israel has not signed the NPT and is no more a nuclear outlaw than any of the "established" nuclear weapons states. The bottom line is that, given a realization of the necessary preconditions, Israel may be willing to lower its guard somewhat by giving up its nuclear ambiguity.[35]

Peace with Syria, regional CBMs, and a defensive alliance with the United States may provide Israel with sufficient confidence that its very existence can never again be threatened by its immediate neighbors. Israel could then begin a deliberate process of denuclearization as envisioned by the VDNES concept. Still, one significant threat would remain: the possibility of a "bolt from the blue" attack by Iran, Iraq, or Libya, with ballistic missiles armed with nuclear, biological, or chemical weapons. In all likelihood Israel's residual nuclear capability would deter Mu'ammar Qadhafi or Saddam Hussein from contemplating such attacks. Deterrence is never 100 percent guaranteed, however, and, if any state in the international system were to carry out a suicidal strike with a weapon of mass destruction, chances are it would come from this group, plus perhaps North Korea. Iraq and Iran exchanged ballistic missiles during their 1988 "War of the Cities"; they also used chemical weapons against each other on the battlefield. Saddam Hussein has deployed chemical weapons against Iraqi Kurds and launched ballistic missiles at Israeli cities. Libya fired missiles at U.S. forces on the Italian island of Lampedusa in retaliation for the 1986 bombing of Tripoli. In sum, Israel can never completely rule out the remote but real possibility of a devastating blow from some quarter.

Three additional security measures would serve to alleviate Israeli concerns about this threat. First, Israeli officials would be likely to insist on an explicit escape clause in the language detailing the rights and responsibilities of VDNES regime members. Such a provision would allow Israel to re-nuclearize if it perceived preparations for a missile attack by any of its more distant neighbors. Second, since virtual deterrence might not be robust enough to dissuade a radical adversary from striking hard at Israel, it may also insist on the enunciation of a U.S. extended deterrent threat to the relevant capitals. Because a U.S. nuclear reprisal would lack credibility in this situation, the threat might instead make reference to a number of conventional options, such as the decapitation of the aggressor's leadership or the destruction of its oil production facilities. Finally, as the ultimate hedge against a bolt-from-the-blue attack, Israel would probably view theater ballistic missile defenses as integral to its new security posture.

INDIA

In theory the preconditions for extending a VDNES regime to South Asia would be significantly less demanding than Israel's. (Indeed, South Asians could point with justifiable pride to the fact that the world's other nuclear powers are finally seeing reason and embracing a distinctively South Asian path to deterrence, in which nuclear weapons *capabilities* dissuade aggression but their unassembled state minimizes the possibility of accidents or nuclear terrorism.[36]) With agreement in principle between the established nuclear weapons states on the broad parameters of the VDNES, India's main precondition for joining such a regime will have been met. India has always touted a global approach to nuclear arms control, one that treats all nations equally, instead of dividing the world into nuclear haves and have-nots. A VDNES regime would link great power arms control (i.e., START) with nonproliferation norms (i.e., the NPT), in a sense leveling the playing field between all nuclear-capable countries.[37] From the standpoint of prestige India would be recognized as roughly at par with China in terms of nuclear (and, by extension, great power) status.

In strategic terms joining the VDNES regime would freeze India's nuclear deterrent capability at much lower levels than China's. Indian calculations would necessarily focus on how much nuclear capability is required to maintain deterrent credibility vis-à-vis a more potent nuclear China. Several factors suggest that India would feel secure with a relatively small virtual nuclear force, of perhaps fifty to sixty weapons. First, India has been satisfied for two decades with a minimal nuclear deterrent capability. New Delhi has never aimed to draw even with China in quantitative terms; rather, it has tried to achieve a very rough qualitative parity in warhead design and delivery capabilities. A VDNES regime would in essence formalize that qualitative equivalence. Although some analysts would argue that an Indian virtual nuclear arsenal of fifty weapons would be at risk of preemptive attack by a Chinese force of five hundred weapons, this thinking underestimates the robust deterrent effect of "first-strike uncertainty."[38]

Second, India's deterrent demands with respect to China have declined in recent years, due to a gradual thaw in relations between New Delhi and Beijing. The prospect of China attacking India with nuclear weapons is vanishingly small, especially given the fact that China has enunciated the world's most explicit nuclear "no-first-use" doctrine. Third, in terms of deterring a Chinese conventional attack, India is for all intents and purposes a different strategic entity than it was in 1962, when Chinese forces rolled into the subcontinent with ease. In addition to its virtual nuclear deterrent, New Delhi now deploys a vast, battle-tested army with some of the world's best-trained and -equipped mountain divisions. Chinese leaders undoubtedly know that a repeat of their 1962 invasion would result in huge casualties and little prospect of victory in any meaningful sense.

Turning to the west, the demands on Indian military preparedness are lower. The available evidence indicates that nuclear weapons deter war between India and Pakistan, which have successfully weathered two major crises in the last decade.[39] In the event that nuclear deterrence were to break down in a future crisis, India could defeat a Pakistani conventional invasion within a matter of weeks. In sum, the only way Islamabad can challenge New Delhi militarily is by continuing what it is already doing: that is, "bleeding" India in Kashmir. From India's perspective, though, resolution of the Kashmir conflict need not precede nuclear arms control, because New Delhi views the insurgency there as primarily a domestic challenge, albeit one exacerbated by Pakistani support for the guerrillas.

What would joining the VDNES regime entail on India's part? India would essentially freeze its nuclear program right where it is and agree to the same inspection regime as every other nuclear weapons state. India's nuclear force is believed to be unassembled but available for assembly on short notice, perhaps within a few days. In other words, India's nuclear deterrent is already virtual in nature. New Delhi has never denied that it has various component nuclear capabilities; all it would have to do now is provide sufficient detail about these capabilities to meet the transparency requirements of the new regime. Indian leaders may be willing to forgo the ambiguity surrounding their nuclear posture in exchange for a truly global approach to nuclear arms control, as envisioned in the VDNES concept.

India's other requirements would likely be minimal compared to Israel's. Regional CBMs, especially agreements on conventional military balances, would stabilize India's frontiers with both China and Pakistan, as well as help to rationalize Indian defense planning in an era of national belt tightening. Since such agreements would no doubt require tortuous negotiations, analysis of suitable conventional force ratios should begin sooner rather than later. New Delhi would no doubt reject the notion of receiving security guarantees from any of the established nuclear weapons states: great powers meet their own defense needs. Nor would India push for ballistic missile defenses. Not only would these be prohibitively expensive, but even the most hawkish Indian strategic analyst would admit that India faces little possibility of a bolt-from-the-blue attack from either China or Pakistan.

PAKISTAN

On paper Pakistan's only precondition for joining an evolving VDNES regime would be India's simultaneous agreement to do so. Islamabad has long maintained that it will match any arms-control measures accepted by New Delhi. As A. Q. Khan, the "father" of the Pakistani bomb, told an interviewer in 1993: "Time and time again our president and our prime minister have a hundred times told the whole world that if India signs the NPT then we will sign the NPT. If they will open their facilities today for inspection by foreign inspectors, we will open ours. From our side there is no hesitation."[40] This posture would presumably extend to the entire VDNES formula. If India were to call Pakistan's bluff, and it indeed turned out to be a bluff, Islamabad would come under enormous pressure from the other nuclear powers to adhere to the regime. Pakistan's only conceivable rationale for not doing so would be to claim that India remains unwilling to settle the Kashmir conflict. This might in turn bring increased great power pressure to bear on India for a resolution of the dispute, but any such pleas are likely to fall on deaf ears. Ideally, nuclear arms control in South Asia should proceed in tandem with overall political reconciliation, but it should not be held hostage to one of the world's last great intractable disputes.

In one sense joining a VDNES regime would represent no fundamental change for Pakistan. Islamabad claims to have halted its production of highly enriched uranium (heu) and nuclear weapons cores in 1991. If this is true, a VDNES agreement would simply formalize the extant situation. There is, however, one significant hurdle blocking Pakistani accession to any nuclear arms-control regime. Islamabad has a smaller fissile material stockpile than the other nuclear weapons states and thus prizes its ambiguity more highly than the others. Pakistan *may* have enough heu for six to eight nuclear weapons; then again, it may not—this is the essence of Pakistani opacity. Pakistani leaders would justifiably worry that disclosing their exact nuclear weapon potential might erode the deterrence they derive from ambiguity. Because of this, Islamabad is likely to push for keeping its precise nuclear capabilities a secret. In turn, Indian leaders might see the virtues of maintaining their own nuclear opacity with respect to both Pakistan and China. It would thus be worth exploring whether a distinctive regional mini-regime might be structured whereby impartial inspectors could periodically declare that neither India nor Pakistan had *exceeded* a certain preset limit on fissile material stockpiles without revealing the exact amount of material they have on hand. Absent such an arrangement, Islamabad would find it politically difficult to join the overall VDNES regime.

Another potential obstacle to Pakistani nuclear arms control is Islamabad's conventional military inferiority with respect to New Delhi. Injecting a greater time buffer into Pakistan's nuclear preparedness would reduce the possibility of accidents or unauthorized nuclear use, but it might also take some of the sting out of Pakistani nuclear deterrence. Because of this, Pakistan is likely to support the negotiation of explicit conventional-force ratios with India. Security along the Indo-Pakistani frontier would be immeasurably enhanced by each side's knowledge that the opposing army had capabilities sufficient to defend the border but not to launch a decisive offensive. Finally, Islamabad would probably try to elicit great power security guarantees, especially if Israel were to conclude a formal defense treaty with the United States. Although a similar alliance is out of the question for a variety of reasons, there might be a way to trigger great power intervention in the event of an escalating Indo-Pakistani crisis. Such an arrangement would chafe against Indian leaders' sensitivity to external involvement in regional security matters, but they would certainly prefer it to a resumption of the U.S.-Pakistani defense relationship of the 1950s and 1980s.

FINAL THOUGHTS

This essay has explored the political and strategic dynamics that would attend the extension of a VDNES regime to the Middle East and South Asia. The bottom line for India, Israel, and Pakistan—as for all nuclear weapons states contemplating the VDNES formula—will be the continued maintenance of deterrence vis-à-vis historical adversaries. If the opaque proliferants join a VDNES regime, will traditional rivals still believe them capable of launching nuclear strikes and thus be dissuaded from aggression? Or is virtual deterrence a wasting asset—a gun that fails to deter robbers because they know the safety catch is permanently engaged? The answer to this question will be crucial as nuclear arms controllers navigate their way through a more complicated world than existed during the bipolar Cold War. To put it bluntly, we would not want to succeed in making a nuclear catastrophe less likely at the cost of making major conventional war more likely.

Two considerations seem especially relevant in assessing the prospects for integrating India, Israel, and Pakistan into a VDNES regime. First, it is important for U.S. analysts to bear in mind that, from the standpoint of resources and technology, nuclear deterrence is not easily replaced in the case of the opaque proliferants. While U.S. strategists can contemplate deterring adversaries with stealthy combat aircraft and cruise missiles, most high-technology conventional deterrence options are not open to less-developed nations such as India and Pakistan. As a result, these countries are likely to view nuclear weapons as cheap political and military "equalizers" well into the future. Second, U.S. arms controllers should remember that, while our transcendent security threat has evaporated, the opaque proliferants still face their traditional security dilemmas. Indeed, the end of *the* Cold War has in some cases exacerbated *regional* cold wars, most notably in South Asia. The loss of superpower patronage has made both India and Pakistan less secure than they were in the 1980s. As a consequence, they are as unlikely to give up their nuclear deterrent forces as were the United States and the Soviet Union during the Cold War.

These observations suggest that nuclear arms control is a long way off in the very regions many U.S. experts believe are most vulnerable to a nuclear catastrophe. While this may be true, there are also positive trends under way: the START process; the indefinite extension of the NPT; nuclear renunciations by Argentina, Brazil, South Africa, Ukraine, Belarus, Kazakhstan, and (tentatively) North Korea; a global consensus on the need for a comprehensive nuclear test ban; and an emerging consensus on the desirability of a fissile material production cut off. Admittedly, much remains to be done. In particular, the START II ratification process must be reinvigorated, and the United States and Russia must begin to incorporate China in the next phase of great power nuclear arms control. As noted in this essay, China's inclusion in a global denuclearization process is crucial for regional arms control in South Asia. With China on board, the vision of a truly comprehensive VDNES regime would assume greater clarity.

In the meantime two areas require sustained attention from strategic analysts. First, we need to push relentlessly for solutions to underlying political disputes in the so-called conflict-prone regions. While the Middle East has seen marked progress on this front in recent years, South Asia has not. If and when the moment for global denucle-arization arrives, success will be more likely in these regions if their core political conflicts have eased. Second, it would behoove us now to start thinking through the security implications of a denuclearized world. In such a scenario countries will have to rely more heavily on conventional means to meet their security needs. Unfortunately, calculations of conventional military balances are notoriously imprecise. Indeed, some have characterized the phenomenon of war itself as a disagreement over relative military capabilities, the implication being that, if two sides were fully cognizant of the "real" military balance between them, the weaker side would always prefer to appease the stronger rather than fight.[41] In regions that have been especially war prone—such as the Middle East and South Asia—agreements on stable conventional military balances may provide a buffer against the proliferation of major conventional wars in a postnuclear era. A VDNES is decades away, but there is plenty of scope in the meantime for preparatory research and analysis.

NOTES

1. The concept of opaque proliferation was first introduced by Benjamin Frankel, in "Notes on the Nuclear Underworld," *National Interest*, no. 9 (Fall 1987): 122-26. It was more fully developed in Avner Cohen and Benjamin Frankel, "Opaque Nuclear Proliferation," in "Opaque Nuclear Proliferation: Methodological and Policy Implications," special issue, ed. Benjamin Frankel, *Journal of Strategic Studies* 13, no. 3 (September 1990): 14-44.

2. I am indebted to James M. Goldgeier and Michael McFaul for this overall conceptualization of the international system. See "A Tale of Two Worlds: Core and Periphery in the Post–Cold War Era," *International Organization* 46, no. 2 (Spring 1992): 467-91.

3. The NPT signatories agreed in 1968 "to pursue negotiations in good faith on effective measures relating to cessation of the nuclear arms race at an early date and to nuclear disarmament, and on a treaty on general and complete disarmament under strict and effective international control." See Leonard S. Spector and Mark G. McDonough, with Evan S. Medeiros, *Tracking Nuclear Proliferation: A Guide in Maps and Charts, 1995* (Washington, D.C.: Carnegie Endowment for International Peace, 1995): 23.

4. Frankel, "Nuclear Underworld," 123-24.

5. Cohen and Frankel, "Opaque Nuclear Proliferation," 17.

6. Ibid., 21.

7. Aziz Haniffa, "CIA on India's Navy and A-Plans," *India Abroad*, March 5, 1993, 10.

8. Cohen and Frankel, "Opaque Nuclear Proliferation," 22.

9. Ibid., 21.

10. Neil Joeck, "Tacit Bargaining and Stable Proliferation in South Asia," *Journal of Strategic Studies* 13, no. 3 (September 1990): 77-91.

11. On this point, see Susan M. Burns, "Preventing Nuclear War: Arms Management," in *Nuclear Proliferation in South Asia: The Prospects for Arms Control*, ed. Stephen Philip Cohen (Boulder: Westview Press 1991): 95.

12. Spector and McDonough, *Tracking Nuclear Proliferation*, 135-36; Leonard S.

Spector, *The Undeclared Bomb* (Cambridge, Mass: Ballinger, 1988): 48.

13. Mitchell Reiss, *Bridled Ambition: Why Countries Constrain Their Nuclear Capabilities* (Washington, D.C.: Woodrow Wilson Center Press, 1995): 185, 192.

14. "India, Pakistan Missile Race Is Serious Concern, Say Officials," United States Information Agency Wireless File, NEA 509, March 10, 1995.

15. Avner Cohen, *Toward a New Middle East: Rethinking the Nuclear Question,* DACS Working Paper (Cambridge: Defense and Arms Control Studies Program, Massachusetts Institute of Technology, 1994): 9. For a more detailed account of Israeli leaders' strategic reasoning in the 1950s, see Yair Evron, *Israel's Nuclear Dilemma* (Ithaca: Cornell University Press, 1994): 5-7, 42.

16. Leonard S. Spector, with Jacqueline R. Smith, *Nuclear Ambitions: The Spread of Nuclear Weapons, 1989–90* (Boulder: Westview Press, 1990): 64.

17. I am indebted to Stephen P Cohen for this observation.

18. Robert E. Harkavy, "After the Gulf War: The Future of Israeli Nuclear Strategy," *Washington Quarterly* 14, no. 3 (Summer 1991): 161.

19. Avner Cohen, "Nuclear Opacity and the Israeli Press: The Gulf Drift," *New Outlook* (Tel Aviv) 34, no. 5 (September-October 1991): 20-21.

20. Evron, *Israel's Nuclear Dilemma,* 208.

21. Cohen, "Nuclear Opacity and the Israeli Press," 19, 21.

22. Shai Feldman, "Middle East Nuclear Stability: The State of the Region and the State of the Debate," *Journal of International Affairs* 49, no. 1 (Summer 1995): 217.

23. See Evron's thoughtful discussion of these and related issues in *Israel's Nuclear Dilemma,* 213.

24. M. Granger Morgan, K. Subrahmanyam, K. Sundarji, and Robert M. White, "India and the United States," *Washington Quarterly* 18, no. 2 (Spring 1995): 164.

25. R. Jeffrey Smith, "Pakistan Can Build One Nuclear Device, Foreign Official Says," *Washington Post,* February 7, 1992.

26. Thomas W. Lippman and R. Jeffrey Smith, "Bhutto: Deliver F-16s or Return Payment," *Washington Post,* April 11, 1995.

27. Interview, 1995.

28. Devin T. Hagerty, "Nuclear Deterrence in South Asia: The 1990 Indo-Pakistani Crisis," *International Security* 20, no. 3 (Winter 1995/96).

29. Gerald M. Steinberg, "Israeli Arms Control Policy: Cautious Realism," *Journal of Strategic Studies* 17, no. 2 (June 1994): 11.

30. Gerald M. Steinberg, "Middle East Arms Control and Regional Security," *Survival* 36, no. 1 (Spring 1994): 130.

31. Steinberg, "Israeli Arms Control Policy," 4.

32. Feldman, "Middle East Nuclear Stability," 211-12.

33. For a concise overview of the war in Kashmir, see Devin T. Hagerty, "Kashmir and the Nuclear Question," in *Pakistan: 1995,* eds. Charles H. Kennedy and Rasul Baksh Rais (Boulder: Westview Press, 1995):159-92.

34. For a concise description of CBMs that might be utilized in the Middle East, including some discussion of measures already implemented there, see Michael Krepon, ed., *A Handbook of Confidence-Building Measures for Regional Security*, 2d ed. (Washington, D.C.: Henry L. Stimson Center, 1995).

35. Of course, the Arab states are likely to insist on complete Israeli de-nuclearization as a condition for a comprehensive regional peace. As a compromise, Israel might then offer to treat the VDNES as a temporary phase (of perhaps ten years) in the transition to a nuclear-free Middle East. That, in turn, raises new strategic issues that are beyond the scope of this essay.

36. See Devin T. Hagerty, "The Power of Suggestion: Opaque Proliferation, Existential Deterrence, and the South Asian Nuclear Arms Competition," *Security Studies* 2, (Spring/Summer 1993): 256-83; and George Perkovich, "A Nuclear Third Way," *Foreign Policy*, no. 91 (Summer 1993): 85-104.

37. Of course, this raises the question of whether a VDNES regime would simply shift the line between the nuclear haves and have-nots, to incorporate eight "legitimate" nuclear weapons states instead of five. The relationship between the NPT regime and a future VDNES regime is well worth exploring but beyond the scope of this essay.

38. On this concept, see Hagerty, "Nuclear Deterrence in South Asia."

39. For an examination of Indian and Pakistani crisis behavior in South Asia's nuclear era, see Devin T. Hagerty, "The Theory and Practice of Nuclear Deterrence in South Asia" (Ph.D. diss., University of Pennsylvania, 1995).

40. Simon Henderson, "'We Can Do It Ourselves,'" *Bulletin of the Atomic Scientists* (September 1993): 27.

41. See, for example, Geoffrey Blainey, *The Causes of War* (New York: The Free Press, 1973): 108-24.

FOURTEEN

VNAs AND THE
CONTEMPORARY
LATENT WEAPON STATE

BRAD ROBERTS

IN SPECULATING ABOUT ALTERNATIVE NUCLEAR FUTURES, attention tends to focus on how the declared nuclear weapons states and especially the United States might adjust to new strategic realities. Less attention is paid to how the undeclared nuclear weapons states might respond. Little or no attention is paid to states that have not so far played in the nuclear game. But many of these states have the potential to do so. Moreover, a far larger number of states has the capacity to make biological and chemical weapons, both of which can credibly threaten massively destructive effects and thus have strategic leverage in some ways analogous to that of nuclear weapons. The narrow focus on the declared nuclear weapons states thus misses important parts of the larger picture.

This chapter focuses on this last category of states—those with a latent capability to make nuclear, biological, or chemical (NBC) weapons. It has two purposes. The first is to assess how their interests and perceptions might be shaped by a move toward virtual nuclear arsenals (VNAs) by the declared nuclear weapons states. Toward this end this essay begins with a depiction of the contemporary latent state phenomenon and then explores how different types of latent states might be influenced by VNAs. The second purpose is to utilize the experience of these states to generate some propositions about how an international system dominated by virtual weapons states might function. The phenomenon of latency in the existing international system offers some useful benchmarks against which to test core propositions of this study and thus serves as a useful supplement to Cold War experience, which otherwise dominates the thinking of most nuclear analysts. Thus, this essay draws some general lessons and offers some speculative thinking about implications.

THE CONTEMPORARY LATENT WEAPON STATE

Latent military capability is an established fact of the existing international system. Yet the existence of a tier of states technically capable of making weapons offering them significant military options in war and political leverage in peace is hardly noticed by political scientists or policymakers.[1]

In fact, this tier of states is sizable. In the nuclear domain the 5 to 9 states equipped with such weapons contrasts sharply with the 40 or so deemed technically capable of building them and the 65 states that operate nuclear reactors;[2] the emergence in the 1980s of at least 15 new exporters of nuclear technologies attests to this diffusion.[3] Moreover, 22 countries currently possess or control separated plutonium.[4] In the biological domain, the 10 to 12 states rumored to have weapons programs contrasts with the virtually global diffusion of the biomedical and fermentation-based industries that put this capability into the hands of many (a process greatly accelerated by the biotechnology revolution of the last two decades).[5] In the chemical domain the 20 to 24 states with weapons programs contrasts with the existence in most countries of the world of petrochemical, fertilizer, and other general industrial facilities in which chemical warfare agents could be produced.[6] This points to the conclusion that only a small percentage of the states technically capable of making NBC weapons have actually chosen to do so.

Moreover, a significant number of states that have built weapons of mass destruction (WMD) have now abandoned or forsworn specific WMD options. This is most striking in the nuclear domain, in which South Africa has declared and destroyed a small nuclear arsenal, while

Argentina and Brazil have made common cause to close nuclear weapon programs, and Belarus, Kazakhstan, and Ukraine have relinquished nuclear assets of Soviet genesis.[7] The biological domain presents similar examples, as in recent decades the United States, the United Kingdom, and France, for example, have abandoned such weapons. So too in the area of chemical weapons, as the United States and other countries have begun to eliminate such weapons under the Chemical Weapons Convention. Of course, many other states participate in the relevant treaty regimes to formalize their abstention from weapons-related activities in these areas.

Looking to the future, it seems likely that the number of states capable on a technical basis of building NBC weapons will only continue to grow. A globalizing economy characterized by rapid technology diffusion, open access to scientific information, and transnational corporations increasingly supersedes the old international economy of trade among states in manufactured goods and raw materials.[8] Moreover, within this economy the very notion of dual-use materials and technologies is changing as the high-technology sectors of the civilian economy provide an increasing number of spin-offs for military applications, a reversal of past patterns.[9]

What picture emerges from these statistics and trends? The means to produce high-leverage weapons have diffused far more broadly than the weapons themselves. Barring a collapse of the global economy, this process seems certain to continue. The orientation of these states toward the weapons potential inherent in their economies and technical infrastructures seems likely to feature prominently in a VNA world, given their salience for issues of arms control, deterrence, defense, and aggression.

To be sure, not all latent states are the same. Some are relatively closer, from a technical point of view, to having deployed weapons than others. Japan, for example, has very strong latent capabilities; indeed, its nuclear weapons capability is often characterized as robust to the point of being virtual or nearly extant. Some states that might possess warhead acumen could not readily assemble the requisite delivery systems, command and control capabilities, and doctrine and training to make readily effective crisis or wartime use of such weapons; this is particularly true in the chemical and biological domains. Many latent weapons states exploit dual-use technologies solely for peaceful, commercial purposes, especially in the biological domain, in which medical or commercial research utilizes technologies and materials sensitive from a military point of view. Some exploit them for military purposes as well, whether for defensive purposes (e.g., vaccine production, as in the UK) or offensive ones (e.g., developmental programs aimed at expanding weapons competence and creating future military options, as in Iran). But, as varied as they may be in terms of weapons competence, these states share the essential attribute of being able to assemble high-leverage weapons largely on the basis of national will.

Such latency is not entirely novel. Historically, few states have mobilized their full military potential for total war. On the other hand, never before have so many states or such a large proportion of the membership of the interstate system been able to build high-leverage weaponry for strategic warfare or to do so as quickly as possible in the dual-use domains. Mobilization of full military potential seems to require a particular set of motivations and economic well-being. That these coalesce relatively rarely should ease our concerns about a future characterized by a quite permissive technology environment. But that they do occasionally coalesce should remind us of our stake in international stability.

LATENT STATES AND VIRTUAL DETERRENCE

What if the United States and the other nuclear weapons states were to join this club, by dismantling their active nuclear arsenals and focusing their nuclear competence on possible future reconstitution and their military competence on conventional weaponry? What would be the impact on the existing latent states?

In seeking an answer to this question, it is useful to disaggregate the contemporary latent state phenomenon and to consider how each category of state might react to VNAs among the nuclear weapons states. This analysis identifies five categories of latent states, each motivated by a different set of security needs and perceptions: (1) states whose latency derives from expectations of a benign international environment; (2) states facing national security problems, for which weapons of mass destruction are deemed irrelevant; (3) states that might deem WMD desirable but which find them too costly; (4)

states whose latency appears short-lived; and (5) states whose latency is made possible largely by the U.S. nuclear umbrella. Each presents different insights into whether and in what conditions a move to a virtual arsenal would be desirable.

The first category consists of those states that have refrained from turning weapons potential into weapons prowess simply because they exist in a regional environment that is benign and believe existing international institutions, broadly defined, to be in the service of their national interests. This category includes states as varied as Portugal and Singapore, for example, both of which possess an economy with high-technology, dual-use sectors and both essentially unthreatened by a military aggressor.

A decision by the United States and the other nuclear weapons states to forswear deployed nuclear arsenals would likely have little or no impact on such states. Their expectations about the durability of their benign environment might conceivably be shaken, however, if such a step were perceived by them to indicate also the loss of benign U.S. influence in world affairs and a weakening of collective security and multilateralism more generally. Portugal, for example, might fear the consequences for European security of a realignment of nuclear influence in Europe and hints of possible U.S. disengagement. Singapore might fear the consequences for East Asian security of VNAs, if it perceives an active arsenal as essential to the U.S. security role in the region and to the balancing effect of U.S. power in the East Asian great power mix. In general, this type of state might have orientations to the nuclear question not anticipated by its nonnuclear status. It may matter significantly to the state that the major powers look unassailable or which powers seem to hold nuclear advantages. It seems unlikely that such states would respond to a VNA regime with weapons programs of their own. But they might see some utility, which they do not today, in research programs that strengthen their mastery of commercial nuclear, biological, or chemical technologies as hedges against a long-term decay of the interstate system.

The second category consists of those states facing tangible challenges to national security for which WMD responses are not commensurate. Many, if not most, states of the world fall into this category. For many developing countries the primary security challenge is domestic and associated with protecting the state from the challenges of "state building"; for such states NBC weapons offer little, except perhaps in the hands of tyrants willing to use them to expunge domestic threats to authority (Saddam Hussein's authorization of chemical attacks on Kurdish villages in the 1980s comes to mind). Other developing countries face the challenges posed by neighbors willing to brandish or use conventional military forces to press claims arising from contested borders. For many developed countries, such as Sweden or Switzerland, the commitment to modern and robust militaries does not mean also an interest in the acquisition of NBC weapons. For states in this category weapons of mass destruction would invite a dangerous escalation of conflict with their neighbors, in the form of either an unintended and thus undesirable arms race or a war in which the costs are grossly disproportionate to the issues in dispute.

A decision by the nuclear weapons states to forswear their arsenals might well be welcomed by these states. They might see it as consistent with the drift of history away from total warfare among developed countries. They might well look upon the arsenals of the nuclear weapons states as little more than expensive symbols of a time now past when those states were thrust into the center of world affairs by events. Or they might see actions by the nuclear weapons states as largely incidental to their own security needs or interests. Or they might fear the long-term destabilizing consequences of actions by the nuclear weapons states that might seem to call into question the credibility of their security guarantees or of collective security principles and thus move into category 5 described in the pages that follow.

A distinct subcategory of this second group consists of those states, noted earlier, that have abandoned nuclear weapons and nuclear weapons programs because they were deemed unnecessary for the security challenges of a new era—Argentina, Brazil, and South Africa, for example. Their experience is particularly germane to the study of a similar step by the declared nuclear weapons states. Three aspects stand out as especially noteworthy. One is the propensity in each society to accept certain risks in the nuclear domain in exchange for other perceived benefits, a propensity born of the emergence of a generation of political leaders committed to national renewal and desirous of more extensive integration into the global economic system and the international political community. Another is the capacity for these states to create mechanisms for joint risk taking with erstwhile adversaries, mechanisms that mix reliance on traditional arms-control measures such as the Nuclear Nonproliferation Treaty (NPT) with experimental approaches, such as the Argentine-Brazilian nuclear accord. The third is the apparent belief, in capitals in which disarmament steps have been taken, that residual potentials for future weapons programs are an adequate buffer against the possibility that accords may not be honored, and helpful in dissuading a potential opponent from taking such steps. This experience suggests that a willingness to engage in prudent risk taking, to experiment with various arms-control mechanisms, and to view residual capabilities as offering deterrent or security benefits could be critical determinants of any future decisions by nuclear-armed states to abandon ready arsenals.

The third category consists of those states that have determined nuclear, biological, or chemical weapons to be too costly to acquire, despite their perceived utility for some problem of national security. This category includes, for example, Ukraine, a state that perceives a threat to its security from Russia for which nuclear weapons might be seen as useful. But it has opted not to hold onto the nuclear weapons inherited from the Soviet arsenal because its need to achieve a stable and cooperative relationship with the West outweighs its need to hedge against Russian armed aggression at this time. This category may also include Iran, a state that perceives strategic deterrence as of growing interest but which appears to have chosen to move gradually to assemble the ingredients of a future nuclear weapons competence rather than to seek nuclear deployment on an urgent basis, which might involve the cost of a backlash within and beyond the region that would harm Iranian interests.

A decision by the nuclear weapons states to renounce their arsenals would likely influence the thinking of such states in contradictory ways. Some might see such a step as removing even residual military threats, although in the case of Ukraine the Russian threat it perceives is as much conventional as nuclear. Others might see such a step as greatly reducing the cost they might expect to pay to acquire and use such weapons, if they come to believe that the major powers are no longer willing to use military force to insure compliance with existing international agreements and norms.

The fourth category of latent weapons states consists of those states whose latency may prove short-lived—in other words, states actively seeking to turn weapons potential into weapons prowess but not yet across the threshold. In the NBC domain at least twenty states are rumored to have weapons-development programs. There is no authoritative list of such states, as most publicly deny the existence of such programs, and the list changes depending on whether one focuses on nuclear, biological, or chemical matters.

Some of these research and development programs may be aimed not directly at deployed weapons but at creating the capacity to deploy such weapons should future circumstances require it. Whether or where Iran fits into this category is a hotly debated subject. It is likely that many of the biological warfare programs of proliferation concern fall into the latter category. Among this category of states are likely to be many different degrees of proximity to the weaponization threshold.

In the current international climate a decision by the nuclear weapons states to forswear their arsenals would likely significantly increase interest within these states in exploiting their weapons potential to create WMD arsenals. In the Middle East, for example, some of the programs seem to be held in check by a belief that such deployments could precipitate an international crisis and confrontation with the United Nations Security Council and/or the United States. A move to VNAs might be perceived as signaling a weakening will among the established nuclear powers to face such crises. This might fuel the ambition of regional hegemons. It might also drive states likely to be the victim of aggression to seek counters of their own, as a result of their diminished reliance on external assistance. Thus, it seems reasonable to anticipate a growing number of research and development programs on weapons of mass destruction as well as an increasing sophistication and scale of those programs if the decision to forswear arsenals suggests to these states growing uncertainty about the drift of international events and the possible emergence of predatory states capable of exploiting their weapons potential for purposes of aggression.

The fifth category consists of those whose capability is latent largely because of U.S. security guarantees. Japan, Germany, and South Korea are conspicuous today as states capable on a strictly technical basis, and sooner or later, of assembling weapons of mass destruction but choosing not to do so. Why not? Because their alliance relations with the United States, backed by the U.S. nuclear umbrella, free them of the obligation of responding to the perceived threats to their security with national WMD programs.

A decision by the United States to forswear its nuclear arsenal would likely raise questions in these countries about the nature of U.S. power and of the U.S. commitment to their security.[10] Debates on these questions might be the catalyst for a decision by these states to move to acquire their own arsenals. They might choose to do so because they fear that such a U.S. step implies a faltering U.S. commitment to active engagement and cooperative defense, thus raising doubts about the credibility of U.S. security guarantees. Or they may take such guarantees as credible but fear that a United States extending deterrence primarily by conventional means would find the cost too prohibitive or would be unable to project power with the speed and decisiveness apparently unique to nuclear weapons. Were these states to build their own arsenals, the implications within and beyond the regions where these states are located could be far-reaching. Japanese acquisition of a nuclear weapons arsenal would cause shock-waves through the region, raising old questions about its ambitions to hegemony and new questions about how the major powers in the region can accommodate one anothers' ambitions. German acquisition would cause similar shock waves and seems possible only in a context in which collective defense and an opening to the East have passed from the scene. South Korean acquisition would signal a loss of faith in the U.S. security role and raise analogous regional questions about how to juggle competitive nuclear interests. Neighboring states might well respond with weaponization of their own, whether in the nuclear, biological, or chemical domains.

But these results of a U.S. commitment to VNAs are not foreordained. Perceptions and interests might change in coming years. U.S. allies might come to believe that U.S. guarantees are credible even absent an on-call U.S. nuclear force, given the other advantages of power enjoyed by the United States and its both de jure and de facto interest in the security of those allies. In other words, they might be confident that a U.S. "bomb in the basement" is good enough. Or they might come to believe that there is no realistic threat to their survival requiring a countervailing strategic threat of whatever genesis. Or, alternatively, they might come to believe that even a United States still in possession of nuclear weapons might not be sufficiently reliable as a security partner and thus opt to make weapons of their own. Or they might come to place higher emphasis on their own latent capabilities as a dissuasive factor of potential aggression against them, perhaps in conjunction with continued U.S. guarantees or perhaps not. But in the mid-1990s the continued strong conviction in each country that the U.S. relationship and umbrella are essential to their security implies that a U.S. commitment to renounce its nuclear weapons could have destabilizing implications where it offers extended deterrence. Such implications are largely unanticipated by the traditional devotees of nuclear disarmament.[11]

The future mix of offense and defense in the U.S. strategic posture is likely to have an impact on the thinking of U.S. allies on these questions. That thinking cannot be predicted with certainty, given the variety of interests and perspectives in the debate on defenses and the likely relevance of catalytic events in shaping both. Some allies may come to believe that a United States invulnerable to missile attack is also a security guarantor that cannot be blackmailed into inaction by a potential aggressor, thus easing their concerns about the U.S. commitment to them and perhaps making them more willing to support VNAs. But other allies might believe that strategic defenses will reinforce isolationist and/or unilateralist tendencies in Washington, thereby weakening alliance relations and diminishing the credibility of U.S. guarantees, whatever happens to active nuclear forces.[12]

In surveying the various extended deterrence roles of U.S. nuclear weapons, a question arises about whether U.S. nuclear weapons serve today only to address nuclear problems. The evidence suggests that they do not. In Europe, U.S. nuclear guarantees historically have had as much to do with the conventional imbalance as with the nuclear one. Also, less well noticed but equally important was the role of nuclear weapons in deterring chemical and biological attack by the Soviet Union and Warsaw Pact.[13] Today, the U.S. nuclear commitment to NATO has as much to do with deterring potential challenges to the status quo from around NATO's periphery as with old problems of central strategic deterrence, challenges by states like Iraq or Libya rumored to be armed with weapons of many different kinds. In South Korea U.S. nuclear guarantees are intended to deter attack from North Korea, attack that might be made with any mix of conventional and unconventional weapons. And in regional contingencies more generally U.S. forces have to contend with a variety of conventional and unconventional threats, some of which might coalesce in ways that make nuclear use by the

United States seem necessary and just.[14] Thus in each region potential nuclear threats constitute only a portion of the larger security challenge that U.S. guarantees, and by implication nuclear capabilities, are intended to address.

This disaggregation of the latent-state phenomenon points to one basic conclusion: significant repercussions among the latent weapons states would accompany any decision by the United States to move to a virtual nuclear arsenal, at least in the present international setting in which U.S. security guarantees play an important role and in which extant arsenals are valued for the existential quality of deterrence they are seen to provide. Particularly important would be the reactions of the recipients of U.S. security guarantees as well as the targets of those guarantees. In the current setting VNAs would likely raise questions for both about the credibility of those guarantees.

But the very complexity of the relationship between U.S. power, interests, regional commitments, and its weapons prowess makes it difficult to predict with certainty the result of U.S. choices. It seems reasonable to conclude that some latent states would welcome VNAs as a step in the "right direction." But others would likely view VNAs as a step in the wrong direction, that is, toward heightened nuclear insecurity.

But this very uncertainty means that a decision to eschew VNAs for the foreseeable future might also have repercussions among the latent states not anticipated today. Many U.S. allies might find little to protest in U.S. nuclear retention from a deterrence point of view. But many are also committed to the strongest possible actions under the NPT to implement Article VI commitments to move toward a nuclear-free future. Failure by the United States to honor its NPT commitments could add to friction in U.S. alliances, especially if deployed U.S. nuclear weapons are seen as ever less relevant to the security needs of those alliances. Such failure might also induce some states possessing latent capabilities to build up NBC arsenals as a way to contest the status quo and a distribution of power internationally, as codified in the NPT, that they perceive as antiquated and unjust.

This disaggregation of the latent-state phenomenon points also to a couple of significant implications. One is that the nuclear weapons problem cannot be separated analytically, politically, or militarily from the larger strategic context. Only in the minds of the nuclear disarmament community are nuclear weapons and the relations among nuclear arsenals discrete and isolated things. Nuclear weapons coexist with other weapons of significant strategic leverage, including other weapons of mass destruction as well as massed conventional weapons. The political realities they create coexist with those derived from the changing relations of major and minor powers as well as the changing nature of power in an evolving interstate system. Getting it wrong on nuclear weapons by treating them as divorced from these other factors may well magnify these other dimensions. The postnuclear era might well be the era of biological weapons; it might be an era in which any state can veto the use of force by any other; or it might be an era in which regional and global patterns of cooperation succumb to the armament programs of "prudent hedgers." Getting it right on nuclear weapons, by integrating the nuclear problem into the larger security framework, may well lead to an era in which all strategic weapons and WMD capabilities are ever more marginalized as historical forces.

The other implication is that in a world of latent weapons states and virtual nuclear arsenals, problems of war and peace will not have gone away; they will have changed. Issues of nuclear deterrence and of deterrence more generally will remain, but in new forms. As Martin Wight, among many others, has long ago observed, "disarmament does not eliminate military potential; it changes it."[15] Might reliance on reconstitution capability and conventional means suffice for the challenges of deterrence and war fighting in the future (which is, of course, a different question from whether they would suffice for the past or for present challenges)?[16] And, because deterrence is a matter of perception, would people by and large believe it to be sufficient? This review suggests only that, on the basis of the contemporary latent-state phenomenon, latent capability does not necessarily or automatically translate into stable, if nonexistential, deterrence. Among the existing latent weapons states not many appear to rely on the weapons potential inherit in their own societies and economies to deter aggression by a potential adversary. In the nuclear domain Ukraine is perhaps the only state in this category. In the chemical and biological domains no example comes readily to mind. Achieving relationships of power and deterrence derived from latent capabilities thus seems likely to require significant departures in thinking in the United States and beyond about how and when military responses to aggression are marshaled.

A FUTURE INTERNATIONAL SYSTEM OF VNAs AND LATENT WEAPONS STATES

The existence in the present international system of a significant number of latent states should also help us to understand something about how a descendant system, characterized by virtual deterrence among the existing nuclear weapons states as well as an even larger number of technically capable states, might function. This section of the paper identifies three features of such a system: (1) strong incentives to cooperate on economic and political matters that will increasingly constrain freedom of maneuver on military matters; (2) the inherent instability related to the potential for wildfire-like proliferation; and (3) the diminished role of the great powers.

The steady diffusion of NBC latency is, as previously argued, tied inextricably to a changing global economy and to the processes of economic, technical, and political development through which most states of the world are passing. This fact complicates the task of reaping military advantages. This economy is by its very nature interdependent and interpenetrating. Capital, technology, and expertise are available today largely in international markets. States desirous of improved economic performance, greater prosperity, and long-term development must find that their freedom for maneuver in the military domain is limited. This is true only to the extent that norms have formed guiding the application of dual-use technologies and materials. In fact, these norms do exist, as codified in the form of the global treaty regimes to control nuclear, biological, and chemical weapons. These norms are not universally held, nor consistently policed by the international community. But they are very broadly held, and the major powers take a special interest in their effective functioning, along with key states in places like Europe, Latin America, and Southeast Asia. Actions inconsistent with those norms and established legal undertakings not to pursue weapons of mass destruction generally result in growing isolation from the global economy and thus a cost in economic and developmental terms. This is a cost that some may be willing to pay in the short term but few seem likely to be able to sustain politically in the long term. This may be part of the reason that there are only a handful of so-called rogue states today.

The world is growing more interdependent and interpenetrated not just economically but politically. States desirous of building coalitions with others, deepening the bases of domestic political stability, and invoking international institutions in service of their national interests may find that their ability to do so is increasingly impaired if they are not party to global norms, institutions, and legal mechanisms. Belligerent rhetoric and behavior might well cast those states in the role of aggressor or renegade, to be feared, not welcomed.

Militarily, too, the desire of most states not to rely on total war strategies to meet existing threats to national security suggests a growing reliance on cooperative and comprehensive approaches to security. Suggestive of these interconnections is the view attributed to former Argentine President Carlos Menem that abandonment of an Argentine nuclear option was in the interest of his nation because it was better to be the last member of the First World than the first member of the Third.

The point here is not that a globalizing economy and global political mechanisms prevent states from acting independently. To be sure, important limits remain on the ability of the United States and the international community to utilize political and economic sticks and carrots to constrain the security behavior of especially powerful states or willful leaders. Rather, the point here is that the globalizing economy and the spread of liberal political values push back these limits. The incentives to cooperate internationally are increasing. The costs of not cooperating are also increasing. Few states want to contemplate the possible collapse of an international system, the stability of which is essential to their economic well-being, political stability, and freedom from the threat of strategic warfare. Most perceive at least some stake in the credibility of both collective security and the guarantees of major powers.

There is, of course, no guarantee that these incentives will continue to operate as described here. A catalytic event of some kind may drive states back to behavior dominated by the self-help principle. The point is simply that an international system characterized by large numbers of states whose well-being depends on cooperation is not a system in which those states are likely to find it easy to turn NBC weapons potential into deployed forces.

A second feature of the future world system seems likely to be its inherent instability in the form of a potential for wildfire-like proliferation. To date, proliferation has appeared as a process of piecemeal accumulation of weapons capacities, weaponry, and weapons states, subject possibly to delay, derailment, and sometimes reversal. But, as more states have the means at their disposal to build high-leverage strategic weapons based on what is available to them in the civilian economy, proliferation becomes a process that might unfold with great speed, as some group of states, whether within a region or across the international system, move suddenly to create hedges against an uncertain future.

Those hedges might include new military research and development programs spun off from civilian NBC activities, more lavish funding for such programs and a push for greater sophistication and weaponization readiness, the construction of "bombs in the basement," the assembly of the full accoutrement of effective military systems, or actual deployment, whether secret or open. The gaps between different states would, of course, create advantages for those farthest along in the process of competitive hedging, and the perception of those gaps could be a significant source of instability. If it were to occur, wildfire-like proliferation would likely be visible and unsettling internationally. But it might also be nearly invisible, and thus doubly pernicious, by suggesting the existence of a stable world moving toward deeper cooperation when in fact world order is weakening and the risk of war is growing.

A catalytic event would be necessary to set this process in motion. This might be a predatory state's success in using WMD to act aggressively and sustain the aggression. Or it might be a decision by a security guarantor (e.g., the United States or the United Nations Security Council) not to act in honor of some commitment, thus calling into question the larger pattern of stability based on the credibility of its guarantees. Different catalysts would, of course, produce different reactions.

This potential for wildfire-like proliferation suggests something also about the nature of stability in such a system. That stability would likely have a number of sources. The risk of wildfire-like proliferation might itself prove to be an added incentive to seek stability by deepening the patterns of cooperation and integration previously noted. Expectations about the credibility of leading states and institutions as security guarantors would also play a significant role. Norms seem likely to play a particularly prominent role as factors structuring a state's choices with regard to its weapons potential. Notions of justice could also be significant: states might opt to exploit their weapons potential for political purposes if they come to believe that the international system is flawed by a fundamental injustice. A distribution of power and authority seen by some latent weapons states as historically outdated or favoring the powerful few or employed only in the service of the interests of a few states could lead them to exploit military potential to contest that distribution and upset that status quo.[17]

A final insight into the possible functioning of a future world system relates to the role of the great powers. Put simply, that role seems likely to diminish. More to the point, it seems likely to diminish further. Great powers no longer play the role they did a century ago, when they "managed" the international system by structuring it along the lines of their competitive interests and fighting periodic wars to eject declining powers or accommodate new ones. Today's great powers seem unlikely to fight wars among themselves, not least because of the impact of nuclear weapons, or to structure and police the international system through their unilateral exercise of military power. Proliferation increases doubts about their capacity to use military means to enforce the position and rights held by them and thus also raises doubts about the very nature of their power. It also conveys an autonomy and independence, at least from a military point of view, to small and medium powers unknown historically.

Of course, big powers and states with broad international interests will not go away. It is their capacity to manage the system that is increasingly in doubt. What this suggests is that leadership of the emerging system will not simply be won by big states of historical significance or bristling with armaments that aspire to manage the system. Instead, it will be accorded to those that earn leadership roles by tying their power to common purposes, by employing multilateral institutions in defense of common security, and by articulating common interests in an era of uncertainty. Others will want to follow leaders only if they have participated in establishing the general direction of the march and the rules by which it is conducted. The capacity of the established major powers to respond positively and imaginatively to the aspirations of states desirous of joining, as opposed to upsetting, the global status quo would likely be a critical determinant of the stability of this system.

The nuclear disposition of the United States seems likely to affect its leadership potential in such an international system. But exactly how is uncertain. Its capacity to manage through military threats and actions seems likely to be of declining value, although certainly not irrelevant, especially from the point of view of key allies. Its political standing may be increased if it were to embrace virtual nuclear deterrence, at least among some constituencies, but for what end and in what context is uncertain. On the other hand, a United States perceived as overarmed and overly reliant on military power and not adept at the use of political and economic instruments may look anachronistic, if not dangerous, to some, especially if its power is not firmly anchored in alliances. It seems obvious that the future of U.S. nuclear capabilities is tied inextricably to its future world role. The credibility of the United States as a guarantor of the security of others, the depth of its engagement in world affairs, and its availability as a benign power to provide leadership to the international community and stewardship of its common interests are all tied inextricably to its nuclear disposition. Whether nuclear weapons themselves are essential to these purposes in the emerging international system is an open question.

Among the other nuclear weapons states continued possession of nuclear weaponry may have a prominence not appreciated in the United States, especially in terms of their claims to continued world prominence and leadership. For Britain, China, France, and Russia nuclear weapons seem to have as much to do with their sense of what it means to be a great power as with any immediate or near-term threat to national survival. Few seem to want to contemplate a world in which the gap between them and the United States has widened even further, a likely result of the sharp movement away from nuclear weapons and heightened reliance on conventional weaponry, in which U.S. advantages, especially future ones, appear uncontested. This focus on the other nuclear weapons states is also a reminder of the importance of relations among those states in determining larger nuclear futures. If there is a falling-out among these states, especially over competing conceptions of the distribution of power and authority internationally, it seems unlikely that they will see making common cause on virtual nuclear arsenals to be in their interests. If one or more of them perceives a strong military threat posed by the proliferation of weapons of mass destruction, the embrace of virtual nuclear arsenals seems especially unlikely.

In summary, then, although we cannot know all of the features of the emerging system, some of its primary dynamics can be predicted with reasonable confidence. The incentives to cooperate will be many, as will the risks of instability—which may themselves prove to be an incentive to deeper cooperation. Questions of political legitimacy seem likely to be especially prominent in an international system in which the status quo is essentially a take-it-or-leave-it proposition. Norms will matter—as the principles governing the will of individual states to turn weapons prowess into weapons potential. Leadership will be accorded states that earn it, not merely on the basis of historical weight but by generating collective action. Collective security will remain a strong interest of many states—and an elusive goal. An international system characterized by large numbers of states, major and minor powers both, that hold military potential in reserve is a world that will hold both peril and promise.

A final thought: this exercise sheds some light on the functioning of the current international system as well as the future one. If latency is already a widespread phenomenon in the international system so too are some of its implications. The risks of instability are manifest, but the means for dealing with them are still dimly perceived. Norms are generally paid lip service today, despite their current relevance for the choices many states make about their weapons potential. Collective security is a strong interest, despite the difficulty of the permanent members of the Security Council in embracing that interest. The great powers continue to have significant, albeit diminished weight in the current international system. That system still requires a few states that take a special interest in its functioning and that lend their weight and power to achieving consensus about modes of behavior and to policing the rules that embody that consensus. Today, few states have the ability to build international political coalitions or to build consensus about shared interests and stakes. Fewer yet have the will to do so. Questions of political legitimacy are hardly noticed in Washington, even as they gain currency in countries that fear a post–Cold War United States either free to intervene impulsively in its unipolar moment or drawing closer to the siren song of isolationism. Finally, the particular character of leadership needed in this system seems little understood.

CONCLUSIONS

The tendency to overlook the latent weapons states in speculating about alternative nuclear futures, and about the drift of international politics, is unfortunate. The actions of these states could be critical determinants of those futures if circumstances compel them to make choices with regard to their NBC weapons potential that could unsettle futures preferred by the nuclear weapons states or upset the drift of politics. Thinking through some of their interests and perspectives points to the following basic conclusions.

First, as the world's leading security guarantor, the United States must understand that its commitments to extended deterrence and its capacity to project force in defense of key allies and interests are tied inextricably with the U.S. nuclear posture, *especially* in the minds of the recipients of those guarantees and of their intended targets (that is, those whom the United States seeks to deter by offering such guarantees). A fundamental change in the U.S. nuclear posture would undoubtedly raise large questions about the will and capacity of the United States to act as a security guarantor and to mobilize international coalitions to overturn brazen aggression. Those questions may have answers that are credible and compelling and that would strengthen the appeal of VNAs. But there is little evidence that either questions or answers have received much critical analytical attention from nuclear experts singularly focused on the nuclear weapons states and especially the United States. Absent such answers, VNAs will look to many states as offering a world system in which the benign influence of the major powers and especially the United States has been stripped away, leaving them vulnerable to the vagaries and predations of an even more anarchic interstate system.

Second, the existence of a large tier of states with latent NBC capabilities in the existing international system offers some insights into how a descendant international system characterized by broader latency and VNAs among the major powers might work. That system would have sources of both order and disorder that are little analyzed today. Most of the debate about whether and what kind of nuclear weapons are needed by the nuclear weapons states seems to occur in the context of an international system that is now passing from the scene. It is one thing to know how VNAs might have worked for the problems of the Cold War. It is another to understand how they might work in a qualitatively new international system. Within that system nuclear weapons, like military power generally, seem likely to offer only diminishing returns as a source of power and leverage. But, in the hands of particularly willful challengers to the status quo, their political effects could be considerable.

Third, VNAs seem likely to contribute to U.S. security and international security more generally only under a number of specific conditions.

If war among *and by* the major powers is effectively obsolete, if the impetus to cooperate economically and politically continues to grow increasingly irresistible, if doubts do not arise about the primacy of benign over predatory powers in the international system, and if U.S. security guarantees are deemed sufficiently credible through a mix of conventional forces and defenses against NBC attack, then the movement toward a pattern of deterrence among the nuclear weapons states based on virtual rather than deployed assets could contribute to the national security of each and the security of the larger international system.

But, if even one of these conditions is not met, the risks of VNAs go up. In the international system of the mid-1990s these conditions do not obtain. Particularly important is the fact that the security extended by the United States through alliances, and to a lesser extent by the permanent members of the UN Security Council through guarantees, is prized because of its existential nature. It seems likely that a decision by the major nuclear powers, and especially the United States, to abandon their arsenals would create insecurity within these allied states. Some might respond by exploiting their dual-use capacities to move closer to a virtual arsenal or to actual deployment. Others might respond by seeking new political alignments with partners other than the United States. Thus, achievement of latent deterrence for the great powers seems for the moment to require either a weakening or abandonment of their guarantees or a resolution of the security concerns of the recipients of those guarantees. Because these concerns seem to have as much to do with conventional military threats as unconventional ones, excising the nuclear dimension appears particularly difficult.

But what of the future a decade or decades hence? If this emerging era is characterized not by competition among the great powers but by cooperation on core interests, they may find it reasonable to balance the uncertainties of new forms of deterrence against a much less demanding security problem and the growing benefits of international economic and political cooperation. The thinking of allies may change as well. But even in an essentially cooperative system such powers seem unlikely to forsake self-sufficient deterrence for collective security, especially if technology diffusion is putting high-leverage weapons into the hands of regional aggressors or others desirous of upsetting the status quo by violent means.

Might forging ahead now with the virtual option push the system in directions that make virtual deterrence more beneficial? The political effect of such a move could perhaps be salutary, if pursued jointly by all the nuclear weapons states and closely tied to efforts to strengthen collective security through other means. The political effect would likely be attenuated if the United States were to pursue this course alone, although its power of example might prove significant. But a premature embrace of virtual deterrence could have the contrary effect of raising so many doubts about the future of strategic deterrence and about the U.S. world role that it would lead to an erosion of even the existing state of international cooperation.

A final conclusion relates to policy priorities, particularly as regards arms control. Two schools of thought on arms control have emerged in the mid-1990s. One posits that arms control has no place in the new era, it being little more than an outdated vestige of the Cold War (and some would say a dangerously foolish vestige at that). The other posits that the most important new function of arms control is to further limit the nuclear arsenals of the nuclear weapons states. On the basis of this analysis both appear wrong.

Arms control has many new functions in the type of international system described here. Its most basic function is to formalize the restraint states already find desirable and to create tools for cooperative risk taking and joint punishment of malefactors. The global treaty instruments and regimes are embodiments of the relevant norms, and they are political tools for marshaling coalitions to meet the challenges of states that defy those norms. Regional arms control has important new functions, although more likely as a tool of confidence and security building than as a tool for structuring force balances. This is not to imply that arms control will function smoothly in this new era. The fact that so many states have a working knowledge of WMD technologies suggests that arms-control instruments will generate ambiguous insights into the activities of states, which is a poor foundation for compliance-related responses, as well as false confidence in behavior of states not complying with the treaty, which is a poor foundation for using arms-control instruments to increase security. Problems of ambiguous data and false confidence can be expected to grow in an international system marked by the wide dispersal of dual-use technologies and expertise. But, in a highly permissive technology environment and given the instabilities associated with wildfire-like proliferation, there seems to be no alternative to working with such mechanisms of formalized restraint.

The importance of bolstering global patterns of formalized restraint suggests, then, that the singular focus of the U.S. arms-control community on nuclear disarmament as the next phase of arms control is to miss the much larger function and the complex and evolving role of arms control in international politics more generally. Restraint by the existing nuclear weapons states only makes sense in the context of more general restraint by all weapons-capable states. One without the other is a recipe for disaster.

NOTES

1. For a detailed discussion of the diffusion of dual-use military technologies and the phenomenon of the latent weapon state in the contemporary international system, see Brad Roberts, *Weapons Proliferation and World Order after the Cold War* (The Hague: Kluwer Law International, 1996).

2. This number 40 was offered by the Iklé-Wohlstetter Commission in 1988, as a prediction of the number of states capable, from a technical point of view, of making nuclear weapons by the year 2000. See Commission on Long-Range Integrated Strategy, *Discriminate Deterrence* (report) (Washington, D.C.: USGPO, 1988): 10.

3. These include Argentina, Brazil, India, Iran, Iraq, Israel, Japan, Libya, North Korea, Pakistan, People's Republic of China, South Africa, South Korea, Spain, and Taiwan. See William C. Potter, "The New Nuclear Suppliers," *Orbis* 36, no. 2 (Spring 1992): 199-210.

4. George Perkovich, "The Plutonium Genie," *Foreign Affairs* 72, no. 3 (Summer 1993): 153-65.

5. See W. Seth Carus, "The Proliferation of Biological Weapons," and Victor A. Utgoff, "The Biotechnology Revolution and Its Potential Military Implications," in *Biological Weapons: Weapons of the Future?*, ed. Brad Roberts (Washington, D.C.: Center for Strategic and International Studies, 1993): 19-34.

6. The Russian intelligence service has specifically characterized the number of states capable of making chemical weapons as about 100. See Y. Primakov, "A New Challenge after the Cold War: The Proliferation of Weapons of Mass Destruction" (Report prepared by the Foreign Intelligence Service of the Russian Federation, Moscow, 1993, translated by U.S. Foreign Broadcast Information Service, February 1993); summary and excerpts made available by Committee on Government Affairs, U.S. Senate, February 24, 1993, and subsequently published in *Proliferation Threats in the 1990s*, Hearing Before the Committee on Governmental Affairs, U.S. Senate, 103d Cong., 1st Sess., February 24, 1993 (Washington, D.C.: USGPO, 1993).

7. Mitchell Reiss, *Bridled Ambition: Why Countries Constrain Their Nuclear Capabilities* (Washington, D.C.: Woodrow Wilson Center Press, 1995).
8. See, for example, Ernest Preeg, "Who's Benefiting Whom? A Trade Agenda for High-Tech Industries," in *New Forces in the World Economy,* ed. Brad Roberts (Cambridge, Mass.: MIT Press, 1996): 139-56.
9. For a discussion of the changing nature of the dual-use phenomenon, see Michael Moodie, "Beyond Proliferation: The Challenge of Technology Diffusion," in *Weapons Proliferation in the 1990s,* ed. Brad Roberts (Cambridge, Mass.: MIT Press, 1995): 71-90.
10. This volume offers some insights into these reactions in the essays on Japan, France, and the United Kingdom. Each author argues that the VNA option would raise significant questions in allied capitals about the nature of the relationship with the United States and the fate of extended deterrence.
11. For more on this connection between U.S. nuclear reductions, extended deterrence, and nuclear proliferation, see George H. Quester and Victor A. Utgoff, "U.S. Arms Reductions and Nuclear Nonproliferation: The Counterproductive Possibilities," *Washington Quarterly* 16, no. 1 (Winter 1993): 129-40.
12. For a discussion of these issues, see the essay in this volume on defenses and VNAs.
13. On the chemical dimension, see *Report of the Chemical Warfare Review Commission* (Washington, D.C.: USGPO, 1985).
14. See Brad Roberts, "Rethinking How Wars Must End: NBC War Termination Issues in the Post–Cold War Era" (Draft report, Institute for Defense Analyses, January 1996).
15. Martin Wight, *Power Politics,* eds. Hedley Bull and Carsten Holbraad (London: Penguin Books and the Royal Institute of International Affairs, 1979). See also Thomas C. Schelling, *Arms and Influence* (New Haven: Yale University Press, 1966): 257. Their work is a reminder that in earlier periods of the twentieth century the challenges of building stable international systems through disarmament measures have been thoughtfully analyzed. Many of their insights are germane to the consideration of whether and how to move toward virtual nuclear arsenals.
16. For a discussion of these themes, see the essays in this volume on reconstitution and mobilization.
17. For an elaboration of this argument, see Brad Roberts, "1995 and the End of the Post–Cold War Era," in Roberts, *Weapons Proliferation in the 1990s,* 453-73.

PART FOUR

REACTIONS

FIFTEEN

EMERGING NUCLEAR WEAPONS POLICY AND THE ROLE OF VIRTUAL NUCLEAR ARSENALS

CHARLES HORNER

THE 1950S AND 1960S featured articles, discussions, and policy documents on the utility of nuclear weapons and strategies for their employment. The most commonly accepted concept involved the use of large nuclear arsenals to deter war in a bipolar world, the central theme that underscored the Cold War. It can be argued that nuclear weapons kept the peace, although veterans of Korea, Vietnam, and Afghanistan might dispute that assertion. At any rate the strategy of mutual assured destruction, whether arrived at by means of rational debate or as a result of a nuclear arms race, seems to have prevented direct military confrontation between the then superpowers while providing some measure of assurance to other nations that they need not acquire nuclear weapons for themselves.

The Defense Guidance tells us that the Cold War is over. Events throughout the world, including the former Soviet Union and today's Russia, indicate that the world is rapidly becoming multipolar. The utility of nuclear weapons in roles outside of superpower deterrence is being called into question. The nations possessing nuclear weapons seem to fall into two categories: those that seek nuclear disarmament and those that seek to possess nuclear weapons. The former hold sizable inventories of these weapons and are evaluating means to reduce the costs and vulnerabilities associated with ownership. The latter, generally denied ownership, intend to own nuclear capabilities and hope that possession of these weapons will serve their purposes for regional deterrence or otherwise confer military strength disproportionate to their own conventional armed forces. The measures of merit used to judge the value of weapons of mass destruction, most notably nuclear weapons, have also changed dramatically with the dissolution of the bipolar world.

The Gulf War in 1991 demonstrated that unacknowledged nuclear-weapons programs were both feasible and ongoing. Added to Iraq's nuclear, biological, and chemical weapons programs were the unstoppable ballistic missile delivery systems and the willingness to use them. It is argued by some that the possession of nuclear weapons by the United States prevented Iraq from using its weapons of mass destruction. Only Saddam Hussein knows, but it is likely that future aggressors on the world scene will conclude that no U.S. president will order a nuclear retaliatory attack with its attendant killing of women and children. As a result, the utility of the United States' nuclear inventory as a regional deterrent is becoming marginal. There may be some value in creating uncertainty in the minds of aggressors while the Cold War deterrent force of nuclear weapons is already in place, but the cost of ownership, the risk of nuclear weapon detonation for whatever reason, and moral principles all argue for elimination of these weapons on a worldwide basis.

Thoughtful people have long argued for the elimination of weapons of mass destruction, especially nuclear weapons—so what is the problem? The problem involves the need for mutual assurances of survival as the former superpowers reduce their inventories, safeguards against a declared owner breaking out of weapons elimination regimes, and prevention of a third nation secretly building a nuclear weapons inventory capable of destroying one of the newly disarmed nations. As troublesome, but not nation threatening, will be the need to induce those nations that might wish to develop weapons of mass destruction from seeking nuclear weapons ownership. Therefore, reduction of nuclear weapons needs to be worked on two fronts: Cold War inventory reduction and elimination of proliferated weapons and/or attendant development programs.

The concept of "virtual nuclear arsenals" has merit in a strategy to eliminate nuclear weapons. For the owners of large weapons arsenals a number of steps have already been implemented; START agreements, on-site inspections, and de-targeting of ballistic missiles are the most well-known measures. A strategy that goes beyond current levels of weapons reduction is needed to include measures that provide for the security of the disarming nations. For example, it is conceivable that Russia and the United States could agree to reducing their numbers of weapons down to levels of a few hundred, thereby greatly reducing the dangers on national survival yet affording some measure of deterrence to attack from other actors such as China. The next step might be that the declared owners of nuclear weapons reduce their inventories to tens of weapons; at this point the concept of deactivated or disassembled weapons becomes a very important tool as a hedge against breakout by one participating nation or surprise from an undeclared nuclear weapons owner.

The ultimate goal of elimination of all nuclear weapons remains; a number of interim steps are needed, however, and the concept of virtual weapons adds value to the disarmament process. In the final analysis the use of a "few" nuclear weapons to deter "rogue" states must be abandoned: first, because the use of nuclear weapons by rational actors is in doubt, and therefore their deterrent role is greatly weakened; second, because they provide little utility other than as a terror weapon used to kill cities and their inhabitants; and, finally, because the moral issues involved in the use of military force are bad enough without the aggravated evil of weapons of mass destruction. Human beings have proven themselves incapable of living together in sustained peace. Conventional military force will be required for the foreseeable future. There has been progress in reducing the horrors of war, as evidenced by a variety of measures such as the Laws of Armed Conflict and the development of precision munitions. Should the major powers get rid of their nuclear weapons, they will still have to maintain strong conventional military capabilities for their own national security purposes. Their conventional forces must be of sufficient size to insure that, once the existing owners of nuclear weapons eliminate their inventories, no other nation's or group's possession or use of these weapons will be tolerated. The nation that in the future seeks to own weapons such as nuclear devices must be deterred from the use of weapons of mass destruction, not by retaliation in kind but, rather, by the sure knowledge that the conventional response will take the perpetrator's political entity apart, totally and without remorse.

The world needs to enact measures to eliminate nuclear weapons, by mutual reductions of the major nuclear powers and by affording incentives to nations with unannounced yet existent nuclear weapons and nuclear weapons development programs. The tools needed are international and national inspection agreements, shared ballistic missile defenses, virtual nuclear arsenals, and strong conventional military forces. The shared danger of weapons of mass destruction, especially nuclear weapons, requires that all nations, whatever their differences, achieve a world free of these devices. To a war fighter they are of marginal utility; the demise of the Cold War eliminated the rationale for former superpower possession, and all nations are endangered by the use of these weapons by anyone due to the effects on the worldwide environment of their intended or accidental explosions. It is a hopeful sign that bright minds are now examining ways to eliminate nuclear weapons rather than employ them. Certainly, there is a place in the disarmament equation for an interim virtual nuclear arsenal.

SIXTEEN

VIRTUAL ARSENALS: A FRENCH VIEW

FRANÇOIS HEISBOURG

THE NOTION OF VIRTUAL NUCLEAR ARSENALS is still novel and tenuous within the U.S. strategic community, where it originated. Therefore, it is not surprising that the concept remains for the time being essentially foreign to the French strategic debate; furthermore, for a variety of reasons that will be discussed, the notion itself may well remain alien to French thinking, even if virtual nuclear arsenals were to become a commonplace item for debate. This does not imply, however, that attitudes on nuclear weapons are static in France: as elsewhere, they have been shifting, essentially as a result of extraneous events.

This essay will therefore examine the reasons behind the shifts in French attitudes and the nature of these shifts (The Actual). Building on this analysis, it will attempt to portray some of the possible reactions to the virtual arsenals concept (The Virtual). Finally, the possible extent of future changes in French attitudes to nuclear weapons and deterrence will be explored (The Plausible).

THE ACTUAL

The most obvious, and far-reaching, cause for French attitudes to nuclear weapons lies in the collapse of the Soviet Empire: in this, France is in a situation similar to that affecting the other nuclear powers polarized within the East-West conflict. Furthermore, many of the secondary effects of the disappearance of the Soviet threat are also identical to those that the United States and the United Kingdom have had to cope with:

- in the military area the elimination of an obvious and constant force-dimensioning adversary;
- in the domestic sphere the absence of a long-standing antagonist whose existence and actions would justify in political terms the mobilization of the nation's resources and energy;
- the mechanical increase in salience that the evaporation of the Soviet threat has given to other risks and threats, not least those related to the proliferation of weapons of mass destruction;
- the global erosion of the legitimacy and political advantage pertaining to the possession of nuclear weapons, once the clear and present danger has passed.

In addition to these generic causes of changing attitudes, France has also had to deal with a more specific effect of the end of the East-West conflict, that is, the reduced value of France's nuclear status in its relationship with other European countries, notably Germany. In the "balance of imbalances" that has characterized the Franco-German couple, nuclear weapons were a powerful asset for the French during the Cold War. With the subsequent devaluation of the nuclear currency as an instrument of power and the rising strength of the Deutschmark (once the initial pain of German unification had passed), the balance of imbalances looks increasingly unbalanced.

What then have been the French reactions to these trends?

FORCE SIZING

The least difficult challenge has been that of the disappearance of the Soviet force-dimensioning challenge. French nuclear doctrine was always that of the "Weak to the Strong," in which the size of the "weak's" nuclear arsenal was not dictated by the size of the "strong's": the dimension of the French force was tailored to the need to be able to inflict a crippling blow to the vital assets (*oeuvres vives*) of the adversary. Defining the minimum level of a credible force (*seuil de suffisance*) was therefore not the result of the correlation of forces analysis but, rather, the answer to the question: What kind and what size of nuclear force do I need in order to inflict massive damage to an adversary's cities, taking into account his first-strike capability and his active or passive defenses? This led to an SSBN-based second-strike nuclear capability: at its peak this consisted of 6 SSBNs of which at least 3 were on patrol, equipped with 16 six-warhead M.4 missiles, capable of dealing with the Moscow ABM system as well as targeting other major population centers, even if a first strike destroyed the other elements of the French nuclear triad.

The emergence of Russia as a successor state has provided France with an *ersatz force dimensioner:* the United States as an ally is naturally not a suitable substitute, whereas Russia, not an enemy but not an ally, plays the role of a benchmark for French nuclear force planning. This is de facto rather than declaratory policy, since Russia is not a "declarable" foe. In this context France is ratcheting down its minimum deterrent without abandoning the "weak to the strong" relationship with the Russian benchmark:

- the disappearance of the massive Soviet threat in Central Europe removes the requirement for operational prestrategic surface-to-surface missiles (Hadès, with its 480-km range, was mothballed as soon as it was produced in 1990);
- the destruction of Soviet INF—and therefore the elimination of potential escalation dominance resulting from the combination of conventional and nuclear Soviet forces—has removed the need to field the 18 IRBMs in the hardened silos of the Plateau d'Albion;
- the elimination of a serious ASW threat in the Atlantic Ocean has made it possible to reduce the number of SSBNs (currently moving to four), of which two are on patrol at any given time.

As a consequence, the trend is one of substantial unilateral force reductions in terms of number of platforms, delivery vehicles, warhead, and megatonnage (see table 16.1).

TABLE 16.1—FRENCH NUCLEAR FORCES

		Platforms[b]	Delivery[c]	Warheads	Megaton-nage[d]
Strategic Forces	1990a	6 SSBNs	96 SLBMs	452	
		18 IRBM silos	18 IRBMs		108 Mt
		18 Mirage NP	18 ASMP		
	2001	4 SSBNs	64 SLBMs	384	57 Mt
Pre-Strategic Forces	1990-91	45 Mirage 2000	45 AMSP	285	
		53 Super Etendard1	60? an-52		
		89 Jaguar bombs			
		40 Pluton launchers	80 Pluton		
					5.6 Mt
	2001	72 Mirage 2000 N?	110 ASMP?	110?	5 Mt?
		38 Super Etendard			
TOTAL	1990		617 ?	737	114 Mt
	2001		174 ?	494?	62 Mt

START counting rules are used throughout; actual numbers may in some instances be significantly lower (e.g., all SSBNs are deemed under START to be fully loaded along "so tested/so counted" lines).

NOTES:
a. 2001: as per force planning contained in 1996-2001 Military Program Bill adopted in 1994.
   The peak year for all categories save megatonnage was 1990-91.
b. Including silos, SSBNs, Hadès launchers, dual-capable aircraft (e.g., Mirage IMP, Mirage 2000 N, Super-Etendard, etc.).
c. S.3 D IRBMs, M.4/M.45 SLBMs ASMP air-to-surface missile, Pluton and Hadès missiles.
d. Assuming the yields provided for warhead types by "The Military Balance, 1990-91 and 1995-96," IISS.

DOMESTIC PRESSURES

In summary French nuclear doctrine has proven sufficiently robust to cope with the disappearance of the threat in military terms. It may not prove quite as easy to deal with the domestic consequences of being deprived of an enemy. For the first five years following the fall of the Berlin Wall there was little political pressure from either Right or Left to put French nuclear doctrine, forces, or spending into question. Although spending on nuclear weapons did actually drop substantially (in contrast to defense spending in general [see table 16.2]), this was not as a consequence of political attacks but, rather, the mechanical effect of downsizing flowing from force-dimensioning considerations. Indeed, these budgetary cutbacks were made against some opposition, successive governments of the Left and of the Right being at pains to prove that they were not jeopardizing national security through ill-considered spending cuts.

This situation came to an end in 1995, with the convergence of two new developments:

- the resumption of nuclear testing, against the opposition of a majority of French respondents to subsequent opinion polls. This opposition is fairly low key and has not translated into any major political attempt to call into question French nuclear doctrine;
- more important, the need to reduce the budget deficit drastically, which has turned all political forces against sustained defense spending, nuclear or otherwise.

PROLIFERATION FEARS

The new visibility that the end of the Soviet Union has given to possible threats from *actual or potential proliferation* has had an impact in French thinking, if not force structures, at least comparable to what has occurred in the United States. Indeed, the prospect of "rogue states" targeting France from the southern or eastern Mediterranean has sometime proven to be, in rhetorical terms, nearly as powerful as the old *Feindbild* of the Soviet juggernaut. "Rent-a-threat" attitudes flourish readily when one lives next to a not-so-pleasant neighborhood.

TABLE 16.2—FRENCH DEFENSE SPENDING, 1990-95

Billion French Francs (% of Total)	1990	1991	1992	1993	1994	1995
Defense Spending, Nuclear	32.1 (17.2%)	31.1 (16.4%)	29.9 (15.8%)	26.4 (14%)	21.7 (11.3%)	20.7 (-11.2%)
Defense Spending, All Others (excluding Pensions)	154	157.4	157.6	162.7	170.5	-164

Indeed, there have been attempts to shift the French doctrine away from the "Weak to the Strong" paradigm, toward doctrines emphasizing the possibility that France could find itself in "Strong to the Weak" situations. More ominously, such a shift has in some cases gone toward employment, as opposed to deterrent, doctrines: a doctrine of "the Strong to the Crazy" (*du Fort au Fou*) would imply, for some of its proponents, the use of high-accuracy, low-yield nuclear weapons in order to target leaders or specific high-value assets rather than cities. In hardware terms the weapon of choice for this school of thought would be an extremely accurate supersonic long-range *air-sol longue portée* (ASLP) as a successor to the existing shorter-range airborne ASMP missile.

This line of thinking has been officially rejected by President Chirac; the ASLP project has not been funded, a decision made easier by the cutbacks in defense spending. Whether or not this rejection is deep and long-lasting remains to be seen. The fact remains that the most visible alternatives to current French nuclear doctrine tend to be of the "we-want-more-and-better-nukes" variety rather than of the "virtual arsenal" kind. On the positive side of the ledger, however, is the fact that the fear of proliferation to the south has increased the priority that France gives to multilateral efforts in this field: scope for further change is substantial.

POLITICAL ADVANTAGE

French attitudes on nuclear weapons have not shifted spectacularly as a result of the reduction of their general *political utility*. Erosion of legitimacy and political advantage does not imply illegitimacy or net political disadvantage. Possession may not be enough to justify continuing membership of the Permanent Five of the UN Security Council, but it certainly does not hurt. Furthermore, renewal of the NTP, if anything, has relegitimized France's status as a recognized nuclear power.

It is in an indirect sense that French attitudes have changed. France knows that it has to be more active than before to hold claim to its seat at the P-5, and it acts accordingly: French participation in the Gulf War and in Bosnia is to a major extent a result of this recognition As the issue of legitimacy becomes more acute—and the resumption of nuclear testing will have played a major role to that effect—greater changes will have to be contemplated beyond France's militant stand in favor of the "zero-option" in the CTBT negotiations.

THE EUROPEAN DIMENSION

This aspect of French reactions to the new situation has led France to contemplate changes in nuclear policy. For close to three decades the French nuclear deterrent was presented consistently as the exclusive domain of French national sovereignty, to be shared with none. Indeed, until the closing years of the Cold War the only powers with which France considered discussing nuclear affairs were other nuclear powers: the covert Franco-American nuclear connection, the attempted Franco-British talks of the early 1970s, the successful Franco-British dialog on doctrine and other nuclear issues since 1987 onward. Vis-à-vis nonnuclear countries, it was not until 1986 that France hinted at the possibility of keeping Germany in the nuclear picture, along "time and circumstances permitting" lines; at the time this was not followed through by the establishment of the corresponding institutional machinery, such as that which kept NATO's Nuclear Planning Group busy during the Cold War. By the time France undertook to express a willingness to "concert" its deterrence (*dissuasion concertée*) with its nonnuclear European partners, in 1995, the political and strategic value of such an undertaking had been substantially reduced by the absence of a clear and present danger. Changes in attitude here are welcome but probably too late, if not too little.

THE VIRTUAL

Potential French responses to proposals for virtual arsenals can be derived from the existing French shifts of attitude toward nuclear weapons in the post–Cold War era. This means that special consideration may be given to:

- the practical impact of virtual arsenals on current French nuclear force structure and spending;
- the effect of virtual arsenals on proliferation;
- the consequences of virtual arsenals on France's special status as a recognized declared nuclear weapons state; and
- the implications for the European dimension of a virtual nuclear posture.

As we shall see, the first three considerations will tend to weigh against virtual arsenals, without those negatives being necessarily outweighed by a possibly positive European dimension.

FORCE STRUCTURE CONSIDERATIONS

By the turn of the century it is unlikely that France will deploy any land-based IRBMs. Its reliance on air-launched nuclear weapons is essentially confined to the so-called no-strategic sphere; even the 18 longer-range Mirage IV P cannot be considered as a fully fledged credible retaliatory strategic nuclear deterrent; furthermore, they will be decommissioned from their nuclear role in 1996. In other words, and unless France decides to develop a long-range air-to-surface nuclear missile (the ASLP concept), France will rely quasi-exclusively on her SSBNs for strategic nuclear purposes.

Therefore, France will have a force structure that lends itself with great difficulty to a transition toward the virtual arsenal concept. Indeed, it is paradoxical to note that the component of the French nuclear array that could be most readily adapted to such a concept, the Hadès SRBM, happens to be the most disputable and least relevant element of the existing force structure. These 480-km-range mobile missiles were developed during the 1980s, along lines akin to that of the Soviet SS-23 or the U.S. Pershing IA, essentially for use on the European central front. Given their range, these rockets would not strike targets significantly beyond the Elbe River. The 30 rockets and their 15 launch vehicles have been mothballed in the east of France, separately from their TN-51 variable-yield warheads, which were manufactured at the same time. Similarly, the airborne prestrategic component—the dual-capable Mirage 2000N and Super Etendard—could transition with relative ease into a "virtual" mode: since the end of the Cold War none of the delivery system has been kept on Quick Reaction Alert; hence, warheads and aircraft are normally kept separate.

In effect, the French—like the British and unlike the Americans, Russians, or Chinese—have put nearly all of their eggs into the submarine basket. As pointed out in Michael Mazarr's essay, a submarine-based virtual arsenal would be rather difficult to verify, unless the missiles were withdrawn from the submarines—which is another way of saying that all missiles would be ground based, which is exactly the force posture that France is moving away from.

Another negative force structure implication would involve strategic defenses. Under current conditions France has no need to invest in the production and deployment of such defenses. The protection of nuclear storage sites and other military uses, as suggested in Mazarr's essay, through the deployment of "several hundred interceptors" to prevent "any nation from acquiring a rapid first-strike capability" would therefore be a major budgetary burden for a country that is currently reducing defense spending: the cost of such anti-missile defenses could well exceed the expense of the nuclear deterrent force.

IMPACT ON PROLIFERATION

Frances' geostrategic position is substantially less enviable than that of the United States or the United Kingdom. By virtue of its location the United States is not susceptible to nuclear strikes from so-called rogue states, and the United Kingdom lies on average 500 miles farther away from potential proliferators in the Mediterranean Basin than does France. The existence of sore points—demographic, religious, and cultural—between France and a number of unstable states to its south give added salience to French fears of proliferation. The virtual arsenals concept must therefore also be considered in terms of its impact on the spread of nuclear weapons. In comparison to the existing paradigm, the virtual paradigm is one that creates doubt on this score in comparison to the existing situation. Today, there is a fairly clear distinction between two categories of states that have signed the NPT and a third set outside of the NPT:

1.   The five "official" nuclear weapons states whose possession of
     nuclear arsenals has been recognized, if not legitimized, in the
     framework of the NPT.
2.   The nonnuclear signatories of the NPT that compose the
     overwhelming majority (180 countries) of the international
     community. Some of these signatories are suspected of imper-
     fect compliance (Iraq, North Korea, Iran); but there is fairly
     little ambiguity on what NPT rules are, thus creating a basis for
     action vis-à-vis possible violators. A number of recent signato-
     ries have possessed nuclear weapons (South Africa) or used to
     have military nuclear programs (Argentina, Brazil); they have
     since joined the fold; then there is the case of those former
     Soviet Republics where Russian nuclear warheads have been
     (Kazakhstan) or still are deployed (Belarus, Ukraine), a case
     similar to that of 5 nonnuclear NATO countries on whose
     territory U.S. airborne nukes are stationed (Belgium, Germany,
     Greece, Netherlands, Turkey). But in none of the cases is there
     any ambiguity today about who controls these weapons (re-
     spectively. Russia and the United States); they have all signed
     the NPT as nonnuclear weapon states.
3.   The last category consists of a handful of states, three of which
     are deemed to be nuclear weapons states (India, Israel, and
     Pakistan). This category is in a sense "fenced off" since the last
     wave of adhesions to the NPT.

In contrast to this fairly stable and clean-cut situation, a virtual
arsenal concept building on the Swedish precedent quoted in Mazarr's
essay would break down the distinctions between these categories. After
all, it would take only a small step for a large number of industrialized
or industrializing states to move from their current nonnuclear status
and posture to a nuclear status (albeit virtual). Countries that had
nuclear military programs (Canada early on, Sweden until the
late1960s) or that considered such programs (Germany and Italy, which
signed a nuclear agreement with France in 1957 that De Gaulle put a
halt to in 1958; Switzerland in the mid-1950s) would be particularly
ready candidates for such a move, as would Japan. In itself this would
probably not be a major worry in military terms from a French
perspective—even if the politics could be less than pleasant—but the

indirect effect would be seen as extremely threatening: if it were legitimate for an NPT state such as Sweden to have the bomb, be it a virtual one, why should Algeria or Libya, also NPT signatories, be precluded from securing a similar status?

EFFECTS ON FRANCE'S INTERNATIONAL STATUS

A logical corollary of the blurring of the status between existing nuclear weapons states and "virtual proliferators" would be an erosion of advantages of membership of the "Club of Five." These benefits are particularly tangible for medium-sized nuclear powers, such as France or the United Kingdom: whereas the United States' specific economic, political, and military weight will give it great power status, irrespective of the nuclear dimension, no such built-in weight pertains to the second-rank nuclear states. Therefore, France has a vested national interest in insuring a clear-cut divide between the nuclear haves and have-nots. The interest is mitigated by the fact that the "exchange rate" of nuclear weapons possession as a "currency of power" has sharply diminished with the end of the Cold War—but it has not disappeared. Virtual nuclear arsenals would further erode France's relative position in the international pecking order.

The general remark also applies in specific bilateral relations. Most important, French possession of nuclear weapons has been perceived in Paris as a valuable balancing element in the key Franco-German relationship, which has become more lopsided as a consequence of the successful implementation of German unification.

The importance that the French will attach to this national interest will depend to a large degree on the extent to which an opposite interest will continue to emerge, that is, that which is implied by the European-ization of French foreign and security policy, hitherto the more or less exclusive prerogative of national decision making.

THE EUROPEAN DIMENSION

Virtual nuclear arsenals would make it easier to move toward so-called concerted deterrence, a part of a situation in which considerations of specific national weight in traditional bilateral relationships would be subsumed by European-scale integration, of which the Franco-German team would be the hard core. Naturally, such an evolution is basically contingent upon the continuation of the process of European unification that began in the mid-1950s, and which has today reached the stage whereby a single currency and a modicum of political union have become stated goals for the turn of the century. Given the difficulties that this process is currently encountering, it would be premature to suppose that even partial unification of foreign security and defense policy will actually occur, but such is the declared objective of the Maastricht Treaty. Therefore, it is also premature to conclude that the imperative of preserving France's specific nuclear status will be overridden by the exigencies of Europeanization.

It is also clear, however, that full Europeanization of security and defense policy would imply a disappearance of stark barriers between nuclear haves and have-nots—in the form of extensive nuclear power sharing (above and beyond what was achieved during the Cold War in NATO's Nuclear Planning Group) and/or of the recognition that nuclear weapons may be owned by all, a prospect made more accessible via the virtual nuclear arsenal concept. Indeed, equality of nuclear status between France and Germany would be a precondition for true nuclear power sharing: in other words, the proliferating effect of the virtual nuclear arsenal concept could become a tool for European unity.

All of this is obviously hypothetical: there remains an immense gap between the essentially national practice of international policy (including its defense dimension) within the European Union and the pooling of interest implied by full political union. In the foreseeable future the need to defend the French national interest (such as membership of a small and distinct nuclear club) will probably take precedence over the advantages on the European scene of nuclear power sharing. This will be all the more the case since the national interest will be seen from Paris as being congruent with the general interest of avoiding the proliferation of nuclear weapons under the guise of virtuality.

THE PLAUSIBLE

In practice French nuclear policy could evolve toward a mix of:

- quantitative reductions

- the elimination of reliance on ground-launched systems
- greater involvement in negotiated arms-control measures
- a degree of concerted deterrence with the European Union partners.

While remaining well short of the virtual concept, the combination of these measures would lead to substantially smaller essentially retaliatory force—under the proviso that the proponents of "doctrine of use" (*doctrines d'emploi*) will not take over. Indeed, the most visible alternative to current trends is not a virtual arsenal but a war-fighting first-strike, ready-to-use, nuclear force relying on high-accuracy low-yield air-launch weapons, with no reliance on a ground-based system.

Quantitative Reductions

It is entirely possible, if no new military threat against France's vital interest emerged, that France, after having peaked at six SSBNs , will not only move down to four boats but could cut out the fourth new-generation SSBN, in effect leading to a three-submarine force, with the capability of keeping one boat ready at any given point in time.

The Plateau d'Albion IRBMs will most likely be shut down, possibly by 2000, and the Mirage IVPs were withdrawn from nuclear service in 1996. There would remain two issues:

- What to do with the 30 mothballed Hadès SSBNs, the only part of the French force which is in a virtual mode. It would make sense to eliminate them altogether, not least since this would release from its duties a full artillery regiment devoted to their custody.
- What type of successor to provide to the 110 Mirage 2000 N and Super-Etendard equipped with ASMP air-launched missiles. This is not an urgent matter, since the warheads and missiles will still be operational toward the end of the next decade. A choice between two options appears most likely:
  - entrusting limited nuclear strikes to the SSBNs, which is what the British have chosen to do as a replacement for their WE-177 gravity bombs
  - undertaking a life-extension program of the ASMP, includ-

ing a renewal of the propulsion systems, which would be given greater range (up to 500 km). This would be a fairly low-cost decision; in itself it would not entail basic changes in the existing doctrine and *modus operandi.*

ARMS-CONTROL MEASURES

France's nuclear status and the credibility of its downsized nuclear forces would not be imperiled by a significantly more dynamic arms-control policy; in a number of instances arms-control policy would have a significant positive impact on France's security situation. In particular, France could seek:

- A multilateralization of the INF treaty (1987 Washington treaty), banning U.S. and Soviet 500- to 5,000-km-range SR/LRINF. This would be entirely feasible with the decommissioning of the Plateau d'Albion IRBMs. Furthermore, France could attempt to amend the INF treaty's lower limit, in order to prohibit SRBMs of 300- to 500-km range: this would make the lower INF threshold coincide with the maximum range (300 km) of allowable missiles exports, as expressed in the multilateral Missile Technology Control Regime (MTCR). Such measures could help prevent avoid the emergence of a new missile threat capable of hitting France.
- A multilateralization of the ABM Treaty of 1972 and its subsequent additional protocols. The integrity of the U.S.-Russian ABM Treaty has from its inception been considered a major French security interest. As the treaty comes under attack in Washington, its extension to other parties such as China, Japan, Israel, and the European Union could reinforce the ABM regime.
- A cut-off in the production of fissile materiel for nuclear weapons purposes. Such a regime would be entirely compatible with French security interests, insofar that recycling of existing military-grade fissile materiel would be permitted.
- International plutonium and HEU storage. This would also be entirely compatible with French security interests, although the burden of verification would be particularly onerous for

France, which has invested heavily in the civilian plutonium cycle.

- Nuclear weapons–free zones. NWFZs have now become as acceptable to France as to the other recognized nuclear powers with the end of nuclear testing. The Rarotonga Treaty, the Pelindaba Treaty, and a possible Southeast Asian NWFZ should be acceptable in principle to Paris (albeit with the usual provisos about transit rights), as would eventual zones in the Middle East and South Asia.

Such measures could constitute the arms-control components of the concerted deterrence concept between France and its European partners.

CONCERTED DETERRENCE IN EUROPE

France will no doubt find it useful to develop the concerted deterrence concept in Europe. This could, in theory, have several types of content, aside from the previously mentioned arms-control measures:

- A commitment to consult European partners "circumstances and time permitting" (to paraphrase the old NATO Athens guidelines) on potential recourse to the threat of nuclear weapons and setting up the machinery to facilitate timely consultation if the need arises.
- A dialog on issues of common nuclear concern: such is the nature of the French-British nuclear relationship as it has developed since 1987; doctrine, nuclear safety, and security; presumably, mutual help in matters relating to the protection of outgoing and incoming patrols of SSBNs could be included; a degree of "de-conflicting" of patrol cycles and targeting may also be possible.
- The formulation of employment options of the NPG variety relating to the use of nuclear weapons in particular areas in specific contingencies: however, for the same reason that the NPG has stopped meeting since 1992, it is difficult to imagine that this type of dialog could take place in the absence of a clear and present danger.

- A commitment to provide extended nuclear deterrence; this is, in a sense, implied by existing treaty commitments (notably the respective Articles V of the WEU and NATO treaties). The difficulties of giving credibility to such a commitment are well known. To these one must add, since the end of the Cold War, the problem of providing relevance to such an undertaking.

In conclusion, it appears most unlikely that the virtual arsenal concept will find any particular appeal in France, whatever the angle of approach: strategic, political, or financial. The only conceivable exception would imply a spectacular advance of the pooling of French defense and security interests within an integrated European Union. This may be desirable; it is hardly likely as a short- to medium-term prospect.

SEVENTEEN

THOUGHTS ON VIRTUAL NUCLEAR ARSENALS

KENNETH WALTZ

WHEN I READ Jonathan Schell's 1984 *New Yorker* essay, "The Abolition," I wondered why anyone would prefer a world in which no one had more than a near-nuclear military capability to the world we had then. More than a decade later I still wonder.

The three main advantages of a system of virtual arsenals are said to be these:

- They would relegate nuclear weapons to the margins of international politics.
- They would remove the danger of nuclear weapons being fired accidentally or without authorization.
- They would strengthen efforts to halt the spread of nuclear weapons and help to solve regional problems.

Seemingly, a system of virtual arsenals would bring substantial advantages. Moreover, it is thought that in such a system not much could easily go wrong. Any country would know that if it began to assemble weapons others would too. Attempts to break out of the system would be seen as self-defeating. If several countries nevertheless reactivated parts of their arsenals, they would, as now, deter one another from using them.[1]

A system of virtual arsenals promises large benefits at low or no cost. On close inspection, however, the benefits begin to dwindle, and the costs appear to grow. It is said that substituting virtual for actual arsenals would move nuclear weapons to the peripheries of international politics, but in an important sense that would leave them right where they are now. Nuclear weapons are useless for fighting wars and even for threatening blackmail.[2] Nuclear weapons have always formed part of the scenery of international politics, which is the appropriate place for weapons suited for deterring rather than for fighting. One may hope, and virtual weaponeers do in fact hope, that nuclear weapons will continue to cast their shadow over international affairs, thus providing a considerable assurance of peace among states enjoying their protection.

If deterrence would work as well with virtual as with actual weapons, then nations should surely agree to eliminate weapons-in-being. Low though the dangers have proved to be, weapons that are ready to fire may go off accidentally, may be exploded without authorization, and may be acquired by "rogue" states or terrorists. One must, however, wonder whether virtual arsenals will deter as readily as actual arsenals have. The argument that virtual arsenals are sufficient for deterrence is especially odd when it comes from those who earlier thought that the requirements of deterrence were endlessly demanding and inordinately expensive to meet, that only a seamless web of capabilities able to dominate an opponent whatever the opponent might do up and down the escalation ladder would deter.

Belief in the difficulty of deterrence was summed up in the widely accepted thought that a strategy inadequate for the fighting of wars cannot deter.[3] Virtual weaponeers nevertheless argue that deterrence will work without weapons-in-being so long as some states retain or develop the ability to assemble them quickly. In the first step toward a system of virtual arsenals the number of nuclear warheads in the hands of the major nuclear states would be drastically reduced. This would be a good thing in itself. Small numbers of warheads are easy to safeguard and control. Some people have long claimed that only small numbers are needed for deterrence, and recently weighty voices have buttressed the claim.[4] If they are wrong, then a system of virtual arsenals can be realized only by moving the world through a forbiddingly dangerous condition on the way to establishing the system. If they are right, then unilateral reduction of weapons to small numbers is possible without further ado. Once this is accepted, warheads numbering in, say, the low hundreds can be deployed and guarded in ways that are highly proof against threat and against accidental and unauthorized firing. The first two virtues of a system of virtual arsenals can be gained without eliminating second-strike forces-in-being.

The minimal deterrence argument—that not much is required to deter—has never been widely accepted. If the leaders of states cannot be persuaded that small numbers are sufficient for deterrence, then surely they cannot be persuaded to go all the way to having no actual weapons at all. If we make the big assumption that finally they can be persuaded, can we then move on to a system of virtual arsenals and safely reap the additional advantages that its advocates promise? For two closely connected reasons a system of virtual arsenals is untenable. First, deterrence without second-strike forces will not work. Second, a system of virtual arsenals would be unstable.

To deter means to dissuade someone from doing something for fear of the consequences. One country's weapons may deter other countries from using their weapons to score gains at the expense of one's vital interests. Nuclear weapons, because they dominate other weapons, are especially good for the purpose.

Virtual weaponeers would substitute "factory deterrence," or "weaponless deterrence," for deterrence with second-strike forces. As Schell puts it, weapons would no longer deter weapons; instead, "factory would deter factory." The ability to make nuclear weapons "would make abolition *possible,* because it would keep deterrence in force."[5] Would it? Factories cannot deter factories from producing their goods. Only the products of factories can serve as instruments of deterrence. Factory deterrence is deterrence one step removed. In a system of virtual arsenals all countries would know that if they secretly made weapons with the factories they were allowed to have, or secretly assembled weapons from parts legitimately on hand, other countries, becoming suspicious, would soon do the same. Presumably, no country would have reason to break with the system. The penalty for doing so would, however, be a mild one: namely, that others might well follow suit. Such a penalty would be easily borne. Countries feeling insecure, and doubting that other countries were strictly following the rules, could safely risk incurring it. The inability of factories to deter would drive states out of the system, that is, away from reliance on it and toward relying on themselves by acquiring second-strike forces.

Virtual weaponeers emphasize that their system will be viable only if deterrence continues to work. Indeed, some of them stipulate that the United States must retain its ability to extend its deterrent to cover U.S. interests abroad. Yet, even when the United States had more than 10,000 strategic warheads, its allies wondered whether the U.S. deterrent would cover them. A latent nuclear force is at best a shaky deterrent at home; it will find no credit abroad.

Virtual weaponeers also stress that a regime for the management of nuclear weapons must promise stability. A system of second-strike forces is highly stable. Indeed, stability is part of the meaning of the term *second strike*. Second-strike forces are nearly impervious to the efforts of others to negate them, whether by seeking first-strike capability or by building defenses. As Harold Brown put it when he was secretary of defense, purely deterrent forces "can be relatively modest, and their size can perhaps be made substantially, though not completely, insensitive to changes in the posture of an opponent."[6]

Because second-strike forces reduce worries about others' military capabilities, surveillance of their forces by intrusive means of inspection is unnecessary. With virtual arsenals, countries would have to worry incessantly lest their capability for rapid production and deployment fall behind the similar ability of others to do so. The possession of nuclear weapons has brought not only security to states individually but also peace among nuclear states collectively. Weapons bringing such benefits are rarely found. States that believe their security endangered will want to keep or to get them. To thwart them will require heroic efforts. States will resist conforming their policies to internationally imposed stipulations that can promise satisfactory levels of security only if all states follow the rules. Believing that heroic efforts will sometimes fail, states will hedge their bets and bend the rules or simply cheat. Virtual weaponeers argue that, because states know that if some cheat others will too, all will have reason not to.

Temptations to cheat grow, however, as the gains from doing so rise and as the chances of being caught fall. Since the security of nations will be at stake, the reasoning of states will reverse the reasoning of virtual weaponeers: some states will feel that they had better cheat, if only because others may be doing so. It is hard to hide battleships; it is easy to hide warheads. No one can know about weapons that may be hidden to the view of even well-equipped and free-ranging inspectors. Because this is so, counsels of prudence would require countries to cheat a little by hiding some ready weapons as a hedge against the possible cheating of others. If states are limited to very low numbers of weapons, and even more so if the number is zero, cheating is both worthwhile and easy. Mazarr is right in saying that a system of virtual arsenals would require "extremely intrusive" inspection.[7] Inspectors would have to certify not only that proscribed weapons do not exist but also that nuclear facilities are incapable of making or assembling weapons in less than a specified time and in more than a specified quantity.

Virtual weaponeers understandably emphasize the importance of intrusive and rigorous inspection. Unstable systems depend on it; stable systems do not. Yet by both common sense and recent experience we know that the reports of inspectors will be thought unreliable. We can hardly expect states to agree to inspections as intensive and thorough as those to which Iraq has been subjected since its 1991 defeat. Yet five years later doubts persist about Iraq's ability to produce, or to resume production of, chemical, biological, and nuclear weapons. In June 1995 the United Nations official overseeing the destruction of weapons told the Security Council that Iraq's biological warfare program is larger than previously thought and that some of its materials are not accounted for. In November 1995 two experts on the control of nuclear weapons expressed fear that Iraq may be perfecting and testing components of a bomb while lacking only the plutonium and bomb-grade uranium needed to assemble nuclear weapons rapidly.[8] Because nuclear warheads are small and light, they can easily be hidden and moved. Inspection is at best an uncertain business. Weaponless deterrence would multiply the uncertainties. Uncertainties by each country about how other countries are doing would breed distrust all around, increase insecurities, and provide strong incentives to strengthen military forces.

Some virtual weaponeers realize this. Having pointed out that extremely intrusive inspection would be required to maintain the system, Mazarr adds that some cheating would be tolerable, since the "state which covertly reassembled twenty or fifty nuclear weapons would have achieved little." Only if it had gained a first-strike capability could it prevent "other states from redeploying their own arsenals."[9] Logically, he may be right. What could a first strike accomplish? And how much would the country that struck first risk losing if the country struck had a secret store of even a few nuclear warheads? Sensible answers to these questions make a first strike all but unthinkable. But some states will think of reasons why other states may do the unthinkable. Paul Nitze imagined in the mid-1970s that the Soviet Union might launch a first strike at us, believing that somehow it had "deterred our deterrent," even though at the time the United States and the Soviet Union had more than 2,000 strategic delivery systems.[10] Less fertile imaginations will be able to invent ways in which states might exploit a "zero-some" gap, and some states will begin to worry that others may do so. Mazarr underestimates how much states worry about such gaps in capability that may be thought to offer "windows of opportunity" to others. States would hasten to equip themselves with nuclear weapons, lest a newly rearmed state somehow gain an advantage from its moment of superiority.

If some countries fear that other countries can move more quickly from virtual to actual weapons than they can, everyone will work on worst-case assumptions. Under such circumstances crises easily develop from uncertainties the system spawns, aside from substantive matters. The parties to crises then find it risky to ride through them without furthering their military preparations, even though doing so predictably heightens tensions all around. The temptation to move first, eliminated by second-strike forces, would be reintroduced by a system of virtual arsenals. By placing a premium on speed of action in crises, virtual arsenals would increase the chances of accidents occurring, including the most important accident of all—the misjudgment of others' acts and intentions. Especially in crises, one's precautionary measures are easily taken by others as preparations to strike. One can scarcely believe that in an unstable system accidents are unlikely to happen. Competition over the ability to move first with decisive force is dangerous, a lesson well learned from the prehistory of World War I. The lesson was taken to heart by nuclear strategists of the 1950s and 1960s. We should not forget it.

The first big problem of a system of virtual arsenals is that deterrence would be problematic; the second that the system would be unstable. A third problem is a more subtle one. With nuclear forces-in-being, a state that has been attacked can choose the time for retaliation. Without nuclear forces-in-being, the attacker can make use of the pause imposed between aggression and retaliation. People would worry again, as they did in the 1950s and 1960s, about the possibility of a "Hamburg grab." (The worry was that the Soviet Union might pounce, secure, and hold an exposed territory and in effect ask whether its limited gain merited a military response.) A country could seize coveted ground, dig in to raise the cost of a counterattack, and announce that it had clandestinely assembled a small nuclear arsenal. The aggressor could then use its deterrent force to protect its illicit gains.

Worrying about a Hamburg grab seems fanciful, yet states have often hoped or feared that time could be used to gain military advantage. Some states may well think of additional ways to exploit an enforced interval between the ability to produce and the ability to use nuclear weapons, and others will fear their doing so. The scope of Egypt's and Syria's combined attack on Israel in 1973 was apparently limited by fear of Israel's nuclear deterrent.[11] If Egypt and Syria had believed that their forces could have joined hands by slicing Israel in two before a retaliatory strike could be mounted, they might have been tempted to try.

If rigorously enforced, a system of virtual arsenals would invite aggressors to use time to secure a military advantage. At this point one may wonder how the virtual arsenals that some states have—the undeclared nuclear forces of Israel, India, and Pakistan—work their deterrent effects. The answer is that everyone believes that those states do, or at least may, have warheads ready to use and that is enough to deter. In the same way cheating may save a system of virtual arsenals. The possibility of cheating would preserve the deterrent effect against major aggression that only weapons-in-being can reliably provide.

Knowing that states would still worry, virtual weaponeers add that states could always construct strategic defenses. With deterrence in abeyance and with the security of states uneasily dependent on a delicate mixture of obedience to rules and efforts to elude them, states will find strategic defenses attractive. A perfect defense against large nuclear arsenals is hard to imagine, but a defense capable of denying entry to warheads fired in small numbers may seem worth building.

A virtual arsenal system would be a rickety one. It would presumably work this way: knowing that others would follow suit, no state would be likely to rearm heavily. That would be of some comfort but not much. The nuclear deterrent would, as now, be the reliable one: fear of retaliation should rebuilt arsenals be used. And, if a country clandestinely readied weapons before other countries could ready their own, missile defenses would provide protection.

Might one then hope that there the system, if it can be called such, would come to rest, with small offensive forces posed against small defensive forces? Such a system would still be unstable with everyone worrying about the comparative quality of offensive and defensive forces and with each tempted to improve its capabilities, if only to make sure that the offensive/defensive balance be kept quite even. Moreover, with the level of insecurity high, all states would fear that one of them might try to exploit a momentary offensive or defensive advantage by striking first.

Under the circumstances, far from strengthening efforts to halt the spread of nuclear weapons, virtual arsenals would set the stage for the proliferation of nuclear weapons that the world has long feared but never seen. An unstable system with deterrence problematic would increase the insecurity of states. Insecure states would want at least to have the virtual arsenals that the new system would permit. The system would stimulate states to construct virtual arsenals and thus put themselves in a position to take the easy step from having the facilities for making the weapons to making the weapons themselves. Instead of halting the spread of nuclear weapons, a system of virtual arsenals would promote it.

States that feel insecure try to protect themselves. Some states believe, understandably, that nuclear weapons are the cheapest, safest, and surest way of doing so. Heroic efforts are required to keep states from getting the weapons they believe essential to their security. Virtual weaponeers admit the truth of this statement when they accept the likelihood of cheating within a system of virtual arsenals. Cheating would restore the effectiveness of deterrence by bringing it into closer correspondence with the system we now have. One wonders, then, why we should not leave well enough alone and why, with its obvious pitfalls, advocates of a system of virtual arsenals should be taken seriously.

The notion that virtual arsenals can be substituted for weapons-in-being is symptomatic of an idea now gaining popularity in the United States, the idea that nuclear weapons can be abolished. The vogue of abolition owes more, however, to the recent shift in world-political forces than to the merits of an idea. Reflecting on the rich experience of half a century at the center of international affairs, Paul Nitze has recently noted that while we once used nuclear weapons to offset the Soviet Union's conventional strength, others now use nuclear weapons to offset ours.[12] Les Aspin, when he was chairman of the House Armed

Services Committee, put the same thought in the following words: "A world without nuclear weapons would not be disadvantageous to the United States. In fact, a world without nuclear weapons would actually be better. Nuclear weapons are still the big equalizer, but now the United States is not the equalizer but the equalizee."[13]

A country's nuclear weapons deter other countries from using force against them much more surely than its conventional weapons can. Against countries that have nuclear weapons, the United States loses much of the advantage of its superiority in conventional weapons. Pointing this out, however, rather gives the game away. Nuclear weapons deter with an effectiveness that conventional weapons do not approach. That is the most important reason for wanting to have them. For illustration, we need look no farther than America's recent war in Iraq. If the United States had thought that Iraq might have had a few bombs, we would have had to manage the Iraq-Kuwait crisis differently, say by employing only an embargo. Invasion *might* have prompted Iraq to dump a couple of warheads on Haifa and Tel Aviv. We would not have wanted to run the risk, and Israel surely would not have complained about our unwillingness to use force in a headlong attack. A big reason for America's resistance to the spread of nuclear weapons is that if weak countries have some they will cramp our style. Militarily punishing small countries for behavior we dislike would become much more perilous.

Nuclear weapons in the hands of the weak limit what the strong can do to them. That is why the spread of nuclear weapons is so hard to stop, and why some leading American military experts have become abolitionists.

Nuclear weapons in the hands of other states depreciate the value of our conventional forces. So long as America's conventional superiority lasts, devaluing nuclear weapons would seem to serve our interests. Enhancing the value of conventional weapons by depreciating the value of nuclear ones would, however, stimulate conventional arms races and make wars easier to start. These results would serve neither our nor the world's interests. Nuclear weapons have helped to preserve the peace where it has been most endangered and prevented wars from getting out of hand in some of the most troublesome areas, as between the United States and the Soviet Union, between India and Pakistan, and in the Middle East. We should be wary of the false hopes held out by advocates of virtual arsenals.

318 KENNETH WALTZ

NOTES

I am grateful to Karen Ruth Adams and Rodha Pathak for their assistance on this essay.

1. Michael J. Mazarr, "Virtual Nuclear Arsenals," *Survival* 37, no. 3 (Autumn 1995): 22. Mazarr's essay provides an excellent summary of the case for a system of virtual arsenals.

2. See Kenneth N. Waltz, "Nuclear Myths and Political Realities," *American Political Science Review* 84, no. 3 (September 1990).

3. Linton F. Brooks, "Naval Power and National Security: The Case for the Maritime Strategy," *International Security* 11, no. 2 (Fall 1986): 71; John P. Rose, *The Evolution of U.S. Army Nuclear Doctrine, 1945 - 1980* (Boulder: Westview Press, 1980): 102-6; Michael Howard, "On Fighting a Nuclear War," *International Security* 5, no. 4 (Spring 1981): 3-17.

4. See, e.g., Bernard Brodie, Robert S. McNamara, and Herbert York, cited in Scott D. Sagan and Kenneth N. Waltz, *The Spread of Nuclear Weapons: A Debate* (New York: W. W. Norton, 1995): 108-09.

5. Jonathan Schell, *The Abolition* (New York: Knopf, 1984): 119-20.

6. Harold Brown, *Annual Report, Fiscal Year 1980* (Washington, D.C.: U.S. Department of Defense, 1979): 75-76.

7. Mazarr, "Virtual Nuclear Arsenals," 18.

8. Christopher S. Wren, "U.N. Expert Raises Estimates of Iraq's Biological Arsenal," *New York Times,* June 21, 1995, A6; Paul L. Leventhal and Edwin S. Lyman, "Who Says Iraq Isn't Making a Bomb?" *International Herald Tribune,* November 2, 1995, 8.

9. Mazarr, "Virtual Nuclear Arsenals," 19.

10. Paul H. Nitze, "Deterring Our Deterrent," *Foreign Policy* 25 (Winter 1976-77).

11. Gerald M. Steinberg, "After the NPT Extension: Israeli Policy Options," *IGCC Newsletter* 11, no. 2 (Fall 1995): 6.

12. Nitze, "Deterring Our Deterrent."

13. Les Aspin, House Armed Services Committee Hearings.

EIGHTEEN

VIRTUAL ARSENALS: A RUSSIAN VIEW

ALEXEI ARBATOV

HISTORICAL AND POLITICAL BACKGROUND

THE UNEXPECTED AND QUICK END OF THE COLD WAR has sent experts and politicians searching for new models of strategic relationships among major powers. Something was needed to supersede nuclear deterrence, which has been so inseparably associated with decades of East/West ideological and geopolitical confrontation. A concept of virtual nuclear arsenals (VNA) is one of the most interesting and substantive products of these intellectual explorations.

Actually, it should have emerged much earlier in various proposals and designs of the partisans of complete nuclear disarmament. It should have been clear that nuclear disarmament, as an end-state, may be not like absolute "zero" on the Kelvin scale but much more like zero by Celsius, below which, after the last warhead is withdrawn from operational service, there are many degrees of deeper and deeper denuclearization, down to Einstein theory in the minds of physicists. With few exceptions, however, it was never seriously explored.[1] Partly it was because "disarmament" served much more as a political slogan or symbol, rather than as a realistic concept of strategic relations among states, and partly it was due to the fact that disarmers were too preoccupied with more urgent and immediate problems of partial

nuclear arms control, weapons reduction, test limitation, and nonproliferation.

Beside the ideal of disarmament, the other parent of VNA was
quite practical. It was the concept, introduced under START I and
START II, of "downloading"—the declared and verifiable removal of
some of the nuclear warheads from a (MIRVed) strategic missile as a
method of reducing the total number of warheads, in contrast to
dismantling whole missiles, as envisioned under SALT I and SALT II.
This method led some experts to suggest downloading to zero some
portion of missiles, while retaining them in operational service, as a
faster, cheaper, and more acceptable way of lowering levels of nuclear
weapons in the superpowers' arsenals.[2]

The end of the Cold War helped the two parents come together,
since serious experts started to think seriously about nuclear disarmament, and total downloading to zero began to look like a more realistic
proposition. Thus was produced the child, called virtual nuclear
arsenals (VNA).

The principal merit of the concept is its circumventing the
traditional objection of "the impossibility of disinventing nuclear weapons" and greatly enhancing nonproliferation and counterproliferation in
the world. Nonetheless, at least two sobering observations of a general
nature are immediately warranted: numerous particular reservations and
counterarguments of a technical, strategic, and political kind.

First, for all the importance of the mutually reinforcing effects of
the Cold War and the nuclear arms race, their coincidence in time was
historically accidental. The invention of nuclear weapons could have
happened long before or after the period of four decades of U.S.-Soviet
bipolarity—geopolitical and ideological rivalry—that came to be identified as the Cold War era. Moreover, nuclear weapons had been initially
conceived and developed against each other not by the United States and
the Soviet Union, but by other enemies: the United States and Germany.
Nuclear bombs were first (and it is hoped it is the last time) employed
in anger between still other forces: the United States and Japan. Since
nuclear weapons were actually born before the Cold War, apart from our
hopes there is nothing historically persuasive to claim that they must die
with the end of Cold War.

Second, the Cold War was the main but not the only set of
confrontational relations during that time. Beside the enmity between the

United States and the USSR—or as it was called by the Soviets, West and East—there were many related but quite genuine conflicts between China and the West (including Japan, South Korea, and Taiwan), China and the USSR, China and India, China and Vietnam (and other Southeast Asian states), Israel and Arabia, Iran and Iraq, each of the two and other Persian Gulf countries, India and Pakistan, Turkey and Greece, South Africa and its neighbors, etc. Some of these vectors of regional hostilities gave birth to their own open, tacit or potential nuclear races.

The end of the Cold War did away only with one, although the principal, global axis of international confrontation, that of East and West, and made it easier to manage some other conflicts. In the future, however, other confrontations might continue, and new ones could erupt and escalate, fueling a nuclear arms race. Of those, renewed hostilities between China and the West and/or China and Russia would be of greatest nuclear significance.

Last, but not least, after several years of euphoria, relations between Russia and the West once again look uncertain and fraught with big controversies, if not outright conflicts. Due to Russia's relative economic, military, and political weakening at present and at least during the next decade, its potential new confrontation with the West can hardly acquire a global scale. If not averted, it could have regional dimensions: with NATO, over redivision of Central and Eastern Europe, and/or with NATO member Turkey over the influence in the Balkans, Transcaucasus, Central Asia, and even Russian North Caucasus. This regional rivalry could lead to renewed hostilities, confrontation, and some revival of the nuclear arms race. Even if for economic reasons (foremost because of Russia's size) there will be no large-scale nuclear competition, tense relations and mutual suspicions would be enough to undercut any new ambitious disarmament design and maybe even the existing arms-control regimes.

Hence, the concept of VNA cannot be considered as merely a technical adaptation of the nuclear powers' strategic relationships to a new and promising post–Cold War era, which we presently witness or expect in the foreseeable future. To implement the option of VNA requires not only resolving numerous concrete problems, but, and much more important, it demands profound improvements in the worlds' political and military environments and in great powers' ability to cooperate and trust one another.

Among other things, this is predicated on domestic democratization and stability in Russia and China as well as on the ability of the United States and some of its principal allies to prevent domestic political shifts toward nationalism, conservatism, and isolationism. In short, for the idea to work, the benign changes in the world that would be needed in the future are of much greater scale and depth than those that happened during the last ten years and which gave birth to the VNA concept in the first place.

GEOSTRATEGIC ENVIRONMENT

Despite the end of the Cold War it looks as if the United States and the Russian Federation (RF) continue to evolve out of sync with each other in terms of their nuclear arms–control policies. In January 1986, when Mikhail Gorbachev made his declaration on doing away with nuclear weapons by the year 2000, this was offhandedly dismissed in the West as yet another piece of Soviet propaganda. Moscow's major breakthroughs from 1987 to 1991 on the INF-SRF, CFE, and START I Treaties, unilateral steps to curtail some weapon programs, and reduction of tactical nuclear arms parallel with U.S. initiatives—all proved that Gorbachev was serious, if not strategically very practical or consistent, about radical measures of nuclear disarmament. In 1991-92 Boris Yeltsin's attitude toward improvement of relations with the West and further nuclear cuts and weapon programs curtailment opened the door for unprecedented denuclearization steps between former "mortal rivals."

The U.S. nuclear policy under the Bush administration, however, was quite conservative and cautious. It never went beyond the START II Treaty, largely formed by the U.S. negotiating position and strategic-forces modernization plans, and it exercised only partial tactical nuclear arms withdrawals and cuts. After a surprisingly conservative Nuclear Posture Review (NPR) by the Clinton administration in 1993, the U.S. position started to change in 1994-95, toward more radical nuclear disarmament, which was manifested, among other things, by a growing interest in the VNA concept.

This evolution was motivated by some pragmatic considerations, centered on U.S. self-interest and hardly taking into account divergent perspectives of others. Unprecedented U.S. and Western conventional superiority over a weakened Russia and concern over Russian "loose nukes" all of a sudden started to change the 50-year-old position held by the United States on the indispensability of robust and overwhelming nuclear deterrence for its security. But some of the new U.S. views against nuclear weapons were exactly the other side of the coin and made nuclear arms more attractive to other parties.

At exactly the same time the Russian position started to change in a reverse direction. After two failed sessions of the Russian Security Council, on March 3 and October 6, the new military doctrine was approved at the Security Council session on November 2. That same day the document "Principle Guidance on the Military Doctrine of the Russian Federation" (PGMD) was officially legalized by presidential decree no. 1833.[3]

The nuclear part of the presidential decree consisted of several main innovations. First, it was stated unequivocally that the "goal of the Russian federation policy in the area of nuclear weapons is the removal of the threat of nuclear war by way of deterring its initiation against the Russian federation and its allies."[4] After several years of utopian concepts of substituting deterrence with something different, this was a positive and realistic point, clearing the issue and theoretically allowing Russian leaders to address real problems without confusion and wishful thinking. Nonetheless, the concrete formula of deterrence was much more dubious and controversial.

In particular, and this was the second point, the 1982 non-first-use (NFU) pledge was officially revoked. It was elaborately stated that the Russian Federation would not employ nuclear weapons against any other state party to the NPT Treaty that: (1) is not a nuclear power, (2) is not an ally of a nuclear power, and (3) does not conduct joint operations with a nuclear power in aggression against the RF, its territory, its allies, or its forces. To put it in a different way, Russia would feel entitled to use nuclear weapons against any nuclear power, any nonnuclear ally, or any nonnuclear nonaligned state, acting militarily in alliance with a nuclear power and any nonnuclear, nonaligned state, not acting jointly with a nuclear power, if this state is not a party to the NPT Treaty of 1968.

Third, there was more confusion, because it did not follow from the text of the PGMD whether this highly permissive formula meant first-use/strike or second-use/retaliatory strike. Further elaborations of the highest officials from the Ministry of Defense and Security Council made it clear, however, that the subject of this part of the decree did refer to the first strike.[5]

Fourth, the strategic requirements were interpreted as "maintaining a structure and state of strategic nuclear forces at the level, providing for assured inflicting of the designated damage on aggressor under any circumstances." Compared to traditional notions of "massive," "crushing," "maximum" retaliation, the new goal sounded more limited and selective, which might indicate recognition of previously overstated damage requirements and of the prospects of deep force reduction (under START II, or even without it, because of obsolescence and curtailment of modernization programs).

Fifth, the technical requirements were stated as "maintaining the whole complex of strategic weapons at the level, ensuring the security of the Russian Federation, its allies, strategic stability, deterring nuclear and conventional war, as well as nuclear safety."[6] This was yet another clear statement, assigning the strategic forces the task of deterring conventional war, which implied a first-use/strike strategy.

The main arguments in favor of the rejection of the 1982 Soviet commitment are as follows:

- The declaration of 1982 was purely propagandistic, and its revocation means realistic adaptation of declaratory doctrine and strategy to practical strategy and force capabilities.
- Other "civilized" states (i.e., NATO states, which impolitely implies that China is not "civilized") have not followed the Soviet example and have not assumed the non-first-use concept.
- Russia's strategic forces and C3I (for economic reasons and as a result of deep reductions either unilaterally or under START II) will be more vulnerable to a counterforce nuclear strike, making second-strike or launch-on warning less reliable for deterrence.
- Moscow's strategic forces will become more vulnerable for conventional precision-guided weapons, because of their further development parallel with strategic force reduction and restructuring.
- Russian conventional forces are too weak, as a result of the disintegration of the USSR, the economic crisis in Russia, and

the transitional stage of current military reforms. They have to be compensated with higher reliance on nuclear weapons, much like NATO had been doing during the Cold War to counter Soviet and Warsaw Treaty Organization (WTO) conventional superiority.

Indeed, after the disintegration of the Warsaw Treaty and then of the USSR, in 1992-93, NATO could have safely adopted the NFU pledge, which would have brought substantial strategic and political benefits in its relations with Russia, regarding nuclear weapons in Ukraine and Kazakhstan, and for NPT enhancement. Having been too cautious, conservative, and preoccupied with inter-NATO affairs, the United States and its allies missed an important opportunity to legalize post–Cold War stability. Unwillingly, they have helped conservative pro-nuclear groups in Russia, all the more so because the NFU question held important political significance within the country.

The future vulnerability of strategic forces and their inability to retaliate after attack is a matter of assumptions and modeling, but it seems exaggerated. Nevertheless, in this case the United States bears part of the responsibility. Washington's conservative attitude to revising nuclear strategy, unjustified continuing reliance on counterforce targeting and options, vagueness about extended deterrence and the first-use concept, as well as reluctance to accept greater restraints on sea-based counterforce capability were not lost on Russian advocates of a first-strike strategy.

Actual (in contrast to virtual) nuclear arsenals, at a time of economic, political, ideological, and military weakness and uncertainty, are perceived by the majority of the Russian new political elite like the only legacy of its former status and influence in the world, making it still formally equal to the United States and superior to all other nations, which helps to compensate for the detrimental effects of Russia's economic and geopolitical vulnerabilities. Under the circumstances a proposition to downgrade the nuclear factor radically through VNA implementation could be perceived in Russia as a plan to deny it the only tangible political and military asset it has retained and to push it far down the international hierarchy.

In spite of its large territory (which puts Russia in the category of Australia and Canada) the civilian economy (GNP size), as a result of

Saxs/Gaidar/IMF "shock therapy," is at the level of Italy or Brazil—to say nothing of Japan, Germany, France or China—and probably lower in terms of military production. In terms of population Russia is smaller than Germany, France, and Britain put together, or smaller than the population of China's northern provinces. Russia's non-Muslim population is smaller than that of Turkey, Iran, Azerbaijan, or the Central Asian former Soviet republics. The Russian army is close to that of the United States in terms of personnel numbers, but is funded at the level of less than 10 percent of the U.S. defense budget. Liberated internal prices and free domestic convertibility of the ruble (while internal prices approach world levels) are having disastrous effects on armed forces morale, combat readiness, maintenance, and equipment.

Many things have to change inside and outside of Russia, including the attitude of the United States and other states, to persuade enough Russians that with a deactivated nuclear arsenal it will receive its due in the international arena.

Beside these general reservations, there are two particular issues bearing directly on the acceptability of the VNA idea to Russia: the Western conventional counterforce threat to Russian strategic forces, and trade-offs between Russia's conventional and nuclear balance and deterrence capabilities.

CONVENTIONAL COUNTERFORCE QUESTION

The increasing vulnerability of strategic forces to conventional precision-guided air-launched and some sea-launched weapons is a matter of growing concern to the Russian military and almost totally neglected by U.S. strategists. The Western capability seems exaggerated, but the United States has been doing virtually nothing to alleviate concerns about it in Moscow.

The experience gained from the military operations in the Persian Gulf clearly demonstrated the effectiveness of precision-guided nonnuclear weapons in destroying military sites, command-control and communication posts, and other hardened point targets in Iraq. In this respect Russian experts naturally raise the question: How far might such a capability present a hypothetical threat to Russian mobile and silo-based strategic missiles and command-control and communication systems, especially given the reductions under START II?

According to some military forecasts, at present about 240 strategic bombers and 5,500 tactical strike aircraft are available to NATO world-wide. By the year 2000 these numbers may be, respectively, 180 and 6,500, of which 25 percent of heavy bombers and 5 to 7 percent of tactical aviation may be realistically allocated for conventional strikes against Russian strategic forces. Of all Russian fixed and mobile missile bases, 100 percent would be within the range of converted heavy bombers and about 40 to 50 percent within the range of tactical aircraft.[7] It is further estimated that during two to three weeks of intensive conventional air strikes, NATO aviation would be capable at present of destroying around 20 percent of fixed ICBM silos and 40 to 50 percent of railway and mobile ICBM launchers. By the year 2003, after implementation of most of START II reductions and planned strategic force modernization, NATO aircraft would be capable of destroying about 60 percent of fixed and 15 percent of mobile ICBM launchers.

What is no less important: by hitting bridges, roads, and fixed structures in mobile ICBM deployment areas, conventional strikes might greatly degrade their mobility, thus "softening" them for potential nuclear counterforce attack, while fixed silos would be vulnerable to such a strike anyway. Even greater damage could be inflicted by conventional strikes on command-control and communication systems.

Apparently, the assumption is that Russia would not respond to conventional air raids with strategic nuclear retaliation against the U.S. homeland. It is somewhat similar to the core problem of NATO strategy in the 1960-80's, which was the degree of credibility of nuclear retaliation to counter Soviet conventional attack, including conventional strikes against NATO tactical nuclear weapons sites. The Russian assumption is that conventional attacks might have some advantages for NATO, compared to a nuclear counterforce strike. In particular, they do not inflict vast collateral damage, provoking all-out nuclear retaliation. The NATO force may repeat the strikes continually to achieve high kill results, while in nuclear attack all targets have to be destroyed in the first attempt. Conventional attacks are most threatening to those forces that are least vulnerable to nuclear counterforce operations: land-based mobile ICBMs. Finally, this is the area of greatest asymmetry in favor of the United States, since Russia virtually lacks any conventional, let alone counterforce, strike capability against the U.S. homeland.

While the conventional counterforce threat still may seem a dubious issue when both sides have combat-ready strategic forces, it would look different under the VNA scenario. Apart from the problem of verification and insuring equal reconstitution time for all the parties, is an issue that has been addressed by Western experts; still more difficult and perhaps more acute would be the problem of conventional strikes against strategic missile and submarine bases, airfields, command and control sites, support and maintenance infrastructure, nuclear warheads storage facilities (or nuclear materials storage facilities), facilities for manufacturing nuclear warheads and transporting and installing them back to delivery vehicles, as well as nuclear power stations and enrichment and reprocessing plants.

Here the danger of immediate nuclear escalation might be safely disregarded by a hypothetical aggressor. Also, in technical, military, and geostrategic categories, the West has a relative advantage. In this respect, for the VNA to be at a minimum palatable to Russians, something should be done to remove the preponderant conventional counterforce capability of NATO. This, however, is just the kind of capability proposed in the U.S. as a substitute for actual nuclear deterrence and as an instrument of counterproliferation, which should be built up and enhanced to a maximum degree.

In order not to make Russians suspicious an unprecedented degree of trust and political cooperation would be needed between Russia and the West, virtually an alliance. Such relations would, of course, greatly simplify the implementation of VNA by Russia and the three Western nuclear powers. But at the same time the whole notion of deterrence would then disappear from their relations (allies do not fear one another's nuclear weapons; they develop joint nuclear policy), together with some basic arguments in favor of VNA and its value as a substitute for operational deterrence.

CONVENTIONAL FORCES BALANCE

The principle of making up for the lack of conventional forces by greater reliance on nuclear weapons in deterrence strategy and operational planning alike is as old as the Dulles "massive retaliation" strategy of 1954. After 1967 and during the next quarter century, in spite of the shift to "flexible response" and its various successive versions, NATO was retaining the first-use option for its forward-based tactical nuclear forces in Western Europe, trying to outweigh the almost triple aggregate numerical superiority of the USSR and Warsaw Treaty Organization in offensive conventional ground and air forces on the continent.[8]

Disintegration of the WTO, breakup of the Soviet Union, deep economic crisis and high inflation in Russia, failure of conversion and military reform in 1991-93, political and administrative turmoil—all these have greatly degraded conventional forces, which were historically the strongest Soviet/Russian point. From a strategic point of view, as it looks from Moscow, for several years shifts of enormous strategic importance have occurred. Their dimension is similar to what happened historically in Europe only as a result of major powers having been defeated in large continental wars.

First, the double blow of disintegration of the Warsaw Pact and of the USSR has led to a deep decline in Moscow's relative military position in the space of only a few years. The East/West balance of conventional forces has been changing and would eventually shift for Moscow from a nearly threefold superiority to an almost threefold inferiority, compared to Western armed forces, and to fivefold inferiority if those are joined by the forces of Central European states and some former Soviet republics. Russia's position in the world nuclear balance is gradually deteriorating for technical and economic reasons as well.

Second, once highly integrated, the defense industry and armed forces of the Soviet Union fell apart as a result of the disbanding of the USSR in 1991 and under the impact of an unprecedented economic crisis in Russia since that time, its social, demographic, and political calamities; and profound failures of the military reforms and defense-industrial conversion. Dismemberment of the former Soviet defense space and structure not only has disproportionately undercut the remaining Russian part (to say nothing of other republics) but also has presented the Russian army with new contingencies emanating from local instabilities and possible outside intervention in the post-Soviet subregions. As the operation in Chechnya in early 1995 showed, the Russian army had been severely disorganized, weakened, and mismanaged—probably at its lowest point since June 1941, when it suffered a catastrophic initial defeat at the hands of the German Vehrmacht.

Third, in a geostrategic sense Moscow's present military power has been drawn back 1,500 kilometers from the center of Europe: from Magdeburg and Prague to Smolensk and Kursk. For the first time in 300 years (in peacetime) the Moscow military district has gone from being the deep rear to the advanced defense line of Russia.

The radical strategic shifts are indeed not to Moscow's advantage. Nevertheless, there are some obvious political and economic benefits of the new international environment. The North Atlantic alliance is being reformed in the direction of greater emphasis on political functions and peace-keeping operations. The role of collective defense is getting smaller; armed forces, weapons, and defense expenditures of member states are being cut; foreign troops are partially being withdrawn from their territories; and programs of cooperation are being developed with NATO former opponents.

The prospect of NATO expansion to the East, however, would once again change Russia's perceptions of Western intentions. NATO enlargement could undermine the prospects of genuine post–Cold War European security.

Russian politicians and the military, instead of implementing radical reforms and redirecting defense to the south and east, would resume their customary task: planning large-scale conventional and nuclear war in the European theatre. Moreover, they would decide that, once NATO without valid reason advances eastward, it is Russia's duty to move its line of defense as far westward as possible. That would influence Moscow's policy in regard to the Kaliningrad region, the Baltic states, Ukraine, Belarus, Moldova, and the countries of Eastern Europe, and would fuel a buildup of forces in the European part of Russia. This, in turn, would lead to a worsening of ethnic and territorial clashes over the division of the military inheritance of the USSR, including the remaining nuclear legacy.

NATO extension would greatly enhance, first, Western conventional capabilities against Russian conventional forces. Second, Western conventional counterforce capabilities against Russian nuclear forces, support infrastructure, maintenance and production facilities, command control, and early-warning assets. Third, it would damage political relations, trust, and the possibility of cooperation between

Russia and the West. All those consequences make the prospects of VNA quite bleak indeed.

In the Far East two powers, Japan and China, may present a threat to Russia. Japan's offensive conventional capabilities against Russia will be quite limited, at least for the rest of the decade. Its attempt to take back the Kuril islands or Sakhalin by force is inconceivable (although VNA implementation could alleviate the Japanese antinuclear syndrome, as one element of their aversion to war and the use of force).

China is a special matter. Its contemporary crash military buildup, geostrategic position, and long history of territorial disputes with Russia and the USSR might in the future encourage Beijing's expansionist policies toward Russia's Siberia and the Far East or against Kazakhstan and Central Asian allies of Moscow. In time it may achieve conventional offensive superiority along the Transbaikal and Maritime borders, thus gaining serious reinforcement advantages and capabilities for the interdiction of Russian reinforcements from its western territory. On the other hand, China will remain inferior to Russia in the number of tactical nuclear weapons and its strategic nuclear capabilities, allowing for Moscow's credible first-use threat and escalation dominance.

Chinese conventional buildup greatly depends on massive imports of weapons and technology from Russia. Thus, besides the nuclear threat, Moscow has effective means of undercutting or at least seriously slowing down the emergence of this hypothetical threat. At a minimum, to deter effectively China's conventional offensive superiority at the theater, Russia might rely on the option of employing tactical nuclear weapons in the border area to thwart the enemy's offensive operations while deterring China's nuclear response at the strategic level by superior (assured destruction) strategic retaliatory capabilities. Then Russia's deterrence would be credible: its nuclear capabilities would be sufficient to deny China's alleged military gains at the theatre but not threatening to its national survival and thus would not provoke its strategic nuclear preemption.

Implementation of the VNA concept may deny Russia this strategy and require an expensive buildup of conventional forces along the border with China. Even if the reconstitution capability could be made effective against the emergence of a nuclear threat, it might be much less impressive as a deterrent against conventional encroachment, if the other side has a reconstitution capability of its own to deter indirect or direct nuclear response. To make VNA acceptable to Russia in view of its problems in Asia, Russia's political and security relations with China, Japan, and the United States would have to improve profoundly (which also implies resolution of some subregional conflicts in Asia and the Asian-Pacific zone) to decrease the attractiveness of actual nuclear deterrence and render VNA an attractive proposition.

TECHNICAL AND POLITICAL ISSUES

A number of considerations of a more practical nature are worth mentioning, if only briefly. First, for the VNA concept to be acceptable, equality in terms of reconstitution capability would be much more crucial and hard to fix, technically, and verify than most Western experts apparently believe. With deployed and combat-ready nuclear forces, various differences and asymmetries among nations are made less significant by sheer destructive magnitude, uncertainty, and the horror of projected nuclear-weapons use. But under VNA the discrepancies in technical characteristics of weapon systems, in force structures, support and maintenance facilities, C3I capabilities, and nuclear production complexes may enormously affect reconstitution capabilities—by days or even months. This could create much more dangerous temptations in preempting reconstitution or even using conventional or nuclear forces to deny reconstitution to others.

Besides, the alliance relationships would play a larger role in creating asymmetries in the speed and scale of reconstitution. This would make VNA quite advantageous to the United States, Britain, and France, and much less so for Russia or China.

Multilateral talks have not yet been tried even on classic nuclear arms reduction measures. Multilateral negotiations of the five legal nuclear powers on the VNA concept would be more, not less, difficult than yet-untried talks on mere arms limitations or reductions. Apart from other problems, at such talks smaller nuclear powers would be concerned about tacit or potential nuclear weapons states such as India, Pakistan, Iran, Iraq, Israel, and Libya, which would have to be involved in the verification regime and limitation procedures while denying that they even possess nuclear weapons.

To summarize, the many problems of strategic asymmetries that have plagued SALT/START negotiators for decades would hit VNA talks much harder, and would be augmented by the effects of asymmetries in support infrastructures, production facilities, conventional counterforce capabilities, tactical nuclear forces, C3I performance, as well as the multilateral character of negotiations.

Second, there is a great difference in the VNA concept of forces just downloaded to zero, with warheads placed in controlled storages, and the VNA version in which warheads are partially or completely dismantled. These two options would imply quite different problems of verification, such as preventing reconstitution preemption and providing for the facilities' survivability against conventional or nuclear attacks.

Besides, the requirement to deal with nuclear weapons obsolescence and produce the warheads or their elements for replacing arsenals in storages would require additional and quite difficult agreements. It would make IAEA tasks more difficult and controversial than just insuring the absence of production or acquisition of weapons-grade uranium or plutonium and verifying the ban on warhead manufacturing.

Third, preventing surprise or preemptive reconstitution would require dealing not only with strategic but also with tactical nuclear weapons and substrategic systems such as SLCMs. Those up to now have been largely beyond the scope of arms-control agreements (except the INF-SRF Treaty). They were a subject of unilateral or parallel reduction and withdrawal commitments with very loose transparency procedures, if any.

This would not be acceptable under the VNA design. And this would imply involving a substantial part of conventional or dual-purpose naval, air, and ground forces' systems, and their operations and support infrastructure, in the regime of limitations and verification. The exhausting saga of START I talks on SLCM limitations is a good illustration of what is in store in this part of VNA. Actually, cruise missile submarines would be among the most threatening systems for possibly violating a VNA regime.

Fourth, the goal of the VNA end-state, if defined and agreed upon by the nuclear powers, would require revision of some principles of the process of phased nuclear arms reductions, which would have to be negotiated and implemented as intermediate steps. As a result, some serious logical contradictions may occur. For instance, shifting the structures of deterrence forces to sea, as embodied in the START I and START II Treaties, may have to be reconsidered.

Ballistic missile submarines are the most controversial systems under the VNA regime. There is no sense in keeping them on patrol (except for training purposes) without nuclear warheads. All proposals of providing for at-sea uploading capabilities look either impractical, threatening in terms of violation, or make SSBNs too vulnerable and thus do not serve their purpose. Keeping them in ports without nuclear warheads or without missiles would make them and their support facilities and storages highly lucrative targets for nuclear or conventional preemption. At the same time, uploading them in ports and deploying them at sea would provide the largest and fastest breakout capability. To some extent the same is true about strategic and tactical aircraft.

The best system for VNA is a single-warhead, silo-based missile with its warhead stored separately. The second best is ground-mobile ICBM. They are less vulnerable, less attractive targets, and at the same time quite easy to verify and monitor under the "downloading to zero" regime. But even MIRV-capable missiles would be preferable to SSBNs, strategic and tactical nuclear-capable airplanes, or cruise missile submarines.

Another crucial matter is whether the VNA concept permits a limited number of combat-ready and deployed nuclear forces (100-200 warheads) as insurance against cheating or breakout. For this purpose the United States and its allies would certainly nominate SSBNs or cruise missile SSGNs, while Russia and China would opt for mobile or fixed land-based ICBMs. In such a version, however, VNA is nothing more than a finite (minimum) nuclear deterrence concept with large-scale breakout capability.

Apart from a possibility of fixing some kind of equality among the five nuclear powers in their combat-ready forces (while preserving U. S. and Russian superiority in reconstitution potential) this does not change in any principal way the traditional strategic relationships of mutual deterrence. Nor does it deviate too far from the traditional arms-control model, aimed at strategic stability at lower force levels. To get down to such levels incrementally from present force numbers would be much easier than to make a quantum jump from finite deterrence to the full VNA end-state.

Fifth, the idea of matching the VNA regime with ballistic missile and air defenses to protect strategic bases, warhead storages, transportation and uploading equipment, and C3I assets against a preemptive strike by a would-be cheater looks very attractive. Unlike the present state of affairs or a potential minimum deterrent relationship, under a full VNA regime the BMD system would not be destabilizing. It would help to protect legal reconstitution capability but would be unable to deny reconstituted retaliatory capability.

As long as strategic relations among nuclear powers remain those of mutual deterrence, BMD systems would be either unnecessary or destabilizing. A full VNA regime would certainly do away with classic deterrence, and hence the effects of strategic defenses could be stabilizing.

Some reservations, however, are still in order. One is that strategic defenses might be effective against minimal nuclear attack against reconstitution facilities but not against massive conventional counterforce strikes, which are among the greatest Russian concerns. Another is that, at least for Russia, protection of such vital and so few sites as warhead storage facilities would create strong interest in nuclear armed interceptors to insure destruction of missile re-entry vehicles and avoid their explosion on impact (if primed this way). Finally, all nuclear powers for economic and technical reasons would have unequal defensive capabilities. This may exacerbate their reconstitution asymmetries or require joint defense systems, with all the problems this implies.

CONCLUSION

The concept of virtual nuclear arsenals as a stage in nuclear disarmament is an extremely interesting and challenging idea. Its main value is that it provides a nonidealistic and practical vision of nuclear disarmament and the possibility of effective nonproliferation and counterproliferation cooperation among major powers. No doubt, it is worth further collective research and intellectual efforts by experts and politicians from different countries.

The United States' propensity, however, to use such concepts to enhance its strategic advantages (that is, conventional superiority and power projection capabilities) might defeat its purpose. Other nations may object to the concept precisely because it looks expedient to the United States.

There is much more to the concept of virtual nuclear arsenals than just technically deactivating nuclear forces and expanding their transparency. The implementation of VNA would require an unprecedented

degree of consensus on mutual interests and cooperation among principal powers. Their relations would have to change profoundly, as would
existing methods of force development and employment, both for
nuclear and conventional forces and systems.

The role of international organizations would have to acquire
qualitatively new dimensions in world politics as well as in establishing
and enforcing new rules of international behavior. The United States
would not only have to observe these rules, like all other nations, but, most
likely, take the lead in introducing them and abiding by their terms.

NOTES

1. See Jonathan Schell, *The Abolition* (New York: Alfred Knopf, 1984).
2. See A. Arbatov, ed. "Implications of the START-II Treaty for U.S.-Russian
   Relations" (Henry L. Stimson Center, Report no. 9, Washington, October
   1993), chap. 6.
3. See "Principle Guidance on the Military Doctrine of the Russian Federation,"
   Izvestiya, no. 221, November 18, 1993, 1-4.
4. Ibid.
5. See interview with M. Kolesnikov, *Segodnia,* December 29, 1993, 9; interview
   with O. Lobov, *Izvestiya,* no. 211, November 4, 1993, 1.
6. Ibid.
7. Heavy bombers of B-52G and B-1B types may be equipped to deliver in each
   sortie 8 to 22 AGM-137A missiles or 38 GBU-11 guided bombs. Tactical
   aircraft of F-15A, F-15C, F-15E, F-16, F-111, F-117, F-22, or Tornado types
   may carry variable loading of 2 to 6 AGM-65 Maverick, 4 AGM-130A, or
   AGM-84E missiles and 2 to 4 GBU-8, GBU-10, GBU-11, and GBU-15
   bombs.
8. Later this ratio was revealed by data exchange relating to the CFE Treaty of
   1990. By accepted arms-control definitions, tanks, armored combat vehicles,
   artillery, combat aircraft (except strategic heavy bombers and ASW aircraft),
   and attack helicopters are considered to be offensive weapons.

Managing Asymmetries and Instabilities in Nuclear Reconstitution

Patrick Garrity

ANY STABLE NUCLEAR "ARCHITECTURE" of the future—whether it involves competition between deployed nuclear forces, the presence of virtual arsenals, or nuclear abolition—must take into account the possibility of changing strategic conditions. In the case of a virtual nuclear weapons regime, allowance will have to be made for reconstituting nuclear forces. The essay in this volume by Michael Wheeler considers many of the major issues concerning the reconstitution and reassembly of a virtual nuclear arsenal. This essay seeks to complement his analysis by considering potential asymmetries and instabilities in the reconstitution process that must be taken into account.

To the extent that virtual nuclear forces would have the advantages of an arsenal-in-being, without the accompanying dangers, the reconstitution process must be visible, predictable, and ultimately stable. This is unlike the case of nuclear abolition, in which the focus and weight of the arms-control regime would be to prevent, or at least provide ample warning of, the recreation of a nuclear capability. In certain respects, at least conceptually, verifying nuclear abolition would actually be an easier task than balancing the risks and advantages of a virtual nuclear weapons agreement that includes a "reconstitution allowance." The necessarily brief analysis in this essay highlights the complexity and challenge of the issue.

To take one example: reconstitution and reassembly may not be the correct concept to apply to a virtual nuclear weapons agreement (although for reasons of consistency we will still use those terms in this essay). *Re* implies that nations that activate their nuclear arsenal would follow the same path—doctrinally as well as technologically—that they followed in creating their original capabilities. The allowance for reconstitution in a virtual nuclear weapons regime, however, must account not only for the predictable but also for the unpredictable, as nations may choose to follow a different path. For instance, if a virtual nuclear power decided to focus its reconstituted arsenal on nuclear effects (e.g., electromagnetic pulse) rather than on physical destruction, the desired size and character of that arsenal might be very different than that of a traditional nuclear force.

POTENTIAL ASYMMETRIES AND INSTABILITIES

Although many potential asymmetries and instabilities would involve technical issues (e.g., the survivability of reconstituted nuclear arsenals), some of the most critical problems could involve political differences. I will summarize some of the most salient topics in the pages that follow.

VIRTUAL NUCLEAR ARSENALS AND NONNUCLEAR STATES

A significant difference will continue between those states that choose to remain or become virtual nuclear powers and nations that are nonnuclear powers. Nonnuclear states will undoubtedly seek security assurances, or to exact some diplomatic price, if they agree to that status, as long as nuclear reconstitution is permitted. The set of bargains between the nuclear and nonnuclear weapons states under the current Non-Proliferation Treaty (NPT) regime would probably not suffice to deal with this fundamental asymmetry.

A first-order question would involve whether the nonnuclear powers should forswear the possibility of constituting their own nuclear force, in the event that a virtual nuclear power legally activated its capability. This asymmetry could be avoided by encouraging all states to become virtual nuclear powers or at least to treat them as such. But such a course would likely prove neither desirable nor acceptable in practice. If international tensions are reduced to the point where a virtual nuclear weapons regime does emerge, Germany and Japan, for instance, would likely have no interest in moving away from a nonnuclear posture. Nuclear powers such as Russia and China, in turn, would probably not accede to a virtual nuclear weapons regime in the event that Germany and Japan sought virtual nuclear equality.

The most likely solution to this basic asymmetry will involve, as in the past, positive and negative security assurances. Such assurances must be robust in the event of a permitted nuclear reconstitution on the part of virtual nuclear powers, and nonnuclear weapons states would always retain the right to reconsider their posture in the event of a nuclear breakout. But, in addition, nonnuclear powers might seek to establish asymmetrical military capabilities of a different sort, to protect themselves in the event of nuclear reconstitution or breakout.

The most obvious route would be that of maintaining an option to produce other types of weapons of mass destruction, but this hedge should hardly be encouraged. Of perhaps more interest to nonnuclear states would be an asymmetrical capability consisting of ballistic missile defenses and advanced conventional military capabilities. Such capabilities, which could be maintained actively under a virtual nuclear arrangement, might be credible—even advantageous—against a reconstituted nuclear power, if the numbers and sophistication of the reassembled nuclear arsenals were limited. Of course, for a variety of reasons some or all of the virtual nuclear powers themselves might well be inclined to maintain highly effective conventional forces, thus maintaining or even widening the military gap between (virtual) nuclear haves and have-nots.

DIFFERENCES AMONG VIRTUAL NUCLEAR POWERS

Important asymmetries concerning reconstitution will undoubtedly exist even among virtual nuclear weapons states. For example, Russia and the United States once fielded diverse nuclear arsenals that were developed by extensive testing programs. These arsenals were also supported by a massive industrial and technological infrastructure. To a greater or lesser degree other virtual nuclear powers would lack these inherent historic strengths, which could be drawn upon for the purposes of reconstitution.

Some of the most significant technical/industrial asymmetries would include:

- Sophistication and reliability of nuclear designs. Presumably, with the very limited numbers of weapons or components allowed under virtual nuclear weapons regime, nations will choose to retain those systems best suited to reconstitution. Some nations (e.g., Russia, the United States) may have an advantage because of their broader "menu" of choices. Or, ironically, those nations that had already planned on a virtual nuclear arsenal (e.g., India, Israel) might be better off.

- Capabilities of reconstituted nuclear delivery systems. Rather than redevelop a dedicated and unique nuclear force structure, at least at first, reconstituting nuclear powers would likely draw upon extant delivery systems that were being used for conventional purposes (e.g., refitting nuclear weapons on cruise missiles). Thus, the stronger aviation powers—which enjoy stealth, accuracy, and large numbers of platforms—would likely have early advantages under a reconstitution scenario.

- Ability/necessity to test. Some virtual nuclear weapons states may be able to retain confidence in their stockpile through advanced simulation and modeling techniques, but others may not have made the necessary investment in these capabilities to sustain a reconstituted stockpile. Safety or reliability questions could emerge even for those states with sophisticated computational capabilities. But even a testing loophole would not necessarily address this asymmetry: some nations may well not retain or have access to an operational test site (e.g., France).

- Survivability of reconstituted forces. Here, everything else being equal, the potential advantage could accrue to those nations that have hedged in a way that allows them to take advantage of geography (e.g., the large size of Russia, China, and the United States; Britain's access to the sea).

- Command, control, communication and intelligence. An asymmetry caused by inequalities in C3I could increase the confidence of some powers that they could carry out a preemptive strike while causing others to fear that their reconstituted nuclear C3I system was vulnerable to conventional as well as nuclear attack.

The playing field for reconstituted nuclear forces can probably be leveled to some extent. Time may itself serve to equalize the ability to reactivate a virtual nuclear arsenal. Ironically, the very sophistication of the U.S. and Russian nuclear arsenals may work against them in a reconstitution scenario. It may prove difficult to reassemble, or remanufacture, complicated weapons that were originally designed to operate close to the margin in terms of yield-to-weight ratio. Nations that produced "cruder" weapons could actually have an advantage, perhaps offsetting other disadvantages in capabilities (e.g., less advanced delivery systems).

The decisive material factor in maintaining a level playing field with respect to reconstitution would concern the supply of weapons-grade nuclear material and tritium. A virtual nuclear world of necessity would be one in which production of plutonium and highly enriched uranium had ceased or was closely controlled. The fissile material available for reconstitution would remain in disassembled weapons or in storage, but it would have to be sized to support only a stockpile of limited number (e.g., several hundred). There would also have to be some means of regulating the supply of tritium (which must be replenished at some point as the radioactive gas decays). Arguably, some nations might seek an agreement permitting them to possess somewhat greater quantities of fissile nuclear materials and tritium, on the basis of their unique weapon design requirements. There would be additional uncertainties associated with fears of cheating, through clandestine storage or new production, for both virtual nuclear powers and for nonnuclear states who decided to enter the game. How great a potential asymmetry in nuclear materials nations can tolerate will be a critical issue in determining the feasibility of a virtual weapons regime.

GENERAL MILITARY-TECHNICAL CAPABILITY

The issue of technological capability extends beyond that of the virtual nuclear arsenal and its supporting infrastructure. Some nations will have, or believe themselves to have, significant advantages in nonnuclear forces, especially those involving advanced conventional weapons. Other nations, in turn, will be, or believe themselves to be, at a disadvantage. The so-called Revolution in Military Affairs, involving the inventive use of information systems and precision-guided weapons, among other technologies, may create a strategic gap between the haves and the have-nots. Other types of extreme changes in the military balance, involving for example biological agents, cannot be discounted.

The state of the nonnuclear military balance may well affect the desirability and configuration of a virtual nuclear arsenal. For the haves, the strategic advantages of revolutionary capabilities may incline them to push for a very restrictive virtual regime, with extremely limited possibilities for reconstitution—if not nuclear abolition altogether. For the have-nots, the attractiveness of nuclear weapons as a counter to advanced conventional forces will increase, to the point where a deployed arsenal is seen as mandatory or at least where reconstitution is relatively quick, easy, and large.

An additional asymmetry for reconstitution involves the presence and sophistication of ballistic missile and air defenses. The more sophisticated and numerous the defensive forces, the greater will be the pressure for a larger reconstitution allowance. But this issue is further complicated by the fact that some nations may possess effective defenses, others more limited capabilities, and still others no defense. A reconstituted nuclear arsenal sized to be appropriate against one level of defense (e.g., Russia against China) may be too large relative to other nations (e.g., against France) but too small relative to others (e.g., against the United States).

DOCTRINAL ISSUES

One of the most important asymmetries during the Cold War involved the differing doctrinal perspectives of the various nuclear powers. For instance, rightly or wrongly, a number of analysts were concerned that American flexible response policy did not take into account Soviet preemptive war-fighting doctrine. That is, an American use of nuclear weapons that was designed to control and limit a conflict might actually have had the opposite effect of triggering a massive Soviet nuclear response.

The degree to which such critical doctrinal differences might emerge in a reconstituting, and later a reconstituted, nuclear world is unclear. If a minimalist perspective became the dominant paradigm as nuclear arsenals are deactivated, their eventual reactivation might not cause any particular difficulty; in fact, reconstitution might offer an important degree of security assurance that would allow a worsening international situation to be managed successfully. But, if a nuclear arsenal were reconstituted according to other doctrinal tenets—for example, to offset the suspected conventional superiority of other states or for coercive purposes—the cure might be worse than the initial disease. Whether by good policy or good fortune, the world learned to cope with an active nuclear competition. The unexpected assertive use of a reconstituted nuclear capability, under what had been posited to be a benign virtual nuclear weapons regime, might provide a shock that could not be contained by the international system.

Of particular concern would be a targeting strategy of a reconstituted force that was directed against the political leadership and C3I of the adversary, in order to create a decisive war-winning advantage. This could only be executed on the basis of excellent intelligence, command and control, weapons accuracy, and the like—military attributes that, as previously noted, would not necessarily be evenly distributed among the states participating in the agreement. Preemption might appear to be a good deal more attractive under such a regime than it did during the Cold War.

By the same token one could argue that it is this very possibility—that a nation might legally reconstitute nuclear forces in search of strategic advantage—that provides the essential ingredient for stability. The prospect that nuclear reconstitution could have unintended and dangerous consequences might encourage nations to keep their nuclear capability inactive and otherwise to avoid waking the sleeping dragon.

POLITICAL REGIMES AND CULTURES

One of the traditional concerns about arms control and disarmament agreements involved the alleged advantages possessed by authoritarian states. Such states, presumably, could (or did) exploit the closed nature of their societies to violate the letter and/or spirit of the agreement and thus potentially steal the march on their more open rivals.

Would such a political asymmetry create difficulties for a virtual nuclear weapons regime under various reconstitution/breakout scenarios? The fact that many nuclear-related activities, including the process of reconstitution, would be designed for transparency under a virtual nuclear weapons regime would help somewhat. Questions would undoubtedly remain, but it is fair to say that the anxiety would not be confined to one side. Revelations, or reminders, that democratic Sweden and Japan pursued the nuclear option during the 1960s indicate that even democratic societies are capable of covertly developing a nuclear option.

Perhaps greater differences might emerge because the political culture of some states would make it easier for them to maintain a virtual nuclear arsenal than would be the case for other nations. For example, Russia and France arguably have a much greater political and psychological attachment to their nuclear establishments, civilian and military, than do the United States or the United Kingdom. Although the same rules about reconstituting a virtual arsenal would presumably apply to all parties, some might thus be in a better position to reassemble a nuclear force. In a situation in which the industrious "ants" had begun the reconstitution process, the "grasshoppers" might feel pressure to make up for their lazy summer by taking steps that undermined efforts to stabilize the strategic situation.

"OLD" AND "NEW" NUCLEAR STATES

Although most nonnuclear weapons states would probably choose to retain that status, it is not impossible that new powers might instead decide to become virtual nuclear powers. Because these powers would start from scratch, as it were, a virtual nuclear weapons regime would have to take account of the development of a virtual nuclear capability, rather than the deactivation of an extant arsenal (as would be the case with today's declared or undeclared nuclear weapons states). This could conceivably lead to certain difficulties: Would the new nuclear power, with presumably a more modern nuclear complex and the momentum behind its construction, enjoy worrisome advantages in the case of reconstitution? Conversely, would the technological experience and more mature infrastructure (e.g., that provided by nuclear testing programs) give the old nuclear powers a destabilizing edge?

Breakout

The notion of a virtual nuclear arms-control regime presupposes the existence of transparent means to reconstitute a nuclear arsenal in a specified manner under agreed-upon conditions. But there will always be the underlying danger that one or more virtual nuclear powers will create a covert capability for nuclear forces outside the permitted reconstitution allowance. And, as is the case with the current NPT regime, nonnuclear powers could conceivably develop a clandestine nuclear arsenal.

The virtual nuclear weapons regime would obviously have provisions to preclude breakout from occurring or at least to provide strategic warning. Depending on the confidence that member states had in such provisions, they might well want to include an additional "breakout allowance" in their deactivated nuclear arsenals for the purposes of reconstituting against a rogue state.

BARRIERS TO RECONSTITUTING NUCLEAR CAPABILITY

If the regulated ability to (re)constitute a nuclear force is an essential part of a virtual nuclear world, then the barriers to reactivation must neither be too low nor too high. Obviously, if it were too easy to reassemble a nuclear arsenal, concern about breakout would probably negate the value of the virtual weapons agreement. But there is the opposite problem: if reconstitution is too difficult, for some or all of the parties, the existential deterrent value of the virtual nuclear arsenal would be lost or seriously weakened. Clearly, reconstitution (e.g., to counter a sudden biological weapons threat) must not appear so difficult that an aggressor nation would assume that it did not have to take the virtual arsenal fully into account.

There are three principal and interrelated barriers to reconstitution: the political will required to maintain a credible virtual capability; the technological, industrial, and military expertise to carry out reconstitution; and the cost of maintaining a virtual arsenal and reactivating it when desired. (In each of these areas successful reconstitution would presuppose the ability to prevent outside agents from interrupting reactivation of a nuclear arsenal.)

For purposes of this analysis I will focus here on the barrier of expense, since political will and technical competence largely, if not totally, would flow from the perceived cost-effectiveness of maintaining a virtual arsenal. At one level the expense of a residual nuclear capability would not seem to be prohibitive: a modest science and technology base; limited facilities for weapons reassembly; access to means of delivery (probably aircraft and cruise missiles, at first); and basic command and control.

Upon closer examination, however, cost looms as a potentially imposing consideration. First, if the overall defense budgets of virtual nuclear powers remain under downward pressure—which is true today of all the declared nuclear weapons states except China—the marginal expense of retaining a nuclear hedge will be evaluated against the need for the modernization and readiness of more immediately "useful" conventional forces. Also, the requirement to deal with possible opponents equipped with significant advanced nonnuclear or biological capabilities, in turn, could further drive up the standards and funding required for nuclear reconstitution.

The key to the affordability of a virtual nuclear arsenal, and an effective reconstitution capability, may ultimately depend on the potential for its integration with nonnuclear forces and infrastructure or with the civilian economy. For instance, could university research centers provide the necessary science and technology base, or is a dedicated and permanent laboratory system necessary? Can the reassembly/remanufacture of some or all nuclear components be assigned to existing industrial contractors? Would the national and operational C3I systems established for nonnuclear forces easily be adapted to managing a reconstituted nuclear arsenal, or would a nuclear-unique system need to be retained or developed?

As noted previously, the political culture and strategic situation of some virtual nuclear powers might incline them to make the investments necessary to create a credible reconstitution capability, while others might let this capability atrophy. Further, it may be difficult for third parties, who might be contemplating aggression, to judge accurately the disposition and means to reconstitute a nuclear arsenal. This uncertainty might work in favor of existential deterrence, but it would undoubtedly weaken over time. The virtual nuclear powers may therefore want to find periodic means to exhibit their commitment to reconstitution and to codify this demonstration process within the virtual nuclear weapons regime, so that it does not itself become destabilizing.

ACCOUNTING FOR RECONSTITUTION UNDER A VIRTUAL NUCLEAR ARMS-CONTROL REGIME

The need to account for asymmetries in a nuclear control regime is by no means unprecedented. During the Cold War, for example, the United States and the Soviet Union sought, through negotiation, to balance various geographical and technological asymmetries and advantages. The NPT bargain itself involves a basic distinction between nuclear and nonnuclear weapons states, with appropriate responsibilities and benefits accruing to each category.

Given the complexities described earlier, it is probably unwise in advance to lay out in any great detail the particulars of reconstitution under a virtual nuclear arms-control regime. The process of establishing such a regime will be evolutionary in character, proceeding from a starting point that all would agree is desirable: moving away from a hair-trigger nuclear posture.

As this evolutionary process proceeds, it may well be discovered that "one size does not fit all." Obviously, the United States would not feel comfortable with a virtual nuclear arsenal—even if Russia too had moved in this direction—while China possessed a deployed and active nuclear force. The "reconstitution disparity" would simply be too great. But, short of this, two or more nuclear powers (e.g., the United States and Russia; China, India and Pakistan) that have traditionally had competitive nuclear relationships could take steps to stabilize the relationship and move in the direction of virtual nuclear arsenals. The de-alerting of U.S. and Russian nuclear forces, with hedges built in, is one example of how the process might evolve.

But to succeed ultimately in creating a virtual nuclear weapons regime, internationally accepted norms must be translated, as appropriate, into formal agreements. The elements of this regime might be designed primarily to create the necessary boundary conditions for giving nuclear states the confidence to de-alert their arsenals in the first place—and only secondarily to regulate virtual nuclear forces and the reconstitution process. That said, the following observations might serve as general guidelines:

- The political and military presumption should be against reconstitution. The emphasis on maintaining strategic stability should be made at the level of virtual, not reconstituted, forces.

- The reconstitution process should be extended in time. Ideally, the reassembly of a virtual nuclear arsenal would be staggered such that a few weapons could be made available on relatively short notice to handle emergencies but that full-scale reconstitution would take some time. (Alternatively, a small deployed international force might take up the slack temporarily to cover an emergency.) Further, this process should be as transparent as possible, with appropriate notifications about the scale and timing of the reconstitution process.

- Reconstituted forces should be limited in number. This will require, above all, controls on the complete nuclear energy fuel cycle, because it is not essential to have either weapons-grade material or tritium for usable weapons (although other types of material might limit the military interest and effectiveness of the designs).

- Although it is difficult to prescribe the precise doctrine of a reconstituted nuclear force, political discussions and military-to-military contacts should press the parties to stay away from preemptive targeting policies.

- The appropriate interlinkage with conventional forces and a reconstituted nuclear arsenal must be considered and perhaps regulated. Ideally, the virtual nuclear power would have easy access to the use of its conventional forces and C3I, for the purposes of making reconstitution credible, but not in such a way as to create dangerous military advantages. Thus, conventional arms control, tailored in part with this problem in mind, may be a necessary part of the virtual nuclear weapons regime.

- Coercive measures and an intrusive inspection regime must be in place against rogue states. The mere presence of a virtual nuclear regime would by no means obviate concern with nuclear proliferation and might make the consequences much worse. The reconstitution process should not be designed to deal primarily with the possibility of nuclear breakout but, rather, with supporting a stable balance among virtual nuclear powers and deterring other threats (e.g., use of biological weapons).

Finally, reconstitution may depend on the ability of virtual nuclear powers to address potential asymmetries by sharing information, technology, and the like. No one virtual weapons state may possess all of the necessary or desirable means to support reconstitution and a reconstituted arsenal—computational capabilities, appropriate delivery systems, nonnuclear or even nuclear test facilities, and the like. But combinations of virtual nuclear powers may be able to do so, and a virtual nuclear regime should not discourage this process. To be sure, the difficulties of international nuclear cooperation in the past have been obvious, and such activity in the future might be worrisome to outside parties who fear collusion among the virtual nuclear powers. But the entire notion of a virtual nuclear weapons regime presupposes changes in the character of international relations, whereby such cooperation becomes possible and useful in its own right.

A JAPANESE REACTION TO THE IDEA OF VIRTUAL NUCLEAR ARSENALS

AKIO WATANABE

AS A NONNUCLEAR STATE, Japan is clearly in favor of marginalizing the nuclear arsenals in international relations. The government of Japan is therefore seriously interested in upholding and strengthening the NPT regime, which at the moment seems the best possible means to achieve a long-term goal of making the world free from nuclear weapons. Such a basic position is reflected in its policy, especially since the Hosokawa government, of a firm commitment to the goals of the NPT.

Japan's commitment to the NPT is composed of the following three elements: (1) its belief in the promise by the established nuclear weapons states of their eventual nuclear disarmament; (2) its belief in the nuclear umbrella of the United States for its allies as long as nuclear arsenals still remain in the hands of potential adversaries; and (3) its belief in the assurance of the NPT regime about the rights of nonnuclear nations for peaceful nuclear programs. The first two points are directly related to security policy of the country, while the last is concerned with its energy policy, but, as explained later, it has important implications for the issue of nuclear weapons.

All these were in fact the issues over which lengthy debates were conducted for the six years between 1970, when the NPT was signed by the Japanese government, and 1976, when the treaty was finally ratified. They were also reiterated in the recent debate prior to the final decision on the NPT extension issue of 1995. Given these contours of Japanese policy debates over the NPT regime, let me here comment on the idea of virtual arsenals by suggesting likely responses that idea would invite from Japanese policy and opinionmakers.[1]

A substantial portion of the influential opinion in Japan was, and still is, skeptical of the treaty by pointing to the "unequal" nature of the regime. People of this school of thought have maintained that the regime, which makes a distinction between the established nuclear weapons states and the rest, is inconsistent with the principle of equality among all sovereign nations. This view is shared not only by those idealistic thinkers who are sympathetic with emerging nations in Asia but also by pragmatic security-oriented thinkers. It was barely counterbalanced by another argument, which emphasizes the importance of Article 6 of the NPT, obligating the existing nuclear weapons states to dismantle their nuclear weapons eventually. In other words, in the latter opinion the regime does not permanently concede privileges to the established nuclear states, and the present inequality would disappear eventually when all nuclear weapons are dismantled.

The latter argument was not very persuasive in the Cold War period, when nobody seriously believed in the practicability of nuclear disarmament. Encouraging progress is being made in recent years toward that goal, affording some grounds for hope among NPT supporters. Still, as long as the established nuclear weapons states remain essentially intact, criticism of the NPT regime on the grounds of "inequality" cannot be completely eliminated. The idea of virtual nuclear arsenals would be helpful in mitigating Japanese dissatisfaction with the NPT regime on that account, because under the proposed regime of virtual arsenals the existing gap between the nuclear and nonnuclear states would be somewhat lessened. This would be welcomed especially by the high-technology states like Germany and Japan. At least for psychological reasons, therefore, the idea of virtual arsenals would be regarded as a positive factor from the viewpoint of supporters of the NPT regime in Japan.

The next point of the past debate was concerned with the reliability of extended deterrence. The opponents to the NPT asked whether we could rely on another state's nuclear guarantee for an indefinite future and argued that, while not advocating nuclear policy as an immediate option for Japan, the present generation had no right to deprive future generations of freedom of choice about a matter of crucial importance like this. Their argument was called the "free-hand" position.

The debate was apparently concerned with a hypothetical situation in some distant future. But in fact it was an indirect way of expressing some reservations, if not strong doubt, about the credibility of the U.S. nuclear umbrella. It is significant that the Japanese government's decision on the NPT ratification was facilitated by the assurance given by President Gerald Ford, who stated, in his joint announcement with Prime Minister Miki Takeo, in August 1975, that "both leaders recognized that the U.S. nuclear deterrent is an important contributor to the security of Japan. In this connection the president reassured the prime minister that the United States would continue to abide by its defense commitment to Japan under the Treaty of Mutual Cooperation and Security in the event of armed attack against Japan, whether by nuclear or conventional forces."

In view of the suspected possession of nuclear weapons by some defiant countries today and tomorrow, the reliability or limitations of the U.S. extended deterrence has assumed new dimensions. As stated in the beginning of this essay, Japan is clearly in favor of the nuclear-free world and therefore welcomes the pursuance by the United States of a "nuclear marginalization" policy. Ironically, however, Japan finds itself recently more uncertain about the credibility and applicability of the United States' nuclear umbrella to protect Japan from attacks by hostile nations in the form of weapons of mass destruction (WMDs). The country is surrounded by two big and one small (suspected) nuclear states possessed with very different political creeds. This characterization applies especially to the present regime in Pyongyang. As long as this basic political question about the Korean peninsular remains unsettled, the Japanese would find it difficult to put their trust in the virtual arsenals scheme.

China and Russia are parties to the NPT, but their future nuclear policies are at best uncertain. China's long-term intention is difficult to read, while its present leaders are firmly committed to a further upgrading of their nuclear arsenals. As for Russia, it is still too early to agree with those who claim that extended deterrence is obsolete because "Europe no longer faces a potential aggressor armed with nuclear bombs. The era of the Russian bear threatening the security of Germany, France, and Britain is over."[2] These remarks about Russia's nuclear arsenals basically hold for East Asia as well, although the Russian factor is less important than in Europe.

Given these many factors of uncertainty in the post–Cold War security situation in East Asia, one of the essential roles for the United States is to uphold the alliance system, if only to prevent the situation from becoming more complex and more fluid. As Lawrence Freedman pointed out, "Few issues in the history of nuclear policy have been more vexed than the credibility of the nuclear guarantees at the heart of this alliance network."[3] The U.S.-Japan alliance had not been so much vexed by this issue as the NATA had been during the Cold War. An irony is that the NPT-related issues, including that of extended deterrence, have become a real test for the viability of the U.S.-Japan alliance after the Cold War, because of the increasing fluidity and complexity of nuclear issues in this part of the world.

More concretely, it would be absolutely necessary for the United States to relieve the Japanese of their anxiety about nuclear attacks/ threats by the defector states while the nuclear marginalization program is under way. One will face here a typical case of prisoners' dilemma, because stakes are so high that one has to be absolutely sure to prevent a defector. Can virtual nuclear arsenals be a hedge against defectors?

For these purposes certain conditions have to be fulfilled. First, as long as we cannot be absolutely sure about the innocence of the North Korean regime, the period of delay of the virtual arsenals cannot and should not be made too long, because it might give a wrong signal to the potential attacker. The risk can be partly reduced by the installation of a theater missile defense (TMD) system. But we must remember that a TMD system, however highly developed, cannot meet the danger perfectly, especially in relation to an attacker close at hand. In general terms a virtual arsenals regime cannot go too far as long as we have a "nondeclared" virtual arsenals state in our neighborhood.

Second, in relation to China and Russia, the security of Japan would be greatly improved if these two declared nuclear states are firmly incorporated into a well-developed virtual arsenals regime. The risk of nuclear war by mistake—no small possibility in case of large-scale political disorder in these countries—would be substantially reduced. What is more, the virtual arsenal scheme, if it is maintained in good shape, would make nuclear weapons less useful as a means of political blackmail vis-à-vis the nonnuclear neighbors.

The period of delay—that is to say, the period that is needed to convert the virtual arsenals into a state of readiness—can be gradually prolonged depending on the accumulation of managerial experience of the regime once all nuclear states have agreed to comply with the rule. A most serious obstacle stands in the way, however: the problem of verification. You may say that all nuclear forces already have some built-in delay imposed by launch procedures and other factors. This may be the case with the Soviet Union and the United States. A symmetrical relation that existed between the two superpowers was instrumental in creating a sort of cooperative spirit as far as the nuclear crisis management was concerned, which resulted in a sharing of the common language and culture regarding nuclear weapons. Does this apply to China, which still suffers from a deep sense of inferiority in the field of military technology and, therefore, cannot be very tolerant of information sharing about military affairs in general and nuclear problems in particular?

Moreover, the proposed virtual arsenals regime would require much more sophisticated methods for verification, even as compared to the MAD system. In order for one nuclear state to feel secure with a limited number (say, two or three) of warheads, it has to have a perfect information about the other side while being strongly motivated to maintain a very high level of invulnerability of its own arsenals. Verifiability and invulnerability are thus mutually exclusive. Country A wants to know everything about Country B's nuclear arsenals, but Country B wants to hide its own nuclear arsenals so that its arsenals can survive the first attack, because secrecy is, after all, the surest means of invulnerability. This logic itself is nothing new. But if one has to rely on a very limited number of arsenals, whether nuclear or not, one has to be completely clear about his opponent's preparedness. The less you have in your arsenals, the more you must have in your intelligence. Redundancy was one essential element of the traditional MAD system. A system based on a nonredundancy principle, like the proposed scheme, requires of us an almost superhuman rationality. In this sense a virtual nuclear arsenals regime would be a far more sophisticated device than the MAD system. Is it realistic to expect that level of sophistication among the present five nuclear states?

A related problem is that of crisis stability. Suppose an equilibrium exists at a relatively low level of arsenals. With the slightest symptom of doubt about the other side's behavior, one would rush to assemble components, resulting in a breakdown of the equilibrium. An equilibrium that can be obtained from a nonredundancy system would be very sensitive and vulnerable, exceedingly subject to political situations. That was exactly the cause of a seemingly absurd situation called the "overkill" in the MAD system.

There is another aspect of the verification issue that is concerned with nonnuclear states including Japan. This is related to what is called "veiled proliferation." There would be only a subtle distinction between virtual arsenals and virtual nuclear capabilities. As said before, the shrinking gap between the established nuclear states and the nonnuclear states would be favorably received in Japan, because it would mitigate the dissatisfaction of those who call for equality among all nations.

Psychological satisfaction apart, however, this situation would create a practical problem in relation to Japan's ongoing nuclear power program. In the aftermath of the oil embargo by the Arab nations in the early 1970s, Japan launched systematic efforts to pursue energy security. As a means of reducing the level of dependency on oil, an ambitious program of building nuclear power plants was adopted. This became an issue, in fact a most serious one, in the debate over the NPT. The opponents took issue on this point by referring to what they regarded as the disadvantages that nonnuclear industrial nations (like Germany and Japan) were likely to suffer vis-à-vis the nuclear industrial nations (like France, England, and the United States). The latter group of countries can be exempted from the various restrictions, if they wish, including submission to inspections by the IAEA.

Under pressure from this school the Japanese government conducted a series of hard negotiations and succeeded in gaining some concessions such as equal treatment comparable to the members of EURATOM. Thus, the Japanese government had by now firmly committed to a policy of nuclear-power programs and gone a long way toward implementing that policy. It was based on the assumption (or, rather, the fact) that the NPT stipulated the "inalienable rights" of the signatories of the treaty to use nuclear materials for peaceful purposes.

Recently, in conjunction with the movement for a nuclear-free world, a call for a total abolishment of all plutonium, either for military or nonmilitary use, is being made more loudly. According to this view, nonproliferation of plutonium itself is an essential condition to insure the nonproliferation of nuclear weapons. Thus, the Japanese government is facing increasing pressure from some quarters of U.S. society, as well as at home, to dismantle the Japanese energy programs, which rely greatly on plutonium.

Given the salience of the energy security issue in Japan, additional pressure for more rigid regulations, or even a total ban, of the plutonium-based energy policy, which is a likely consequence of the virtual arsenal scheme, would encounter strong resistance from the Japanese government. The government has no intention of using its nuclear energy program for the veiled purpose of developing nuclear weapons. Even so, some overseas observers are alluding to that interpretation. If the distinction between virtual nuclear powers and those close to virtual weapons capability becomes thinner, suspicions about Japan will grow and, with that, increased pressure for a total cancellation of the plutonium-based energy program.

The solution to this problem lies in two areas. First, Japan's plutonium is to be placed under a multilateral regional regime such as ASIATOM. Second, a virtual nuclear arsenals scheme is to be supplemented and reinforced by additional regimes such as the MTCR. The latter would place the possession of medium- and long-range missiles under strict surveillance, thus serving as a hedge against veiled proliferation.

In conclusion, the proposed scheme is attractive because we need one device or another with which security can be guaranteed during a transitional period. One can easily fall into errors when moving from one established system to another. Nuclear marginalization is a great idea, but utmost care is needed in the process of transition. In theory no one wants to live in a world full of nuclear weapons. The problem is not defining the goal but the way in which one can reach that goal. The idea of virtual arsenals encourages us to think about the way.

One of the outstanding characteristics of the scheme is the confident belief in the rationality of the human mind. The present writer is not so sure about it. He agrees with a statement that arms control is clearly a political process. A real test for the scheme is, therefore, more political than technological. Much depends on whether political leaders of the nations concerned can build a new world order based on a "concert of powers" among themselves. A highly sophisticated regime like the one proposed here cannot operate unless and until they exercise prudence in dealing with one another. Technical difficulties that plague the scheme can be overcome only if this prerequisite is satisfied.

NOTES

1. As for Japan's policy and the surrounding debate on the NPT, see Niacin Takeshi (division chief for Disarmament and Arms Control of the Ministry of Foreign Affairs), "NPT and Japan's Response" (in Japanese), *Kaigai Jijo* (July-August 1994): 22-40. The responsibility about interpretation falls entirely on Watanabe.
2. Michael H. Shuman and Hal Harvey, *Security without War: A Post–Cold War Foreign Policy* (Westview Press, 1993): 199.
3. Lawrence Freedman, "Great Powers, Vital Interests and Nuclear Weapons," *Survival* 36, no. 4 (Winter 1994-95): 35-52.

TWENTY-ONE

VIRTUAL VISIONS, PAST AND FUTURE

PHILIP ZELIKOW

Virtual nuclear arsenals is an innovative and ambitious concept for multilateral nuclear disarmament. With the end of the Cold War and the rise of a new international system in 1990 and 1991, such an idea deserves a fresh, serious evaluation. The rise of a new international system, in fact, provoked the very first consideration of the idea of virtual nuclear arsenals, in 1945 and 1946. Many of the questions raised at that time have still not found satisfactory answers, even though the circumstances and concerns today are quite different.

THE ACHESON-LILIENTHAL PRECEDENT

In the autumn of 1945 Henry Stimson, then the secretary of war, was joined by deputy secretary of state Dean Acheson in an effort to persuade President Harry Truman to propose a plan of multilateral nuclear disarmament to Stalin based on some form of international control over the means of producing atomic weapons. Truman and British Prime Minister Clement Attlee were persuaded to the point of asking Acheson to run a group that would develop a plan for international control entrusted to the new United Nations. Acheson in turn engaged a group of technical consultants headed by David Lilienthal, which included J. Robert Oppenheimer, the former head of the Los Alamos laboratory that had developed the atomic bomb. The Acheson-Lilienthal groups, strongly influenced by Oppenheimer, produced a report in March 1946 that detailed a plan for an international agency that would control all aspects of atomic energy production. Enforcement would be achieved by insuring that the assets for producing atomic weapons were disseminated to a number of states so that, if any one of them seized international assets to begin producing weapons, several other states would be positioned to retaliate in kind.[1]

The logic, then, of the Acheson-Lilienthal plan was conceptually quite similar to the logic of the current idea for virtual nuclear arsenals. The current idea would place the components of nuclear weapons "under international inspection."[2] The term *inspection* understates what is envisioned. The inspectors, or the means of their controls, would be so omnipresent that, as in the Acheson-Lilienthal plan, the nuclear materials would be under the effective, constant control of the international agency. The mechanism for self-enforcement is also similar: violation by one state would allow others to build offsetting weapons of their own.

The Acheson-Lilienthal plan did not fare well. Concerns about enforcement dogged the plan from the start. When the financier Bernard Baruch was asked to take charge of the issue for the Truman administration, Baruch—not part of the Acheson-Lilienthal deliberations—insisted that violators receive immediate and sure punishment that could not be blocked by a Security Council veto. In other words, he was unconvinced by the logic of self-enforcement through the threat of mutual rearmament. He was not alone. A plan providing for such veto-proof enforcement was anathema to the Soviet Union, which vetoed the idea once it was presented in the United Nations. Though some commentators still think an opportunity for disarmament was lost, it is hard to reconcile the hopes of Stimson, Acheson, and the others with any serious examination of the attitudes and policies of Stalin's government.[3]

The story of what happened to the Acheson-Lilienthal plan is less important than the analytical process that surrounded its development and consideration in the U.S. government. Mark Twain is supposed to have said that "history does not repeat itself, but sometimes it rhymes." Since the

Acheson-Lilienthal groups analyzed the problems associated with their proposed plan with some depth and skill, the latter-day proponents of virtual nuclear arsenals should build on that work or at least cite it.

VIRTUAL NUCLEAR ARSENALS IN PRINCIPLE

Virtual nuclear arsenals, and the associated abandonment of plans for the first use of nuclear weapons in a crisis or conflict, have several possible advantages. Production, possession, and operational deployment of nuclear weapons are inherently dangerous for the United States and anyone else. A regime of multilateral disarmament might reduce the danger of weapons of mass destruction (WMD) proliferation, thereby accentuating the salience of the current U.S. superiority in conventional fighting power. The containment of WMD proliferation would be enhanced even more if a virtual arsenal regime made Russian custody of nuclear weapons material and technology more secure.

Since the autumn of 1945 American military planners have identified two reasons to maintain relatively large peacetime stockpiles of nuclear weapons and to consider the possibility of being the first to use them in a conflict. One reason was the need to offset the larger conventional military strength on land in Eurasia of the Soviet Union and China. The second reason was to protect an option of preemptive attack if a nuclear strike against the United States or its allies seemed imminent. These considerations sometimes included analysis of preventive war options, though such a policy was never endorsed by the U.S. government. Operational nuclear weapon requirements were then driven upward in the 1950s and 1960s by contemplation of large-scale nuclear war fighting on a tactical and strategic level and then by the desire to insure coverage of many (often hardened) targets by the fraction of forces that could be relied on to survive a massive enemy attack.

THE WORLD IN 2010 AND BEYOND

To consider the value of a virtual nuclear arsenal plan we must consider the world of the future. Let us assume, optimistically, that the convention is signed in the year 2000 and that the interim target (with retention of limited nuclear arsenals) is reached by 2005 with the plan fully in force (all arsenals in virtual form) by about 2010. Meanwhile, countries have been working for years to create armed forces that are appropriate for a world of only virtual nuclear arsenals. The full implications of their new plans may not become evident until the years after 2010.

This perspective affords some distance from concerns that preoccupy us now. The problem of Russian nuclear custody, to the limited extent that it is affected by a virtual nuclear arsenal plan,[4] is likely to be substantially settled, for better or worse, a decade or more from now. The political situation, especially in Asia and the Near East, may be quite different from what we know today.

This focus on the future could strengthen arguments for virtual nuclear arsenals. The threat of WMD proliferation could be greater by then; hence, larger benefits could accrue to the United States from the containment of this threat. But return to the 1945 rationales for building up U.S. nuclear forces; first, the sense of conventional weakness.

The current debilitation of Russia and Russian armed forces may have turned to a period of recovery and rapid growth. Chinese armed forces are growing at a rate that, if continued, could present a rather formidable picture by 2010. The situation in the Near East and North Africa is even harder to foresee. It is possible that U.S. conventional forces will be more than adequate to protect American and allied interests in 2010 and beyond. But a convincing analysis to support such a conclusion has not yet been offered by proponents of virtual nuclear arsenals. Such an analysis would project scenarios for the size of United States' allied, and possible hostile, forces at least ten to twenty years into the future, as applied to various regional settings.

In 1945 U.S. planners worried about preempting a possible nuclear attack against the United States. That worry remains valid. Leaving aside the issue of preventive strikes with conventional or redesigned nuclear forces,[5] it is not hard to imagine a situation in which the United States learns of preparations for an imminent attack against American or allied territory using WMD and can only thwart the attack with weapons that have long-range ability to destroy promptly a very hard target or targets, possibly deep underground.

Traditional deterrence theory would suggest that the adversary might be deterred from attack by the threat that the United States would reassemble nuclear weapons and retaliate against an attacker. The virtual nuclear arsenal plan, however, introduces at least two new challenges. First, reassembly is not consistent with an operational requirement for a prompt strike.

Second, and more important, the decision to reassemble introduces a new, distinct step in the ladder of escalation. The adversary could threaten the use of weapons that already exist if the United States merely orders the assembly of weapons that do not. If the United States ignores the threat and orders reassembly, the adversary could still back down before the United States takes the next step and launches its weapons. If the United States heeds the threat and does not reassemble, the adversary would prevail.

THE PROBLEM OF ENFORCEMENT

The threat of mutual rearmament was the driving idea behind the Acheson-Lilienthal plan. There were two great concerns with the idea. The first was that the United States was giving up a less stable but superior nuclear posture in exchange for a presumably more stable posture at the equal level of zero. In 1946 attention correctly focused on the USSR. In the future the same argument is more likely to focus on China. Given the standards the Chinese seem to be setting for their own nuclear program, they undoubtedly consider their current posture inadequate and greatly inferior to that of the United States.[6] Is it in the United States' interest to give Beijing a far rosier assessment of the relative strategic balance? The answer certainly turns in part on judgments about China's future over the next ten to twenty years. But these judgments are so problematic that we must pause before developing any policy that relies on a particular conclusion, especially an optimistic one.

The argument about the disadvantage of equality has been made so far only from an American perspective. The Russian view is likely to be far stronger. Lacking superior and long-reach conventional forces, a large nuclear arsenal has become more important to Russian defense plans even as its salience to Washington has declined.

The other great argument against Acheson-Lilienthal was that violators could not be punished except through national military action unconstrained by UN vetoes. This, of course, led to the Baruch additions to the plan that helped seal its diplomatic fate. The reply, which perhaps Baruch did not understand, was the self-enforcing concept of mutual rearmament inherent in widespread possession of virtual nuclear arsenals. But is this sanction adequate?

Good arguments can be made that the sanction is adequate against nuclear breakout. The arguments rest on the presumption, which has some basis, that violators cannot build up substantial operational nuclear arsenals without timely detection.

The more troubling version of the argument in 2010 and beyond, however, is in the relationship between biological and nuclear weapons. The United States and its allies have forsworn retaliation in kind against the construction of biological weapons. This resolve has already been tested by the past and possibly present existence of a Soviet biological weapons program developed in contravention of international agreements. Iraq and other countries are similarly engaged in active biological weapons work. It is difficult to be too optimistic about the status of these programs ten or twenty years from now. It is also difficult, given past experience, to be overly optimistic about how much Washington will know about what is going on.

Unless the United States changes its biological weapons policy, it must rely on either conventional or nuclear weapons for a military response to the threat or use of biological weapons. There is thus a synergy between nuclear disarmament and biological disarmament that has not been adequately considered by proponents of virtual nuclear arsenals. Mazarr understands that the prospects for biological disarmament must greatly improve for the nuclear proposals to be tenable,[7] but there is almost no evidence to support optimistic assumptions on this score and a good deal of evidence the other way.

Mazarr also argues that one can threaten the reassembly and use of nuclear weapons in retaliation against biological attack. But he must also deal with the different logic of biological breakout, in which we lack the same confidence about timely detection of massive weaponization that we have in the nuclear case. This means that a biologically armed adversary may perceive various advantages in escalation dominance after the capabilities are revealed in a crisis. The old problems of extended deterrence could arise in a new, menacing form if an adversary could feel that biological weapons could be used against a U.S. ally while, meanwhile, the United States was immobilized by being threatened with direct biological attack if it tried to reassemble, much less use, its virtual nuclear weapons.

One response to these problems would be a change in international norms for both nuclear and biological weapons development. In the Acheson-Lilienthal plan, for instance, international control was so comprehensive that even the national seizure of a uranium mine could be considered prima facie of hostile intent and would be enough to justify international action against the would-be aggressor. In other words, the burden of proof was shifted so that the suspect had to prove its innocence rather than requiring the international community to prove guilt.

Pervasive international controls and inspections, combined with similar shifts in the international burden of proof, would legitimize preventive or preemptive conventional military action against violators. This greater freedom to police national behavior with conventional forces might reduce the need to retain sizable nuclear forces as a hedge. Yet, just as more vigorous enforcement provisions doomed the Baruch plan to rejection by a Soviet Union that may well have intended to violate it, such enforcement addenda are also likely to complicate the already poor prospects for international acceptance of a sound plan for virtual nuclear arsenals.[8]

NOTES

1. For an introduction to the Acheson-Lilienthal analysis and the discussions it stimulated, see the report itself, published as *A Report on the International Control of Atomic Energy* (New York: Doubleday, 1946); and Dean Acheson, *Present at the Creation* (New York: W. W. Norton, 1969): 151-56; David E. Lilienthal, *The Journals of David Lilienthal*, vol. 2: *The Atomic Energy Years, 1945-1950* (New York: Harper and Row, 1964): 16-34; Richard Hewlett and Oscar Anderson, *The New World: A History of the United States Atomic Energy Commission, 1939-1946* (Berkeley: University of California Press, 1990): 531-619; and Melvyn P. Leffler, *A Preponderance of Power: National Security, the Truman Administration, and the Cold War* (Stanford: Stanford University Press, 1992): 114-16.

2. Michael J. Mazarr, "Virtual Nuclear Arsenals," *Survival* 37 (Autumn 1995): 7, 14.

3. For a recent revival of the "lost opportunity" thesis, see James Chace, "Sharing the Atom Bomb," *Foreign Affairs* 75 (January-February 1996): 129. But, for a dash of cold water, spend some time in the world described in David Holloway, *Stalin and the Bomb: The Soviet Union and Atomic Energy, 1939-*

1956 (New Haven: Yale University Press, 1994), esp.150-65. Holloway actually understates the potential difficulties since he thinks Stalin's policy did not include support for revolutions in Europe and Asia. Recent evidence affords a more ominous view of Soviet intentions, especially as they evolved during and after 1947. For a partial (principally for Asia) but convenient summary of this evidence, see Douglas J. Macdonald, "Communist Bloc Expansion in the Early Cold War: Challenging Realism, Refuting Revisionism," *International Security* 20 (Winter 1995-96): 152.

4.   Most of the dangerous Russian nuclear material is not to be found in the nuclear warheads deployed on operational systems. Further, the operational systems are the most secure portion of the Russian custodial system.

5.   On the nature of preventive and preemptive options, see Philip Zelikow, "Offensive Military Options," in *New Nuclear Nations: Consequences for U.S. Policy,* eds. Robert D. Blackwill and Albert Carnesale (New York: Council on Foreign Relations Press, 1993): 163 n. 1, and, more generally, 162-95.

6.   Mazarr, "Virtual Nuclear Arsenals," 21.

7.   See Alastair Iain Johnston, "China's New 'Old Thinking': The Concept of Limited Deterrence," and Banning N. Garrett and Bonnie S. Glaser, "Chinese Perspectives on Nuclear Arms Control," both in *International Security* 20 (Winter 1995-96): 5-42, 43-78.

8.   Among the most important diplomatic issues to be considered before the United States could even announce the wish to seek virtual nuclear arsenals would be the obstacles or prices associated with acceptance of a sound plan by Russia, Israel, Pakistan, France, and Britain. Japan, South Korea, and Taiwan will also have a view on the effects of such a plan on regional stability vis-à-vis China.

PART FIVE

CONCLUSION

TWENTY TWO

VIRTUAL NUCLEAR ARSENALS: A SECOND LOOK

MICHAEL J. MAZARR

THE PRECEDING ESSAYS HAVE, it is hoped, conveyed the enormous complexity, promise, and, in the view of some, peril inherent in the idea of virtual nuclear arsenals. As noted in the introductory essay, not all the contributors to this volume think VNAs are a good idea. A few are supportive; many are open-minded but skeptical; some are staunchly opposed .

In assembling the book, it was our conviction that a dialog among commentators with such a range of views would be most helpful, both to the reader and to the evolution of thinking about VNAs. The concept remains at such a rudimentary stage of analytical development that no final case for it can yet be made, and the arguments of skeptics and opponents must be first understood and fully appreciated before they can be answered. Such was our purpose with this book—to provide a forum for a more in-depth examination of VNAs than any yet accomplished and thereby to advance the debate on the concept.

As an advocate of VNAs, however, my purpose in editing this volume has been more ambitious. Believing as I do that the case for VNAs is a sound one, it has been my hope that further discussion and analysis will improve its chances for acceptance. I will therefore take the opportunity of this final essay to advance the argument in favor of the idea. In an earlier essay I made an introductory case for virtual arsenals;[1] here I will make an updated argument, taking into account the issues raised in this book—a "second look" at VNAs in the light of the superb research and analysis contributed by the authors.

I should make clear in the strongest possible terms that the authors of this book should not necessarily be associated with these final arguments. It is not a summary of the volume or a consensus conclusion. It is my own argument for VNAs, responding to or using the work done by others as part of the analysis.[2] In making this case, I will focus on four issues from the framework of subjects laid out in my opening essay: the context for arms control; the design of a VNA system; verification; and stability.[3]

ISSUE 1: THE CONTEXT FOR ARMS CONTROL

The first question raised at the end of the introductory essay focuses on the context for arms control over the next decade or two, including such issues as the role of force in the international system and the status of reform projects in Eastern Europe and China. Would this context be supportive of a transition to VNAs?

It is impossible to predict the course of world politics even over the next two or three years, let alone the next two decades. But merely to state the obvious—to say that nasty things could happen in the world that would rule out dramatic arms-control ideas like VNAs—is not to make an argument against them. For all we know, souring U.S.-Russian relations might even continue to rule out ratification of START II, as well as any steps beyond it. Clearly, any global arms-control scheme will presume a certain amount of cooperation among the major powers during the transition period. A more meaningful question relates to the *nature* of that cooperation, how absolute it must be in order to allow a transition to VNAs. Must it be something dramatically different and more harmonious from the world we have experienced from 1989 roughly through 1996?

My answer is no: participating states need not view one another in fundamentally different ways from the way they did in the wake of the Cold War in order to accept VNAs. Governments will demand reassurances about verification and reconstitution; they will want to try the idea out a piece at a time, over many years; and until the very last stage they will probably want to keep some hard core of a deployed, fully operational nuclear reserve. But these demands and concerns have to do with accustoming states operating in existing patterns of world politics to the idea of living without nuclear weapons ready for use on a day-to-day basis. They do not imply that these same governments must decide that the nature of international relations has somehow fundamentally changed and become more cooperative.

The way in which the governments of the United States, Russia, China, and so on viewed one another in, say, 1993 or 1994 is perfectly cooperative and harmonious enough to support a drawn-out transition to VNAs. At their core VNAs aim to offer precisely the sort of guarantee that would allow states in an uncertain and potentially conflictual world to adopt them: the promise of a reconstituted nuclear arsenal when one is deemed necessary. Given that the United States and the Soviet Union (more the latter than the former) found themselves able to live with "virtual" nuclear forces not ready for immediate use during the first years of the Cold War, it is hardly utopian to suggest that suspicious but essentially unaggressive great powers could make the same choice again. As Michael Brown stresses in his essay, the nuclear powers continue to have a "deep attachment" to their operational nuclear forces, but, if a broad process of arms control could weaken that attachment over a decade or two, nation-states could well come to see the value of a de-alerted nuclear world.

If the international system in which VNAs are to be employed remains roughly the same as the one we know today, then it follows that traditional means of pursuing national security, such as deterrence, will remain in force. Virtual arsenals must therefore be able to deter as well, or nearly as well, as operational nuclear forces without enjoying their advantages of readiness. I will argue below that VNAs can pass this test.[4]

ISSUE 2: DESIGN OF A VIRTUAL ARSENAL

One particular outline of a VNA emerged from the analysis of this book as probably the most likely foundation of a virtual nuclear world: separating warheads from launchers. Such a step represents the minimum necessary condition of the shift from actual arsenals to virtual ones. Until the warheads are divorced from their delivery vehicles, the nuclear weapons remain ready for use in very short order. At the same time, the steps beyond mere warhead separation—taking apart the warheads themselves and removing the fissile material—may be vastly more difficult to reverse.

While the designs of U.S. nuclear warheads (and those of the other declared and undeclared nuclear powers) are highly classified, one can assume that their workings are intricate enough that simply taking them apart would be a complex challenge—and putting them back together again would be even more difficult. Thus, while removing warheads from missiles might create a relatively predictable delay of several days before the weapons could be reassembled and used, disassembling the warheads themselves would be a much more fundamental step, perhaps creating delays of weeks before weapons could be reconstituted for use and introducing many possible complexities and asymmetries into the process. Not all warheads, for example, have the same design, and nations with more "modular" warheads whose fissile material could be removed more easily might have important advantages in a reconstitution race. This is not to suggest that a VNA scheme would never call for the dismantlement of warheads but merely to recognize that it will probably have to wait until the later stages of the VNA regime to be implemented.

Once the parties to a VNA accord have removed the warheads from their delivery vehicles, the weapons would be taken to agreed (though perhaps secret)[5] storage points and placed under international inspection. The details of the verification scheme will be outlined in the following pages; in broad terms it might involve the warheads being taken to designated storage sites and "tagged" with electronic homing devices, connected to a network via both wireless communication devices and physical cables. The state whose weapons were being verified would control security at the site itself; it would then be surrounded with a perimeter monitoring system manned by multilateral or international inspectors.

PRECONDITIONS FOR VNAS

It is important to stress two critical preconditions for warhead separation: a robust arms-control regime that controls warheads in addition to launchers and some broad accounting of weapons-grade fissile material.

Even the START II Treaty continues the practice established in the 1970s of counting *launchers* rather than *warheads*. It allows each side not a certain number of warheads per se but, instead, a number of launchers with the capability of delivering a given number of warheads, and its verification provisions are designed to monitor these delivery vehicle limits. This distinction has little import under traditional modes of deterrence but, when one contemplates a transition to VNAs, the risk posed by excess, uncounted, fully assembled warheads becomes obvious: such weapons would undermine the warhead counting and verification that would accompany warhead separation. If one state removed all warheads from its strategic missile force, for example, and put them under international inspection but retained a secret reserve of 500 or 1,000 assembled warheads not known to the inspectors, it could perhaps conduct a secret reassembly of some number of operational missiles and attempt to blackmail other states. A parallel verification program targeted at delivery vehicles, which I will propose in these pages, would attenuate this risk, but it is clear that the transition to a VNA regime will demand an extension of arms-control agreements to cover numbers of specific warheads in addition to delivery vehicles.

In a similar vein, as Pat Garrity stresses in his essay, states considering a VNA agreement will want as firm an assurance as possible about the status of fissile material stocks among the declared and undeclared nuclear powers. Hidden fissile material does not pose quite the same risk as fully assembled warheads—jury-rigged weapons constructed in underground warhead factories, for example, might not be completely reliable—but their symbolic and coercive power could not be denied. A VNA agreement would therefore also demand as preconditions a ban on the production of new fissile material for weapons purposes and as comprehensive an accounting as is possible of past fissile material production. The Comprehensive Test Ban Treaty (CTBT) now under negotiation will provide an important adjunct to fissile material controls by helping to reduce the perceived reliability of new warheads by preventing them from being tested.

TRANSITION ARRANGEMENTS

As suggested by Robert Manning and others,[6] the final transition point to VNAs might involve a small, operational deterrent based on survivable platforms, such as submarines, and a larger virtual force. This residue of an operational deterrent would offer a hedge against the collapse of the system and would reassure the participating states of their security during the transition. As one example, a post–START II agreement might call for reductions in U.S. and Russian forces to 1,000 warheads each, place a cap on second-tier arsenals of 300 weapons each, and implement strict warhead and fissile material controls. Once the nuclear weapons states had implemented that agreement, they could take the first step toward a virtual nuclear world: agreeing to dismantle all but a small minimum deterrent force, which might be 200 or 300 U.S. and Russian weapons and 100 each for the second-tier powers (or an equal number for all five).[7] In this way the declared nuclear powers could gradually become comfortable with the verification scheme for virtual arsenals while retaining a sufficient operational reserve force to guarantee their security.[8] If, after a period of years, the arrangement and verification of the dismantled portions of each nuclear power's arsenal worked well, this arrangement would open the door to a complete dismantling of all operational weapons—the ultimate goal of the VNA proposal.[9]

This discussion of transition stages holds two lessons. First, it offers an instructive caution about the likely time frame necessary to implement VNAs. Merely achieving the arms-control preconditions for virtual arsenals—post–START II reductions, a CTBT, a warhead accounting system, and fissile material controls and production bans—could easily consume a decade or more. Then comes the final transitional agreement, dismantling the majority of the remaining weapons and leaving a small operational reserve and then leaving it in place long enough for the nuclear powers to become accustomed to the VNA verification scheme, anywhere from five years to another decade or more. Although it is possible to imagine this entire process being compressed into a decade—if we assume, for example, sudden and dramatically positive turns in Russia and China—it is much more likely to take at least twenty years. This fact again emphasizes the importance of avoiding discussion of VNAs as any kind of current policy option; they are not.

But, second, the very fact that the transition to VNAs is likely to be extended helps answer the basic criticism that "nuclear weapons states would never consider them." Of course, they would not, today. But after fifteen years of progressive arms reductions, including several years of watching the operations of a verification system controlling hundreds or thousands of dismantled warheads, the context for a decision about VNAs will be very different. Some critics have suggested that VNAs are hardly feasible and that minimum deterrence should be the ultimate goal of arms control.[10] Yet I would argue that nuclear powers willing to move to a regime of a few dozen or a few hundred nuclear weapons would almost certainly consider the further step of VNAs.

Indeed, given the precedent established in START of preserving large reserve forces in addition to smaller operational ones, it is nearly *inevitable* that minimum deterrence would be backed by some form of virtual reserve arsenal. Yet, because the deployed force will be so small, states participating in the minimum deterrence regime will demand stringent controls on dismantled reserve weapons, and once those controls are established, if they work well, a transition to VNAs might hardly seem radical; it would represent the logical next step. Far from being a true alternative to VNAs, therefore, minimum deterrence contains within it the seeds of a VNA agreement and, by the same token, VNAs do not argue against or rule out minimum deterrence; they demand it as a transitional stage.

A final issue in VNA transition arrangements is missile defenses—what kind and how many the nuclear powers allow and when they erect them. I will discuss this issue in the section on stability.

RECONSTITUTION REQUIREMENTS

A VNA accord would have to lay out very clear and specific standards for reconstituting a nuclear force. If any nation determined for some reason that it had to reassemble several (or several hundred) nuclear weapons, the resulting process would have to be transparent and stable for the overall scheme to work. How much confidence the nuclear powers have in advance that reconstitution could be accomplished in a stable and secure fashion—even if they hope never to execute it—will be a critical determinant of how readily they accept the proposal.

In general, as suggested in the opening essay, a state wishing to reassemble any weapons from its virtual arsenal would be required to deposit a notification of this intent at some international body, such as the United Nations. The notice would presumably make clear when the nation intended on reassembling its weapons and how many it would reconstitute. The architects of a VNA regime would face a critical question about such a notification: Would it require a certain waiting period, say thirty days, before the withdrawing state could actually reassemble its weapons? A waiting period might enhance stability, by giving other states a chance to match the reconstitution and thus prevent the withdrawing state from gaining an advantage. A waiting period might also make an actual reassembly less likely by providing the world community with an opportunity to address the causes of reconstitution and prevent it from happening. The nuclear powers, however, might be reluctant to agree to a waiting period in advance: if a threat emerged very rapidly, national leaders might believe, they would want assembled nuclear weapons to use very quickly. Governments accustomed to relying on nuclear weapons on a day-to-day basis might be unwilling to allow a cooling-off period of a full month before reassembling their arsenals, even in the face of a major threat.

Yet there are answers to these concerns. The mere announcement of an intent to reassemble would become a powerful deterrent tool in a virtual nuclear world—as powerful, if not more so, as overt threats of nuclear use are today. It is highly unlikely that a threat to a major world power, a threat totally unforeseen and thus unmet until the last minute, could emerge in the space of thirty days. Even if one did, however, the threatened state could immediately apply for reconstitution, and this threat would convey the seriousness of its resolve and thus begin to answer the threat without actually reassembling a weapon.

Even more fundamentally, a VNA accord might contain a clause offering a reconstitution exemption in case of military attack on a virtual nuclear power. If Russian aircraft started bombing Paris, for example, France would not have to wait thirty days; it would be freed from its constraints under the treaty and could reassemble and use nuclear weapons immediately. (Of course, it would do so anyway in such circumstances, but clarifying this point in advance would help make clear to aggressors that they would not necessarily be free from nuclear retaliation for the first month of a war.) The problem then shifts from one of reconstitution to one of survivability—insuring that a virtual arsenal would not be subject to a preemptive attack. I will examine this question in the following pages.

The accord might also contain another hedge: a clause stipulating that, if any nation suddenly admitted that it had been cheating on either the VNA agreement or the Nonproliferation Treaty and possessed some nuclear weapons—and at this stage, every nation in the world would belong to one or the other of those treaties—all other parties to the VNA accord would be free to reassemble as quickly as they thought necessary. The accord might demand notification of this decision, but the usual thirty-day waiting period would not apply.

In fact, the nuclear powers need not wait until VNAs have been implemented in order to put some system like this in place. The United States and Russia intend to keep several thousand nonoperational nuclear weapons in reserve under the START II Treaty, and no procedures currently exist to encourage a notification or other formal statement of intent to reconstitute those reserve forces. Such a procedure might represent an important confidence-building measure; if U.S.-Russian relations deteriorated and a crisis erupted, both sides might begin to worry that the other was dipping into its reserve force to bolster its operational arsenal. To address this danger the United States and Russia might agree today to provide a formal notification to the United Nations Security Council if either decides to bring into service any decommissioned nuclear weapons. Verification of this promise would require the sort of warhead accountability regime mentioned earlier, and it would lay the groundwork for the broader notification system that would be required in a virtual nuclear agreement.[11]

ISSUE 3: VERIFICATION

Verification is arguably the most important single issue that will determine the feasibility and desirability of virtual nuclear arsenals. As Kenneth Waltz and other authors in this book have stressed, an unverifiable VNA regime would be a useless one. At the same time, monitoring an arms-control accord of such unprecedented completeness will demand verification measures of equally unprecedented intrusiveness; whether the parties to a VNA agreement are willing to allow such a troublesome level of monitoring will play a major role in determining whether virtual nuclear arsenals could ever be adopted.

As previously suggested, two important preconditions for a transition to VNAs—arms-control accords that should be agreed, put in place, and allowed to operate for several years before full dismantlement could occur—are a convention controlling and monitoring nuclear warheads and one controlling and prohibiting new production of warhead-usable fissile material. These accords would lay the groundwork for the even more elaborate verification requirements of a VNA.

As I will argue, one can imagine the general characteristics of a VNA verification system without too much difficulty. But those characteristics are secondary to a larger issue, for the verification of a virtual nuclear regime is first and foremost a *political* rather than a technical question. When one asks the question of verification experts—could you design a system that would theoretically be able to verify a VNA agreement?—the answer is almost uniformly yes. The real question is whether states would accept such an intrusive monitoring regime, a question that, in turn, depends on the state of great power relations, the perceived value of a VNA agreement, and other factors. Thus, it is meaningless, as well as factually incorrect, to say that a VNA agreement could not be verified. One could say that a regime that sought to prevent cheating at the level of one bomb could not be verified, but the same claim could not be made against VNAs. The issue is whether the nuclear powers will see enough urgency in the task of nuclear reductions that they allow the necessary procedures.

CRITERIA FOR VERIFICATION

As they make their decisions, the nuclear powers will consider, among other things, the criteria they would ask the monitoring system to meet. The states involved could conceive verification criteria so rigidly that no VNA monitoring scheme could meet them. Imagine, for example, the implications if the U.S. Department of Defense issued the following standard: "A VNA verification system should be capable of detecting cheating at the level of a single warhead or the fissile material capable of manufacturing one." It is quite obvious that no verification system could meet this standard. American diplomacy has been unable to enforce it in North Korea, a country believed only to have a few bombs' worth of plutonium at most; it would simply be impossible to apply it to declared nuclear powers, each of which probably has unaccounted fissile material capable of manufacturing hundreds, if not thousands, of nuclear weapons. Hence, Michael Wheeler's conclusion that "it will be impossible to verify with high confidence that all nuclear weapons and fissile materials are in monitored storage."

Critics will argue that, in a virtual nuclear world, even one covert bomb would provide a cheater with substantial leverage. Some will say an Iraq, reinvading Kuwait in 2020, and capable of flashing around two or three nuclear warheads and threatening their use against U.S. or allied forces, would gain important leverage. So would a China threatening Taiwan again in 2015 and able to discover a handful of assembled nuclear devices ready for use in any regional conflict.

This, of course, is one of the most venerable arguments against disarmament—the risk of rogue states hiding a "bomb in the basement." It is in such circumstances, Waltz contends in his essay, that "cheating is both worthwhile and easy." Yet the VNA scheme is designed precisely to answer such threats: under the clause in the VNA agreement mentioned earlier, open cheating would free any VNA parties to reassemble some number of weapons as rapidly as possible. As long as the cheater did not acquire by their cheating a first-strike-capable nuclear force—and rogue states like Iraq certainly could not—the United States could simply take a few days or a couple of weeks to reassemble a small deterrent force, and the cheater would have achieved absolutely nothing.

Nothing, that is, *relative to the status quo*—a distinction that is worth making. For even today the threat of a single Iraqi or North Korean nuclear weapon poses a major challenge to deterrence theory and practice. In the event of a war against either of these two states, presuming they are nuclear armed, the United States would have enormous difficulties in deterring the use of their nuclear weapons. Any U.S. nuclear retaliation against nuclear use would be meaningless— what would U.S. forces do, annihilate Pyongyang? Furthermore, either or both of these regimes might be fighting for its very existence and thus might view its nuclear arsenal as true weapons of last resort.

The key fact, however, is that these problems already bedevil U.S. deterrent policy. The difficulties with nuclear retaliation in such cases have already encouraged the U.S. military to begin thinking about nonnuclear means of defense, retaliation, and preemption to address small-scale nuclear threats, and such means, when more fully developed, will provide the basic answer to low-level cheating under a VNA agreement. And, of course, if U.S. officials or those of other VNA parties deemed such measures insufficient, they would have the right to reconstitute an active nuclear force to deal with the threat. The only remaining advantage for a cheater, then, might be to strike quickly and hope that, by the time the victim has reassembled its weapons, the passionate urge to retaliate has died away; one must ask, however, if such a change would not actually be in everyone's best interests—presumably the victim would find some nonnuclear way of punishing the aggressor but without needlessly killing tens of thousands of innocent civilians with a nuclear riposte.

Let us imagine, then, a less rigorous standard for verification, such as this: a VNA monitoring system "should be sufficient to prevent cheating on a scale that would provide the cheater with a militarily usable, first-strike capable advantage in nuclear weapons." Here the focus is on preserving stability in the traditional, second-strike manner (as stressed, for example, by Waltz) guaranteeing that all parties to the VNA agreement would be able to detect cheating before it would render them vulnerable to a disarming first strike.

A standard such as this nicely illustrates the important fact that verification is, as it has always been in arms control, intimately connected to survivability. If a VNA were truly survivable against a first strike—as I will suggest that it could be—then even a certain amount of cheating might not provide an aggressor with a significant advantage. This would not suggest that the monitoring system should be any less stringent; obviously, it should be as rigorous and intrusive as possible. But a survivable VNA would offer the added assurance that, even in the event that cheating occurred, it would not be militarily useful.

And, when we turn our attention to the dangers of preemptive strikes, delivery vehicles become far more important than warheads. Warheads are useless for first-strike purposes without a delivery vehicle to take them to the enemy, and so a VNA verification regime designed to meet the final criterion outlined here might focus heavily on aircraft, missiles, and ships capable of carrying nuclear weapons. Intercontinental ballistic missiles—the "fast-flyers" that constitute the core of any preemptive nuclear attack—would remain of special concern, and, indeed, as I will suggest, a VNA agreement might be well complemented by a complete ban on such missiles.

A VNA VERIFICATION SYSTEM

One can imagine dozens of verification provisions designed to enforce a VNA accord, at both the level of warheads and that of delivery vehicles. As David Kay, Michael Wheeler, and others in this volume suggest, once the warheads are separated from their delivery vehicles, they could be placed in guarded storage sites. Actual possession of the warheads would be retained by the nuclear power; multilateral or international inspectors would man an outer ring of perimeter monitoring to insure that no warheads could leave the complex without notification.

In addition, each warhead could be "tagged" with an electronic identification system. The system would have several purposes: to supply an accurate count of known warheads; to identify the location of each individual warhead (perhaps through a Global Positioning System link); and to verify that the warhead remains unmated to any delivery vehicle (which could be accomplished through sensors located in various places on the warhead). The system would send its information out in various ways: through a computer cable, hooked into a central database; through a wireless communications transmitter; and through direct inspection at random intervals.

As noted, a VNA regime's monitoring system would also pay close attention to delivery vehicles. Inspectors would probably take up residence at missile fields, bomber bases, and submarine ports to track the status of these systems. The agreement might require that intercontinental-range missiles, SLBMs as well as ICBMs, be taken from their silos and stored separately so that they would not be available for preemptive attacks. All delivery vehicles could be tagged, as warheads were, and any requirement to use one, even for conventional missions, would have to be preceded by a notification at the United Nations similar to the reconstitution notification.

Finally, verification must have teeth—the enforcement provisions of a VNA agreement, the prior agreements of what parties would do if the monitors discovered one or more states cheating on the treaty. Obviously, much depends on the nature of the cheating and whether it threatened to produce an operational nuclear weapon. The minimum penalty might be to free other parties to the agreement from its restrictions, thus allowing them to reconstitute parts of their own nuclear arsenals. The cheater would therefore not have achieved a first-strike advantage or any other measurable military or political gain.

Presumably, too, any state that cheated on a VNA agreement would face substantial international outrage if its cheating were discovered. The hostility that greeted the 1996 French announcement of renewed nuclear testing suggests that the seeds have been firmly laid for a robust antinuclear consensus, and a VNA accord would create a far more powerful basis for it than exists today. Knowing in advance that, if it were found to be cheating, it would provoke a worldwide backlash that could well lead to political, economic, and military sanctions, a state might be deterred from beginning the process.

One major question for virtual nuclear arsenals is how fully these potential worldwide sanctions could be included in the treaty as formal commitments. To do so would establish a kind of collective nuclear security; any of the major powers that cheated would face the combined anger, and possibly military forces, of all the other major powers and quite a few medium and small ones as well. If China decided to develop a covert force, for example, it would then know that, if it ever made the force public, the United States, Russia, Japan, the European Union, India, and dozens of smaller states would join in condemning the action and promising a sort of mutual defense if China used its illicit arsenal for aggressive purposes.

This sort of collective response would be the most powerful answer to cheating. If it were strong and reliable enough, such a system could constitute a *decisive* response, for even a secret arsenal of 100 or 200 nuclear weapons would not counterbalance the military power of the rest of the world combined—especially when at least several other nations would quickly reconstitute their own VNAs. And yet it is hard to say, at this point, how willing nations will be to establish such a system of collective security. To do so might require rather fundamental changes in the international system of the sort that I have decided not to assume for the purposes of this analysis.

But collective enforcement might be possible even in a situation of mixed conflict and cooperation among the great powers. For one thing it would offer a fairly absolute answer to cheating by rogue states such as Iraq or North Korea, whose small nuclear arsenals would pose a threat to the status and influence of the great powers. One can easily imagine Russia, China, the United States, Japan, Germany, France, and so on agreeing wholeheartedly to punish Iraq in a severe fashion if it were found to be cheating in a virtual nuclear world. And, further, even great power cooperation on this issue might represent the collective pursuit of self-interest rather than some unprecedented level of trust in other nations. *If* the great powers saw significant advantages in a virtual nuclear world—as I am arguing that they should—and if they began considering the mechanics of a transition to such a world, a collective promise to punish cheaters would be a logical, rational choice for states operating even within an essentially anarchic world in which hostility remains possible.

This discussion has made clear, I hope, that it is not enough for critics of VNAs to suggest, as Waltz does, that in a virtual nuclear world "clandestinely rearming thus appears as a risk one can afford to run." This simply assumes that a VNA system could not be verified, and yet there are highly sophisticated verification and enforcement schemes that would make cheating extremely difficult as well as very risky. The argument, moreover, that the potential capability to cheat will automatically lead to cheating assumes that state behavior is so conflictual that no cooperative agreement can go unviolated—an assumption that seems to have been disproven by a number of recent arms-control agreements. Again, I would argue that if nuclear weapons states saw a VNA regime as desirable, they would allow the kind of verification necessary to implement it. The task then becomes one of convincing their governments of the value of radical arms-control proposals—no small task but arguably less utopian than fighting against the myth that arms control is somehow alien to the nature of world politics.

ISSUE 4: STABILITY

Along with verification the perceived stability of a virtual nuclear deterrent will go a long way toward determining its acceptability. The nuclear powers presumably would not abandon operational nuclear forces for a highly insecure and unstable alternative. This is not to say that the nuclear powers ten or twenty years hence will view stability in precisely the same way that they do today; indeed, the process of arms control required before a transition to VNAs can even begin would necessarily transform great power attitudes toward nuclear arms.

Nonetheless, because I am not assuming fundamental changes in international relations, any VNA proposal will have to meet certain basic stability criteria.

Stability in a virtual nuclear world has several elements, including survivability and reconstitution. Essentially, VNAs attempt to answer these concerns by offering a survivable, reconstitutable arsenal that promises a less operational form of the same kind of stability that exists today—stability through threat of retaliation in kind. A number of authors in this book refer to the value of second-strike forces in preserving deterrence during the Cold War; the question is whether VNAs would perpetuate or undermine it.

It is worth noting that the sort of collective nuclear security regime envisioned here, in that all the major powers pledge to punish any one of their number that cheats on a VNA agreement would offer perhaps the most robust form of stability to the overall system. The burden of stability in a VNA world is to establish enormous costs and disincentives against individual states' breaking out of the agreement and to deny them any potential advantages for doing so. As I will suggest, this can theoretically be done on a bilateral basis. But it would be much stronger if grounded in multilateral pledges—if a predator state knew that its aggression would provoke reactions from all the other major military powers in the world or at least the vast majority of them. Such a situation would override nearly all calculations of first-strike potential, VNA survivability, and so on; it would create a circumstance in which breaking out of a VNA agreement for aggressive purposes is useless and counterproductive. As such, some form of collective agreement to respond to cheating or nuclear aggression stands out as perhaps the single most absolute guarantee of stability in a virtual nuclear world.

SURVIVABILITY

Yet, even without such a collective security regime, I would argue that a system of VNA storage and monitoring that both guarantees verification and provides for a secure, survivable deterrent is perfectly feasible. Designing it will be no small challenge. The very act of dismantling a nuclear arsenal would render it at least somewhat vulnerable to a first strike; with the warheads separated from missiles or other delivery vehicles and stored at fixed locations, a cheater that had acquired even a few dozen illicit ICBMs might be able to launch a disarming preemptive attack. Hence, Michael Wheeler in his essay concludes that "nuclear weapons in monitored storage will be more vulnerable than nuclear weapons that are operationally dispersed." Avoiding this risk will be a major preoccupation of the architects of a VNA regime.

One can imagine dozens of ways in which participating states might make their virtual nuclear components survivable, a few of which I will outline. These various tactics obviously need further study: some might be more technically feasible, politically acceptable, or affordable than others. My point in offering these various options is to indicate clearly that many possibilities do exist to insure VNA survivability, possibilities limited only by the imagination and courage of states participating in the accord.

- Silos and hardened warhead shelters. Missiles, absent their warheads, could remain in hardened silos; their warheads could be stored nearby at hardened underground (and monitored) storage sites. The system would be designed to ride out a first strike and then allow warhead remating, probably through an underground passageway. As suggested, accord monitors would fit both warheads and missiles with sensors to insure that they had not been remated before an attack.

- Shelters in mountains and tunnels. As Peter Wilson suggests in his essay, both warheads and missiles could be stored in underground shelters built into mountains and designed to withstand a first strike. The two systems would be stored separately to insure warhead separation but would both be maintained at the same site. After an attack they could be remated, rolled out, and fired.

- Mobile missiles and warhead carriers. Single-warhead mobile missiles could be left deployed in the field, as they are today, and hardened vehicles could be designed to carry their warheads, vehicles that would also be allowed to roam. Monitors would fit sensors to both to verify that remating had not occurred and might also physically inspect a random set of missiles and warheads each week or month, enough to establish a statistical improbability that more than a handful could even theoretically be remated at any given time. The overall system would be as immune to first strike as existing mobile missiles.

- Submarine missiles without guidance sets. As suggested in the opening essay, guidance sets could be removed from SLBMs and stored on attack submarines. Verification might be both by random call-ups and electronic queries. If participating states were willing to develop a new, more modular missile design, SLBMs could be fitted without warheads, which themselves might be carried on attack submarines.

An interesting complementary accord that might help insure survivability in a virtual nuclear world is a ban on all intercontinental ballistic missiles, perhaps accompanied by a global ban on intermediate-range missiles (extending the U.S.-Soviet INF Treaty globally). Fast-flyers like ICBMs are responsible for much of the instability in the current nuclear balance and would certainly pose the greatest danger to VNA stability: even a few dozen covertly reassembled ICBMs could represent a serious threat to vulnerable stocks of dismantled warheads and delivery vehicles. The missiles might be able to arrive before stockpiled warheads could be removed from storage, much less remated with their own delivery vehicles for a retaliation.

Thus, a ban on all missiles of intermediate range or greater, and perhaps a complementary ban on any yet-to-be-designed intercontinental cruise missiles, might help bolster the stability of a VNA regime. Nuclear forces would be limited to bombs carried by aircraft and cruise missiles of intermediate range (roughly 1,500 km) or less. Even if such weapons were covertly reassembled, they would be far less capable of a first strike because they would take too long to arrive. Such a ban has always had significant practical problems—the threat of a rapid and certain retaliation, delivered by missiles, has arguably helped to strengthen deterrence—but the proposal would be worth a new look in a VNA.

Some critics have argued that, in a virtual nuclear world, even conventional weapons could threaten the survivability of virtual nuclear forces. Long-range, highly accurate smart weapons of the sort used by U.S. forces in the Persian Gulf War could conceivably provide an aggressor with a nonnuclear first-strike capability against a VNA arsenal, if that arsenal were dismantled and stored in vulnerable locations. The response to this worry is obvious enough: if the participants of a VNA agreement take steps to insure the survivability of their dismantled forces—by using, for example, some of the measures suggested here— then the VNAs would presumably be as immune to conventional attack as nuclear. Nonetheless, the role of conventional forces in a nuclear exchange, even given current nuclear deployments, may be growing with the advent of the "revolution in military affairs," and the designers of a VNA regime must take careful account of their effect on stability.

Finally, modest or robust missile defenses could also play an important role in preserving the survivability of virtual nuclear forces. As Keith Payne points out in his essay, defenses could raise the level at which cheating would become influential, thus discouraging it—though a ban on ICBMs and SLBMs might achieve the same thing much more inexpensively. More fundamental questions attach to the role of strategic defenses in a VNA world, questions that I will briefly touch on in the following pages.

RECONSTITUTION

A final stability issue relates to the period of reconstitution. If states ever find the need to reconstitute part or all of their nuclear force, the VNA agreement must outline procedures to allow it to happen in a stable and predictable fashion. Designing these procedures for reconstitution is one of the major challenges facing VNAs, but a close analysis suggests that it can be done. One key to this process is to insure that no state could achieve enormous leverage by sprinting out of the reconstitution starting gates and rapidly acquiring a handful of operational weapons. Guarding against this risk demands both stringent verification and a survivable core of all VNA deterrents.

Kenneth Waltz suggests, in his superb and important essay, that, because of these reconstitution dynamics, VNAs would exacerbate the "premium on speed of action in crises" and thus increase the risk of accident. This is an important point, but one can question the severity of the accident being made. If reconstitution can allow states to reacquire a survivable deterrent, why would the speedily reassembled arsenals be less stable than existing ones? The risk of war would only increase if participating states adopted nuclear doctrines that called for reconstituted forces to be launched as they were reassembled, a highly unlikely decision. And, of course, these responses do not even assume that a disassembled arsenal could itself be survivable, as I have argued, for, if it can, the premium on speedy response to possible cheating declines substantially. Finally, I would contend that Waltz underestimates the risks of accidental war inherent in operational forces, especially when one or more actors have launch-on-warning policies—as we now know Russia does.

Several writers in this volume, perhaps especially Pat Garrity, have pointed to another danger: the risk of long-term, rather than short-term, reconstitution asymmetries. If one state could win a large-scale rearmament race over a period of a year or two, reconstituting (and perhaps building from scratch) hundreds or thousands more weapons than its adversary (or intended victim), it would seem destined to gain important political and military leverage and perhaps could even acquire a first-strike capability. Appreciating this risk in advance, many states might hesitate to commit themselves to a VNA world that could turn so quickly against them.

And yet, on closer examination, the risk of long-term reconstitution disparities looks like a rather easy problem to solve. A handful of straightforward and easily verified measures could address this danger decisively.

First, for such long-term reconstitution competitions to produce instability, we have to assume that they would be asymmetrical, and fundamentally so. But once one nation abandoned the agreement, so would the others. And, while differences in nuclear infrastructures and other capabilities could produce a few months' lead for one or another state here or there, there is no reason to suppose that these would be decisive: marginal differences of a few hundred weapons would not produce a first-strike capability for any side.

Second, to tamp down those asymmetries as far as possible, a VNA agreement would presumably restrict quite stringently the number of dismantled weapons each state could possess. More important, it would go on to control fissile material that might be used to manufacture more. In this way the accord might create a clear gap of a year or more before the initial reconstitution of virtual forces and any state's ability to begin mass-producing new warheads, and, unlike today, there would be no "reserve" arsenal bridging that gap. I would think that this is the sort of situation Pat Garrity has in mind when he recommends a requirement for "staggered" reconstitution.

If Russia decided to break out of a VNA accord, for example, and sought to outrace its opponent(s) in long-term reconstitution, it might initially be able to reassemble its allowed virtual force—say, 300 warheads. If the VNA regime's short-term reconstitution procedures were sound, this opening reassembly would not cause any instabilities; other states could simply match it and return to active deterrence. Given that a VNA agreement would not allow member parties to stockpile large amounts of fissile material, Russia then would be faced with the prospect of acquiring such material from civilian nuclear plants or other sources and manufacturing it into weapons. If a VNA accord had also shut down and dismantled all existing nuclear production facilities, this task would take many months. Meanwhile, any nuclear powers possibly threatened by the Russian buildup would have generous time to match the Russian reconstitution.

Third, the survivability of a fully reconstituted VNA force would address the risk of a longer-term buildup. If Russia began the theoretical breakout and the United States reconstituted its 300 active warheads in highly survivable deployment modes such as submarines at sea, Russia could build more warheads virtually forever and never achieve a first-strike advantage. This hard core of a survivable deterrent offers very substantial guarantees against long-term reconstitution asymmetries, just as it does against smaller, short-term cheating.

Fourth, and finally, missile defenses could help answer the threat of a reconstituted nuclear force by undermining the coercive value of the first several hundred or thousand weapons redeployed. For this purpose defenses might offer an additional guarantee, even if the VNA accord had banned intercontinental missiles—for in an all-out reconstitution race the nuclear powers might well abandon that restriction and begin manufacturing missiles again. Yet defenses also carry a more fundamental price in a more fully reconstituted world than they do in the early stages of reassembly: the process might well pass through stages in which the offense-defense ratio was highly unstable and offered a substantial advantage to an aggressor. I do not have space here to examine this question in detail; suffice it to say that the exact role and size of missile defenses in a virtual nuclear agreement need much more detailed study.

THE PROMISE OF VIRTUAL NUCLEAR ARSENALS

Clearly, the subject of virtual nuclear arsenals is enormously complex and needs a great deal more investigation. But just as clearly, in my view, it offers enormous potential, both in the long term and the short term. In the long term, some decades from now, VNAs could offer a promising means of dramatically reducing the danger to humanity posed by nuclear weapons. And in the short term they can help spur serious thinking about the requirements of a more fundamentally denuclearized world. Such has been the purpose of this volume: to investigate seriously the potential to remove nuclear weapons from operational service among the nuclear powers. We hope that it will spark a renewed debate on the long-term goals of nuclear arms control—a debate that is sorely lacking in the nuclear weapons powers today yet one that is critical to the future of humanity.

NOTES

1. Michael J. Mazarr, "Virtual Nuclear Arsenals," *Survival* 37, no. 3 (Autumn 1995): 7-26. For several very thoughtful letters to the editor on the essay and my response, see *Survival* 37, no. 4 (Winter 1995-96): 184-89.

2. It is worth noting that I was encouraged to prepare this essay in this way by other authors in this volume, not all of whom agree with the idea of VNAs. A strong updated case for the concept, they suggested, would be a useful and provocative tone on which to end the book, even if they might take issue with that conclusion.

3. One issue I will not treat at length is the need for VNAs. In his very thoughtful contribution to this book Kenneth Waltz argues that deterrence with operational nuclear forces has worked well, so why alter it? Endless debates about the true dangers inherent in alert nuclear forces would not resolve the issue, and I have already made this case in the opening essay. I would only add that the history of the Cold War, as it emerges from newly declassified documents and newly released memoirs, suggests to me at least that the risk of nuclear war was at several points very real.

4. I would take issue, however, with the claim, made, for example, by Pat Garrity in his thoughtful essay, that states would somehow want *more* potential nuclear capabilities than they currently possess to deal with the threat of breakout. While analysts of VNAs must be careful to force the concept of adhering to the same standards of stability and deterrence as existing nuclear forces, we must take care not to impose on them unfairly *tougher* standards.

5. One major question is whether warhead storage sites could be kept secret, at least from other nuclear weapons states. I can imagine a scheme in which verification officials are drawn from states other than the nuclear weapons powers and during their work are allowed to inspect only one storage site—so that, even if they sold their secrets, they would betray but one location. Similarly, the identity of inspectors could be kept secret from the nuclear powers. Yet the potential for abuse in such a system is obvious, and governments would be loathe to entrust the security of their nuclear sites to the whims of a largely unknown cadre of international inspectors. An alternative arrangement might be to have inspectors brought essentially blindfolded to the storage sites; they would not know where they were, but they would be able to count the requisite number of warheads. Again, the potential for a cheater playing an elaborate shell game is probably too severe, and it is likely that storage sites would have to be publicly revealed.

6. Robert A. Manning, *Back to the Future: Toward a Post-Nuclear Ethic* (Washington, D.C.: Progressive Policy Institute, 1994). I should stress very strongly that Manning does not advocate a full VNA system, and he may or may not agree with the proposal.

7. The United States and Russia might agree to an equal minimum deterrent force of roughly 300 weapons if they knew that they each had 700 more weapons capable of being reconstituted in a matter of days—the virtual remnant of the rest of their 1,000-warhead forces—an option that did not exist for the second-tier powers.

8. This minimum deterrent reserve would not, it is worth noting, be forced into the arguably incredible policy of targeting cities and other civilian areas: as I have argued elsewhere, a 300-warhead force could perform "counterpower" targeting, holding at risk the conventional military forces of a potential enemy. See Michael J. Mazarr, "Military Targets for a Minimum Deterrent: After the Cold War, How Much Is Enough?" in *Toward a Nuclear Peace,* eds. Mazarr and Alex Lennon (New York: St. Martin's Press, 1994): 113-41.

9. Even in its policy toward the START II Treaty, the United States is taking a very similar approach. In addition to the 5,000 active nuclear weapons it will keep in operational status, as Bruce Blair noted in his essay, the United States is planning to keep some 5,000 more in reserve—3,000 in active, reconstitutable reserve and 2,000 "on the shelf." The U.S. Department of Defense considers these reserve weapons an important hedge against a newly resurgent and hostile Russia. The precedent, therefore, for smaller operational forces backed by a larger reconstitutable reserve has already been established. All that the transitional arrangement for VNAs would do is adjust the numbers downward.

10. See, for example, the "Letter to the Editor" by Roger Molander, in *Survival* 37, no. 4 (Winter 1995-96): 184-85.

11. A VNA accord would also have to address the status of the three opaque nuclear powers—India, Israel, and Pakistan. Would they be admitted as full members to the agreement, subject to the same verification and other requirements?

Would there be some provisional status for them? These questions probably cannot be answered in detail in advance. The key requirement in a virtual nuclear world would be twofold: capping the opaque arsenals at their current status and verifying this limitation. Whether this goal would be achieved through admitting the three states as full parties to a virtual agreement or—which seems more likely, for symbolic reasons alone—including them in some sort of special status would depend upon political considerations. Either way, however, it is clear that a transition to VNAs would change the balance of power between the five declared nuclear powers and the three opaque powers. How fundamentally it would do so and in what specific ways are subjects that clearly demand further attention.

Contributors

FRED C. IKLÉ is distinguished scholar at the Center for Strategic and International Studies. Dr. Iklé served as Under Secretary of Defense for Policy in the Reagan administration and from 1973 to 1977 as director of the U.S. Arms Control and Disarmament Agency.

MICHAEL J. MAZARR is director of the New Millennium Project at the Center for Strategic and International Studies, and Editor of *The Washington Quarterly*. Dr. Mazarr also worked on Capitol Hill as defense and foreign policy advisor to Representative Dave McCurdy.

MICHAEL BROWN, a Fellow at the Center for Science and International Affairs, Harvard University also serves as Managing Editor of the Center's journal, *International Security*. Before coming to Harvard in January 1994, he was for six years a member of the Directing Staff and a Senior Fellow at the International Institute for Strategic Studies in London. Brown has also been a Research Fellow at the Center for Strategic and International Studies in Washington, and the Brookings Institution.

BRUCE BLAIR is a Senior Fellow at the Brookings Institution in Washington, D.C.. A former project director at the U.S. Congress's Office of Technology Assessment, and former visiting professor at Yale University, he specializes in arms control, crisis management, national security policy, nuclear proliferation, U.S. and foreign nuclear forces, and command and control safeguards.

PETER WILSON is a consultant with RAND, and has worked with the Institute for Defense Analyses (IDA), Science Applications International Corporation (SAIC), the Central Intelligence Agency (CIA), and the Department of State.

DAVID KAY is with the Science Applications International Corporation (SAIC) in McLean, Virginia. Dr. Kay has also served as the Chief

Inspector, United Nations Special Commission (UNSCOM), monitoring weapons of mass destruction facilities in Iraq.

MICHAEL O. WHEELER is a member of the Special Projects Division of the National Security Studies and Systems Group of Science Application International Corporation (SAIC) and serves on the Strategic Advisory Group to the U.S. Strategic Command (USSTRATCOM). Previously Dr. Wheeler worked for Systems Planning Corporation (SPC) for three years, following 24 years in the U.S. Air Force with a variety of staff and field assignments.

KEITH PAYNE is President of the National Institute for Public Policy, and Adjunct Professor, Georgetown University in Washington, D.C.

KONSTANTIN SOROKIN is director of the Center for Geopolitical Studies at the Russian Academy of Sciences, Institute of Europe, based in Moscow, Russia. In his former capacity as head of section, International Security and Arms Control Studies at the Institute, he frequently advised the Russian Security Council and the Duma.

TAEHO KIM is the Senior China Analyst at the Korea Institute for Defense Analyses in Seoul, Korea.

PHILIP H. GORDON is a Senior Fellow in the U.S. Strategic Studies program at the International Institute for Strategic Studies (IISS) in London, England. He is also Editor of *Survival,* the policy journal of IISS.

STUART CROFT is Professor in the Security Studies Research Programme at the University of Birmingham in the United Kingdom.

DEVIN T. HAGERTY is Lecturer in International Politics, Department of Government and Public Administration, University of Sydney. His book, "The Consequences of Nuclear Proliferation: Lessons from South Asia," will be published by the MIT Press in 1998. Hagerty is now writing a book on Asia-Pacific security after the Cold War.

BRAD ROBERTS is a member of the Research Staff at the Institute for Defense Analyses in Alexandria, Virginia. Dr. Roberts is a former Editor of *The Washington Quarterly,* and a former fellow at the Center for Strategic and International Studies.

GEN. CHARLES HORNER, before his retirement from the U.S. Air Force, served as Commander in Chief, North American Aerospace Defense Command and the United States Space Command, and Commander of Air Force Space Command. As commander of both the 9th Air Force and the United States Central Command Air Forces he commanded all U.S. and allied air assets during Operations Desert Shield and Desert Storm.

FRANÇOIS HEISBOURG is Senior Vice President of Strategic Development at Matra Defense/Space in France.

ALEXEI ARBATOV is a Member of the State Duma of Russia, and sits on its Committee on Defense.

KENNETH WALTZ is Professor Emeritus at the University of California - Berkeley.

PATRICK GARRITY is a political scientist with the Los Alamos National Laboratory in Washington, D.C., and is also a Professorial Lecturer at the Johns Hopkins University's Paul H. Nitze School of Advanced International Studies, also in Washington.

AKIO WATANABE is Professor at the Ayoama Gakuin University in Japan.

PHILIP ZELIKOW is associate professor of public policy at Harvard University. A former trial lawyer in Texas, he became a career diplomat with the Department of State and served on the staff of the National Security Council (1989-1991) before coming to Harvard. He is a member and Deputy Director of the Aspen Strategy Group, a program of the Aspen Institute, and has been appointed to the Department of State's Advisory Committee on Historical Diplomatic Documentation.

INDEX

italic t *(t)* in page numbers indicates table

rogue states, 82, 146, 297
Russian nuclear policy, 34, 42, 48,
    58-59, 201-202
    conventional forces and, 326-
        332
    extended deterrence in, 24-25
    former Soviet allies and, 38, 44,
        62, 201, 325
    new military doctrine and, 44,
        62, 201, 323, 325
    political issues and, 332-335
    and reconstitution, 181
    START II and, 39, 146-149,
        179-180, 184, 203
    technical issues and, 332-335
    verification and, 22, 180-181
    and virtual nuclear arsenals,
        319-326

safety, operational, 55, 57, 67-68
SALT. See Strategic Arms Limitation
    Treaty.
Schell, Jonathan, 16-17, 149, 309,
    311
Schelling, Thomas, 7, 126
SCUD missiles, 247
SDI. See Strategic Defense Initiative.
Semenov, General, 201
Shamir, Yitzhak, 247
Shastri, Lal Bahadur, 245
short-range ballistic missiles
    (SRBMs), 306
    Hadés, 296, 300, 305
Singapore, 267
Singh, Vishwanath Pratap, 248
SLBMs. See submarine-launched
    ballistic missiles.
Sorokin, Konstantin, 199-206
South Africa, 114, 258, 264, 268,
    302
South Korea, 186
    as latent nuclear state, 270-272
    reliance on U.S. deterrence, 161,
        176
Southeast Asian NWFZ, 307

Soviet Union. See Russian nuclear
    policy.
Spaak, Henri, 140
SRBMs. See short-range ballistic
    missiles.
SS-19, 201
SS-23, 300
SS-25, 201
SSBNs, 295-296, 300, 305, 334
stability issues, 77
    in deterrent relationships, 24
    virtual nuclear arsenals and, 81-
        82, 91-94, 383-389
Stalin, Joseph, 359-360
START. See Strategic Arms
    Reduction Treaty.
Steinberg, Gerald, 249
Stimson, Henry, 359-360
storage sites of nuclear components,
    15-16, 93-94
Strategic Arms Limitation Treaty
    (SALT), 145, 147-150, 320
Strategic Arms Reduction Treaty
    (START), 10-11
    START I, 42, 79, 104, 112, 117,
        148-149, 322, 333
    START II, 44, 112, 146, 201,
        216, 320, 322, 377
        deactivation of weapons, 57
        provisions of, 62, 327
        Russian perspective on, 39,
            146-149, 179-180,
            184, 203
        and theater missile defense,
            153
    START III, 38, 201, 203
Strategic Defense Initiative (SDI),
    146-149, 235
strategic defenses, 88-89, 145-152,
    215
    advantages of, 150, 160-163
    disadvantages of, 21, 160-163
    virtual abolition regime and, 88-
        89
    virtual nuclear arsenal regime